# SURVEY OF
# UNITED STATES
# INTERNATIONAL FINANCE
# 1953

BY

GARDNER PATTERSON

JOHN M. GUNN, JR.

AND

DOROTHY L. SWERDLOVE

ASSISTED BY

MARY B. FERNHOLZ

INTERNATIONAL FINANCE SECTION
DEPARTMENT OF ECONOMICS AND SOCIAL INSTITUTIONS
PRINCETON UNIVERSITY

PRINCETON UNIVERSITY PRESS

Printed in the United States of America
by Princeton University Press, Princeton, New Jersey

# PREFACE

This is the fifth and final volume of an experimental series begun in 1949. The International Finance Section has been pleased with the comments received from those who have used the earlier volumes, but interest in them does not seem to warrant the continued expenditure of effort and money needed for their preparation.

The present report covers the calendar year 1953, and frequent references are made to earlier volumes for background information. It is a survey; no subject is treated exhaustively. To help those who wish to explore a given issue more thoroughly, citations have been made to the most useful and important sources, especially original documents. It must be noted that during 1953 the Executive Branch of the U.S. Government provided less data to the public than in previous years. As a result, more than the usual number of gaps exist in the record as presented here.

This survey's objective is the limited one of presenting an accurate and orderly report of the international economic and financial activities and policies of the United States. The authors have refrained from introducing any analysis of their own on the various activities, but have attempted to order the record so as to bring out shifts in policy, progress toward stated goals, and, where they existed, important conflicts and inconsistencies.

Again, the reader is warned that many of the statistical data on international economic transactions are estimates, subject to considerable error and frequent revision. The most recent estimates available to the public as this document went to press have been used, and some of the statistics for years prior to 1953, as given here, differ—though usually by only relatively small amounts—from those given in previous volumes. It is not unusual for one Government agency to publish statistical data on a given transaction that differ from the information published by another agency. Considerable pains have been taken here to reconcile such differences. When reconciliation has not been possible, the reports of the Department of Commerce, if available, have been used.

Much assistance in the preparation of this volume was received from Miss Dorothea Collins, Librarian of the Pliny Fisk Library of Economics and Finance, and from Mr. Robert Turner, Librarian of the International Relations Collection, both of the Princeton University Library. Several persons in official positions have checked parts of the manuscript for accuracy. Our debt to them is great, but it would be improper to cite them by name; their help was requested, and given, on an informal basis and no one of them saw the final draft. Full responsibility for accuracy, for the selection of material to be included, and for the form of presentation is borne by those credited on the title page.

GARDNER PATTERSON, *Director*
INTERNATIONAL FINANCE SECTION

*Princeton University*
*May 1954*

# CONTENTS

# LIST OF TABLES

# INTRODUCTION

FOR several years prior to 1953 the overriding objective of United States international economic policy had been to strengthen the defenses of the free world against possible further aggression by the Soviet bloc. The Presidential campaign and the knowledge that the new year would bring with it a new Administration and a new Congress resulted in something of a paralysis in policy formulation during the latter half of 1952, and there was evidence, in the United States and abroad, of a growing dissatisfaction with many of the current practices and policies.

The most important economic device being used by the United States to deter the spread of Communism was the provision of various kinds of aid to friendly nations and to those more or less uncommitted in the East-West struggle. From the end of World War II through 1952 a net of nearly $38 billion of grants and loans had been provided other nations by the U.S. Government, but sentiment in Congress and among the public in favor of drastically reducing the amount of official assistance and virtually terminating all aid except military items was noticeably stronger in 1952 than in the preceding years. In the early postwar period the aid had been designed primarily to relieve human suffering and to hasten economic recovery and reconstruction abroad. Following the Korean invasion the objective shifted to strengthening directly friendly military forces abroad, and during 1952 well over half the aid was in the form of military supplies, equipment, and services, with much of the remainder characterized as "defense support." The Western European countries received approximately three quarters of the total aid actually utilized in 1952 and during the postwar period as a whole, it having been decided that these nations were not only capable of making effective use of such assistance but that their loss would so strengthen the relative military potential of the Soviet bloc as to force the United States to assume a more costly mobilization posture. For several years some Americans had bitterly criticized this concentration

1

on Europe, and following the outbreak of fighting in Korea greater emphasis was put on helping non-European nations. As compared with Europe, a larger proportion of this aid was designed to hasten the economic development of these areas, on the assumption that the danger of internal subversion and the appeal of Communism would decline as economic well-being rose.

Deliveries of military equipment and supplies through 1952 were far below the levels of Congressional appropriations and of the hopes and expectations of the recipient nations. The flow was at a faster rate as the year ended, but it was generally agreed that there was an urgent need to find methods for expediting deliveries. Although the European members of the North Atlantic Treaty Organization were increasing their own production of military equipment and the number of men they had under arms, they had not fully met the 1952 goals set by the North Atlantic Treaty Organization Council. Moreover, in Europe there seemed to be growing sentiment that the threat of Soviet aggression was less imminent than American authorities believed it to be and that the previously planned mobilization goals were beyond the European economic-political capabilities unless the level of United States aid were increased. Many in Congress, on the other hand, expressed keen disappointment at the pace of rearmament in Western Europe, and some believed it justified a reduction in the amount of American help. The creation of a European Army had become a major objective of United States policy, and both the Legislative and Executive branches, as well as much of the vocal American public, were especially critical of the failure of the affected nations to ratify the treaty creating the European Defense Community. As 1953 began, sentiment in official circles for applying additional pressures to secure ratification appeared strong.

Support of the Point Four Program for helping the so-called underdeveloped areas of the world improve their production and productivity continued to be substantial, both in and out of Congress, although there was as yet little evidence that the Program was accomplishing its stated objectives. Many observers at home and abroad held that experience under the Program had conclusively demonstrated that technical assistance could be effective only if it were accompanied by much larger amounts of capital assistance than were being provided. Congress, however, was determined that the U.S. Government must reduce its foreign "economic" aid, and in 1952 it cut drastically the Administration's request for the Point Four Program, stressing that it should concentrate on providing technical assistance and, except in special and rare circumstances, should not involve the provision of commodities beyond amounts necessary for demonstration purposes. In keeping with this policy, official spokesmen for the United States vigorously opposed the efforts in the United Nations of representatives from the poorer countries to create new international financial institutions to make loans and grants for economic development purposes. The position of the United States in these frequently bitter debates was that the International Bank and the Export-Import Bank were able to meet the legitimate needs for noncommercial-type foreign loans and that the bulk of the foreign capital required by the poorer nations must come from private sources. The U.S. Government continued various efforts to expand the outflow of private investment funds but achieved little success.

The United States balance of payments remained in severe disequilibrium during 1952, but during the latter part of the year a noticeable trend toward greater balance emerged. During the year the rest of the world accumulated some $1.2 billion in gold and dollar assets in its transactions with the United States as official aid continued on a large scale, as nonmilitary merchandise exports declined more than imports, and as expenditures abroad by the Defense Establishment increased by nearly 50 percent over 1951. The improvement in the dollar position of many foreign nations rested in part on what were regarded as "extraordinary" conditions, but it was also clear that many countries, especially those in Western Europe, had made substantial economic progress, due in part to the economic aid granted by the United States in earlier years. With the improvement in their reserve position and their ability to compete more successfully with the United States in third markets, some foreign countries— notably the United Kingdom—began late in the year actively to seek ways to restore the convertibility of their currencies. It was made clear, however, that action here would depend in part on the United States' easing access to its markets and the International Monetary Fund's easing access to its resources. The return to convertibility of foreign currencies had long been a major objective of American policy, but the outgoing Administration left to its successor the decisions on specific responses to the foreign proposals.

The desire to facilitate convertibility for foreign currencies, the concern over the growing inadequacy of domestic sources of many raw materials, the widely held conviction that it was neither feasible nor desirable to continue official aid on the levels of recent years but that maintaining export markets of something like the current dimensions was important, and the feeling that American efforts to curtail trade between Western Europe and the Soviet bloc carried with them responsibilities for providing alternative markets and sources of supply—for many these gave a sense of urgency to the need for the United States to lower import barriers. Authority to make large changes in the nation's import policy rested in Congress. Action by that body during 1951 and 1952 was in the direction of increasing rather than decreasing import restrictions, and the United States was found to have violated some of its commitments under the General Agreement on Tariffs and Trade. Many observers concurred as 1952 ended that there was a clear and urgent need for a new foreign trade policy, but there was no evidence of agreement as to the shape that policy ought to have.

The incoming Republican Administration had found much to criticize in the international economic and financial policies of its predecessor and had promised a thorough revaluation and reformulation of all the major policies. The rest of this volume surveys what was done by the new Administration during its first year to find answers to the problems facing it when it assumed office and to the new problems which emerged during the year.

# I · MILITARY ASSISTANCE

HUGE official foreign-aid programs have been an outstanding characteristic of United States international economic policy during and since World War II. From mid-1945 to the end of 1952 a net of nearly $28 billion had been provided other countries on a grant basis, and net official loans, excluding the operations of the International Monetary Fund and International Bank, totalled another $10 billion. For several years these activities were carried out under a variety of separate programs and agencies, but in 1951 most of the grants were lumped together in the so-called Mutual Security Program and placed under the administration of a single Mutual Security Agency.

In the years immediately following the war, most of the aid was designed to provide emergency relief to war-devastated areas and to help friendly foreign countries regain their ability to produce goods and services for civilian consumption and investment. Beginning in 1949, however, increasing amounts were given for the purpose of helping other countries to improve their military defenses against Russian aggression. After the outbreak of the war in Korea in 1950, the objective of American assistance was determined primarily by considerations of military defense rather than of economic recovery, and the bulk of American aid was intended to strengthen directly the military capacity of the recipients. At the same time, it was believed by most of those having responsibility for national policy formulation that aid designed to raise standards of living in many of the so-called underdeveloped areas of the world and to meet the emergency needs of countries suffering from natural disasters was justified not only on humanitarian grounds, but also because it was a feasible means of lessening the appeal of Communism to the people in these countries. Grant assistance for directly building up military strength is discussed in the present chapter, and the other types of grants are discussed in Chapter II. The official loans made by the U.S. Government and the development of policies in connection with them are discussed in Chapter III.

## A. *LEGISLATIVE ISSUES*[1]

The postwar foreign-aid programs of the U.S. Government were, in general, conceived and executed by Democratic Administrations. The debates on them in Congress, however, were not notably partisan, and it was the Republican-dominated Eightieth Congress that enacted the legislation providing assistance to Greece and Turkey in 1947 and that approved the Economic Cooperation Act of 1948. In 1953 a Republican Administration took office under the leadership of President Eisenhower, with narrow Republican majorities in both Houses of Congress. The election victory of the Republican Party had followed a campaign in which that party had not questioned the desirability, under certain conditions, of aiding America's allies to strengthen their defenses against Communist aggression but had been critical of the ways in which some of the past programs had been administered; it had also stressed the need to reduce Government expenditures and to balance the federal budget. Furthermore, many

[1] Most of the material presented in this section was taken from the following official documents: Mutual Security Act of 1953 (P.L. 118, 83d Cong.), July 16, 1953; Mutual Security Appropriation Act, 1954 (P.L. 218, 83d Cong.), August 7, 1953; "The Mutual Security Program for Fiscal Year 1954: Basic Data . . . ," *Revised Committee Print*, Senate Committee on Foreign Relations and House Committee on Foreign Affairs, 83d Cong., 1st Sess., June 5, 1953; "Mutual Security Act Extension," *Hearings on H.R. 5710*, House of Rep., Committee on Foreign Affairs, 83d Cong., 1st Sess., March-June 1953; "Mutual Security Act of 1953," *Hearings*, U.S. Senate, Committee on Foreign Relations, 83d Cong., 1st Sess., May 1953; *H. Rpt. No. 569*, Parts 1 and 2, 83d Cong.; *S. Rpt. No. 405*, 83d Cong.; *S. Rpt. No. 444*, 83d Cong.; *H. Rpt. No. 770*, 83d Cong.; "Communication from the President of the United States Transmitting Estimates of Appropriation . . . ," *H. Doc. No. 209*, 83d Cong.; "Mutual Security Appropriations for 1954," *Hearings*, House of Rep., Subcommittee of the Committee on Appropriations, 83d Cong., 1st Sess., 1953; "Mutual Security Appropriations for 1954," *Hearings on H.R. 6391*, U.S. Senate, Committee on Appropriations, 83d Cong., 1st Sess., 1953; *H. Rpt. No. 880*, 83d Cong.; *S. Rpt. No. 645*, 83d Cong.; and *H. Rpt. No. 1056*, 83d Cong.

The debates on the authorizing act were printed in the *Congressional Record* (daily edition), June 18, 1953, pp. 7048-7087; June 19, 1953, pp. 7096-7143; June 29, 1953, pp. 7781-7793; June 30, 1953, pp. 7871-7883, 7892-7897, and 7903-7963; and July 1, 1953, pp. 7995-8015 and 8017-8028. The debates on the appropriation act are found in the *Congressional Record* (daily edition), July 22, 1953, pp. 9712-9746; July 29, 1953, pp. 10657-10695; July 31, 1953, pp. 10921-10928; and August 3, 1953, pp. 11273-11277.

members of the Republican majority in Congress were known to support the pursuit by the United States of a security policy that would be less dependent on other nations of the non-Communist world than was the so-called "Truman-Acheson" foreign policy.

Upon taking office, however, the new Administration gave strong support to continuing the Mutual Security Program along established lines, and it did not meet strong dissent in Congress. Many of the legislative issues concerned specific aspects of the Program, but there were also a few broad policy issues relating to the Program as a whole. As in the previous year, the more important of these were not concerned with whether the Program should be continued, but with how much foreign assistance should be provided, how the aid should be distributed among the various areas, and in what form and under what conditions it should be extended.

## Broad Policy Issues

In justifying a continuation of the Mutual Security Program, the new Administration relied on essentially the same arguments as had been advanced by their predecessors.[2] Administration spokesmen emphasized that the basic purpose of the Program was to strengthen the long-term security of the United States and that this security could not be assured by the military strength of the United States alone but depended in important part on the ability of other free nations to resist aggression. It was further asserted that other free peoples would develop their strength and unity more effectively if the United States provided strong leadership and material aid and that this country could obtain a greater degree of security through the Mutual Security Program than through the expenditure of equivalent additional sums on the nation's own Defense Establishment. As in earlier years, it was also stated that the Program was designed not only to build up the defensive military strength of the free world but also to permit a steady advance in standards of living in the aided countries, which in turn, it was said, would reduce the dangers of aggression from within.

[2] For an account of the development of the Mutual Security Program in the years prior to 1953, see Chapter I of *Survey—1952*, and the references cited there.

The Administration's proposals were not submitted to Congress until May and were in the form of changes in the Mutual Security Act of 1951, itself an extension and amendment of previous legislation.[3] Administration spokesmen agreed that it would have been desirable to prepare new enabling legislation but explained that time had not been available for this. In his original proposals the President requested $5927 million in new appropriations for the Mutual Security Program for fiscal year 1954.[4] In addition to asking for these new funds, the President proposed that any monies appropriated in previous years which were unobligated at the end of June 1953 be carried over to the new fiscal year. While the hearings were in progress the request for new funds was cut, to the pleasure of Congress, by $354 million. The reduction was explained as representing "savings" in executing existing programs and chiefly affected military aid for Western Europe. A second revision redistributed slightly among major areas the sums recommended.

This revised request of $5573 million compared with an appropriation of $6143 million for the previous year, as shown in Table 1.[5] Nearly $5 billion of the total funds requested were designated for military end-items and economic aid intended to support directly the rearmament programs abroad; just under $500 million were designated for economic-development programs; and the remaining $100-odd million were set aside for various

---

[3] All legislation covering the Mutual Security Program, as amended to the end of the First Session of the Eighty-third Congress, may be found in "Mutual Security Legislation and Related Documents," *Committee Print*, House of Rep., Committee on Foreign Affairs, 83d Cong., 1st Sess., December 1953.

[4] Prior to leaving office on January 20, the outgoing President presented to Congress a budget for fiscal year 1954, as he was required by law to do, proposing new obligational authority of some $7600 million for the Mutual Security Program. This proposal was commonly regarded as little more than a formality. For the relevant portion of Mr. Truman's Budget Message, see *Congressional Record* (daily edition), January 9, 1953, pp. 304-305.

[5] The total for fiscal year 1954 includes $98.4 million in foreign currencies already held by the U.S. Government. In order to make the comparisons between the two years more valid, the previous year's appropriations have also been adjusted, by adding $141 million of expenditures in foreign currencies made during that period. These foreign currencies were the local-currency counterpart of previously granted foreign aid. Prior to mid-1953 these counterpart funds had been expended by the Mutual Security Agency without specific legislative authorization, but the Supplemental Appropriation Act of 1953 provided that after June 30, 1953, foreign currencies or credits owned by the U.S. Treasury would be available for expenditure by agencies of the U.S. Government only as provided annually in appropriation acts. (Sect. 1415, P.L. 547, 82d Cong., July 15, 1952.)

# I. MILITARY ASSISTANCE

## TABLE 1

*Mutual Security Program Funds, Fiscal Years Ending*
*June 30, 1953, and June 30, 1954*
(millions of dollars)

| Program and Area | 1952-1953 Congressional Appropriation[a] | Revised Presidential Request[b] | 1953-1954 Congressional Authorization | Congressional Appropriation[c] | Congressional Reappropriation of Unobligated Balances |
|---|---|---|---|---|---|
| I. Military Assistance | | | | | |
| Europe | 3047[a] | 2237 | 2180 | 1860 | 1812 |
| Near East and Africa | 506[a] | 408 | 355 | 270 | 318 |
| Asia and the Pacific | 542 | 1084 | 1082 | 1035 | 257 |
| Latin America | 52 | 15 | 15 | 15 | 51 |
| II. Mutual Defense Financing | | | | | |
| Europe, defense support | 1433[a] | 311 | 250 | 220 | 116[d] |
| Formosa and Indochina, defense support | 166 | 84 | 84 | 84 | 18 |
| Manufacturing in France | — | 100 | 100 | 85 | — |
| Manufacturing in the United Kingdom | — | 100 | 100 | 85 | — |
| Force support for Indochina[e] | — | 400 | 400 | 400 | — |
| III. Mutual Special-Weapons Planning | — | 250 | 100 | 50 | — |
| IV. Technical Assistance | | | | | |
| Near East and Africa | 51 | 44 | 44 | 34 | — |
| Asia and the Pacific | 105 | 72 | 72 | 51 | 11 |
| Latin America | 20 | 24 | 24 | 22 | — |
| Basic materials | 64[a] | 50 | 8 | 19 | — |
| V. Special Economic Assistance | | | | | |
| Near East and Africa | 70 | 194[f] | 194 | 147 | — |
| Palestine refugees | 60 | ([f]) | ([f]) | — | 44 |
| India and Pakistan | — | 94 | 94 | 75 | — |
| VI. International Organizations and Other | | | | | |
| Movement of migrants | 9 | 10 | 10 | 8 | — |
| Multilateral technical assistance | 9 | 14 | 14 | 10 | — |
| Children's welfare | 7 | 9 | 9 | 10 | — |
| Ocean freight | 8 | 2 | 2 | 2 | * |
| Korean reconstruction | — | 71 | 71 | 51 | — |
| Total | 6143[a] | 5573[b] | 5256[g] | 4532 | 2121 |

Details may not add to totals because of rounding.

* Less than $500,000.

a) Adjusted for the transfer of $125 million by the Mutual Security Agency from military assistance to defense support for Europe. Also included are expenditures of $141 million in local-currency counterpart funds reserved for United States use. These were not subject to Congressional appropriation prior to June 30, 1953, but are included in this table to permit a more accurate comparison with data for fiscal year 1954. The local-currency expenditures in 1952-1953 were: $70 million in Europe for military assistance and defense support, $7 million for military assistance to the Near East and Africa, and $64 million for basic-materials development.

(*Notes continued on next page*)

multilateral economic and relief programs. In general, the relative distribution of aid among major programs was the same as during 1952, but comparisons with previous years are difficult because of the overlapping purposes for which aid was provided and the differences in classification.

On an area basis, over $2700 million were requested for Europe (excluding the $400 million requested to reimburse France in dollars for military end-items to be furnished by France to the forces fighting in Indochina), $646 million were requested for the Near East and Africa, $1734 million for Asia and the Pacific (including the above noted $400 million), and $39 million for Latin America. Multilateral aid programs were allocated $106 million, and $300 million were requested for special-weapons planning and for helping to expand the production of scarce basic materials.[6]

---

b) The figures shown here include revisions made by the President during the course of the hearings. Also included are the equivalent of $98 million in local-currency counterpart funds owned by the U.S. Government. In addition to new funds requested, the Administration recommended that any funds unobligated as of June 30, 1953, be carried over to the new fiscal year; the amounts reappropriated are shown in the final column of this table.

c) After enactment of the authorization bill, the President requested appropriations of only $5189 million.

d) Of this, $75 million was to be available only for aid to Spain and $37.5 million only for facilitating aircraft production in Italy.

e) Represents military aid to be furnished by France to the forces fighting in Indochina, for which France would be reimbursed in dollars by the United States.

f) In requesting $194 million for special assistance in the Near East and Africa, President Eisenhower stated that $30 million of the amount was programmed for Palestine refugees, but that this $30 million would not be requested for appropriation because of the large unobligated balances available for this purpose.

g) Includes $98 million undistributed by area or program (the local-currency funds requested by the President).

In addition to the amounts shown, authority to transfer excess equipment and materials to any countries eligible for aid under the Mutual Defense Assistance Act of 1949, as amended, was increased in 1953 by another $200 million, raising the cumulative authority for transfer of such matériel to $1400 million. This does not require appropriation.

Sources: S. Rpt. No. 645, 83d Cong.; H. Rpt. No. 770, 83d Cong.; and Mutual Security Appropriation Act, 1954 (P.L. 218, 83d Cong.), August 7, 1953.

---

[6] Although not so specified, it was probably planned that most of the $250 million requested for special-weapons planning would be spent in Europe. The $50 million for the basic-materials program, half in dollars and half in local currencies, was to be spent mostly in Africa, but some was also to go to Asian and European countries.

The request for Europe was approximately two-thirds the previous year's appropriation and represented only about half the total Program for 1953-1954, compared with three quarters of the total during the previous year. Latin America had in the past received only small amounts of aid under the Program and its share for 1953-1954 was again small. The amounts requested for the Middle East and Africa were about the same as in the previous year's appropriation, and so were a larger proportion of the reduced total Program. Asia and the Pacific, however, were scheduled to receive more than double the amounts provided for them in 1952-1953. This shift in emphasis from Europe in favor of the Far East was a continuation of a movement begun by the Democratic Administration, but was at a sharply accelerated pace. Witnesses for the new Administration vigorously denied that Europe was regarded as less important than it had been, explaining the accelerated trend toward more aid to Asia as the result of the new Administration's focussing attention on the world as a whole. The Senate Committee on Appropriations cited also the facts that the forces in Europe were already becoming large and that great amounts of aid to Europe were in the pipeline.

In justifying their request, Administration spokesmen argued that these amounts represented their best judgment as to the proper reconciliation between the military requirements for the security of the United States and its allies and the free world's economic and political capabilities. They noted that their request was some half billion dollars less than had been appropriated for the previous year and that the programs had been determined after an intensive three-month study of national security policy, together with evaluations of past and present programs, by the National Security Council. They stressed that the proposed Program was based on a new concept: namely, that it was impossible to forecast the time of maximum military danger and that the defense build-up must therefore be such that the military strength of the Western nations could be maintained on a "sound" economic basis for an indefinite period of time. This meant that the *immediate* force goals for the countries of the North Atlantic Treaty Organization (NATO) had been revised downward but that the ultimate goals were unchanged and until they were attained the Western nations would be taking a calculated risk.

United States military leaders played a prominent role in justifying the Administration's request.[7] They testified that there was every indication that Russia was continuing vigorously to develop and modernize her forces and that her atomic capabilities were rapidly improving. They stated that the Soviet bloc's land and air forces greatly exceeded those of the European NATO countries and that, while the size of these forces had not increased significantly since 1949, their effectiveness had been greatly improved, particularly by increasing mechanization. General Bradley, Chairman of the Joint Chiefs of Staff, stated that the force goals established by the North Atlantic Treaty Council were for defensive forces and there was no thought of going beyond that, but that Western Europe could not defend itself unless it was supported through a program of aid from the United States. He declined to name a sum that would represent the minimum military aid required but testified that the amounts recommended to Congress were "considerably" less than the Joint Chiefs of Staffs had contemplated for military assistance and that, from the military point of view, he wished the United States were doing more than was provided in the legislation under discussion.

As in previous years, members of Congress did not take issue with the testimony of the military leaders as to the size of the Soviet threat and the military forces necessary to meet it. But many did question whether the nation could support an aid program of the size requested in view of the budget deficit, the heavy tax burdens, and the inflationary pressures existing at that time inside the United States. Some, noting that the United States had supplied most of the foreign troops in the United Nations forces in Korea, also suggested that at least a part of the requested funds might more effectively strengthen the security of the United States if they were made available to the nation's own Military Establishment, especially the Air Force.

Spokesmen for the Administration admitted concern over the burden this Program imposed on the United States but said that it was within the nation's capabilities, that it was consistent with moving toward a balanced budget, and that any appreciably

[7] The testimony of the military personnel was notable, however, for its caution in nonmilitary matters; they frequently declined to answer questions having to do with economics and finance.

smaller Program would be dangerous to the nation's peace and security. Secretary of the Treasury Humphrey said he was distressed that the federal budget would not be balanced during the coming year but that "I just do not want economy at the expense of security."[8]

In answer to the suggestion that at least some of the funds might more effectively be used to strengthen the forces of the United States, President Eisenhower declared: "Unequivocally I can state that this amount of money judiciously spent abroad will add much more to our Nation's ultimate security in the world than would an even greater amount spent merely to increase the size of our own military forces in being."[9] He was supported by Secretary of State Dulles, who cited the lower cost of maintaining troops of other countries and the fact that these troops were already located in strategic areas.

On the other hand, a few members of Congress asked whether the request was adequate, and they were assured by the Administration that the proposed amounts were "safe," given the requirements for maintaining "sound economies" in the United States and abroad. In this connection, Mr. Dulles denied that the amount requested had been affected in any way by the reported Soviet "peace feelers" following the death of Premier Stalin.

Again in 1953, some members of Congress argued for less aid on the ground that the allies of the United States were not "doing their fair share" in the common security program. In support of this contention, they cited the facts that defense expenditures of most European nations were a smaller percentage of their gross national products than was the case in the United States and that in some countries the periods of compulsory military service were shorter than this country's. They pointed to large social welfare programs as evidence that some of the nations could devote greater expenditures to defense purposes. It was also alleged that the continued heavy votes given to members of the Communist Party, especially in France and Italy, showed that the Program had been a failure, or at least evidenced a "lack of gratitude" for the help.

Administration witnesses replied by asserting that the Euro-

[8] "Mutual Security Act of 1953," *Hearings, op.cit.*, p. 171.
[9] "The Mutual Security Program for Fiscal Year 1954: Basic Data . . . ," *op.cit.*, p. X.

pean countries were making contributions "to the limit of their resources and in some cases a little bit beyond their resources. . . ."[1] They pointed out that the defense expenditures of the European NATO countries had more than doubled between 1950 and 1953 and were expected to reach the equivalent of nearly $15 billion in 1954. They also argued that the higher per capita wealth and income in the United States enabled this country to devote a greater percentage of its income to defense purposes, and they reminded the Congressmen that in several European nations the tax rates were higher than in the United States.[2]

A major issue in Congress in 1953 revolved around the fact that for several years the obligation and expenditure of funds for foreign-aid programs had lagged behind appropriations. At the time of the 1953 hearings and debates, the record showed that of the $32 billion provided for the Mutual Security and preceding programs during the previous four years, some $3.3 billion had not been obligated and more than $11 billion had not been spent.[3] Some members of Congress interpreted these balances as evidence that there was no need for all the requested new appropriations, and they also expressed concern lest such large balances result in Congress's losing its control over Governmental expenditures. The Administration explained that the large amounts of unobligated funds resulted primarily from the diversion of military goods originally intended for the aid programs to American forces in Korea and to strategic reserves within the United States, together with difficulties in negotiating contracts for offshore procurement. In addition, the large unexpended balances were

[1] *Hearings on H.R. 5710, op.cit.*, p. 184. For some details on European defense expenditures, taxes, etc., see *S. Rpt. No. 403, op.cit.*, pp. 18-21.

[2] Although most of the discussion of the Mutual Security Program was conducted without reference to commercial policy, at one point an Administration spokesman referred to the Mutual Security Program and the Reciprocal Trade Agreements Program as a "package," and Mr. Stassen, Director for Mutual Security, testified that the computations of aid requirements for fiscal year 1954 were based on the assumption that the Trade Agreements Act would be extended for one year without change and that no increase would be made in obstacles to imports to the United States. Few Congressmen, however, showed much interest in, or understanding of, the interrelationships between American commercial policy, the balance-of-payments problems of foreign countries, and needs for American aid.

[3] For detailed data on obligations and expenditures, see *S. Rpt. No. 403, op.cit.*, pp. 10-12, and "Mutual Security Appropriations for 1954," *Hearings, op.cit.*, pp. 84-92 and 784-787.

said to result from delays in production due to design changes and strikes, and to the long "lead time" necessary to produce such modern military equipment as tanks, aircraft, electronic equipment, and naval vessels. The Administration officials assured Congress that they planned to reduce this overhang, that obligations and expenditures were proceeding at an increasing rate, and that actual deliveries of military goods had recently begun to reach impressive dimensions. The Administration reminded Congress that new obligations could not legally be undertaken until funds to cover them had been appropriated and that the requested new funds were necessary to insure continuity in the Program and to prevent delays in delivery of long-lead-time equipment in the following years.

Congress finally reappropriated virtually all of the nearly $2.2 billion of previously appropriated funds which had not been committed by the end of fiscal year 1953. However, a number of Congressmen made clear their dissatisfaction with the explanations given for the large unobligated and unspent balances, and the existence of these funds was used as justification for some of the reductions made in the Administration requests for new appropriations.

A few in Congress argued once again that some or all of the aid being extended should be in the form of loans rather than grants. The Director for Mutual Security, Mr. Stassen, stated that the Administration had requested no authority to make grants where loans would be appropriate, that a loan implied the ability to repay and if this ability did not exist extending aid in the form of loans invited continuing problems between creditors and debtors. This point was accepted by most members of Congress, and no concerted attempt was made to require that a portion of the military assistance should be extended on a credit basis. Subsequently, the Randall Commission recommended that "where support is needed to maintain military forces . . . beyond the economic capacity of a country to sustain, grants should be made, not loans."[4]

Although the Administration spokesmen were frequently complimented by members of Congress for their presentation of the

[4] Commission on Foreign Economic Policy, *Report to the President and the Congress*, Wash., D.C., January 1954, p. 9.

case for continued aid, sentiment on the floor of both Houses in favor of pruning the requests ran high. Many, especially on the Republican side, emphasized the urgent "need" to balance the United States budget and reminded their colleagues of the promises their party had made to reduce taxes. Others felt that the European Recovery Program had achieved enough so that the European nations could carry a larger share of the common defense burden than was assumed in the Administration's requests. And many saw an excuse for not appropriating the full amounts requested in the existence of the large balances from previous appropriations. In the end, Congress appropriated $4532 million in new funds—about $1 billion less than the Administration had requested—and, as noted above, reappropriated $2121 million of the unobligated balances of previous appropriations.

The increasing concern over the policy of making large official grants was reflected not only in these efforts to reduce the appropriations but also in the questions raised by many as to when the program would be terminated. During the debates some Congressmen asserted the Executive Branch had given assurances on the occasion of each request for foreign-aid funds since the British loan in 1946 that the request would enable the recipient countries to proceed without further assistance from the United States. Virtually everyone who spoke to the point, both in Congress and in the Administration, agreed that the U.S. Government should plan to reduce foreign aid in future years and that "economic" aid should be terminated quickly. Administration witnesses, however, refused to give specific estimates as to when they thought foreign aid would no longer be needed. Secretary of the Treasury Humphrey stated it was his belief that it would be advantageous to make such transfers so long as the United States could thus better its security position at less expense than by increasing its own forces. Secretary of State Dulles said he thought "economic" aid should be ended very soon but saw no reason why military aid should not continue so long as there was a serious threat of war; and he compared the latter with taxes for the support of a police force. The House Committee on Foreign Affairs specifically commended the spokesmen from the Executive Branch for their candor in thus discussing the future, but a few in Congress who in the past had supported the Program warned that they would not again vote for foreign aid on such a scale.

In order to provide for administrative flexibility and to permit the Administration to meet unforeseen developments, Congress continued the authority of the existing law whereby the President could transfer up to 10 percent of the funds appropriated for any area to the same type of assistance for any other area, and could transfer up to 10 percent of the funds appropriated for military or economic assistance for any given area to the other type of assistance for the same area, provided the total of transfers from any section in the Act did not exceed 10 percent of the funds appropriated under that section. Also continued was the President's authority to use up to $100 million, of which no more than $20 million could be allocated to any one country, without regard to legislative limitations, upon his finding that such use was important to the security of the United States. This authority was broadened in the new legislation by making it applicable to the unspent funds appropriated for previous fiscal years.

Large exports of agricultural commodities in surplus supply in the United States had been financed under the Mutual Security Program and its predecessors, but the legislation prior to 1953 had not specified that the disposal of surplus farm products was a purpose of the Program.[5] The Administration proposed no change in the law in this respect, but in the hearings and debates much attention was given by members of Congress to the problem of agricultural surpluses in the United States and to ways in which these commodities could be used in foreign-aid programs. Various proposals were considered, and Section 550 of the authorizing act specified that not less than $100 million or more than $250 million of the funds authorized should be used to finance the export of surplus agricultural commodities. The appropriation act stated that not less than $100 million of the funds made available, other than funds provided for defense support, should be used to carry out this provision. As one means of fulfilling this requirement, the authorizing act gave the President authority to enter into negotiations with friendly countries for the sale to

[5] For the period July 1, 1952–May 6, 1953, for example, Mutual Security Program funds financed the export of $284 million of surplus agricultural commodities, mostly cotton, bread grains, and coarse grains.

them of surplus agricultural commodities for local currencies, these currencies to be used in turn to provide military assistance to countries eligible under the act and for certain other specified purposes. It was directed that any agreement negotiated under this authority include precautions designed to avoid displacement of customary exports, to obtain prices "consistent with maximum world prices of like commodities," to provide for the use of private trade channels to the maximum extent practicable, to give emphasis to developing new market areas, and to seek to prevent the reexport of the commodities purchased to a third country.[6]

The administration of the foreign-aid programs of the U.S. Government was reorganized by the President during the summer. The Department of State was relieved of virtually all operating responsibilities, the most notable instance being the Point Four Program, and was henceforth to have only policy-making functions. The Mutual Security Agency was reconstituted as the Foreign Operations Administration. It became the operating agency for most of the aid programs but was directed to obtain major policy guidance from the Department of State and, where appropriate, from the Departments of Defense and the Treasury. The Office of the Special Representative in Europe was replaced by a new Mission to the North Atlantic Treaty Organization and to the various regional European bodies. The chief of the diplomatic mission in each country was given responsibility for coordinating and directing all activities of the U.S. Government within that country.[7] Congress welcomed the concentration of the administration of aid programs in a single organization. Some, however, questioned whether the policy-making and operating functions could, in fact, be separated and suggested that the operating organization should be a subordinate unit within the Department of State. Secretary of State Dulles opposed this suggestion.[8]

[6] The 50 percent American flag provision, requiring that insofar as practicable at least half of the gross tonnage of commodities shipped abroad with the funds provided by Mutual Security appropriations be shipped in American flag vessels, was continued in the new appropriation act.

[7] For the text of the various reorganization orders and related documents, see Department of State *Bulletin*, June 15, 1953, pp. 849-856, and August 24, 1953, pp. 240-242.

[8] Congress again expressed displeasure over what it regarded as excessive personnel engaged in administering the Mutual Security Program. In spite of assurances by the Administration that the size of the Agency's staff was being

## Direct Military Assistance

The new Administration, continuing the practice of its predecessors, proposed to grant to foreign nations, for purposes of directly strengthening their defenses, aid of two broad categories: (a) military end-item assistance, including training, and (b) other types of goods and services designed to maintain and increase the internal military efforts of the recipients. In addition, in 1953 the Administration recommended aid of a third category: for the development of special weapons. The second category, which was frequently referred to as "economic" aid, had been officially called "defense support" in 1952 and was labelled "mutual defense financing" in 1953. Distinctions between the first two types of military assistance were often blurred, but the first has for some time been administered by the Department of Defense and the second by the Mutual Security Agency and its successor. The present section is concerned with the first category, for which the President requested some $3700 million: $2237 million for Europe, $408 million for the Near East and Africa, $1084 million for Asia and the Pacific (not including $400 million to be provided by France for which that country was to be reimbursed in dollars under the "mutual defense financing" category), and $15 million for Latin America.[9]

a. EUROPE

From the beginning of the military assistance program in 1949, Western Europe had been the largest recipient of aid, primarily on the grounds that the countries of that area were able and willing to make effective use of the aid and that their security was vital to the security of the United States. The same considerations prevailed in 1953. United States aid to Europe was given to individual countries but was directed toward strengthening the common defense of the West under the coordinated planning of the

---

reduced, Congress saw fit to write into the law a provision specifying that four months after its enactment the number of civilian employes should be at least 10 percent less than the corresponding number on January 1, 1953. The appropriation act also provided that not more than $58 million of the money made available should be used for administrative purposes.

[9] These data include $57 million in local currencies for Europe, $3 million for the Near East and Africa, $2 million for Asia and the Pacific, and $0.1 million for Latin America.

North Atlantic Treaty Organization (NATO). The well-publicized "Lisbon goals" for rearmament, which the North Atlantic Council—composed of Ministers of the Governments of member countries—had set in February 1952, had not been fully reached by the end of that year, and there was growing sentiment among most of the member nations that the scheduled rearmament pace was beyond their economic and political capabilities.[1]

In April 1953, prior to the submission by the Administration to Congress of its Mutual Security Program, the North Atlantic Council met in Paris to review past accomplishments and to plan for the future. As noted in the previous section, United States officials had decided that inasmuch as it was not possible to forecast the date of maximum military danger, the defense build-up must be at a rate which could be maintained on a "sound economic basis" for an indefinite period of time. The United States delegation also gave notice that the levels of United States aid in the future would be less than some of the potential recipients had expected. The goals set for 1953, while not made public, were below the earlier goals tentatively set for that year, but they still called for a "substantial" increase in military strength, with emphasis on improving the quality of existing forces and on amassing reserves of military matériel, especially ammunition.[2] Agreement was also reached at that time on, among other things, the multinational production of some $560 million of jet aircraft, for which the United States would pay not quite half the costs, and the remainder of the "fourth slice" and a tentative "fifth slice" of the infrastructure program, subject to the approval of Congress and the other legislative bodies concerned.[3]

[1] See *Survey—1952*, pp. 31-46, and the references cited there for the progress toward European rearmament under the North Atlantic Treaty Organization in 1952.

[2] For the text of the official communiqué of the April meeting of the North Atlantic Council and a speech by Secretary Dulles about the meeting, see Department of State *Bulletin*, May 11, 1953, pp. 671-674.

[3] "Infrastructures" are military installations, especially airfields and storage facilities, to be used by the collective forces of NATO, and the costs of construction are shared by the members. This program was begun in 1950 by five European nations. The United States first participated in the "second slice," undertaken in 1951. The total cost of the first four segments was estimated to be a little more than the equivalent of $1800 million, of which the United States had agreed to pay $470 million, net of direct taxes to European governments. The

# I. MILITARY ASSISTANCE

In support of the military funds requested for Europe, General Ridgway, then Supreme Allied Commander for Europe, testified that the Western land, naval, and air forces were still inadequate in the face of Russia's known capabilities and well-established pattern of aggression, and that continuation of military assistance to Europe was essential to the United States' own security, as well as to that of the other NATO members. Another spokesman stated that about 80 percent of the funds requested for Europe would be used to provide military hardware and training, with the balance going for packaging and handling, the infrastructure program, and administrative expenses. It was stated that assistance was to be provided only for forces that conformed to NATO plans; that combat forces were being so equipped as to approach performance capabilities comparable with those of similar United States units; that items supplied usually consisted only of those intended for direct military application, especially combat weapons, and that such items as food, clothing, and motor fuel were furnished only in special circumstances; that spare parts were not usually provided; and that no items were sent to any country unless they could not otherwise be obtained within periods of time appropriate to NATO defense plans.

projected "fifth slice" was to cost up to the equivalent of $700 million, of which the United States agreed to contribute up to $264 million, net of taxes.

United States financing of the infrastructure program had been met in fiscal 1952 by an allocation of $220 million of Mutual Defense Assistance funds and in fiscal 1953 by an allocation of $140 million of funds appropriated to the military public works program of the Defense Department. Of the funds requested for the Mutual Security Program for fiscal 1954, the Administration said it planned to use $180 million for the United States contribution to the infrastructure program. There was scattered opposition in Congress to the United States' helping to finance such installations, some believing that unnecessary duplication was involved, some thinking it unwise for the United States to make such expenditures in view of the uncertainty as to the future of the European Defense Community, and some thinking no new appropriations were necessary in 1953 inasmuch as less than half the previous allocations had been spent. General Ridgway made a special plea for long-term, "businesslike" planning, and he stated that he regarded the progress in airfield construction as one of the "significant achievements" of NATO. Congress did not in the end write into the law any prohibition on United States contributions to infrastructure installations.

For some Congressional discussion of the infrastructure program, see *Hearings on H.R. 5710, op.cit.*, pp. 509-549, and "Mutual Security Act of 1953," *Hearings, op.cit.*, pp. 854-866. For a statement by the Executive Branch concerning negotiations with foreign countries involving United States commitments to furnish assistance for more than one year into the future, see *Hearings on H.R. 5710, op.cit.*, pp. 1283-1286. This statement is also relevant to the multilateral aid programs of the United Nations to which the United States is a party.

These guidelines were not criticized by Congress, but many members expressed disappointment at what they regarded as the slow rate of rearmament in Europe, some referring to the NATO forces as "a paper army" and, as noted above, some doubting that Europe was doing its "fair share." However, General Ridgway stated that in his opinion the NATO countries were "capable within the reasonably near future of creating and maintaining that necessary minimum military strength."[4]

Permeating the discussion of military aid to Europe, as in the previous year, was the question of the role of Germany and, in particular, of the European Defense Community. From the beginning of the organized efforts of the United States after the war to strengthen the defenses of Western Europe, both the Executive and Legislative branches have insisted that large-scale German participation was necessary. After a short period of skepticism, both branches of the American Government gave wholehearted support to the 1950 proposal of the then French Premier, René Pleven, that this be accomplished, in such a way as to minimize the danger of resurgent German nationalism, by creating a European Defense Community. In general, under this plan most of the armed forces of France, Germany, Italy, Belgium, Luxembourg, and the Netherlands would be merged into a single European Army which would serve under an integrated command and be under the general direction of a supranational authority. It was planned that the forces would be assigned to the European commander of the North Atlantic Treaty Organization. A treaty establishing the Community was signed by the six prospective members in May 1952, but at the beginning of 1953 none of them had ratified the treaty, and there was strong opposition to it within most of the countries concerned, especially in France and Germany.[5]

In the hearings on the Mutual Security Program, witnesses for

[4] "Mutual Security Act of 1953," *Hearings, op.cit.*, p. 590.

[5] For a discussion of the more important provisions of the treaty and of some of the issues that held up its ratification in 1952, see *Survey—1952*, pp. 46-50, and the references cited there. See also Walton, C. C., "Background for the European Defense Community," *Political Science Quarterly*, March 1953, pp. 42-69.

At the time the treaty was signed, France, the United Kingdom, and the United States also signed a "contractual agreement" with Germany, to come into force at the same time as the European Defense Community, restoring to West Germany virtually complete control over her foreign and domestic affairs.

the Administration voiced keen disappointment at the failure of the countries concerned to establish the Community, and they stressed anew its importance to the security plans of the United States and its allies. The essence of the Administration's position was the same as that of its predecessor: adequate defensive strength in Europe could not be reached without a military contribution by West Germany, and the European Defense Community was the most feasible means by which this contribution could be obtained. Secretary Dulles stated that the Administration's recommendations for aid to Europe were predicated upon the coming into being of the European Army. When asked what the Administration would do if the treaty failed of ratification, he gave his answer off the record; but he warned publicly later in the year that such failure would "compel an agonizing reappraisal of basic United States policy."[6]

Congress did not need to be convinced of the desirability of the Community, and, as in previous years, many favored applying pressure on the nations concerned by making part of the proposed American aid to Europe conditional upon the creation of the Community. Spokesmen for the Administration agreed that it might be desirable for Congress to make its sentiments in favor of the Community known but advised against the proposed action on the grounds that it might serve to strengthen the opposition in Europe and to damage relations between the United States and its allies. Congress, however, was in no mood for caution. An amendment was adopted on the floor of the Senate authorizing the President to withhold up to $1 billion of the military assistance authorized for Europe until the Community was established, it being argued that this would greatly strengthen the bargaining position of the Administration.[7] The House bill went further; it included a provision that 50 percent of the funds authorized for military assistance for Western Europe should be made available *only* to the European Defense Community. A few members of Congress questioned the wisdom of such amendments and warned, as the Administration had done, that such "coercive" tactics might well have the opposite effect from that intended. Supporters stated they regarded the action not as "coercion" but as an "in-

[6] *New York Times*, December 15, 1953, p. 14.
[7] See *Congressional Record* (daily edition), June 30, 1953, p. 7878.

centive" and "legislative encouragement." A variation of the House amendment was finally approved, and the Mutual Security Act of 1953 provided that half of the funds appropriated for military aid to Europe could be transferred only to a European Defense Community or to countries that were members of it, unless Congress, upon the recommendation of the President, should thereafter provide otherwise.

Spain is not a member of NATO; nonetheless, in 1951 and 1952 Congress had specified that $125 million of the Mutual Security funds should be provided to that country on a grant basis. (In 1950 Congress had authorized a loan to Spain of $62.5 million.) At the time of the 1953 debates on the Mutual Security Program, none of the authorized grants had been transferred, the Administration explaining the delays as resulting from the fact that bilateral assistance agreements—one for military aid, one for economic and technical aid, and one for United States use of bases in Spain—were only then in the final stages of negotiation. The new Administration apparently had fewer doubts than its predecessors as to the desirability of aiding Spain, and military leaders stressed the importance to the United States of having bases behind the Pyrenees. Congress was asked to reappropriate the unobligated $125 million and was told that the Administration also planned to use approximately $100 million of the new funds requested in helping that country.[8] A few in Congress opposed aid to Spain because of its dictatorial Government, and some were irritated by what they regarded as hard bargaining by General Franco in negotiating the bilateral agreements. However, the majority appeared to be more impressed by the fact that the Spanish Government was anti-Communist and that bases in Spain were in the United States' interest. Virtually all of the unobligated funds were reappropriated, and while there was no explicit provision for Spain in the new appropriations, Congress did indicate approval of expenditures in that country at the level proposed by the Administration.

Yugoslavia, which had received large amounts of American aid after the rupture with Russia, was also a subject of controversy in

[8] Administration spokesmen said it was tentatively planned that of the $225 million, $140 million would be for "military" aid and $85 million for "economic" aid.

Congress. The Administration, stressing the important contribution the thirty-odd Yugoslav divisions could make to the defense of the Balkans and welcoming the recent understandings between Yugoslavia, Greece, and Turkey on military matters, stated that it proposed to spend $217 million of the request for new "military assistance" funds plus $45 million of the requested defense-support funds in aiding that country. As in the case of Spain, some Congressmen opposed aid to Yugoslavia because of the authoritarian character of its Government; others opposed aid to any country espousing Communism, albeit a non-Russian Communism; and some questioned the reliability of Yugoslavia as an ally. The majority in Congress, however, accepted the view of the Senate Committee on Foreign Relations that, although aware of the adherence of Spain and Yugoslavia to forms of government that were inconsistent with American concepts of freedom, they believed both countries would resist Soviet aggression, and therefore it was in the interests of the United States to support their defenses.

Late in 1951 the United States initiated a major change in policy when it began a program of using large amounts of foreign-aid funds to purchase abroad military end-items to be given to foreign countries as military assistance. This "offshore procurement" program was expanded in 1952, and at the time of the Congressional discussions of the 1953 Mutual Security Program nearly $1.5 billion in contracts had been let for offshore purchases, most of them in France, the United Kingdom, and Italy.[9] The offshore procurement program had been welcomed by foreign countries and the "Evaluation Teams" of businessmen sent abroad in early 1953 by the new Director for Mutual Security recom-

[9] For a table showing detail of offshore procurement contracts placed, by country, see *S. Rpt. No. 403, op.cit.*, p. 28.

Contracts let in France up to May 1953 totalled $608 million, of which $268 million represented contracts originally placed by the French Government for its own military procurement but which that Government subsequently had planned to cancel because of internal financial difficulties. The United States took over these contracts under the offshore procurement program in order to prevent the loss of production involved, about two thirds of which was intended for forces in Indochina. Some in Congress questioned whether this practice would not encourage European nations deliberately to "overcommit" themselves in the expectation that the United States would pay for the excess. Witnesses for the Administration stated that the annual review of NATO would hinder such action and that the United States had tried to make it clear that this was an exceptional case.

mended its extension.[1] The Administration informed Congress that it proposed to enlarge this program, suggesting that perhaps as much as two fifths of the funds requested for direct military assistance might be so spent, mostly for ammunition and spare parts but also for aircraft, electronic equipment, vehicles, and naval vessels. Funds spent for this purpose were called "triple duty dollars" by the Administration, the claim being that (1) they procured military matériel, and probably at lower cost than if it had been purchased in the United States, (2) they would serve to increase the capacity of the recipient countries (mostly European) for defense production and give impetus to the creation of self-supporting mobilization bases abroad, including replacement and maintenance facilities, and (3) they would supply dollars to foreign governments.[2]

The offshore procurement program was enthusiastically supported by most members of Congress, although a few voiced criticism of the practice. Some of its opponents charged that it was merely a device for providing Europe with unneeded economic aid of a type that Congress had disapproved in the past. More serious was the objection that in administering the program too much attention had been given to placing contracts in countries facing serious international balance-of-payments problems and not enough to such factors as prices and delivery dates.[3] Some

---

[1] For this and other recommendations of the Evaluation Teams, see Office of the Director for Mutual Security, *Evaluation Report*, Wash., D.C., March 24, 1953.

[2] Other advantages claimed for the program were that it would foster multinational planning by the NATO staff and the individual countries and that it would help to relieve unemployment in some areas, particularly France and Italy.

A notable feature of the offshore procurement program was the multinational purchase of aircraft arranged by the NATO headquarters. The United States, the United Kingdom, France, Belgium, and the Netherlands joined together to contract for the purchase of some 1700 jet aircraft at a total cost of some $560 million, of which the United States' share was $282 million. This program involved international subcontracting and represented an important step toward international specialization of European military production, a goal sought by many on the grounds that it would permit economies of scale and would be a safeguard against intra-European aggression. NATO was preparing plans in 1953 for similar coordinated multinational procurement of ammunition, electronics equipment, and transport vehicles.

[3] The Randall Commission echoed this criticism in its report of January 1954 and recommended that the program "should not be used as a form of general economic aid." Commission on Foreign Economic Policy, *Report to the President and the Congress*, op.cit., p. 9.

Congressmen criticized the program as depriving American producers of markets, but little attention was given this aspect in the spring of 1953, when the level of production in the United States was high. On the other hand, some members of Congress noted with approval the saving in American resources (at least, in the first instance) and asked why all American foreign aid could not be handled in this way. The Administration replied that there was a limit to the amount of production that European resources could support; that some items had to be produced in the United States for strategic reasons; that, also for strategic reasons, it was necessary to keep certain United States production facilities in operation; and that some items could be produced in this country with greater efficiency.[4]

In 1951 Congress had enacted the "Kersten Amendment," authorizing the use of $100 million of the Mutual Security Program funds for Europe to help escapees from Iron Curtain countries, by forming them into elements of the NATO military forces or in other ways. This authority was continued in 1952. In the 1953 discussions a few in Congress voiced criticism that only about $5 million had been spent under this authority, chiefly for resettlement of refugees in the western sector of Berlin and other areas, and some expressed disappointment that no action had been taken to form such escapees into military units. Although there was some effort in Congress to amend the existing law so as to provide that not less than $100 million should be used for the purposes specified, the majority agreed with the Administration that this should not be made a major program, and the legislation was continued unchanged, except for the addition to those eligible for assistance of escapees from Communist-occupied and Communist-dominated areas of Asia.[5]

b. NEAR EAST AND AFRICA

The bulk of the $408 million requested by the Administration for military assistance to the Near East and Africa was, as in

---

[4] For some Congressional discussion of the offshore procurement program, see *Hearings on H.R. 5710, op.cit.*, pp. 437-464, 469-490, and 497-509, and "Mutual Security Act of 1953," *Hearings, op.cit.*, pp. 817-854.

[5] For Congressional discussion on this issue, see *Hearings on H.R. 5710, op.cit.*, pp. 1052-1062 and 1156-1162; "Mutual Security Act of 1953," *Hearings, op.cit.*, pp. 559-564; and "Mutual Security Appropriations for 1954," *Hearings, op.cit.*, pp. 174-181.

earlier years, scheduled for Greece and Turkey, both members of NATO and recipients of aid since 1947, and for Iran. The programs for Greece and Turkey were a continuation of existing efforts, and both the Administration and Congress regarded these two countries, and especially Turkey, as excellent examples of the United States' obtaining a great deal of national security for very little cost. Authority was also requested to give military aid to the other nations in the area, including the Arab States, Israel, Libya, and Ethiopia, as well as Pakistan. (None of these nations had previously received military aid under the Program.) Pakistan was included in order to make possible its association in areawide defense plans.

Administration witnesses stressed the strategic importance of the Near East area, both for its location and for its petroleum reserves, and said that in view of the poverty and political and social unrest in most of the countries there it was necessary to give aid to resist subversion from within and aggression from without. The Executive Branch stated it hoped, as had the previous Administration, that a regional defense organization could be created in the Near East. It recognized that the United States faced attitudes of uncertainty, mistrust, and even hostility in the Arab States, that Arab-Israeli tensions made formation of a Middle Eastern Defense Organization difficult, that the Anglo-Egyptian dispute over the Suez greatly complicated the issue, and that the Arab States felt they already had a regional defense arrangement in the Arab League. Nonetheless, the Administration hoped that these problems could be overcome and asked for authority to transfer aid directly to a regional defense organization should one be organized.

Many in Congress were as anxious as the Administration that a regional defense arrangement be created in the area, but the prevailing opinion was that it was premature to appropriate large funds for such an organization in 1953. Considering also that there were large amounts of previously appropriated funds for that area that had not yet been spent, Congress appropriated only $240 million for military assistance to Greece, Turkey, and Iran, giving the President authority to utilize up to 10 percent of it for other countries in the area. An additional $30 million was made available for any regional defense organization that might be created, or for members thereof, but it was specified that these funds could be used to aid any nation in the area if the President found such assistance would be important to the defense of the area and to the security of the United States.[6]

## C. ASIA AND THE PACIFIC

The Far East was characterized in the Congressional hearings and debates on the Mutual Security Program as an "area full of trouble," and the Administration requested new funds for military assistance to the area (excluding Korea) of nearly $1100 million—plus $400 million of aid to Indochina to be furnished by France but financed by the United States.[7] Most of the increase in military aid proposed for the Far East—only slightly more than $500 million had been appropriated for such assistance in the previous fiscal year—was intended to go to Indochina and Formosa.

The Senate Committee on Foreign Relations reported that it had received evidence of "notable improvement" in both military and economic conditions on Formosa since the establishment of the Nationalist Chinese Government there at the end of 1949. Many in Congress stated that the United States must honor with continued aid its commitment to support that Government, and the majority favored providing more than the Administration proposed. Only a small minority publicly expressed doubts as to the effectiveness of this aid in enabling the recipients to resist aggression and in reducing the appeal of Communism. A few voiced concern over the limited possibility for recruitment in Formosa, and one Congressman went so far as to comment that Formosa would soon not have a military force but an "old soldiers' home."

Beginning in late 1951 the U.S. Government had given a high priority to aiding the French and Vietnamese forces fighting in

[6] Under another law Congress authorized the loan of two submarines to Turkey for a period of not more than five years, costs of activation of the submarines to be charged against funds programmed for Turkey under the Mutual Security appropriations. (P.L. 214, 83d Cong., August 7, 1953.)

[7] The cost of military operations by United States forces in Korea and aid to other United Nations forces fighting there were not included in the Mutual Security Program but were financed from funds appropriated for the Defense Establishment. Virtually no financial or economic details of the Korean War were made public and they are *not* reported in this *Survey*. Assistance for reconstruction in Korea is discussed in the following chapter.

Indochina. It was believed that a military victory for the Communists there would be a major loss for the free world, while the defeat of the Communist forces would reduce the huge drain on French manpower and resources and so permit an increase in French strength in Europe. The new Administration subscribed to these views and proposed to increase the rate of assistance in fiscal year 1954. Except for some criticism charging inefficient use of the military supplies granted in the past and some doubts as to whether anything less than many times the aid suggested could be effective, there was virtually no opposition in Congress to the Administration's proposals.

One of the more delicate questions in the proposed Mutual Security Program for fiscal 1954 was that of military aid to Japan. The constitution adopted by Japan after World War II (in the formulation of which the U.S. Government played a dominant role) renounced war and threat or use of force as means of settling international disputes and prohibited the maintenance by Japan of land, sea, and air forces. A 1951 "security treaty" between the United States and Japan permitted the stationing of United States troops there to safeguard Japan against aggression, and a "National Safety Force" with an authorized strength of 110,000 men had been created. Prior to 1953, this national police force had been provided with a "substantial amount" of equipment by the U.S. Army from funds available to it, but Japan had received no military items under the Mutual Security Program.

The Administration was negotiating a bilateral agreement for aid under the Mutual Defense Assistance Act of 1949, as amended, at the time of the 1953 hearings on extending the Mutual Security Program. In those hearings Administration spokesmen recommended military assistance to Japan in an amount not revealed in the public record. They argued that such aid would permit Japan to bear an increasing portion of the burden of its own defense. The only alternative, it was said, was an indefinite occupation of Japan by United States troops at a cost of "5 to 10 times as much" and with the continuous frictions always incident to foreign occupation of a sovereign nation. They reported that the British Government favored a gradual development of Japanese defense forces, but that Australia and New Zealand were skeptical as to its wisdom. They emphasized that the intent was not to "rearm" Japan but to strengthen her "defense forces." Some members of Congress regarded this as violating the Japanese constitution and as being contrary to the will of many Japanese people, but the opposition was small and the majority favored the Administration proposals.[8]

Congress showed little disposition, on balance, to reduce the Administration's request for aid to Asia and the Pacific and, as Table 1 shows, virtually the entire amount requested by the Administration was appropriated. The appropriation act stipulated, further, that 20 percent more than the sum proposed by the Administration should be available to the Nationalist Government of China.[9]

d. LATIN AMERICA

Military assistance to Latin American nations was authorized by the Mutual Security Act of 1951 upon a finding by the President that such aid would contribute to the defense of the Western Hemisphere. More specifically, the purpose of this aid was primarily to make more secure the access to strategic materials in that area and to lessen the probability of having to station large numbers of United States troops there in time of crisis. At the time of the hearings on the Mutual Security Act of 1953, however, bilateral agreements for such aid were in effect only with Brazil, Chile, Colombia, Cuba, Ecuador, and Peru. Additional agreements had been signed but not yet ratified with

[8] For a Japanese editorial urging that Japan should accept Mutual Security assistance in the spirit of promoting the security of the free world, see *Journal of Finance and Commerce* (Tokyo), June 15, 1953, p. 1; see also the article on pp. 11ff. of this issue.

[9] Under separate legislation the President was authorized, upon the advice of the Secretary of Defense after consultation with the Joint Chiefs of Staff, to lend or otherwise make available, with or without reimbursement, up to twenty-five naval vessels of the destroyer type or smaller, plus such minor craft and training services as he deemed proper, to "any friendly foreign nation in the Far Eastern area." This authority expires on December 31, 1956.

This legislation also authorized the loan of two submarines to Italy for a period of not more than five years, for the training of Italian units in anti-submarine warfare, and of a small aircraft carrier to France until six months after the cessation of hostilities in Indochina, or for a maximum of five years. Expenses involved in the activation and preparation of all these vessels for loan or other transfer are to be charged against Mutual Security funds programmed for the countries receiving them. (P.L. 188, 83d Cong., August 5, 1953.)

the Dominican Republic and Uruguay, and Mexico had declined military assistance from the United States.[1] Despite the lack of enthusiasm in Latin America for the program and the slowness with which it was being implemented, the Administration requested $15 million in new obligational authority and the reappropriation of unobligated balances. Witnesses pointed out that little modern military equipment is produced in Latin America, and they stated that failure to make any new appropriations would serve to lend credence to the statements of Communist and nationalist propagandists in these countries that the United States was not interested in helping the people of Latin America to defend themselves. There was only minor opposition in Congress to this request and it was honored in full.

### Mutual Special-Weapons Planning

In addition to requesting the military end-items described above, the Administration asked Congress in 1953 to appropriate $250 million for "mutual special-weapons planning." These funds, it was said, would be used to help finance the development of new weapons, not including atomic weapons, that might be discovered by allies who did not have the means to develop and produce them; it was thought the funds would also provide a stimulus to research. Administration spokesmen testified that this new activity was in support of a desire to place more emphasis in the international security program on new weapons and that the aid would be given other countries only upon a finding by the President that it would be in the security interests of the United States.[2] It was also specified that any weapons developed and produced under the program would be provided to other countries only upon the same findings, plus assurances that the benefiting nation would safeguard the secrets.

The majority of Congress found little to criticize in this new program, but they concluded that the Administration's plans were not sufficiently advanced to justify providing the amount requested, and only $50 million was appropriated.

---

[1] See *Survey—1952*, pp. 53-54, for a short statement of some of the opposition in Latin America to receiving such aid.

[2] General Bradley testified that the Joint Chiefs of Staff had not been asked to analyze the request for special-weapons assistance. ("Mutual Security Act of 1953," *Hearings, op.cit.*, pp. 188-189.)

# I. MILITARY ASSISTANCE

## Mutual Defense Financing

Following the formal termination of the European Recovery Program at the end of 1951, Congress had repeatedly stressed its determination to reduce sharply and to terminate quickly the extension of so-called "economic aid" for other than (1) disaster purposes and (2) small amounts for technical assistance to underdeveloped areas. In 1952 the Executive Branch had persuaded Congress to appropriate some $1.5 billion for "defense support" by insisting that this amount would result in the recipients' producing, themselves, additional military goods of more than this amount and so permit them to expand the defense efforts "for our common security."

In 1953 the new Administration designated its request for $995 million (including $11 million of local currencies) for nonmilitary assistance to Europe, Formosa, and Indochina as "mutual defense financing" and justified it on much the same general grounds as had been used by its predecessor, taking care to point out that it was well below the amounts requested and appropriated in earlier years.[3] Of this total, $311 million (including $11 mil-

[3] Countries receiving economic and technical assistance from the United States on a grant basis had been required for several years to deposit local currency in special accounts in amounts equivalent to the dollar cost of such aid. These local-currency deposits—so-called counterpart funds—were reserved in small part for the use of the United States, with the bulk of them being available for use by the countries depositing them for purposes approved by the United States. During the period of the European Recovery Program, the Administration had regarded these deposits as an effective anti-inflationary device when they were allowed to accumulate, and as a means of exercising considerable influence over internal investments when they were spent. (See *Survey—1951*, pp. 55-56, and the references cited there.) The Evaluation Teams sent abroad soon after the new Administration took office in 1953, however, recommended the abolition of the counterpart system. They argued that the concept was "fundamentally and psychologically wrong," that the United States should not attempt to "operate the economies" of other countries, and that, in any case, the system was not effective, inasmuch as other countries "jockeyed around" their budgets until they found expenditures the United States would approve for counterpart funds and then used other funds to finance activities for which the United States had not approved the use of counterpart funds. ("Mutual Security Act of 1953," *Hearings, op.cit.,* pp. 744-748 and 756, and Office of the Director for Mutual Security, *Evaluation Report, op.cit.,* pp. 8-9.)

The Administration, however, did not recommend in 1953 the abolition of the system, the importance of which was decreasing as the amount of "economic and technical" aid provided by the United States declined. There was some criticism of the uses to which counterpart funds had been put in the past, especially of their being used directly or indirectly to help meet "normal" government expenditures, and the law was changed to specify that no counterpart funds

lion in local currencies) was requested for continuing "defense-support" aid to Europe, including the financing of imports of raw materials, machinery and equipment, foodstuffs, and other civilian supplies. The largest amounts were intended for Britain, Turkey, and Yugoslavia.

The Administration also requested $100 million of "mutual defense financing" for the manufacture of aircraft in Great Britain and a similar amount for the manufacture of artillery, ammunition, and semiautomatic weapons in France. This new type of financing, it was pointed out, differed from offshore procurement in that the United States would not take possession of the items produced but would simply pay the British and French Governments for items produced in their countries for the use of those of their own forces that were committed to NATO. Aid of this type was justified on the ground that facilities existed in these countries for such production but that neither country felt able to finance it.

Another innovation in the Administration's 1953 proposals was a recommendation that Congress appropriate $400 million for financing the manufacture in France of military end-items that France would in turn provide to French and Associated States

---

generated from American aid should be used to pay interest or principal on foreign governmental debts.

In 1951 Congress, through the "Benton Amendment," had directed that the Mutual Security Act be administered in such a way as to encourage free private enterprise, discourage cartels and monopolistic practices, and encourage the development of free trade unions. In 1952 the "Moody Amendment" had been added, providing that not less than $100 million in counterpart funds be used for implementing the "Benton Amendment." Officials of the Mutual Security Agency had attempted to implement these provisions by establishing revolving loan funds for extending credit to small businesses for productivity improvements, by making grants for the training of managers, technicians, and trade union officials, and by other means; but they reported that they had not been successful in observing the spirit of the law, much less the letter of it. Moreover, late in 1952 the "Sawyer Mission" had recommended repeal of these amendments as "unworkable," and similar recommendations were made in 1953 by members of a Congressional study mission to Europe and by the Mutual Security Evaluation Teams. These facts were brought out in the hearings on the 1953 Mutual Security Act, but the Administration stated that it did not wish the statement of objectives contained in the Benton Amendment repealed. Congress did repeal the Moody Amendment, with the stipulation that any commitments already made under it could be carried out, and it reworded the Benton Amendment by removing the words directing that the Act "be administered in such a way . . . ," and replacing them with a declaration that it is "the policy of the United States . . . to encourage the efforts of other free countries" to encourage free enterprise, discourage monopoly, and support the development of free trade unions.

forces fighting in Indochina. This aid, it was stated, would not only serve the purpose of strengthening the forces actually combatting Communism but would also ease the heavy pressures on the French domestic budget and the French balance of international payments.[4]

Finally, the President requested $84 million for defense support to Formosa and directly to Indochina, about three fourths of it being scheduled for the former area. Most of this aid, it was said, would be in the form of consumer goods—fertilizers, raw cotton, machinery, etc.—but a part would also be used to rehabilitate various public utilities.[5] That is, this aid was more akin to Marshall Plan assistance than to most of the defense-support aid requested for Western Europe. It was justified on the grounds that relief of the civilian population would increase the stability of the governments and improve the effectiveness of the armed forces of these two countries.

Many in Congress declared their opposition "in principle" to the United States' continuing to supply "economic aid," especially to Europe; it was not always clear, however, just what critics of this type of aid included in the term, and only a few in Congress showed an understanding of the frequent artificiality of distinctions between "economic" and "military" aid. Members of Congress were especially vehement in insisting that the United States should not grant aid for the purpose of easing balance-of-payments problems abroad or of assisting other countries in the solution of internal budgetary problems. Administration spokesmen agreed that economic aid should be reduced, and terminated as soon as possible. They stated that further reductions in such aid

[4] Several Congressmen took this occasion to express impatience with the failure of France to go further toward granting independence to the Associated States. Amendments were proposed from the floor designed in one way or another to use American aid as a lever on the French Government to take such action. All of these were defeated, their opponents arguing that such measures constituted "officious meddling" in the affairs of another state and might encourage the French to withdraw from Indochina completely, leaving the United States with heavier responsibilities for prosecuting the war there. (For discussion of the issue of independence for Indochina, see *Congressional Record* [daily edition], June 30, 1953, pp. 7882, 7894-7897, 7907, 7910-7911, and 7921, and July 1, 1953, pp. 7996 and 8010-8020.)

[5] In addition to the funds requested for defense support, the Administration planned to spend some of those asked for military assistance in Asia for the construction of such common-use facilities as highways that would serve both military and civilian purposes.

were planned for the following year, but they declared that "special" needs made it to the interest of the United States to grant the particular assistance requested. They insisted that in no case were these requests governed by balance-of-payments or internal-budgetary considerations; in every instance they were intended directly to increase the military efforts of the countries benefited.

There was relatively little objection in Congress to providing the full amount requested for defense-support aid to Formosa and Indochina, and this $84 million, as well as the entire $400 million requested to finance French procurement of equipment and supplies for Indochina, was appropriated. Congress, however, reduced the other requests in the "mutual defense financing" category, showing particular reluctance to continue defense-support aid to the United Kingdom. It appropriated only $85 million each to the United Kingdom and France for financing manufactures for their defense forces, and it approved $220 million in new funds and $116 million in reappropriations for defense support to Europe.[6]

## B. *IMPLEMENTATION*[7]

The value of deliveries of military end-items (including disbursements for military training and contributions to the Euro-

[6] Of the reappropriations $75 million were specifically made available for economic aid to Spain and $88 million for offshore procurement of aircraft in Italy.

[7] The more important official sources used in the preparation of this section were: Mutual Security Agency/Foreign Operations Administration, *Report to Congress on the Mutual Security Program*, Wash., D.C., June 30, 1953, and *Report to Congress on the Mutual Security Program*, Wash., D.C., December 31, 1953; Kerber, E. S., "United States Foreign Aid in the Fiscal Year 1953," *Survey of Current Business*, October 1953, pp. 15-20, and "Foreign Grants and Credits of the United States Government in 1953," *Survey of Current Business*, April 1954, pp. 17-22; and "The Foreign Operations Administration: Report of Senator Mike Mansfield," *Committee Print*, U.S. Senate, Committee on Foreign Relations, 83d Cong., 1st Sess., November 1953.

More detailed statistical data may be found in U.S. Department of Commerce, *Foreign Aid by the United States Government*, issues of March 31, 1953, and June 30, 1953, and *Foreign Grants and Credits by the United States Government*, issues of September 1953 and December 1953.

See also the following publications of the Mutual Security Agency/Foreign Operations Administration: *Monthly Report to the Public Advisory Board*, issues of March-June 1953, and *Monthly Operations Report*, issues of July, August, and December 1953 and January 1954; *Procurement Authorizations and Allotments* (monthly through July 1953); *Paid Shipments* (monthly through July 1953); and

pean infrastructure construction program) totalled $4.4 billion in 1953, nearly two-thirds more than in 1952.[8] During the last half of the year, as Table 2 shows, the outflow of such grants fell to an annual rate of $3.4 billion. All major areas shared in the increase of military end-item assistance but the relative predominance of Western Europe declined somewhat as shipments to Indochina were placed on a "high-priority" basis. From the enactment of the Mutual Defense Assistance Act of 1949 through 1953 more than 5300 aircraft, 31,000 tanks and combat vehicles, 175,000 transport vehicles, 30,000 artillery pieces, almost 2,-000,000 units of small arms and machine guns, about 35,000,000 rounds of artillery ammunition, and 1,100,000,000 rounds of small arms ammunition, among other items, had been provided foreign countries under the military assistance program.[9]

*Allotments, Authorizations, and Paid Shipments* (monthly from August 1953).

For information about the foreign-aid programs in years prior to 1953, see earlier issues of this *Survey*; Brown, W. A., and Opie, R., *American Foreign Assistance*, Wash., D.C., 1953; U.S. Department of Commerce, *Foreign Aid by the United States Government, 1940-1951*, Wash., D.C., 1952; and Behrman, J. N., "Political Factors in U.S. International Financial Cooperation, 1945-1950," *The American Political Science Review*, June 1953, pp. 431-460.

[8] The 1953 figure includes some $91 million of United States contributions to the multinational construction program of NATO and $174 million of vessels transferred to Japan, France, and the Netherlands under authority other than the Mutual Security Act: P.L. 467 and P.L. 510, 82d Cong., and P.L. 188 and P.L. 214, 83d Cong. These vessels were transferred with the expectation that they would eventually be returned but were reported as being on an "indeterminate basis" and were classified as grants, not loans.

In addition to the military matériel transferred to friendly governments as grants, the United States assists such governments in the procurement of military equipment from American producers under a system of reimbursable aid. These orders are merged with the procurement of the U.S. Department of Defense in order to insure better coordination of production of military equipment within this country. By the end of 1953, forty-six of the fifty-four countries eligible under the law to make such purchases had contracted to procure $677 million, most of it prior to 1953, and had deposited with the U.S. Government $543 million toward these contracts, of which $162 million was paid during 1953. The remaining contracts were on a "dependable undertaking" basis. Deliveries against these orders were $147 million in 1953, as compared with $124 million during the previous year. Canada, which was receiving no net aid under the Mutual Security Program, was the principal purchaser of American-produced equipment through the reimbursable-aid device, and the bulk of all such purchases were by Western Hemisphere countries.

[9] During the thirteen-month period ending on December 31, 1953, shipments included about 3,000 aircraft, 12,000 tanks and combat vehicles, 75,000 transport vehicles, 10,000 artillery pieces, 600,000 units of small arms and machine guns, 25,000,000 rounds of artillery ammunition, and 600,000,000 rounds of small arms ammunition.

At the end of 1953 over 33,000 allied personnel had completed or were cur-

# I. MILITARY ASSISTANCE

## TABLE 2

### Gross Military Grants Utilized, 1952-1953a
#### (millions of dollars)

| | 1953 | | | | | 1952 |
|---|---|---|---|---|---|---|
| | 1st Quarter | 2nd Quarter | 3rd Quarter | 4th Quarter | Total | |
| Europe, including Greece and Turkey | 1023 | 1127 | 689 | 704 | 3544 | 2260 |
| Asia and the Pacificb | 262 | 246 | 132 | 134 | 774 | 391 |
| Latin America | 5 | 61 | 15 | 7 | 87 | 59 |
| Unallocable, including administrative expensesc | 8 | 14 | 4 | 4 | 29 | 37 |
| Total | 1299 | 1447 | 840 | 849 | 4434 | 2747 |

Details may not add to totals because of rounding.
a) Represents military end-items provided by the Defense Department under the Mutual Security Program, as well as contributions to the NATO infrastructure program and certain military equipment transferred on an "indeterminate basis."

Grants "utilized" represent shipments when goods are procured by U.S. Government agencies and cash payments by the Government when other methods of procurement, including offshore procurement, are used. Excess equipment provided on a grant basis is included at original acquisition value. When such equipment is sold under the reimbursable provisions of the Mutual Security Act, the excess of original cost over the amount received from the sale is included as a grant. This item has been of greatest importance in the case of Latin America.
b) Excludes the value of military items supplied the United Nations forces in Korea. Includes the small amount of military aid provided Iran and Ethiopia.
c) Includes both counterpart funds and dollars used by various agencies of the U.S. Government in administering the military aid programs.
Sources: U.S. Department of Commerce, *Foreign Grants and Credits by the U.S. Government*, Wash., D.C., December 1953, Appendix Table 2.

Military end-item aid, having surpassed economic aid during the last quarter of 1952 for the first time since 1945, held this lead throughout 1953. For the year, aid other than military end-item assistance, including both net loans and grants, totalled just over $2.0 billion, compared with nearly $2.4 billion in the previous year; net grants alone totalled $1.8 billion in 1953, as compared with nearly $2.0 billion in 1952. From data available to the public

rently enrolled in training courses under the Mutual Security Program. These training courses, some of which were held in the United States, were designed to maintain high operating and servicing standards for the equipment supplied by the United States. Approximately 1½ percent of the expenditures under the Mutual Security Program have been for these purposes and have been concentrated on training jet aircraft pilots.

it appeared that none of the funds appropriated for "special-weapons planning" had been utilized during the year.

## Europe

### a. MILITARY END-ITEM ASSISTANCE

At $3544 million, the nations participating in the North Atlantic Treaty Organization, plus Yugoslavia, received some four fifths of the military end-item grants provided by the United States in 1953.[1] The increase of nearly 65 percent over 1952 in actual shipments to Western Europe was the result of two major factors. First, items such as aircraft, completion of which follows by many months and even years the placing of orders, began to be delivered in large quantities; and second, the competing demands for matériel by United States forces declined as hostilities slackened and then stopped in Korea and as the domestic stockpiles of military goods approached more closely the level regarded as adequate by United States military leaders.

No explanations have been found to account for the fact that military aid supplied Europe during the last half of the year was some one-third less than during the first half. Various Administration spokesmen, however, emphasized that Europe's own produc-

[1] No deliveries were made to Spain during the year under the military aid program for that country, but the first shipments were announced in January 1954.

Following long and difficult negotiations, three agreements finally were signed with Spain near the end of September 1953, covering military aid, economic and technical assistance, and the construction and joint use of air and naval facilities within Spain. (For the texts of these agreements, see Department of State *Bulletin*, October 5, 1953, pp. 435-442. For some comment on them by the United States ambassador at Madrid, see *ibid.*, December 7, 1953, pp. 798-796.) The press reported that General Franco, through "obstinate" bargaining, obtained more aid than the United States had originally offered but less than he had expected. The Spanish Government was also reported to have obtained a larger voice in the operation of the joint bases than the United States had planned, but there was no intention of admitting Spain to NATO.

Drawing on the earlier appropriations plus some of the new funds appropriated to the Mutual Security Program in 1953, the Foreign Operations Administration planned to obligate a total of $140 million for military aid to Spain in the fiscal year ending in mid-1954 and $85 million for economic aid. Priority in the economic aid program was to be given to projects that would support the joint military programs, including, insofar as possible, provision of goods and services designed to counteract the inflationary effects of the base construction program. Counterpart funds were to be required for the economic aid, 10 percent being reserved for the use of the United States, and part of Spain's portion being used to help finance the construction costs of the joint military facilities.

tion of military end-items increased substantially during the year and, at an annual rate of the equivalent of $3 billion, was some four times the pre-Korean rate. Late in the year the Director for Mutual Security reported that Western Europe had advanced to a point where the nations of that area could maintain their current defense budgets and "sound" economies with a "considerable" reduction in United States military aid and, with a few exceptions, the termination of economic aid.

b. OFFSHORE PROCUREMENT

The offshore procurement program was greatly expanded during 1953, and a total of about $1.5 billion in contracts was placed with foreign firms, all during the first half of the year, for the production of matériel for delivery to friendly nations under the military assistance program. This raised the total contracts placed since the program began to about $2200 million. Only about $300 million were actually disbursed under these contracts, as compared with some $75 million in 1952, but the rate was increasing as the year ended.[2] Of the total contracts placed, about half were in France, nearly a quarter in the United Kingdom, and about one fifth in Italy. Other important recipients were Belgium, the Netherlands, and Greece.[3] The principal items for which these contracts were placed were ammunition, aircraft, naval vessels, radio and radar equipment, tanks, artillery, and spare parts.

The Department of Defense continued to encounter difficulties in placing contracts abroad, some arising from unfamiliarity with foreign legal practices and institutional conditions. Others were occasioned by the uncertainty on the part of some European producers as to whether they could meet the specified delivery dates unless they enlarged capacity more than they wished to do or unless their own governments would agree to a postponement

[2] As noted in Chapter III, France borrowed $100 million from the Export-Import Bank in 1953 against future payments by the Defense Department on offshore contracts. This loan was repaid in March 1954, and only $24 million of the $154 million which had been borrowed for similar purposes in 1952 remained unpaid as of the end of March 1954.

[3] Contracts of $88 million had also been placed in Japan and Formosa. Canada is not included in the formal offshore procurement program but "extensive" purchases were made in that country by the Defense Department, apparently both for use by United States forces and for transfer to third countries under the Mutual Security Program.

of deliveries to themselves.[4] About half of the contracts placed through 1953 were open to competitive bidding, and the other half, covering primarily aircraft and vessels under procurement in France, were negotiated with specific producers.[5]

The Administration reported that the offshore procurement program not only was expanding the mobilization base in Europe, and thus improving that area's ability to sustain armies in the event of war, but was also improving the foreign-exchange position of countries receiving contracts. Nonetheless, the Randall Commission, while supporting this program in general, was critical of some of the past practices and recommended that the program "should not be used as a form of general economic aid" but that contracts should be placed on the basis of cost, availability, and quality of items purchased, or on broad strategic judgments as to the character and location of military production.[6]

## C. DEFENSE SUPPORT

Nonmilitary grants to Western Europe, virtually all being designed to support directly the defense activities of the countries aided, declined from a gross of $1528 million in 1952 to $1210 million in 1953.[7] As compared with shipments during the period

[4] The Foreign Operations Administration reported that orders for goods under this program were being coordinated with the European governments' own military procurement by the staff of the North Atlantic Treaty Organization.

[5] With a few exceptions, the prices paid under these contracts were not more than 10 percent above the prices for equivalent items in the United States, this 10 percent being approximately equal, on the average, to freight charges on shipments from the United States to Europe.

[6] Commission on Foreign Economic Policy, *Report to the President and the Congress, op.cit.,* p. 9.

[7] Up to the end of 1953, only $8 million of surplus agricultural products had been shipped under Section 550 of the Mutual Security Act, as amended in 1953—tobacco to the United Kingdom—but larger amounts were shipped during the early part of 1954. Such sales, which require the payment of dollars by the Foreign Operations Administration to the Commodity Credit Corporation, are not classified as grants, but expenditures of the local-currency receipts are so classified. Apparently none of this sterling had been spent during 1953.

Negotiations under Section 550 were held during 1953 with fourteen countries in Europe, the Near East, and Asia. It was reported that at year's end arrangements had been completed for the sale of $55 million of such commodities (mostly tobacco and fats and oils) to Great Britain and of about $2 million each to Norway and Germany. These sales were generally to be at prevailing United States prices, private trade channels were to be used to the maximum extent possible, and the purchasers agreed not to reexport the commodities without prior United States approval. (See Department of State *Bulletin*, November 9, 1953, pp. 638-640. For a criticism in the British press, charging that Section 550

of the European Recovery Program, as Table 3 shows, the commodity composition of this aid continued the trend, evidenced in 1952, away from food, feed, and fertilizer, and toward raw

TABLE 3

*ECA-MSA-FOA–Financed Shipments to Europe, by Major Commodity
Groups, 1948-1953*
(percentages)

| Commodity Groups | 1953 | 1952 | 1948-1951 |
|---|---|---|---|
| Food, feed, and fertilizer | 15 | 17 | 36 |
| Fuel | 11 | 21 | 16 |
| Raw materials and semifinished products | 47 | 42 | 33 |
| Machinery and vehicles | 25 | 19 | 14 |
| Miscellaneous | 2 | 1 | 1 |
| Total | 100 | 100 | 100 |

Sources: Mutual Security Agency, *Monthly Report to the Public Advisory Board*, Wash., D.C., December 31, 1951, pp. 42-43, and December 31, 1952, p. 53, and Foreign Operations Administration, *Allotments, Authorizations, and Paid Shipments*, Wash., D.C., December 31, 1953, p. 19.

materials, semifinished products, and machinery and vehicles. Practically all of the 1953 shipments under the food, feed, and fertilizer categories were wheat and various coarse grains, especially corn; the fuel was mostly petroleum products but small amounts of coal were also supplied. Raw cotton accounted for over a third of the raw materials and semifinished products, while nonferrous metals accounted for a quarter of the total, followed by metallic ores and minerals, iron and steel products, and chemicals. Vehicles accounted for less than 15 percent of the category "machinery and vehicles."[8]

sales amount to "tied" offshore procurement, expressing foreign nations' fears that this device would be used to "develop" United States surpluses, and emphasizing that such sales should not displace usual marketings of the United States *or other countries*, see *The Economist*, October 24, 1953, pp. 266-267.)

The above figure on grant aid to Western Europe does *not* include the several million dollars of foodstuffs distributed during the year in Berlin to people from the Soviet sector.

[8] The Mutual Security Act specified that at least 50 percent of the FOA-financed shipments from the United States and of home-bound cargoes of strategic materials financed with dollars or counterpart funds, by cargo ship, liner, and tanker, be in United States bottoms, if available. The nonavailability clause was invoked for a few months during the year with respect to dry-bulk vessels but for the year as a whole the requirements were exceeded. From the beginning of the Mutual Security Program through October 1953 some 66 percent, on the average, of all the relevant cargoes were carried in American flag vessels. The Randall Commission recommended that this statutory provision be re-

The rate of actual shipments was about one-third smaller during the last half of the year than it was during the first six months, and new economic aid was terminated during the course of 1953 for Austria, Denmark, Iceland, the Netherlands, and Norway, their economies having improved to the point where economic aid was no longer thought necessary by United States officials.[9] Aid of this type had been terminated earlier for Belgium, Ireland, Portugal, and Sweden. Many of these countries, of course, continued to receive small amounts of goods that were in the pipeline and might continue to receive aid on a small scale through the technical assistance program. The major economic aid recipients during 1953 were France and the United Kingdom, together accounting for just over half the total, followed by Italy, Yugoslavia, and Western Germany. Yugoslavia was the only European country receiving more aid in 1953 than in 1952 but this assistance virtually ceased during the last quarter of the year. Most of the aid to Western Germany went to the Allied sectors of Berlin.

The only Western European countries still receiving new allotments of economic aid at the end of 1953 were France, the United Kingdom, Italy, Greece, Yugoslavia, Western Germany, Turkey, and Spain. The intention of the Administration to curtail sharply aid to these countries was underscored by the fact that new *allotments* from funds that had been appropriated for defense support amounted to only $66 million during the last half of 1953, more than half of this being for agricultural commodities to be sent to the United Kingdom and most of the remainder being divided between food for Eastern Germany and the Spanish aid program.[1]

---

pealed and that the aid deemed necessary to support a merchant marine adequate for American national requirements be provided by "direct means."

[9] For Western Europe as a whole, industrial production was at an all-time peak in 1953, about 5 percent greater than in the previous year and an estimated 40 percent greater than in 1948. The situation varied from country to country, however, and Western Germany accounted for the greater part of the 1953 increase. Agricultural production in 1953 equalled the peak year of 1951, about 15 percent above the immediate prewar average, but this increase was offset by a comparable increase in population. Inflationary pressures had been largely eliminated in most countries and the area's gold and dollar reserves increased by about $2.5 billion, including the sterling area holdings.

For a report of projects directed to the expansion and improvement of industrial facilities in Europe during the postwar period whose financing was assisted through United States foreign aid, see Mutual Security Agency, *Monthly Report to the Public Advisory Board*, Wash., D.C., April 30, 1953, pp. 1-42.

[1] For some nonofficial evaluations of the results obtained by economic aid from

The Randall Commission minimized the need for continued aid to Europe (and elsewhere) outside the military field and, while leaving the door ajar for exceptional circumstances, recommended that "economic aid on a grant basis should be terminated as soon as possible."[2]

As noted in Section A of this chapter, the Administration regarded its program of "mutual defense financing" as of great importance, but during the year no payments were made from the $85 million that Congress had appropriated for financial assistance in the manufacture of military goods in France, from the $400 million that had been appropriated to help defray the French costs in Indochina, or from the $85 million that had been provided for facilitating the manufacture of military aircraft in the United Kingdom.

Each country receiving economic and technical—as distinct from military end-item—assistance on a grant basis under the Mutual Security Program must deposit, in special accounts, local currency (called counterpart funds) in amounts equivalent to the dollar cost of the aid received.[3] Between 90 and 95 percent of these deposits are reserved for use by the governments making the deposits and the remainder are set aside for the use of the U.S. Government. In accordance with the 1952 amendments to the Mutual Security Act, the funds accumulated in Europe could be spent only for purposes for which dollar aid would have been available under that Act. New deposits of such funds during 1953 amounted to the equivalent of $1027 million, of which $90 million were reserved for United States use. During the same year $1038 million of current and past accumulations set aside for use in Europe were released. Well over half the amount was used for the production and procurement of military matériel and other direct military purposes. Large amounts were also used to finance

---

the United States in the postwar period, see Ellis, H. S., "American Economic Aid to Europe in Retrospect," *Kyklos*, Vol. VI (1953), No. 1, pp. 3-20, and Berolzheimer, J., "The Impact of U.S. Foreign Aid since the Marshall Plan on Western Europe's Gross National Product and Government Finances," *Finanzarchiv* (Tübingen, Western Germany), Vol. 14 (1953), No. 1, pp. 114-140.

[2] Commission on Foreign Economic Policy, *Report to the President and the Congress, op.cit.*, p. 8.

[3] Statistical detail on these funds may be found in Mutual Security Agency/Foreign Operations Administration, *Local Currency Counterpart Funds*, Wash., D.C. These reports were issued monthly through June 1953 and quarterly thereafter.

expansion of industrial capacity and to promote productivity. The funds reserved for United States use were employed to help defray various operating and administrative expenses of U.S. Government agencies in Europe or were transferred to the Defense Materials Procurement Agency.[4]

Although it was not formally a part of the European defense-support program, President Eisenhower, following an expression of concern by West German Chancellor Adenauer over the food shortage in Eastern Germany, offered $15 million of food for distribution there by the Soviet Government. The Soviet Government refused to accept the food and the President then offered it directly to the German people, to be distributed in the Western sector of Berlin. The West German Government acted as distributing agent and bore the local handling costs. Over a three-month period beginning in late July, and amidst much publicity, nearly a million residents of East Germany crossed the border to receive some 18,000 tons of food in individual food parcels. The total cost to the United States apparently was about $8 million.[5]

[4] Although the "Moody Amendment" was repealed in 1953 and the "Benton Amendment" modified, the Mutual Security Act of 1953 (see Section A, above) provided that any commitments already made under the former could be carried out. The equivalent of some $94 million in local currencies had been committed under the "Moody Amendment," in agreements with eleven European countries. These funds were transferred to individual country productivity programs and, together with small amounts of United States dollars, to the European Productivity Agency, established by the Organization for European Economic Cooperation. About three fifths of the funds under the individual country programs were for loans, on favorable terms, to small and medium-size businesses, and the balance were to be made available as grants for modernization of factories, training of workers, and other activities designed to increase productivity. Under agreements reached between the U.S. Government and the eleven countries concerned, beneficiaries of these funds were required to increase wages and lower the prices of their products as productivity increased, thus sharing the gains from productivity with labor and consumers, according to the spirit of the Benton-Moody amendments. (Details on some of these agreements and procedures will be found in *The Economist*, August 8, 1953, p. 406, and Department of State *Bulletin*, March 9, 1953, p. 381.)

[5] These funds were taken from those appropriated for "defense-support" purposes in Europe.

A special food-parcel distribution at Christmastime to certain needy families in Europe, the Near East, and Latin America involving foodstuffs in abundant supply in the United States was financed from funds made available under the President's authority in the Mutual Security Act to transfer $100 million to any project consistent with the purposes of the Act.

The other transfer provisions of the Mutual Security Act were also used several times during 1953. On May 5 the President transferred $125 million from military aid to Europe to defense support for Europe. These funds were

d. PACE OF EUROPEAN REARMAMENT

The goals set at Lisbon in early 1952 to be reached by the end of that year—making available to the NATO command fifty divisions of troops, half active and half readily mobilizable reserves; 4,000 combat aircraft; and 1600 naval vessels (plus Greek and Turkish forces)—had not been met in full.[6] At the meeting of the foreign ministers of the NATO countries in April 1953, new "firm" force goals were established for that year calculated to make up the deficiencies and to add "several" divisions and "several hundred" aircraft and naval vessels. Moreover, higher performance standards for existing forces were set, and the Organization reported that achievement of these goals would result in a "30 percent increase" in the combat effectiveness of NATO forces over 1952. The most widely publicized decision taken at that time, and one in which the U.S. Government played a leading role, was to set lower force goals for 1953 than had been earlier planned. The decision was based on the conviction that the threat of Soviet aggression must be faced over a long period and that rearmament goals must therefore be of a scale which could be maintained for a number of years while permitting the members to continue their present rate of economic and social development.

The second annual report of the Supreme Allied Commander for Europe, issued at the end of May, stated that NATO still lacked the resources for "adequate chances of success against a major attack"; that airpower, in spite of a "considerable increase" during the previous year, remained the "weakest link" in the collective defenses of the West; and that the growth in land forces

to be used as follows: $50 million for the stockpiling of food, fuel, and industrial materials in Western Berlin, $15 million to relieve suffering caused by severe drought in Yugoslavia, and $60 million to ease a dollar-payments and budgetary crisis in France that threatened that country's military effort in Indochina. Later in the year $7.5 million were transferred out of defense-support funds for Western Europe for the purpose of furnishing economic aid to Bolivia and for ocean-freight subsidies on private relief parcels. In September the President approved the transfer of $20 million from Western European military aid to emergency financial assistance for Iran. (See the following chapter.)

[6] For a brief discussion of the shortfall and the reasons for it, see *Survey—1952*, pp. 42-46.

For several articles critically discussing various aspects of the North Atlantic Treaty Organization, see the American Academy of Political and Social Science, *The Annals*, July 1953, pp. 2-189; *Current History*, February 1953, pp. 65-114; and the special NATO section of the *New York Herald-Tribune*, April 19, 1954.

was "encouraging" but not yet satisfactory. This report also asserted that the support facilities for the military forces were much improved, that substantial progress had been made on the infrastructure program, but that military stocks had not been built up at the planned rate.[7]

Deliveries of United States military aid, as noted above, were much increased in 1953; expenditures by the Western European nations for defense purposes were reported to have been the equivalent of $11.5 billion, more than double the 1950 rate, and just over a quarter of these were for the purchase of so-called military "hard goods." At the end of 1953 the European members of NATO had 3.3 million men under arms, up almost a million from mid-1950. The number of planes available to the NATO command was nearly two and a half times as large as in 1951 and most of the piston-driven craft had been replaced by jets. The number of airfields—a large part of the infrastructure program —which were available for at least limited use had increased sevenfold over 1951.

Foreign Ministers of the NATO countries held their annual review in December and reported that the 1953 force goals had been "completely met" for land forces and had been met "to a substantial extent" for air and naval forces. The Ministers stated that the gap between Russia's offensive strength and the defensive strength and retaliatory capacity of the West had "clearly" been reduced during the year. A few weeks earlier the Supreme Allied Commander, General Gruenther, had declared that the NATO forces had reached a degree of strength such that Soviet troops then located in Occupied Europe could not launch an attack with "any reasonable certainty of success," but that the North Atlantic

[7] For excerpts from the annual report, see Department of State *Bulletin*, June 29, 1953, pp. 899-904. For some criticism of this report in the foreign press, see *The Economist*, June 13, 1953, p. 722.

General Vandenberg, then Chief of Staff of the Air Force, testified that the United States Air Force had been forced to concern itself "principally" with the defense of the United States after the cut in its projected size from 143 to 120 wings. (See "Department of Defense Appropriations for 1954," *Hearings on H.R. 5969*, U.S. Senate, Committee on Appropriations, 1953, Part 1, pp. 265, 315-317, and 480-481.) Secretary of Defense Wilson, however, testified that the proposed reduction in the number of wings would not affect the ultimate airpower of NATO, although it might cause delays in reaching stated goals. (See *ibid.*, pp. 559-561.)

forces still did *"not have adequate strength to defeat an all-out Russian attack."*[8]

At the December meeting the Foreign Ministers reaffirmed their confidence in the "stretch-out" policy agreed upon the previous April. (In the official statements, this was usually referred to as a policy of emphasizing quality rather than quantity of armed forces.) The Ministers agreed upon "firm" force goals for 1954 and upon "provisional" goals for 1955 and "planned" goals for 1956. Details were again not published, but it was stated that the 1954 objectives called for a 5 percent increase in the number of army divisions, a 15 percent increase in naval vessels, and a 25 percent increase in the number of aircraft. The plans also called for higher standards of combat-readiness for active units and higher training levels for reserves. Agreement was also reached at that time on the expenditure of $251 million of the projected "fifth slice" of the infrastructure program. Approximately half of this new construction was to be for aviation fuel pipelines and storage facilities, with the remainder allocated for airfields, signal communications, and ports.[9]

Late in the year there were many rumors in the press that the United States planned to withdraw some of its forces from Europe and replace them with "modern," presumably nuclear, weapons.[1] These reports were officially denied by the Administration.

Although spokesmen for the Executive Branch expressed general satisfaction throughout the year with the rearmament efforts

[8] Department of State *Bulletin*, November 9, 1953, pp. 683-684 (italics in the original).

For the text of the NATO Council's December communiqué and some statements by Administration officials, see Department of State *Bulletin*, January 4, 1954, pp. 8-9. For an unofficial assessment of the Organization at the end of the year, see *The Economist*, December 19, 1953, pp. 865-866. This article notes the increased strength of the Organization, but states that the strategy of NATO would still have to be a "fighting retreat" in the event of war and poses the question of how the cost of maintaining the full NATO forces, once attained, can be met without continued United States aid.

[9] During the year international competitive bidding was initiated on various NATO construction projects, and American firms won several contracts.

In addition to the regular infrastructure program, it was agreed during 1953 to undertake a $28 million construction program for military facilities within Western Germany. This program would be financed under arrangements to be agreed upon between the Federal Republic of Germany and the various NATO members.

[1] The existing United States commitment to NATO was six army divisions and an unpublished number of naval and air units.

of the Western European nations, they were highly critical and impatient over the failure of the affected countries to bring into being the proposed European Army.

e. EUROPEAN DEFENSE COMMUNITY

Throughout 1953 United States military, executive, and legislative leaders continued vigorously to press for the ratification of the European Defense Community Treaty and issued numerous hopeful predictions, none of them fulfilled. Shortly after taking office Secretary of State Dulles and Mutual Security Director Stassen visited each of the EDC nations and urged ratification at once. President Eisenhower reportedly supported his Cabinet members in talks with various European officials who visited Washington during the year. As noted above, Congress chose to make half the funds appropriated in 1953 for military aid to Europe depend upon the establishment of the Community.[2] The official communiqués issued after both of the 1953 meetings of the North Atlantic Council of Ministers again called for early ratification of the Treaty.

In their public statements executive officials of the signatory governments were almost unanimous in supporting the Community, but there was little enthusiasm, and often strong opposition, in their parliaments. One of the keenest supporters of the Community was West German Chancellor Adenauer, and under his leadership both houses of the German Parliament approved the Treaty during the spring. Ratification was not completed because of a minor conflict with the Federal Republic's constitution, and the Chancellor did not press for immediate resolution of this conflict in view of the delays being encountered in France and Italy. The reelection during 1953 of Adenauer, with an increase in the strength of his party in the legislature, after a campaign in which the Community was an important issue, led most observers to conclude that the constitutional issue could

[2] Although United States officials emphasized the importance of the Community as a device for incorporating German troops in the Western Defense system, most of them also welcomed the related efforts of the six governments to work out a treaty to establish a European political community which would absorb both the European Army and the Coal-Steel pool and be charged with establishing a freer movement of goods, capital, and people among the participating nations. No such treaty had been signed by the year's end.

easily be resolved in favor of the Community. The lower houses
of both the Netherlands and Belgium also approved the Treaty
during 1953, by large majorities, and early in 1954 the Netherlands became the first nation to complete ratification. However,
opposition continued strong throughout the year in France and
Italy. In France the widespread fear of a rearmed Germany in
any context was made more acute by the knowledge that a significant portion of the French military forces were engaged in
Indochina, leaving France, many felt, in such a weakened position
within the proposed Community that Germany could easily
dominate the instrument conceived to control it. Early in the year
the French legislature approved a series of protocols to the Treaty
designed to overcome this fear. In November the National Assembly debated the Treaty but took no action. The press reported
that French ratification could not be expected until additional
protocols safeguarding France's position within the Community
were signed, the Saar question was settled on terms recognizing
that the area would continue to be economically linked with
France, a firm commitment was obtained from Great Britain to
keep troops on the Continent and otherwise to cooperate closely
with the Community, and a pledge was made by the United States
to keep troops on the Continent. Negotiations on these issues
apparently moved slowly, in part because of the several political
crises in France in which the question of the Community was a
major issue. At year's end, opposition to the Treaty in France
appeared as strong as ever.[3]

In Italy ratification of the Treaty was also forestalled by opposition and inaction in the legislature, arising largely from a
hesitancy to give up this degree of national autonomy, from the
wish to obtain a prior settlement of the Trieste question, and
from the difficulties in forming a stable government. In both
France and Italy the opposition of the Communist Party was an
important factor. Even more important were the hopes held by
many that the Soviet Government was sincere in its many state-

[3] In mid-April 1954 President Eisenhower stated that United States troops
would stay in Europe as long as needed to check "any threat to that area," and
the British Government agreed to cooperate much more closely with the
European Defense Community than had been the previous intention and in
effect gave a pledge to maintain British troops on the Continent. (See New
York Times, April 13, 1954, p. 4; April 14, 1954, p. 1; and April 17, 1954, p. 1.)

ments during the year that for Western Europe, including Germany, rearmament was unnecessary inasmuch as Russia wanted only to live in peace with the West, and the widespread fear that a rearmed Germany would encourage, rather than discourage, aggressive action by Russia.[4]

Many interpreted the various statements by United States officials during the year (especially Secretary Dulles' statement that the failure to create the European Army would call for an "agonizing reappraisal" of United States policy) to mean that if the Community were not soon approved the U.S. Government would support the creation of national German armed forces. Late in the year, however, the Secretary of State declared that no satisfactory alternative to the European Army had been proposed, and President Eisenhower characterized as "feeble" all other proposals for German participation in the collective security system of the West.[5]

## Near East and Africa

The part of the military assistance program directed toward building area-wide security in the Near East and Africa, with links to South Asia, was officially described in mid-1953 as one showing "substantial, if partial, success." The "substantial success" aspect of the program was a continued strengthening of the military forces of Greece and Turkey, both of whom had received large amounts of United States military aid since 1947. As in earlier years, these two nations, members of the North Atlantic Treaty Organization, received nearly all of the slightly over $800

[4] For a discussion of some of the issues involved in the reunification of Germany, the rearmament of Germany, and the European Defense Community as seen by a German citizen, see Von dem Bussche, A., "German Rearmament: Hopes and Fears," *Foreign Affairs*, October 1953, pp. 68-79.

For one expression of a view current in the West that establishment of the Community would make it virtually certain that Russia would not agree to any reunification of Germany on terms acceptable to the West, see the letter by H. J. Morgenthau in *The Economist*, July 11, 1953, pp. 93-94.

[5] For the Dulles statement, see Department of State *Bulletin*, January 4, 1954, pp. 5-7.

Throughout the year *The Economist* carried many informative items on the European Defense Community. Some of the more important were in the following issues, all in 1953: February 21, p. 474; June 20, pp. 795-796; July 18, pp. 183-184; July 25, pp. 264-265; November 7, pp. 407-408; November 28, p. 646; and December 19, pp. 871-872. Also February 20, 1954, pp. 545-546, and March 13, 1954, pp. 749-751 and 786-787.

million in deliveries of military end-items to the area (as well as $110 million of defense-support aid); their portion was included in the data given for Western Europe in the previous section of this chapter. Of the other nations in this oil-rich, tension-ridden area, only Iran and Ethiopia actually obtained grants of military supplies under the Mutual Security Program during 1953. The Iranian program, begun in 1950, was on a modest but undisclosed scale, and it was designed primarily to strengthen the nation's ability to withstand internal subversion. A small military aid program for Ethiopia was begun in mid-1953, but neither Israel nor her Arab neighbors had yet received military supplies under the Mutual Security Program.

Although Greece and Turkey could offer "powerful resistance" to direct attack, the military aid program for the Near East and Africa was only a "partial success" because the other nations continued to exhibit great military weakness. Following a trip to the area in the spring, Secretary Dulles characterized a Middle East Defense Organization as a future rather than an immediate hope.[6] He found a "vague desire" in the area for such an arrangement but declared that some of the nations were so engrossed in disputes with Israel and Great Britain and France that they had little concern for the Communist threat.[7] Nonetheless, American officials continued to hope that some form of regional defense organization might be created. Late in the year the press reported that arrangements were being discussed to bring Pakistan into a defense arrangement with the Near Eastern states. Representatives of the Indian Government immediately attacked this scheme, declaring it a threat to peace in Asia. Despite this criticism, early in 1954 Turkey and Pakistan announced their intention to conclude a mutual defense pact. The U.S. Government welcomed the announcement, described the pact as an additional step toward security in the free world, and announced plans to grant military assistance to Pakistan. At the same time it offered military aid to India, which was refused, and sought to reassure that country by insisting that the aid to be provided to Pakistan would be used only for defensive, and not aggressive, purposes.[8]

[6] For a brief account of earlier United States support for such an organization, see *Survey—1952*, pp. 50-51.

[7] See Department of State *Bulletin*, June 15, 1953, pp. 881-885.

[8] For an article on the military situation in the area in general, see Jernegan

## I. MILITARY ASSISTANCE

### Asia and the Pacific

Although an armistice was reached in Korea in late July 1953, the fighting in Indochina continued to rage and the Far East received an increasing amount of attention under the Mutual Security Program. The value of military end-items and services supplied the area on a grant basis totalled $774 million in 1953, nearly double the amount provided in the previous year, but it was at an annual rate of only $530 million during the last six months.[9]

Data on military assistance to individual countries were not made public, but it was known that Indochina was a major recipient. Shipments to that area, in which active but indecisive fighting had been going on for seven years between the Communist forces of the Viet Minh and the forces of the Associated States and France, were some 50 percent greater than in the previous year. The principal items furnished by the U.S. Government were vehicles, artillery pieces, communications equipment, and some types of aircraft. In addition to this direct aid, the U.S. Government also contributed to the forces fighting against Communists in Indochina by means of aid given to France; the press reported that the U.S. Government was, by the end of the year, covering in one way or another nearly 90 percent of the costs of the matériel being expended by France in Indochina. As noted in the first section of this chapter, Congress earmarked $400 million in 1953 for disbursement to France to finance production in that country of military end-items furnished by the French Government to forces in Indochina. In September the Administration announced that it was making available up to an additional $385 million of other Mutual Security funds for the specific purpose of supporting the so-called "Navarre Plan" to terminate quickly the war in Indochina. However, none of the $400 million

---

J. D., "The Middle East and South Asia—the Problem of Security," Department of State *Bulletin*, March 22, 1954, pp. 444-448. For some unofficial discussion of the issue of Pakistan in the Middle Eastern defense arrangements, see *The Economist*, November 21, 1953, pp. 569-570.

[9] This military end-item assistance, as in the previous years, was provided only to the Associated States of Indochina, the Republic of China on Formosa, the Philippines, and Thailand. The above data *exclude* the value of supplies and services furnished to the United Nations forces fighting in Korea. Such aid was made available from appropriations to the Department of Defense and its amount was not made public.

had been disbursed by the end of the year and data are not available as to the $385 million. The Eisenhower Administration, like its predecessor, regarded the fighting in Indochina as especially important, not only because of the threat of Communism in that area, but also because the termination of the war there would permit France to increase her contribution to the North Atlantic Treaty Organization.

The other principal recipient of military aid in the Far East, as in previous years, was the Republic of China on Formosa, and particular emphasis during 1953 was placed on the delivery of jet planes. Formosa continued to receive the lion's share—$88 million—of the "defense-support" aid to the Far Eastern area. The major commodities were food, raw cotton and textiles, various types of machinery, and medical supplies. The Associated States of Indochina received $25 million of economic aid under the Mutual Security Program, divided about equally between food, fuel, and machinery and vehicles. Some of these commodities were delivered directly to the armed forces.

The Philippines and Thailand continued to receive small amounts of United States military aid for modernizing and equipping their armed forces. In addition, the Philippines received nearly $26 million and Thailand $6 million in defense-support type economic aid and technical assistance.[1]

Negotiations were begun in July with Japan for a Mutual Defense Assistance agreement that would permit the sending of military aid to that country. No accord had been signed at the year's end, but the negotiations were reported near conclusion and Japan had been provided with over $127 million of naval vessels, on an "indeterminate basis," under authority other than the Mutual Security Act.

So far as the public could determine, little attention was given by the United States during 1953 to the question of creating new regional security arrangements in the Far East and Pacific area. The Council of ANZUS—the mutual defense group composed of Australia, New Zealand, and the United States, developed in 1951 upon the signing of a "security treaty"[2]—held a meeting

[1] Local-currency counterpart funds were required in the Far East again, some, but not all, of the economic aid provided by the United States. Specific data on accumulations and uses in 1953 are not yet available.

[2] See *Survey—1952*, pp. 52-58, and the references cited there.

during the year. It reviewed the problems associated with the wars in Korea and Indochina and other matters affecting Pacific security, and it reaffirmed the defensive nature of the group. The members expressed a willingness to consider wider defense arrangements in the Pacific but decided against enlarging the group at that time.[3]

## Latin America

Military assistance valued at $87 million was furnished on a grant basis in 1953 to eight Latin American nations, which had been found by the President to be necessary participants in the Western Hemisphere defense plans and which had concluded bilateral military assistance agreements with the United States. Some $53 million of this was, however, offset by return of equipment and reverse grants. Five of these nations were already receiving aid at the beginning of the year,[4] while Brazil and Uruguay completed ratification of assistance agreements signed in 1952 with the United States, and an agreement with the Dominican Republic was signed and ratified during 1953.

These eight countries were using substantial amounts of their own funds to support the United States military aid program, paying part of the costs of United States personnel assigned to their countries to direct the program, and purchasing some military equipment in the United States through the reimbursable aid program.[5] By and large, the United States aid continued to be designed to help prepare the recipient nations to perform certain tasks of hemispheric defense which otherwise would fall on United States forces. The Latin American states again received no defense-support-type aid during the year.

[3] See Department of State *Bulletin*, September 28, 1953, pp. 414–418.
[4] Chile, Colombia, Cuba, Ecuador, and Peru.
[5] On military assistance to Latin America, see Department of State *Bulletin*, March 30, 1953, pp. 463–467.

# II · ECONOMIC AND TECHNICAL ASSISTANCE GRANT PROGRAMS

In addition to military assistance and economic and financial aid intended directly to strengthen the defense forces of the Western nations, described in Chapter I, the U.S. Government has for several years carried on other foreign-aid programs. The largest of these in the years after 1950 were the various programs of economic and technical assistance designed to increase production in the so-called underdeveloped countries of the non-Communist portion of the world, but there were also, from time to time, special activities directed to relieving famine and other emergency situations abroad. Beginning in 1950-1951 these were regarded by the U.S. Government as integral parts of the Mutual Security Program, in that they sought to eliminate or ameliorate the economic conditions in which it was thought Communism flourished. Several of these programs had been carried out on a bilateral basis by the U.S. Government, while others had taken the form of international activities, usually under the general supervision of the United Nations.

## A. *BILATERAL ECONOMIC AND TECHNICAL COOPERATION PROGRAMS*

### *Legislative Issues*[1]

In presenting its request to Congress for the programs of economic and technical assistance to the so-called underdeveloped

[1] Most of the material in this section was taken from the following official sources: Mutual Security Act of 1953 (P.L. 118, 88d Cong.), July 16, 1953; Mutual Security Appropriations Act, 1954 (P.L. 218, 88d Cong.), August 7, 1953; "The Mutual Security Program for Fiscal Year 1954: Basic Data . . . ," *Revised Committee Print*, Senate Committee on Foreign Relations and House Committee on Foreign Affairs, 88d Cong., 1st Sess., June 5, 1953; "Mutual Security Act Extension," *Hearings on H.R. 5710*, House of Rep., Committee on Foreign Affairs, 88d Cong., 1st Sess., March–June 1953; "Mutual Security Act of 1953," *Hearings*, U.S. Senate, Committee on Foreign Relations, 88d Cong., 1st Sess., May 1953; H. Rpt. No. 569, Parts 1 and 2, 88d Cong.; S. Rpt. No. 405, 88d Cong.; H. Rpt. No. 770, 88d Cong.; "Communication from the President of the United

countries, the Truman Administration in 1952 had emphasized the interdependence between the two types of aid and had, in general, argued that in most cases it was neither useful nor practical to attempt to distinguish between the provision of "pure" technical services and the provision of some commodities necessary to make the technical aid effective. The majority of Congress, however, had insisted on drawing a more or less sharp distinction between providing goods on the one hand and services on the other, the feeling of many being that unless such a distinction were made there was grave danger that under the guise of technical assistance the U.S. Government would become involved in a new series of large-scale "give-away" programs. The Eisenhower Administration took cognizance of this Congressional sentiment and in its 1953 requests separated "technical assistance" and "economic assistance," making separate justifications for each.

a. REGULAR TECHNICAL ASSISTANCE PROGRAM

The concerted and widely publicized effort by the U.S. Government to aid economic development of the poorer areas of the world through applying the methods and technology already in use in the more advanced nations was begun under the Act for International Development of 1950. The program evolved slowly, and by the beginning of 1953 less than $80 million had been spent implementing it.[2] Several operating principles, however, had become well established and had been approved, and in some cases directed, by Congress. Among these were the following: the transfer of "know-how" was to be carried out primarily through sending abroad technicians, with demonstration equipment, and by bringing foreign nationals to the United States for training; aid was to be given only when requested by local governments, and

States Transmitting Estimates of Appropriations . . . ," *H. Doc. No. 209*, 88d Cong.; "Mutual Security Appropriations for 1954," *Hearings*, Subcommittee of the Committee on Appropriations, House of Rep., 88d Cong., 1st Sess., 1958, especially pp. 209-477 and 616-618; "Mutual Security Appropriations for 1954, *Hearings on H.R. 6391*, U.S. Senate, Committee on Appropriations, 88d Cong., 1st Sess., 1958; *H. Rpt. No. 880*, 88d Cong.; *S. Rpt. No. 645*, 88d Cong.; and *H. Rpt. No. 1056*, 88d Cong.

[2] *Survey—1951*, pp. 71t and 81, and *Survey—1952*, p. 68, showed expenditures of $85 million in 1951. This figure was in error in that it included expenditures under the program of aid to Israel which were not properly attributable to technical assistance.

the host governments were expected to "cooperate" by paying what Congress liked to term their "fair share" of the costs of the projects, a fair share usually being defined as equal to at least half the total cost; insofar as possible the actual work was to be performed directly with people rather than with government officials; capital requirements other than for demonstration and pilot-plant equipment were to be met primarily from local sources, through international private investment, or through governmental borrowing, including loans from the International Bank; private agencies and institutions were to be employed to the fullest extent practicable in carrying out individual programs; and the major emphasis in the first years was to be in increasing food production, improving health and sanitary conditions, and in raising levels of education.[3]

The U.S. Government had stressed that the fundamental purpose of the technical assistance program was the humanitarian one of assisting other peoples to improve their standards of living and general welfare, but it was expected that it would also serve the interests of the United States by helping to prevent the growth of Communism in the underdeveloped areas, by increasing the foreign trade of the United States, by enlarging the sources of raw materials in short supply in the free world, and by contributing to world peace through the strengthening of representative governments.[4]

In supporting the Administration's request for $140 million in new funds for the United States bilateral technical assistance program in 1953, Mr. Stanley Andrews, then Administrator of the Technical Cooperation Administration, reminded Congress that it had made technical assistance a permanent part of United States foreign policy in 1950 and that the program was by nature

[3] For a summary of the types of activities for which funds were requested, see *H. Rpt. No. 569, op.cit.,* Part 1, pp. 38-39. For some illustrative programs for individual countries, see "Mutual Security Act of 1953," *Hearings, op.cit.,* pp. 385-418.

[4] For a fuller account of the development of the technical assistance program prior to 1953, see *Survey—1952,* pp. 55-72, and the references cited there.

In the first years of its operation the technical assistance program had been widely known as the "Point Four Program," taking its name from its position in President Truman's inaugural address of January 1949. This term was less frequently used in the official literature in 1953, apparently in a conscious effort to dissociate the program from the Truman Administration.

a long-term one which was just getting under way. He stated that if Congress did not intend to continue appropriations of the order of $100 million a year for at least three to five years, it should terminate the program at once. He and other official witnesses emphasized that the long-run objective was one of helping others to help themselves reduce poverty, and the program's justification did not depend on the existence of a Communist threat. He expressed concern lest the established goals of the program be obscured in the discussion of the national security issues which were, of course, the paramount concern of the Mutual Security Program.

Administration witnesses pointed out that the amounts requested were about $30 million less than had been appropriated the previous year. This met with general approval in Congress, although the comparison was at best of questionable validity inasmuch as the 1952 appropriation had included some items which were comparable to requests made by the new Administration under the separate title of "special economic assistance"; indeed, if the 1953 requests for both economic and technical aid were added, they exceeded the corresponding appropriations in 1952. This decrease in technical assistance funds—if it was in fact a decrease—was explained as resulting from the fact that some projects had high initial costs that were not recurrent and that experience had shown that the amount requested in 1953 was all that could be spent "wisely." The Administration declined to make any commitment as to whether the amounts requested would decline in future years, but stated that it planned for the proportion of total costs of any given project borne by the United States to fall. It reported that the average ratio of payments by all recipient governments to the United States contribution would be about one to one in 1953 and would increase to three to two in 1954. This too was in keeping with Congressional intent as expressed in earlier years and as repeated in 1953.

Slightly more than half the technical assistance funds, as Table 1 shows, were scheduled to be spent helping the countries of Asia and the Pacific, most of them to go to India, Pakistan, and the Philippines, with smaller amounts planned for Thailand, Indonesia, Afghanistan, and Nepal.[5] The particular justification

[5] No economic and technical assistance was proposed for Japan. Economic

for the aid to this area was that in many of these countries recently established, democratic governments were on trial and technical assistance from the United States would help these governments meet the rising expectations of their people for higher standards of living—expectations which if not met might greatly strengthen the appeals of Communism. The request for the Near East and Africa totalled $44 million; Iran and Egypt were each scheduled to receive slightly more than a quarter of the total, on the ground that the United States had great strategic interest in the independence and stability of both countries. Much smaller expenditures were planned for nine other countries in this area.[6] Latin America was scheduled to receive the remaining $24 million of the request.[7] It was stated by the Administration that past expenditures in this area, where technical assistance had been provided for several years prior to the formalization of the Point Four Program, had been well used in increasing production,

---

and technical aid to Indochina and Formosa was included in the "defense-support" category discussed in Chapter I. Aid to the Philippines and Thailand also was essentially of the defense-support type and has been included in that section of this *Survey*. No aid to Korea was scheduled under this program, but substantial amounts were requested through other programs and are discussed below. Aid to Ceylon under the program had been suspended in 1952 because that country had sold rubber to Communist countries, and no aid for her was proposed in the new program. Burma had terminated its technical assistance agreement with the United States as of June 1953 and was not scheduled to receive any aid in fiscal year 1954. Most of the discussion on this termination was off the record, but one witness said that it was related to a political crisis in Burma arising from the presence in that country of Chinese Nationalist troops, who in the minds of the Burmese public and the local press were supported by the United States.

[6] Greece and Turkey were to receive technical assistance from the "defense-support" funds appropriated for aid to Europe and are discussed in the previous chapter. Syria declined technical assistance from the United States in protest against American aid to Israel; nonetheless, funds for Syria were included in the recommendations, to be spent if the necessary agreements could be negotiated.

[7] The Administration planned to spend some $1 million of the aid for helping the twelve Latin American dependencies of European countries. An agreement had already been signed with the United Kingdom covering British dependencies, although no aid had been requested of the United States at the time of the hearings. Negotiations were proceeding with the Netherlands at that time, but France had shown no interest in technical assistance for her territories in Latin America. The Administration planned to continue providing small amounts for technical assistance in the Asiatic dependencies of the European countries.

The Administration requested a special appropriation for dependencies of European nations in Africa; see "Special Assistance to the Near East and Africa," below.

had been appreciated by the public, and had played an important role in fulfilling the good-neighbor policy of the United States. It was also said, in justification of the proposed program for Latin America, that senior officials of the Eisenhower Administration believed the United States should give more attention to that area than had been shown by their predecessors.[8]

In response to Congressional queries as to the "accomplishments" of the technical assistance program to date, Administration witnesses replied that it was virtually impossible to make precise quantitative measurements of the success of the program as a whole. They did, however, cite many specific instances of improvements in health and of increases in production which could be traced to the program.[9] At the same time, they said, in most countries the program had not yet been in operation long enough to admit a confident assessment of its effects in improving the economic welfare of the people or in strengthening democratic political institutions. The Administrator was frank in acknowledging that the program had accomplished little in carrying out the Congressional directive that the program be so administered as to encourage private foreign investment in the aided countries. In addition to the hostility to private foreign capital frequently encountered in these areas, born in part of memories of what was regarded as colonial exploitation in the past, he stated that one of the difficulties was that he was "not quite sure what our overall Government policy is in this particular area of activity."[1] He said that a more precise statement of Congressional policy on this issue would be helpful, but Congress did not attempt to change the existing law in this respect.[2]

[8] In June and July the President's brother, Dr. Milton S. Eisenhower, led a much-publicized special mission to study United States relations with Latin America. His report recommended, among other things, the expansion of the technical cooperation program, continued support to the technical assistance activities of the Organization of American States, and technical assistance in the preparation by these countries of applications for development loans from international lending agencies or institutions of the U.S. Government. The full text of Dr. Eisenhower's report is published in Department of State *Bulletin*, November 23, 1953, pp. 695-717.

[9] For some examples, see "Mutual Security Act of 1953," *Hearings, op.cit.*, pp. 426-427.

[1] *ibid.*, p. 382.

[2] See Chapter III for a discussion of United States policies and activities in the field of private foreign investment in 1953.

As with other parts of the Mutual Security Program, at the time of the hearings relatively large amounts of funds previously appropriated for technical assistance had not yet been spent; many in Congress therefore argued there was no need to appropriate the full amounts requested. Spokesmen for the Administration reported that the rate of spending was increasing rapidly and said that the new appropriations were necessary in order to provide continuity to the program. They pointed out that new projects could not be started until new appropriations were made and that successful projects frequently created urgent demands for supplementary projects, in which cases it was highly desirable to maintain the momentum and enthusiasm achieved. They reported that the delays in the past in spending the funds had been occasioned primarily by the time required to negotiate specific project agreements, including agreements as to the contributions to be made by foreign governments. Delays were also occasioned by the time required to recruit technical personnel to be sent overseas, to obtain security clearance for them, and to train them. The majority in Congress agreed that the reasons for the delays were "understandable," but they also concluded that the Administration could not effectively use the funds requested for fiscal year 1954 in that period.

Although, as noted above, the Administration in 1953 separated its requests for funds to carry out technical assistance programs from its requests for "economic" aid, many in Congress still questioned whether the technical assistance program was not being used to provide "capital" assistance. Administration spokesmen insisted that they had no such intention, but they defended the using of a part of the technical assistance fund to provide "demonstration" equipment and argued that at least small amounts of such capital goods were necessary in order to make the technical assistance effective. Congress had no objection to such expenditures provided they were *only* for demonstration or pilot-plant projects, or for similar purposes. The Randall Commission, in its early 1954 Report, stated that many technical assistance operations could not be successful unless such supplies were available for demonstration purposes, but, they concluded, in the past this "commodity component" had been unnecessarily large and had become economic aid rather than technical assistance. The Commission went on to recommend that the technical assistance program should be pressed forward vigorously but should not involve capital investments.[3]

The Administration stated it planned to continue the policy of the previous year and to concentrate on helping others expand their production of food and improve their health and education facilities. There was relatively little criticism of these plans in Congress. Again in 1953, only incidental attention was given to the question of whether these activities would serve to increase greatly the population of the recipient nations rather than to reduce poverty. There was no discussion of possible conflict between the technical assistance program and American farm policies during the hearings on this program, but in the hearings on extending the Trade Agreements Act the Secretary of Agriculture was asked whether the development of agriculture under the Point Four Program might not serve to reduce the markets for United States farmers. The Secretary replied that most of the agricultural development would be in countries that historically had not been large importers of United States farm products, although their imports of certain farm products from the United States might decline as a result of these activities. But, he stated, the over-all purchasing power of the aided nations would increase and it was to be expected that their total imports from the United States would be larger than before. He agreed that competition to American farmers in third markets might increase but said this would be difficult to measure.[4]

Most members of Congress approved of the U.S. Government's showing the poor peoples of the world how to improve their production and agreed that this should be a long-term program, provided the cost remained small. Many found that the performance under the program had not matched their expectations. It was recognized that this failure was due in part to the unavoidable delay, noted above, in getting projects started. The majority

[3] See Commission on Foreign Economic Policy, *Report to the President and the Congress*, January 1954, p. 12.

The program was also criticized in Congress, and by the Randall Commission, for having too many administrators and too few technicians. The House Committee on Foreign Affairs reported that this "error" was being corrected.

[4] "Trade Agreements Extension Act of 1953," *Hearings on H.R. 4294*, House of Rep., Committee on Ways and Means, 83d Cong., 1st Sess., April-May 1953, pp. 746-749.

believed that, given the amount of unspent funds from previous appropriations, the amounts requested by the Administration could not be "effectively" used in the next fiscal year. The final appropriation therefore provided only $107 million as against the $140 million requested by the President, plus the reappropriation of $11 million of unobligated balances.

### b. BASIC-MATERIALS DEVELOPMENT

In earlier years considerable emphasis had been placed by the Government on the contribution which the technical assistance program could make to increasing the production abroad of strategic and critical materials needed by the United States. The available evidence indicated, however, that the various technical assistance missions had not given much attention to this problem. Beginning in 1949 the Economic Cooperation Administration had made loans, both in dollars and in counterpart funds, for the development abroad of basic raw materials, and the Mutual Security Act of 1952 had authorized the Mutual Security Agency to initiate projects for, and to assist in procuring and in stimulating the production of, materials in which deficiencies existed in the free world. No appropriations were specifically set aside for this activity, however,[5] and with the sharp curtailment in "economic" activity by the Mutual Security Agency it was foreseen that this assistance for raw materials development would also taper off.

The new Administration included in its proposals for technical assistance a separate recommendation for $50 million, half of it in dollars and half in local currencies, for the development of foreign sources of basic raw materials. It was proposed that about three fifths of this sum be spent in dependent territories of European countries in Africa, a fifth in Europe, and a fifth in Asia. The Administration stated that the funds would be used principally to assist in the establishment of new mines, in the enlargement of existing mines, and in facilitating the construction or improvement of transport facilities. For these purposes it proposed to furnish both technical assistance and capital equipment.[6]

[5] See *Survey—1952*, pp. 220-221, and the references cited there.

[6] It was also stated that a part of the funds to be spent in the Far East would be used to increase food production.

Administration spokesmen testified that this program would serve high-priority security interests of the United States and would help to meet the increasing demands of the nation and its allies for imported minerals and metals. Whereas help for these purposes in the past had been given on a loan basis, to be repaid in materials, it was planned that at least some of the new funds might be provided as grants.

A few members of Congress expressed concern lest the program serve to create additional competition for certain domestic mining operations which were able to meet all the current domestic demand, but the Administration gave assurances that it was not planned to encourage production abroad of materials for which anticipated production would be "in excess" of forecasted demand. The majority of Congress, aware of the growing dependence of the United States and Western Europe on foreign sources of many raw materials,[7] were mildly sympathetic with the objectives of the program but asked, and secured, assurances from the Administration that no project was included that was likely to be financed by private capital, the International Bank, or the Export-Import Bank and that none could safely be postponed.

In the end, in part because of its urgent desire to reduce the size of the Mutual Security Program, in part because of the reluctance to increase in any way the competition faced by domestic mines, and in part because of a feeling that this program was in danger of overlapping other activities under the Mutual Security Program, Congress appropriated only $19 million for basic-materials development and indicated that it wished this sum to be spent for projects directly related to such strategic and critical materials as uranium, cobalt, and manganese.[8]

C. SPECIAL ECONOMIC ASSISTANCE TO INDIA AND PAKISTAN

The Truman Administration had tried in 1952 to include in the so-called technical assistance program for India and Pakistan relatively large amounts for commodities, as distinct from services,

---

[7] For a detailed study of the increasing dependence of the United States on foreign sources of raw materials, see the President's Materials Policy Commission, *Resources for Freedom*, Wash., D.C., 1952.

[8] For more information about the basic-materials program, see *Hearings on H.R. 5710, op.cit.*, pp. 1096-1118 and 1126-1180, and "Mutual Security Appropriations for 1954," *Hearings, op.cit.*, pp. 888-418.

on the grounds that the political and economic conditions in those countries made it necessary to "speed up" the Point Four Program. These proposals had met with strong objections from many in Congress, who interpreted them as an attempt to change the fundamental character of the Point Four Program from one of "grass-roots" help to large-scale economic and financial support, and the Administration's request was more than halved in a move specifically designed to restrict the Point Four Program to what Congress regarded as its original purposes.[9]

The Eisenhower Administration in 1953 also proposed sending relatively large amounts of commodities to these two countries, but it presented this part of the aid separately from the technical assistance noted above and asked for a special appropriation of $94 million (of which India was scheduled to receive $80 million and Pakistan the rest) for providing goods to help accelerate the pace of economic development there. The Director for Mutual Security told the Congressional committees that the Administration planned to request a slightly greater amount for the same purpose in 1954 and probably a slightly smaller amount in 1955. He made it clear, however, that the Administration was not asking Congress at that time for a commitment for future years.

Arguments of the Administration in justifying this request were essentially the same as those used by its predecessor the year before. It was stated that the Indian people felt, rightly or wrongly, that economic progress had been in large measure denied them prior to their independence, and now that their affairs were in their own hands they expected rapid improvement in their economic well-being. These expectations led the Indian Government to believe that a large-scale development program was necessary to its continuing in office, and a five-year plan initiated in early 1951 was being executed with urgency. This plan emphasized expanding food production; increasing irrigation facilities and electric generating capacity; improving and extending transportation and communication facilities; and expanding social services, including education and public health. The total cost of the plan was estimated to be the equivalent of $4250 million,[1] of

---

[9] See *Survey—1952*, pp. 62-67.

[1] The Indian Government was reported as hoping that the plan would produce an additional $3500 million of private investment.

which India expected to finance about $2600 million from internal sources and some $610 million from its sterling balances. India had already received some $320 million from the United States Government, from the International Bank, and under the Colombo Plan, but a gap of about $700 million remained.

The Administration spokesmen said they agreed with the Indian Government that the latter's stability was dependent on that nation's reaching the goals of the five-year plan. They testified that in their view the peoples and governments of many of the Asiatic and African nations looked to India for leadership and were comparing developments there with those in the Communist-dominated areas. For these reasons the Administration proposed that the U.S. Government give further aid in the financing of India's five-year development plan and a smaller but otherwise comparable plan in Pakistan.

With their fears of distortion of the technical assistance program proper thus allayed, the majority in Congress were more sympathetic than they had been in 1952 to granting economic aid for development programs in India and Pakistan.[2] Some members of Congress thought there was likely to be some overlapping between this aid and the technical assistance scheduled for India and Pakistan, but the Administration gave assurance that this would not be the case. The final appropriation act provided $75 million for special economic assistance to these two countries. The cut in the request reflected more the desire of Congress to reduce Government expenditures than disapproval of the Administration's plans.

### *Implementation*[3]

In mid-1953 the Technical Cooperation Administration, which, under the general supervision of the Department of State, had

[2] Some, however, expressed the belief that the proposed aid could not be effectively used so long as there were serious disputes between India and Pakistan over Kashmir and over the use of the waters in the Indus River system. It was agreed that the United States should not "interfere" in these disputes, but Congress did provide in the law that the President should extend the aid in such a way as to assist the countries in solving their mutual problems.

There was little criticism during the hearings of India's policies toward Russia and China, such as had marked the 1951 debates on the emergency food loan to India. See *Survey—1951*, pp. 105-108.

[3] Much of the information in this section was taken from the following publications of the Mutual Security Agency/Foreign Operations Administration: *Report to Congress on the Mutual Security Program*, Wash., D.C., June 30, 1953; *Report*

administered the Point Four Program since its inception, was liquidated and its functions transferred to the Foreign Operations Administration. There were also a large number of new appointments to the senior administrative positions in the technical assistance program, and the press carried many reports that the program was in danger of being "smothered" under the military aid programs and its purpose in danger of being diverted from the original objective of "enlightened humanitarianism" to that of directly strengthening the military might of the recipient nations and of the United States. Administration spokesmen, including the President, denied these allegations; they declared that the integration of the technical assistance and other forms of aid, where the latter were being furnished, had increased the effectiveness of both types of assistance and that the new Administration was giving more emphasis to technical cooperation than had its predecessor.[4]

Official data released to the public during 1953 were presented in such summary form as to make it impossible for an outsider to assess the charges that the purposes of the program were being changed, but such information as was available on activities in individual countries indicated few if any shifts in the general types

to Congress on the Mutual Security Program, Wash., D.C., December 31, 1953; Economic Strength for the Free World: Principles of a United States Foreign Development Program, a report by the Advisory Committee on Underdeveloped Areas, Wash., D.C., May 1953; and Conclusions and Recommendations of the International Development Advisory Board, Wash., D.C., December 1953. Other sources were Kerber, E. S., "United States Foreign Aid in the Fiscal Year 1953," Survey of Current Business, October 1953, pp. 15-20; Kerber, E. S., "Foreign Grants and Credits of the United States Government in 1953," Survey of Current Business, April 1954, pp. 17-22; U.S. Department of Commerce, Foreign Aid by the United States Government, issues of March 31, 1953, and June 30, 1953; and U.S. Department of Commerce, Foreign Grants and Credits by the United States Government, issues of September 1953 and December 1953. See also Andrews, S., "The United States and the Underdeveloped Areas," Department of State Bulletin, February 28, 1953, pp. 306-310, and Hunter, J. M., and Knowles, W. H., "Ten Problems of Point Four," Inter-American Economic Affairs, Summer 1953, pp. 64-81.

For summary information about the program in years prior to 1953, see the earlier issues of this Survey.

4 See New York Times, September 24, 1953, pp. 1ff.; September 25, 1953, p. 6; and September 26, 1953, p. 4, for a series of articles appraising the changing character of the Point Four Program. See also ibid., November 6, 1953, pp. 1ff., and Foreign Operations Administration, Conclusions and Recommendations of the International Development Advisory Board, op.cit. For the statement by the President, see Department of State Bulletin, June 15, 1953, pp. 850-851.

of projects being supported. Statistical data on the scale of operations were presented in such a way as to make precise comparisons with earlier years impossible, but it appeared that expenditures under what was commonly regarded as the Point Four Program amounted to approximately $140 million in 1953, as compared with about $63 million in 1952.[5] Three countries, however—Iran, India, and Pakistan—accounted for most of the increase, and aid extended to these countries under "special" economic assistance programs in both years is included. The nations of the Near East and Africa apparently received about $55 million of the total, those of South Asia $65 million, and those of Latin America some $20 million.

The program continued to concentrate on increasing agricultural production, especially that of food; improving standards of health; and raising educational levels. Important sums were also being spent for the improvement of transportation and communication facilities, the training of officials in public administration, and the development of mineral resources. There was as yet little evidence as to the achievements of the program with respect to the major goals set for it, and reports on its accomplishments were still expressed in terms of individual projects, such as the number of persons protected from malaria in one area and the increases in yields of wheat or rice in another.[6]

The Administration reported that the problem of recruiting qualified technicians, which in earlier years had been a major obstacle to carrying out the program, became somewhat easier during 1953 and that "increasingly productive cooperative rela-

[5] *Not* included in these figures are the value of various forms of technical assistance provided the European countries, or the value of goods and services supplied the Nationalist Government of China (Formosa), Indochina, the Philippines, and Thailand. These are included in the data presented in Chapter I.

Also not included are administrative expenses not allocated to particular areas; these amounted to several million dollars in both years.

[6] For a view of a former Point Four official that the total impact of the program had been slight up to 1953, but that the potential effect of the work already completed might be much greater, due to various "multipliers," as well as for some suggestion of measures the United States should take to improve its effectiveness, see Hayes, S. P., Jr., "An Appraisal of Point Four," *Proceedings of the Academy of Political Science*, May 1953, pp. 81-46. See also Blaisdell, T. C., Jr., "Problems of Evaluating the Effectiveness of Development Measures," *Economic Development and Cultural Change*, January 1954, pp. 286-296.

For a more comprehensive appraisal of the program, see Bingham, J. B., *Shirt-Sleeve Diplomacy: Point 4 in Action . . .* , New York, 1954.

tionships" had been established between American technicians and officials of foreign governments.[7] By the end of the year under review almost 1650 American technicians were serving abroad, an increase of about 250 during the year, and about 900 foreign personnel were being trained in the United States. The earlier practice of employing private agencies, including colleges and universities, to execute individual projects under the program was expanded in 1953, but details were not published. Officials of the new Administration repeatedly asserted throughout the year that they believed private agencies could and should take over much of the work previously performed by the Government.

Iran received nearly two thirds of the $55 million of economic and technical aid provided the Near East and Africa in 1953. No one of the other nine participating nations in this area received as much as $2.5 million in Point Four aid, but, except for Libya, all the countries received more than they had in 1952.[8] Particular emphasis was given in the Near East to land development, improved water utilization, and irrigation. The Foreign Operations Administration reported that the host countries increased their participation in the programs, both in the provision of facilities and in the provision of money. In addition to this type of aid, Israel, the nations sheltering Palestine refugees, and Iran received large amounts of other economic assistance under separate programs, and Jordan and Libya received wheat under special famine relief legislation; these programs are discussed in subsequent sections.

India received over half of the assistance provided Asia under the economic and technical cooperation program during the year, followed by Pakistan, which received about one sixth of the total.[9]

[7] For a discussion of some of the problems faced by foreign technical experts operating in the underdeveloped countries, see Morgan, T., "The Underdeveloped Area Expert: South Asia Model," *Economic Development and Cultural Change,* April 1953, pp. 27-31.

[8] The participating nations were Egypt, Ethiopia, Iran, Iraq, Israel, Jordan, Lebanon, Liberia, Libya, and Saudi Arabia. Certain African dependencies of European countries also received very small amounts of aid. Syria continued to decline technical assistance from the United States, in protest against American aid to Israel, but did accept aid under the United Nations technical assistance program.

[9] Only scattered information is available as this document goes to press on the $75 million "special economic assistance" program for India and Pakistan which, as noted above, was regarded as an extension of the technical cooperation

The balance went to Burma, Afghanistan, Nepal, Indonesia, and unspecified "other" countries. The programs in India and Pakistan were coordinated with those countries' five-year development plans; most of the American aid was used to help increase food production, encourage village industries, and assist in the development of irrigation and power projects.[1] There was no public evidence that any efforts were being made in the technical cooperation program to ensure that the increases in production resulting from this aid would not be absorbed by increases in population, but in India local officials showed increasing concern over this problem and some American officials discussed the issue publicly.[2]

All the independent Latin American countries except Argentina participated in the technical assistance program in 1953, and toward the end of the year programs were begun on a very small scale in some of the dependent territories of the European powers. These programs were all small, the largest, in Brazil, involving expenditures by the United States of just under $3 million. In general, the activities in Latin America were directed toward "total country development," with major attention being given to overcoming the problems arising from food shortages, dependence

program although funds for it were separately requested and appropriated. Expenditures under this program have been included in the above data on Point Four expenditures. Nearly $58 million had been "programmed" for India by the end of the year, some $26 million being for the import of 200,000 tons of steel (to be sold in India and the local-currency proceeds used for development projects) and the remainder for the import of 100 locomotives and 5,000 freight cars (with India undertaking to spend an equivalent amount in local currency on mutually agreed projects). Published data do not indicate whether any shipments actually took place during the year. Just over $11 million had been "programmed" for Pakistan, more than half of it for the import of fertilizer and the construction of a fertilizer factory. At least $8 million of fertilizer was shipped during the last quarter of 1953.

As noted above, Formosa, Indochina, the Philippines, Thailand, and Korea received economic assistance that is not reported in this section but is described elsewhere in this volume.

[1] For a list of the specific projects undertaken in India up to mid-1953, involving a total commitment of United States funds of almost $90 million, see *Foreign Commerce Weekly*, October 5, 1953, p. 5. For a discussion of the five-year plan without particular reference to the United States' part in it, see Anjaria, J. J., "India's Five Year Plan," *Current History*, June 1953, pp. 321-326.

The Ford Foundation continued its support of various economic development programs in India, and in 1953 made additional grants for these purposes totalling more than $1 million.

[2] See Anderson, S. W., "The Effect of Population Trends on Economic Development," *Foreign Commerce Weekly*, October 12, 1953, pp. 10ff.

on one or a few export commodities, and limited transportation facilities and energy sources. Not only did the Latin American nations continue to increase the ratio of their expenditures to those of the United States, but during 1953 full responsibility for financing several of the individual projects inaugurated under the Point Four Program or its predecessor had been assumed by the local governments, and some projects were entirely staffed with their nationals.[3]

Late in the year the President of Bolivia wrote President Eisenhower that the sharp decline in the world price of tin, the export of which normally provides about 60 percent of Bolivia's foreign-exchange earnings, was creating a critical situation in his country, and asked for help.[4] President Eisenhower responded by allocating an additional $2 million of Point Four funds to Bolivia for use in increasing food production, by transferring $4 million for special economic aid from funds appropriated for defense support in Western Europe, and by authorizing a gift of $5 million of wheat and wheat flour from stocks of the Commodity Credit Corporation.[5] Just under $1 million of this aid had actually been utilized by the end of the year.

Only scattered data are available as this *Survey* goes to press on the "basic-materials-development" program, for which Congress earmarked $19 million in 1953. Most of the projects were still in the "planning" stage at year's end, but the Foreign Operations Administration had made available, on a loan basis, the equivalent of $3 million to France and $0.6 million to Germany.

## B. *UNITED NATIONS EXPANDED PROGRAM OF TECHNICAL ASSISTANCE*[6]

The United Nations Expanded Program of Technical Assist-

---

[3] See Rowe, C. O., "Cooperative Spirit in Latin America Contributed to Success of Point 4 Program," *Foreign Commerce Weekly*, May 4, 1953, pp. 15ff.

[4] For the exchange of letters between the two Presidents, see Department of State *Bulletin*, November 2, 1953, pp. 584–586.

[5] The gift of wheat was made under the authority of P.L. 216, 83d Cong., which is discussed below.

The $4 million grant was to be used for the import of cotton, lard, cottonseed oil, and other commodities, and to pay for the ocean freight on the wheat. This was the first occasion since World War II of such special "economic aid" being granted to a country in the Western Hemisphere.

[6] For more complete information on the United Nations Expanded Program, see "Fifth Report of the Technical Assistance Board," UN Economic and Social

ance was organized in 1950, following the announcement of the Point Four Program and largely upon United States initiative.[7] The Expanded Program took form slowly, but by the beginning of 1953 some sixty-five nations had contributed the equivalent of $36 million to it, including $22 million paid by the United States. The equivalent of $22 million had actually been spent, over three fourths of it in 1952.[8] The general objectives of the United Nations Program and the Point Four Program were similar, but they differed in that the former provided only very small amounts of material and equipment, nearly all of its funds being spent for salaries of technicians and expenses incident to their work. Only four countries received as much as $1 million in aid in 1952, and no one received as much as $1.2 million.

The UN General Assembly late in 1952 set a goal of $25 million for the Expanded Program in 1953. In February United States officials pledged up to $14.7 million, subject to the usual condition that the American contribution would not exceed 60 percent of the total and that the provision of funds beyond those still available from previous appropriations was subject to Congressional

---

Council, *Official Records*: Sixteenth Session, Supplement No. 10; UN General Assembly, *Official Records*: Eighth Session, Second Committee, 249th-257th Meetings, September 28–October 12, 1953; and UN Docs. E/2394, E/2497, E/TAC/SR.29 to SR.57, E/TAC/L.28 to L.55, E/TAC/3 to 30, E/TAC/84, E/TAC/89, E/2450, and E/2512. Detailed data on activities of the Program in 1953 are not available as this *Survey* goes to press.

For a review of comparative United States and United Nations experience in technical cooperation, see Sharp, W. R., "The Institutional Framework for Technical Assistance," *International Organization*, August 1953, pp. 342-379.

[7] Prior to 1950 the United Nations and several of its specialized agencies had been providing their members with technical assistance on a small scale, financed out of their regular budgets. This "regular" technical assistance was continued after the organization of the Expanded Program, but is not reported in this *Survey*. For information on these programs, see the various reports of the specialized agencies, especially the Food and Agriculture Organization, the World Health Organization, and the United Nations Educational, Scientific, and Cultural Organization. The International Bank and the International Monetary Fund also provide various types of technical assistance to their members and these are described in their annual reports.

[8] For summary accounts of the activities in earlier years, see *Survey—1952*, pp. 72-77, and the references cited there. For more detailed reports on the Program in 1952 than were available when the last issue of this *Survey* was published, see UN Docs. A/C.5/546 and E/2414.

During 1952, 451 experts (of whom 140 were American) served in the field and 729 nationals of underdeveloped countries received training abroad. These figures are less than those given in our *Survey—1952*, p. 75n, which information now available shows were for "approved," rather than actual, programs.

action. Shortly thereafter the Administration asked Congress to appropriate, as part of the Mutual Security Program, $13.75 million for the United States contribution to multilateral technical cooperation programs in calendar year 1954, including $1 million for the program of the Organization of American States,[9] and later made a supplementary request for $4.6 million already authorized but not appropriated for 1953.

The justification given by the Administration for providing a part of American technical assistance funds through international organizations was similar to that offered in earlier years: certain problems were regional rather than national in character and so were more efficiently attacked by regional organizations; in some cases multilateral aid was politically and psychologically more acceptable than bilateral aid; multilateral programs often cost the United States less than bilateral activities and reduced the drain on American manpower; and some problems could best be handled by foreign technicians. Mr. Stanley Andrews, then Administrator of the Technical Cooperation Administration, testified that in his opinion the United States should, as time went on, provide an increasing proportion of its technical assistance through the United Nations.[1] He acknowledged that in the past there had been some duplication in the two programs but asserted

[9] The United States in 1953, as in the two preceding years, pledged up to $1,000,000 to the technical cooperation program of the Organization of American States, but specified again that its contribution should not exceed 70 percent of the total. Total pledges for the year for this program from eighteen participating nations were the equivalent of about $1,400,000. During 1953 the United States actually transferred $921,000 to the Organization. The purposes of the technical cooperation program of the Organization of American States are comparable to those of the Point Four Program and the United Nations Program, but the latter two concentrate on individual projects in individual countries while the Organization of American States establishes and supports regional training centers for local personnel. In 1953, centers were operating in the fields of agricultural extension, low-cost housing, child welfare, economic and financial statistics, and animal husbandry. It was planned to establish similar centers for rural education and natural resource development when funds became available. (For more information on the technical cooperation activities of the Organization of American States, see the various issues of *Annals of the Organization of American States*. See also UN Doc. E/2471.)

[1] He stated, however, that before the United Nations could carry out a much larger program than it was then operating, its officials would "have to get themselves organized to administer it," that their organization was then "loose jointed" and "scattered," but that "the boys know it and are trying to tighten it up." ("Mutual Security Act of 1953," *Hearings, op.cit.*, pp. 529-530.)

that this had been eliminated and that there was "enough for everybody to do."

The majority in Congress did not question the policy of contributing to the multilateral programs, but, as with all multinational aid programs, there was strong sentiment for reducing the proportion of total costs borne by the United States.[2] Many spoke in favor of limiting the United States contribution to not more than one third of the total. No such restrictions were written into the law, but Congress appropriated a total of only $9.5 million for multinational technical assistance. This was sufficient, with the funds still available from the 1952-1953 appropriation, for the United States to meet its pledge, and during the calendar year $11.9 million was transferred to the United Nations Program.

New projects amounting to $25 million were approved for the United Nations Program in 1953, with scheduled local-currency expenditures by host governments on these projects equivalent to one and one half to two times this figure.[3] Total pledges by participating governments for the year were the equivalent of just $22.4 million, and only $20.7 million was actually paid on these and earlier pledges.[4] In midsummer the planned Program

[2] The majority of the Randall Commission early in 1954 recommended continued support of the United Nations and Organization of American States technical assistance programs. They further stated that some expansion of the United Nations Program would be desirable but that the share of the United States in the cost should be reduced.

[3] There were complaints by some of the participating countries that the costs to host countries of foreign experts under the United Nations Program were greater than for experts available elsewhere, particularly under the Colombo Plan; representatives of some of these countries argued in the discussions at the United Nations that host governments should pay a smaller proportion of the living expenses and other local-currency costs of foreign technicians than they were paying, and some argued that they should not pay such costs at all. The United States representative and others urged that the recipient nations should pay a larger share of these costs, arguing that the purpose of the Program was to help the underdeveloped countries to help themselves and that if the host governments paid a larger part of the local costs of experts the Expanded Program could provide a greater number of experts. Several procedural and accounting changes were introduced, under which host governments would pay a slightly smaller proportion than they had been paying (See UN Docs. E/2395, E/TAC/SR.30 to 32 and 34; UN Economic and Social Council, *Official Records*: Fifteenth Session, 687th Meeting, April 15, 1953; and UN Economic and Social Council Resolution 470 [XV], April 15, 1953.)

[4] Considerable publicity was given in the summer to the pledges made by Russia and Poland, this being the first time any of the Soviet-bloc countries had offered financial support to the Program. Russia pledged the equivalent of

for the year was slightly curtailed because of a shortage of funds. This, to say nothing of the inability of the United Nations to undertake all the projects for which aid was requested by members, provided the occasion for strong expressions of disappointment by representatives of some of the underdeveloped countries over the failure of the Program to develop at the rate they had earlier anticipated.[5] Many called for an increase in the scale of operations, alleging that the gap in living standards between the poorer countries and the richer nations was increasing and that the latter had a moral obligation to assist the development of the poorer areas of the world. Spokesmen for the wealthy nations, supported by some from the underdeveloped countries, insisted the project was a voluntary one and that they recognized no "obligation" to support it. None of the official spokesmen seemed to expect any substantial increase in the Program in the near future.[6]

Actual disbursements by the United Nations for its technical assistance program during 1953 totalled the equivalent of $19.8 million. As in earlier years, this assistance was principally in the fields of agriculture, health, education, transportation and communication, and public administration. The underdeveloped countries themselves gave increasing evidence of being capable of helping each other; at mid-1953 about a quarter of all the experts in the field came from other underdeveloped countries and an eighth of the international fellows were studying in such countries. Experience had shown that in many cases the training and experi-

---

$1,000,000 in rubles, calculated at the nominal rate of exchange, and Poland the equivalent of $75,000. By the year's end, however, these amounts had not been paid, inasmuch as no way had yet been found to use the funds under the conditions attached to the pledges.

[5] The midsummer cutback also caused some criticism that the Technical Assistance Board and the participating specialized agencies had undertaken new programs that were too large for the funds available. Spokesmen for some of these agencies replied that they were only carrying out the instructions of the General Assembly and the Economic and Social Council to accelerate the Expanded Program. A working party was appointed to review the Program's financial procedures, with the purpose of preventing overcommitments in the future.

[6] As compared with previous years, little time was given in the discussions of the technical assistance program to urging large-scale capital assistance. In other discussions, however, the underdeveloped countries vigorously sought such capital assistance through the establishment of a Special United Nations Fund for Economic Development and an international finance corporation. (See Chapter IV.)

ence received in other underdeveloped countries were more easily and satisfactorily transferred than training obtained in the more highly industrialized nations. At the end of 1953 there were just over 1,000 experts serving in the underdeveloped countries, of whom almost a fifth were United States nationals, and nearly 600 fellows were in training abroad. Most of those who spoke to the point acclaimed the help given by United Nations experts. United States officials expressed general satisfaction with the program but suggested that even better results might be obtained if the efforts in most of the countries were concentrated on fewer, but larger-scale, projects.

Considerable criticism of the expense of administering the program was voiced during the year, some citing data indicating overhead was in excess of 20 percent of the total cost. Spokesmen for the Technical Assistance Board stated that part of the expenditures charged to central administration were actually operating costs that could not be allocated to individual projects. Nonetheless, they recognized a need for greater administrative efficiency and agreed that there should be a reduction in the size of the administrative organization if the program were not going to grow to the size for which the administrative machinery was designed. Involved in this discussion was the more controversial issue of the employment of "resident representatives" of the United Nations in the host countries. The tasks of these persons were to advise the local governments on economic development matters, to coordinate the activities of the various participating specialized agencies, and to submit reports to the Technical Assistance Board. Spokesmen for a few of the underdeveloped countries urged the elimination of this position, leaving to the governments of the aided countries the entire responsibility for determining what aid was needed and for coordinating the work of the technicians. Led by the United States, the chief contributors to the program recognized the necessity of formulating programs at the country level but successfully insisted that the system of resident representatives be continued. The major argument offered was that this was an efficient way of insuring the coordination of the various activities, but it was clear that an important consideration was the desire to have a United Nations representative screen the recipient countries' requests.

In 1952 the General Assembly had requested the Economic and Social Council to study the feasibility of planning the technical assistance program for periods longer than one year. The program was generally recognized as being a long-term one, but, in the absence of estimates of future contributions, planning for more than one year had been found exceedingly difficult. The Council published no report of this matter in 1953, but a working paper of the Technical Assistance Board pointed out that while many governments were prohibited by their constitutions from making appropriations for more than one year in advance, it would be helpful if executive and administrative authorities declared their intent to support the program and stated the scale of financial contributions they would recommend to their legislatures. Subsequently, a resolution was approved by the Economic and Social Council declaring that a more orderly development of the program would be possible if nations would give assurances of financial support for periods longer than one year, even though exact amounts might not be committed, and inviting participating governments, within their constitutional limitations, to do so.[7]

In late summer and early autumn the General Assembly and the Economic and Social Council passed resolutions asking member governments to contribute to the 1954 program so as to meet its needs "to the maximum extent possible" and urged that total contributions be at least the equivalent of about $25 million.[8] Serious operating difficulties were encountered in 1953 because of the late pledging (and payment) of funds, and the pledging conference for the 1954 program was therefore held in November. At this conference and subsequently, 71 governments pledged the equivalent of $24.3 million. The United States delegate announced that his Government would contribute up to $14.75 million, part of this subject to Congressional appropriation, but that its contribution would not exceed 60 percent of the total payments to the program up to the first $21.25 million, or 40 percent of the next $5 million.

[7] See UN Economic and Social Council Resolution 492 C (XVI), August 5, 1953. See also UN Docs. E/TAC/10 and E/TAC/SR.86 and 87.
[8] UN Economic and Social Council Resolution 492 C (XVI), August 5, 1953, and UN General Assembly Resolution 722 (VIII), October 23, 1953.

## C. SPECIAL ASSISTANCE TO THE NEAR EAST AND AFRICA

### Legislative Issues

In addition to funds for the regular Point Four Program, Congress in 1952 had appropriated $70 million for special economic assistance to Israel and $60 million for helping to resettle the refugees from the 1948 war in Palestine, who were then living in various of the Arab States; the latter funds were to be made available to the United Nations Relief and Works Agency for Palestine Refugees in the Near East. Beside the humanitarian considerations, this "emergency" aid to Israel and the Arab refugees was justified, as in prior years, on the general grounds that an improvement in economic conditions would reduce internal political instability in the various countries, encourage a political settlement between Israel and the Arab States, help to make this strategic area self-supporting, and increase the area's ability to assist in the defense of the free world. The aid to Israel was further defended on the ground that the United States had an obligation arising from its "acquiescence" in the creation of that nation and in the policies of encouraging unlimited immigration of Jews into Israel. By the end of 1952 Israel was far from being viable, and virtually nothing had been achieved in "resettling" Palestine refugees.[9]

The new Administration asked Congress in early 1953 for new appropriations of $164 million for special economic assistance to the Near East and Africa, plus reappropriation of the unexpended funds previously made available for helping resettle the Arab refugees.[1] Administration spokesmen testified that it was tentatively planned to spend some $24 million of the total request

[9] See *Survey—1952*, pp. 79-87 for a more detailed statement of the justification of these programs and a brief account of what had been accomplished under them.

[1] The Administration requested an authorization of $194 million, including $80 million for the Arab refugees, but stated that it did not plan to ask for an appropriation of this $30 million inasmuch as funds were on hand to cover expected expenditures for the fiscal year beginning in mid-1953. This authorization was asked, and received, on the ground that it was desirable to give evidence of continued United States interest in the plight of these refugees and as a precaution against the possibility that an appropriation would be asked later in the year if expenditures by the United Nations Relief and Works Agency for Palestine Refugees should warrant it.

for technical assistance in developmental projects in the African dependencies of European countries, and some $10 million for economic assistance in support of the technical assistance program in Iran. The remaining $130 million, they said, were to be spent for the benefit of Israel and the Arab countries. In contrast with earlier years, Administration spokesmen did not publicly state how they proposed to distribute the total as between Israel and the Arab States; it was said, however, that the proportion of the total planned for Israel was not as great as in the preceding year. The major reasons given for not dividing in advance the requested funds as between the two areas was that the new Administration proposed wherever feasible to treat the whole area as a unit and to concentrate on area-wide projects that would benefit both the Arab States and Israel, it being held that this approach would permit a more economical use of limited resources and would help resolve the political conflicts within the area.[2]

Most of the justification for the aid to Israel and the Arab States was given in executive session, but in the public hearings the request was supported on the same grounds as in 1952. It was planned that the aid to Israel would, as in previous years, include both consumer goods and capital goods. As for the Arab States, it was planned that, in contrast to earlier years, some of the economic aid would be provided on a bilateral basis rather than through the United Nations Relief and Works Agency and would concentrate primarily on equipment and supplies to be used in such projects as river valley development, irrigation, and highway construction. Congress was assured that the Administration did not propose to grant large-scale aid to countries having large revenues from petroleum, and Syria, Lebanon, Jordan, and Egypt were cited as nations not having such revenues. The majority in Congress agreed that the interests of the United States in the Near East justified providing more than ordinary technical assistance and felt that special economic aid to Israel and the Arab States, as well as to Iran, should be continued. There was but little criticism in either House of the proposed program, most regarding the "area approach" as wise, and no serious effort was

[2] For a discussion of political tensions in the area and their significance for United States policy, see Department of State *Bulletin*, February 8, 1954, pp. 209-214; February 22, 1954, pp. 274-281; March 1, 1954, pp. 328-338; and March 8, 1954, pp. 865-871.

made, at least in public, to insure that either Israel or the Arab States received a certain portion of the total. Some questioned the advisability of spending $24 million in aiding Europe's African dependencies, in view of the delicate political situation and rising nationalism in many of these territories, and thought that the American people should not be taxed to help "solve the colonial problems" of the United Kingdom and France. The Administration replied that economic betterment would ease political and social problems and that the European nations, burdened with rearmament programs, could not spare as much of their resources for the development of their dependent territories as the residents of these territories were demanding. Many in Congress, however, were not impressed by these statements, and the final appropriation for special assistance to the Near East and Africa provided only $147 million (plus a reappropriation of the $44 million in unspent balances for the United Nations Arab refugee program); it was made clear that most of the reduction from the Administration's recommendations was intended to fall on the dependent overseas territories.

### Implementation

Except for a few thousand dollars of assistance to French Morocco and Tunisia, there was no evidence in the publicly available data that the Foreign Operations Administration extended any economic assistance during 1953 directly to the African dependencies of the Western European nations. Bilateral aid to the Arab States was greater than in 1952, and the rate during the last quarter of the year under review was well above that of the previous months. Nevertheless, no one of these States received as much as $2.5 million directly from the United States, including aid under the Point Four Program. The total economic and technical assistance grants by the U.S. Government to Egypt, Iraq, Jordan, Lebanon, and Saudi Arabia during 1953 were less than $10 million; this amount was included in the discussion of economic and technical cooperation assistance in Section A of this chapter.

Similarly, it was not possible from the available data to distinguish the aid received by Iran under the technical assistance program and that received under the appropriation for "special economic assistance." Late in the summer, following a period of violence, a new government assumed authority in Iran and the new Premier asked the U.S. Government for additional aid, stating that the Iranian Treasury was empty, the reserves of foreign exchange exhausted, and that, in general, the national economy was in a critical state. The press reported that the Administration in Washington believed the new government in Iran was likely to be more friendly to the West than its predecessor, and shortly after the request from Iran was received it was announced that President Eisenhower had authorized an "emergency" grant to Iran of $45 million, in addition to the economic and technical aid already planned for that country. Over half of the $45 million grant was scheduled to be used to finance the immediate shipment of sugar and certain other urgently needed consumer commodities, with the balance being for "direct budgetary support" and other purposes. By the end of the year a total of more than $56 million had been transferred to Iran, four times the amount of aid extended in 1952. Of this amount, $36 million was from funds appropriated for technical assistance and "special economic assistance" and is included in the totals given in Section A, above. The remaining $20 million, transferred from funds appropriated for military aid to Western Europe, was apparently provided to the Government of Iran as budgetary support.[3]

Israel, on the other hand, received only about one half as much grant aid from the United States during 1953 as in the preceding year—$35 million under the special economic assistance program plus $9.4 million of donations of surplus foodstuffs by the Department of Agriculture, as compared with nearly $82 million in 1952. A large part of this aid was used to purchase foodstuffs and other consumer goods, fuel, and raw materials, with the balance being used for the import of capital goods, mainly for the expansion of irrigation and for housing construction. As in the previous year, these grants included funds used to liquidate maturing short-term debts that Israel had previously accumulated in importing goods later determined eligible for financing under the aid program. In October the U.S. Government announced suspension of new

[3] Discussions were renewed late in the year looking toward a settlement of the Anglo-Iranian Oil Company dispute, but agreement had not yet been reached as the year ended.

allocations of aid to Israel, following a report by a United Nations truce supervision team that the Israelis were undertaking certain construction work in the demilitarized zone that would divert the waters of the Jordan River in a manner contrary to the armistice agreement with Syria. The Government of Israel denied that the construction adversely affected the economic interests of its neighbors, but nevertheless suspended construction pending further investigation. The U.S. Government then announced a large new allocation of aid.[4] Available public evidence indicated that Israel made some progress toward becoming self-supporting during the year, but that foreign aid of one kind or another would be needed for a long time if consumption levels in that country were to be maintained.

Virtually no progress was reported during the year in resettling the Arab refugees from Palestine.[5] In its annual report for the year ending in mid-1953 the Agency for Palestine Refugees stated that 870,000 persons were still on the relief rolls, a decline of only about 10,000 during the year despite the fact that Israel had assumed responsibility during 1953 for the nearly 20,000 refugees settled within its borders. The Agency had been successful in resettling a few of the refugees, but this had been more than offset by the excess of births over deaths. By the end of the year the Agency had finally signed agreements with the Governments of Jordan, Syria, and Egypt for resettlement projects, mostly irrigation, designed to cost a total of $111 million. But only trivial amounts had actually been spent on these projects, with most of

---

[4] For information on United States action in suspending new allocations of aid, see Department of State *Bulletin*, November 2, 1953, pp. 589-590, and November 16, 1953, pp. 674-675. For reports on action in the United Nations Security Council, see UN Docs. S/3108/Rev. 1 and S/3122, with Annexes I-III, and *United Nations Bulletin*, December 1, 1953, pp. 506-509, and February 1, 1954, p. 126.

[5] For official reports on this program for the period ending in mid-1953, see "Annual Report of the Director of the United Nations Relief and Work Agency for Palestine Refugees in the Near East," UN General Assembly, *Official Records*: Eighth Session, Supplement No. 12; UN General Assembly, *Official Records*: Eighth Session, Supplement No. 6B; UN General Assembly, *Official Records*: Eighth Session, *Ad Hoc* Political Committee, 23rd-30th Meetings, November 2-12, 1953; and UN Doc. A/2470/Add. 1. A summary of the proceedings of the *Ad Hoc* Political Committee may also be found in *United Nations Bulletin*, December 1, 1953, pp. 529-534. See also Pevsner, L. W., "The Arab Refugees," *Journal of International Affairs*, Vol. VII (1953), No. 1, pp. 42-50, and other articles in this issue; Vernant, J., *The Refugee in the Post-War World*, New Haven, 1953; and *The Economist*, May 9, 1953, pp. 840-842.

the Agency's $26.8 million of expenditures during the year having been for outright relief.

In explaining its failure to make progress in permanently re-settling the refugees, the Agency reported that, although some of the refugees themselves appeared less unwilling than in the past to resettle elsewhere, the majority of them and the officials of the Arab States continued to insist upon the rights of the refugees to repatriation and to regard this as the principal solution, while the Government of Israel continued to show no signs of accepting this as a solution. The Arab States were also reported to be reluctant to provide economically attractive sites for resettlement projects, continuing to reserve such sites for development plans that were not related to the specific problem of the refugees. The Agency also stated that, although the resources of the Middle East were such that their most economical use frequently involved area-wide development, it had not been possible to obtain the cooperation between Israel and the Arab States necessary to undertake such projects.

The United States spokesman in the United Nations expressed great concern over the failure to make progress in solving the refugee problem and stated that his Government was not prepared to continue bearing so large a share of the United Nations pro-gram if Israel and the Arab States continued to show so little initiative in settling this problem. He asked Israel to reconsider its responsibility for repatriation and to take immediate steps to compensate the refugees for properties left in Israel, and he called upon both sides to take "bold measures" to resettle the refugees. As a first step he urged that agreement be reached on the use of the waters in the Jordan River and its tributaries.[6] In the latter part of the year President Eisenhower sent Mr. Eric Johnston to the Near East to study the problem of economic aid to that area, and especially to emphasize to the governments the importance the United States Administration attached to a project for the large-scale development of the Yarmuk-Jordan River Valley pre-pared at the request of the United Nations by an American engineering firm, under the supervision of the Tennessee Valley Authority. On his return Mr. Johnston reported that the govern-ments were studying the plan "with an open mind." Administra-

[6] See Department of State *Bulletin*, November 30, 1953, pp. 759-761.

tion officials later stated that the United States would not withhold aid from the area if the Yarmuk-Jordan plan were not accepted by the governments of the area but made it clear that the level of future United States aid would depend upon the availability of "sound" and "suitable" development projects, especially ones to improve water use.[7]

The United Nations General Assembly late in the year adopted a resolution recognizing that progress in resettlement had not come up to expectations, extending the United Nations Relief and Work Agency for one year to mid-1955, and authorizing the Agency to adopt a budget for relief for the year ending in mid-1954 of $24.8 million and a provisional relief budget for the year following of $18 million. The General Assembly considered that the $200 million planned for resettlement projects in the original three-year program begun in mid-1951 should be retained intact, and the Near Eastern governments were urged to continue to seek projects that would enable these funds to be used for the purposes intended. The original plan provided only $50 million for relief during the three-year period, but inasmuch as this sum had been exhausted by mid-1953, the new relief authorizations had the effect of increasing the $250 million, three-year program to a $293 million, four-year program. The Negotiating Committee for Extra-budgetary Funds was therefore requested to take account of the need for increased pledges. The United States delegate supported this resolution.[8]

The U.S. Government showed increasing reluctance to grant funds to the United Nations Agency to be used for purely relief purposes and during the year transferred only $9 million to it,

[7] See Department of State *Bulletin*, October 26, 1953, p. 558; November 80, 1953, pp. 749-750; December 28, 1953, pp. 891-893; and February 8, 1954, p. 211; and *The Economist*, October 31, 1953, pp. 888-889.

[8] UN General Assembly Resolution 720 (VIII), November 27, 1953.

For a statement of the U.S. Government's position, see Department of State *Bulletin*, June 8, 1953, pp. 822-824. Later in the year a Special Refugee Survey Commission, established by the Director of Foreign Operations at the direction of the Mutual Security Act of 1953, in an interim report also endorsed the decision to extend the Agency. (See Department of State *Bulletin*, January 18, 1954, pp. 95-102.)

For additional material on the Agency and the U.S. Congress, see "Palestine Refugee Program . . . ," *Committee Print*, U.S. Senate, Subcommittee of the Committee on Foreign Relations, 83d Cong., 1st Sess., July 24, 1953, and "Palestine Refugee Program," *Hearings*, U.S. Senate, Subcommittee of the Committee on Foreign Relations, 83d Cong., 1st Sess., May 20-25, 1953.

$8 million during the first quarter. This compared with $22 million in 1952 and brought the total United States contributions to the United Nations refugee program to $90 million, of which $43 million had been paid prior to the beginning of the three-year program. However, an additional $20 million was in a special U.S. Treasury account on which the United Nations Agency could draw for resettlement programs.

Late in the year the acting director of the United Nations Agency, together with its Advisory Commission, stated that "in spite of all efforts it is now clear that the rehabilitation of all the Arab refugees, in existing economic and political circumstances in the Near East, is for all practical purposes impossible."[9]

## D. *KOREAN CIVILIAN RELIEF AND RECONSTRUCTION*

In the years between the end of World War II and the invasion of South Korea in mid-1950, the U.S. Government had provided some $353 million of economic aid to that country. Most of this was in the form of civilian supplies provided by the Defense Department under its program of Government and Relief in Occupied Areas, but after the formal recognition of the Republic of Korea by the U.S. Government in early 1949, the Economic Cooperation Administration assumed responsibility for administering economic aid. A proposed three-year recovery program was necessarily abandoned when fighting began in mid-1950, but the hostilities increased the need for civilian relief supplies. Although such relief was thereafter handled by the Unified Command in Korea, the great bulk (probably well over 90 percent of the total) was filled out of United States Army stocks and financed out of Department of Defense appropriations. Through 1952 some $260 million of such civilian relief supplies had been furnished the South Koreans; another $119 million were transferred during 1953, but the rate fell very sharply during the last quarter. Foodstuffs were the most important type of goods furnished under this program, although substantial amounts of clothing, textiles, and agricultural supplies were also provided.

Two days after the attack on South Korea the United Nations Security Council passed a resolution calling upon the members

[9] UN Doc. A/2470/Add. 1, pp. 1-2.

of the United Nations to help the Republic of Korea, and subsequently, with strong United States support, the UN General Assembly voted that the United Nations should assume responsibility for post-hostilities relief and reconstruction. For this purpose it created a United Nations Korean Reconstruction Agency. A $250 million program was approved for the Agency's first year of full-scale operations, for which the U.S. Administration pledged $162.5 million. Late in 1952 it was agreed that the UN Agency should undertake at once a reconstruction program on such a scale as military operations would permit, it being concluded that any further delay in starting reconstruction would endanger the United Nations political and economic objectives in Korea.[1]

At the time of the 1953 hearings on the Mutual Security Act, the U.S. Government had already contributed some $51 million to the United Nations Korean Reconstruction Agency, $41 million of it in early 1953. President Eisenhower asked Congress to appropriate $71 million in cash for additional United States contributions to the Agency and to reduce from $67.5 million to $40.8 million the amount of supplies authorized to be transferred, at the time hostilities ceased, from the U.S. Army pipeline to the United Nations Agency.[2] There was widespread support in Congress for assisting the reconstruction of heavily devastated Korea. The authority to transfer civilian supplies in the Army pipeline was set at the amount requested, but only $50.7 million in new funds were appropriated; the reduction from the Administration's request was justified on the grounds that the funds and supplies provided would be adequate for such action as could be undertaken during the year.

On the same day the armistice agreement was signed in Korea, July 27, 1953, the President asked Congress for authority to use for emergency rehabilitation and economic aid to the Republic of Korea up to $200 million of the funds already appropriated to the Department of Defense. He stated that the cessation of hostilities would permit a substantial reduction in planned ex-

---

[1] For more information on the assistance program to Korea prior to 1953, see *Survey—1952*, pp. 90-93, and the references cited there.

[2] These requests plus the previously expended funds totalled the United States pledge of $162.5 million for the first year of the UN program.

penditures by the Defense Department for military operations in Korea, that the needs of Korea for economic assistance were critical, and that here was an opportunity for the free world "to prove its will and capacity to do constructive good in the cause of freedom and peace."[3] Apparently it was planned that these funds would be for the beginning of a program which would be in addition to the UN program and the emergency relief activities of the Unified Command. Congress quickly approved this request.[4] Shortly thereafter the President appointed an "Economic Coordinator" to serve on the staff of the United Nations Command and charged him with seeking to coordinate, and to avoid duplication in, the various assistance programs to Korea. Through 1953, only a few million dollars of this special $200 million authorization had actually been used, but large shipments of food, cotton, rubber, and fertilizer were scheduled for early 1954.

The United Nations Korean Reconstruction Agency began active operations in early 1953.[5] With the armistice agreement in late July, the Agency took "immediate steps" to launch its full-scale reconstruction program and planned activities estimated to cost $130 million for the fiscal year ending in mid-1954. The ultimate objectives of the program, provisionally estimated to require at least five years and to cost the equivalent of approximately $1 billion, were to attain levels of production sufficient to support per capita consumption levels comparable to those of 1949-1950; to achieve balance in Korea's international payments; to establish fiscal and economic policies conducive to economic development; and to develop managerial, technical, and administrative skills. It was planned to carry out reconstruction and development in virtually every sector of the Korean economy and to do it in such a way as not to make more difficult ultimate economic union with North Korea.

[3] Department of State *Bulletin*, August 10, 1953, p. 193.

For a summary of a report of a special mission to Korea, presented prior to the President's request, see *ibid.*, September 7, 1953, pp. 318-316.

[4] P.L. 207, 83d Cong., August 7, 1953, Chap. VII.

[5] For details on the activities of the UN Agency, see "Report of the Agent General of the United Nations Korean Reconstruction Agency for the Period 15 September 1952 to 30 September 1953," UN General Assembly, *Official Records*: Eighth Session, Supplement No. 14; UN General Assembly, *Official Records*: Eighth Session, Supplement No. 6C; and UN General Assembly, *Official Records*: Seventh Session, Supplements No. 19A and 19B.

By early autumn of 1953, however, the Agent General reported that experience to date had shown that the 1953-1954 program of $130 million could not be fulfilled. By year's end the target had been reduced to $85 million in the face of difficulties encountered in "crystallizing" the program (due in part to great differences of opinion between Korean authorities and officials of the Agency as to what the most urgent needs were) and the failure of several of the contributing countries to pay their pledges. The United States transferred nearly $56 million to the Agency in 1953, only $15 million of it during the last half of the year, raising the total of such assistance from the creation of the Agency to $65.8 million. These American contributions accounted for about three fourths of all the funds made available. Actual delivery of supplies, mostly foodstuffs and agricultural equipment, by the Agency to Korea amounted to only $30 million during 1953, the bulk of it during the first six months. Nonetheless, the Agency was generally praised in the United Nations debates. Near the end of the year the General Assembly approved the programs which had been prepared for the future but noted "with concern" that sufficient funds were not available to implement the proposed programs and urged all governments to give consideration to the "prompt payment" of pledges already made or "to the making of contributions within their financial possibilities if they have not already taken such action."[6]

## E. *SPECIAL FOOD PROGRAMS*

In addition to the shipments of agricultural products under Section 550 of the Mutual Security Act, the East German food program, and the Christmas food packages, all parts of the Mutual Security Program and all mentioned in Chapter I, the U.S. Government distributed foodstuffs abroad during 1953 under three other programs, such shipments being made from Government-held surpluses.

Pakistan is normally self-sufficient in wheat but in 1953, for the second consecutive year, experienced a severe drought. In response to a Presidential request, Congress in mid-1953 enacted a law providing authority until mid-1954 for the granting to

[6] UN General Assembly Resolution 725 (VIII), December 7, 1953.

Pakistan of 1,000,000 long tons of wheat from Government-held surplus stocks.[7] Up to 700,000 tons of this was authorized for immediate famine relief, with the remainder to be used for building reserve stocks in Pakistan. In view of the large wheat surpluses held by the Commodity Credit Corporation and the general agreement that Pakistan deserved American support because it was a new democratic nation which had repeatedly shown friendship for the United States, there was virtually no opposition in Congress to the grant. It was specified that the wheat was to be provided without cost to individuals unable to pay for it, with the remainder to be sold at prevailing local prices and the local-currency receipts used for projects designed to increase food production. The law specified that at least half of the shipments were to be made in American flag vessels.[8] Almost 600,000 tons of the wheat, valued at $71 million, had been shipped by the year's end, and the Foreign Operations Administration reported that this aid had "prevented a calamity" in Pakistan.

Shortly after the passage of the Pakistan Wheat Bill, the President requested Congress to give him general authority, "within appropriate limitations," to transfer abroad Government-held surplus agricultural commodities for purposes of meeting famine and other urgent relief requirements. The President stated that this authority would be especially useful when Congress was not in session, that its objectives were essentially humanitarian and should not be confused with those of the Mutual Security Program, and that it would involve no competition with normal commerce inasmuch as the food would be for people who would otherwise go hungry. Congress granted the President authority, until March 15, 1954, to transfer abroad up to $100 million of surplus agricultural commodities held by the Commodity Credit Corporation, the terms and administrative procedures to be determined by the President.[9] The law stated that foodstuffs could be sent

[7] To help relieve the distress in 1952, Congress had approved a loan of $15 million of wheat to Pakistan.

[8] P.L. 77, 88d Cong., June 25, 1958. For the legislative history of this Act, see "Wheat to Pakistan," *Hearings on H.R. 5659* . . . , House of Rep., Committee on Agriculture, 88d Cong., 1st Sess., June 15-16, 1958; *H. Rpt. No. 570*, 88d Cong.; and *S. Rpt. No. 404*, 88d. Cong.

[9] P.L. 216, 88d Cong., August 7, 1958. For the legislative background of this authority, see "Famine Relief," *Hearings on H.R. 6016*, House of Rep., Com-

not only to friendly foreign nations, but to any other nation, provided it were ascertained that the commodities so shipped would be used to alleviate distress among the people. Shipments of wheat and wheat flour, valued at $2.2 million, were made to Bolivia, Jordan, and Libya during the last quarter of the year; larger shipments took place in early 1954.

Still other food distributions abroad were made under the authority of the Agricultural Act of 1949. This law authorizes the Secretary of Agriculture to make available for various purposes, including grants to needy persons in foreign countries, stocks of surplus agricultural commodities held by the Commodity Credit Corporation which are in danger of spoilage.[1] During 1953 butter, dried milk, and cheese valued at $37.4 million were made available to private relief organizations for distribution to twenty-eight foreign countries. Western Germany, Israel, and Italy accounted for over three fourths of the total. This may be compared with only $1.4 million of such donations in 1952 and a total of $92 million from the passage of the Act through 1953.[2]

## F. *MIGRATION AND ESCAPEE ASSISTANCE*

For several years during and after World War II the United States played an active role in various international efforts to care for and resettle war refugees, especially those in Europe.[3] By 1951, however, the U.S. Government concluded that the major "emergency" problems had been solved, and it was instrumental in having the International Refugee Organization terminated, although it did support the creation of an Office of the United Nations High Commissioner for Refugees.[4] The U.S. Government

mittee on Agriculture, 83d Cong., 1st Sess., July 22-24, 1953; *H. Rpt. No. 983*, 83d Cong.; *S. Rpt. No. 631*, 83d Cong.; and *Conf. Rpt. No. 1070*, 83d Cong.

[1] P.L. 439, 81st Cong., Sect. 416.

[2] Costs of ocean transportation of all these special distributions of foodstuffs were paid from Mutual Security Program funds and are not included in the data given here.

[3] For a brief account of United States policies and activities concerning the refugee problem in earlier years, see *Survey—1952*, pp. 95-99, and the references cited there.

As noted elsewhere in this chapter, the United States made large contributions to helping solve the refugee problems in Israel, the Arab States, and Korea.

[4] The United Nations High Commissioner for Refugees was given the general task of protecting refugees, including the 400,000 "hard-core" cases left by the International Refugee Organization. The new organization has concentrated on

became increasingly concerned at about that time with the problems created for European economic recovery by the "surplus" population in several of the European countries, and there was organized in late 1951, largely upon United States initiative, a provisional agency that later became the Intergovernmental Committee for European Migration—not formally affiliated with the United Nations. This Committee, of which some twenty-odd governments are members, hoped to be able over a period of several years to help at least 3 million Europeans, mostly from Germany, Austria, Italy, the Netherlands, and Greece, migrate to areas where manpower was in greater demand. During 1952, with a contribution of $9 million from the U.S. Government, it assisted in the movement of some 78,000 persons, about half of them from Western Germany and about half coming to the United States. The Committee had set a target for 1953 of 120,000 emigrants, but during the first nine months only 61,000 persons had been transferred, and in September it was estimated the total for the year would not exceed 82,000. As in 1952, about half came from Western Germany, but the United States received only about 4,000; Canada, Australia, and some of the Latin American countries received most of the balance. The U.S. Government contributed $6.8 million to the program in 1953, and total contributions to the Committee from all sources were the equivalent of $24.3 million, about a third short of its goal.

President Eisenhower asked Congress to appropriate $10 million for the United States contribution to the Intergovernmental Committee for calendar year 1954. Despite the general support in Congress for the program (the House Committee on Foreign Affairs characterized the Intergovernmental Committee as a

---

attempting to obtain citizenship for the refugees and is operated on a small budget, the funds coming from the United Nations general budget plus some donations from governments and private sources. The U.S. Government has made no special contribution to the organization, but in 1952 the Ford Foundation granted $2.9 million to it, stipulating that these funds should be used for projects aimed at finding a permanent solution for the refugee problem. Most observers agreed that there was a continuing need for international action on behalf of refugees, and in 1953, with United States support, the United Nations General Assembly extended the life of the Office of the High Commissioner through 1958. (UN General Assembly Resolution 727 [VIII], October 23, 1953. For details on this organization and its work, see "Report of the United Nations High Commissioner for Refugees," UN General Assembly, *Official Records: Eighth Session*, Supplement No. 11.)

"creature of Congress"), only $7.5 million was appropriated, the reduction being in keeping with the intent of Congress to reduce Government expenditures. Although spokesmen for the U.S. Government argued that the failure of the Committee to meet its goals for 1952 and 1953 was "confusing" to governments and damaging to public confidence in the Committee and urged that stated future objectives be more modest, the governing body of the Committee late in 1953 set a goal of moving 118,000 persons in 1954.[5]

In 1952 Congress had been unwilling to contribute to the refugee and migration problem either by liberalizing the United States immigration law or by authorizing the emergency admission of persons over and above existing quotas. In 1953, however, in response to a Presidential request, it enacted special legislation permitting up to 214,000 immigrants beyond the quotas to enter the United States through 1956. The Refugee Relief Act of 1953 specifically allocated the nonquota immigration visas, most of them to residents of Western Germany, Austria, Italy, and Trieste.[6]

As noted in Chapter I, Congress took the initiative in 1951 of authorizing the use of up to $100 million of the funds of the Mutual Security Program to assist escapees from Iron Curtain countries, including helping to form them into military units within the NATO forces. The authority was continued in both 1952 and 1953. The Executive Branch had made no effort through 1953 to form such escapees into military units, but an undisclosed amount of funds had been used to permanently resettle some 7800 persons, about 5,000 during calendar year 1953. About 70 percent of the escapees had come to the United States, with most of the rest going to Australia, Canada, and Brazil. More than half of the 17,500 persons registered under the program as of the end

[5] For more details on the Intergovernmental Committee for European Migration, see Department of State *Bulletin*, June 22, 1953, pp. 879-882; July 27, 1953, pp. 117-121; and January 4, 1954, pp. 26-30. See also "Progress in Refugee Resettlement," *The World Today*, October 1953, pp. 449-459. A recent discussion on the refugee problem in general and international measures which have been taken to solve it may be found in Rees, E., "The Refugee and the United Nations," *International Conciliation*, June 1953.

[6] See Department of State *Bulletin*, August 24, 1953, pp. 281-285, and December 21, 1953, pp. 859-863; *H. Rpt. No. 974*, 83d Cong.; and *Congressional Record* (daily edition), June 30, 1953, pp. 7892ff.

of 1953 were located in Western Germany and Austria. A few persons from China, eligible for the first time in 1953, were receiving care under the program at the end of the year, but none had been resettled.

## G. *UNITED NATIONS CHILDREN'S FUND*[7]

The United Nations International Children's Emergency Fund had been created in 1946 with United States support, and during its first three years it concentrated on providing relief aid to children in Western Europe. In 1950 the United Nations extended the Fund for three more years, although at that time there was strong sentiment in the U.S. Government for creating a more permanent body which would concern itself less with emergency relief needs and more with fundamental child welfare problems, especially in the poorer areas of the world. The United States continued to give financial support to the Fund, although it cut its contributions to one third of the total during 1951 and 1952, as compared with over two thirds in the previous years. After 1950 the Fund shifted its emphasis from relief projects in Western Europe to attempts to create continuing maternal and child welfare services in the underdeveloped countries of the world, more or less in line with the suggestions made by the United States.

In 1953 the Administration asked Congress to appropriate $9.8 million that had been authorized but not appropriated in 1952 for American contributions to the fund for calendar year 1953 and another $9 million for contributions during calendar year 1954. Many expressions of public support for this program were received by Congress, and in the authorization bill for the Mutual Security Program the Senate went so far as to increase the sum to be provided for 1954 to $13 million; however, this increase was removed in conference. Congress finally limited its appropriation to $9.8 million for 1953, the House Committee on Appropriations insisting that no appropriation should be made

[7] The more important official sources used in the preparation of this section were: UN General Assembly, *Official Records*: Eighth Session, Supplement No. 6A; UN Economic and Social Council, *Official Records*: Sixteenth Session, Supplements No. 6 and 6A, and Eighteenth Session, Supplement No. 2; and the several series of United Nations Documents the first part of whose designation is E/ICEF/.

for 1954 inasmuch as the United Nations had not at that time taken action to continue the Fund beyond 1953. This $9.8 million was transferred to the Children's Fund during the last quarter of the year, increasing United States contributions from the beginning to $97 million out of a total Fund income of about the equivalent of $186 million.[8]

At the meetings of the UN General Assembly and the Economic and Social Council in 1953 the Children's Fund, then supporting more than 200 projects in 75 countries, was widely acclaimed as one of the most constructive activities of the United Nations. Officials of the Fund reported that it was pursuing policies of concentrating on programs of disease control, maternal care, and child nutrition; of giving aid only where imported supplies were necessary; of supporting programs that were within the estimated capability of local governments to maintain after withdrawal of international aid; and of placing the actual administration of projects in the hands of local authorities. Nations receiving assistance from the Fund were more than matching its expenditures, at a ratio of about three to two.[9] In recognition of the continuing need for the humanitarian work of the Fund and because of the belief that it helped create favorable conditions for other economic and social programs of the United Nations, the mandate of the Children's Fund was renewed on a permanent basis, with full support of the United States Government, and its name was changed to United Nations Children's Fund.[1]

## H. *MISCELLANEOUS OFFICIAL GRANTS*

The U.S. Government during 1953 made a grant of United States-owned counterpart funds in an amount equivalent to $12.9

[8] The 1953 contribution by the United States was about 60 percent of the total during that year, but Congress raised no objection to the departure from the practice of the previous two years limiting the United States share to one third of the total.

[9] Data on expenditures by the Fund for each year are not released until long after the end of the year. Expenditures in 1952 were the equivalent of $18.5 million.

[1] UN General Assembly Resolution 802 (VIII), October 6, 1953. The old symbol, UNICEF, was retained.

For more information on the U.S. Government's position in 1953, see Eliot, M. M., "The United Nations Children's Fund: Symbol of Free World Cooperation," Department of State *Bulletin*, August 31, 1953, pp. 288-292.

million to the "Berlin Investment Fund."[2] As in earlier years, the U.S. Department of Agriculture continued to help Mexico eradicate foot and mouth disease, the prevalence of which resulted in an embargo on the import of fresh and frozen meat from that country; the value of the United States contribution to this program was placed at $2.3 million, raising the total since the end of World War II to $90.4 million. The U.S. Army continued to furnish civilian supplies to the people in the Ryukyu Islands, on which are located large American supply depots and airfields, under the Government and Relief in Occupied Areas Program. The amount fell from $27.6 million in 1952 to $7.8 million in 1953, and shipments during the last half of the year were at an annual rate of less than $1 million.

## I. *TOTAL UNITED STATES GOVERNMENT GRANTS*

Gross U.S. Government grants to foreign nations during 1953 totalled over $6.3 billion, as shown in Table 4. This was the largest sum in any year since the end of World War II and raised the total of official aid provided on a grant basis since mid-1945 to nearly $37 billion, compared with just over $48 billion of grant aid by the U.S. Government during World War II.

The above data are gross; $165 million of return on grants and reverse grants was received by the United States during 1953, of which $110 million represented counterpart-fund deposits reserved for United States use and the balance returns of Lend-Lease ships and certain other military equipment. For the postwar period as a whole, the United States had received $1.4 billion of such reverse grants and returns on grants, and $2.3 billion of the grants had been subsequently converted to credits, including $1 billion of the postwar aid to Germany which was so converted in 1953. Thus *net* U.S. Government foreign grants during 1953 were nearly $6.2 billion (or $5.2 billion if account is taken of the German conversion operation) and they totalled $33.2 billion for the postwar period as a whole. Similarly, the *net* grants

---

[2] Directly and indirectly the U.S. Government has provided a great deal of aid to Berlin, but most of it is lumped in the official data with aid to West Germany. This particular grant was to initiate a new program of equity financing, to be administered through the Berlin Industrie Bank and aimed primarily at providing risk capital to small firms and new businesses. (For details, see Department of State *Bulletin*, April 19, 1954, pp. 585-586.)

# II. ECONOMIC AND TECHNICAL ASSISTANCE

## TABLE 4

*United States Government Gross Foreign Grants, 1945-1953*ª
(millions of dollars)

| | 1953 | 1952ʳ | July 1, 1945–Dec. 31, 1953 |
|---|---|---|---|
| *By Major Program* | | | |
| Mutual Security | | | |
| Military supplies and services[b] | 4435 | 2747 | 9255 |
| Bilateral economic and technical aid[c] | 1549 | 1809 | 14248 |
| Multilateral economic and technical aid | | | |
| Movement of migrants | 7 | 9 | 16 |
| Technical assistance | 13 | 18 | 86 |
| Palestine refugees relief | 9 | 22 | 90 |
| Korean reconstruction | 56 | 10 | 66 |
| Wheat for Pakistan | 71 | — | 71 |
| Emergency Famine Relief | 2 | — | 2 |
| Civilian Supplies to Occupied Areas[d] | 127 | 167 | 5783 |
| United Nations Relief and Rehabilitation and Post-UNRRA and Interim Aid | — | — | 3443 |
| Lend-Lease | — | — | 1906 |
| Greek-Turkish Aid | — | — | 659 |
| Philippine Rehabilitation | — | 4 | 684 |
| Agriculture Department Surplus Donations | 87 | 1 | 92 |
| International Children's Emergency Fund | 10 | 7 | 97 |
| Other[e] | 15 | 8 | 489 |
| Total | 6881 | 4792 | 36887 |
| *By Major Area* | | | |
| Western Europe and Dependencies[f] | 4754 | 3788 | 26448 |
| Other Europe[g] | 8 | — | 1045 |
| Near East and Africa[f] | 130 | 128 | 360 |
| Asia and the Pacific | 1259 | 724 | 7689 |
| Latin America[h] | 110 | 79 | 405 |
| Unspecified Area | 70 | 73 | 940 |
| Total | 6881 | 4792 | 36887 |

r) Revised.
a) In most instances these data represent shipments where goods are procured by U.S. Government agencies, and cash payments by the Government where other methods of procurement are used. They include the ECA-owned counterpart funds spent for administration and other services deemed of benefit to the countries concerned. Dollar costs for administering all aid programs are included. Aid extended on a credit basis is *not* included here, but in Table 10.
b) Virtually all of this represents military equipment, supplies, and services provided by the Defense Department under the Mutual Defense Assistance Act and the Mutual Security Act. Included are United States contributions to the NATO infrastructure program and the value of certain military equipment transferred on an indeterminate basis. Military grant aid extended to China prior to 1951 under the China Aid Act is also included. *Not* included, however, is the value of military supplies and services provided Greece and Turkey prior to 1951 under the Greek-Turkish Assistance Act or the value of military matériel supplied on a grant basis to various nations under the

*(Notes continued at bottom of next page)*

during the World War II period were $40.2 billion. It may be noted, however, that taking into account both *net* grants and *net* loans, the U.S. Government in the period between June 30, 1945, and the end of 1953 extended $44.3 billion in aid to foreign countries, as compared with $41 billion during World War II.

## J. MISCELLANEOUS GOVERNMENT UNILATERAL TRANSFERS

In addition to operating these varied grant programs, the U.S. Government made miscellaneous unilateral transfers to the rest of the world during 1953 amounting, net, to $141 million. Details on these transfers are not available, but apparently the bulk

Lend-Lease program in the period immediately following World War II. Available data do not permit a breakdown of the aid provided under these programs as between "military" and "economic." The Department of Commerce has, however, reported that the gross value of all "military grants" from the end of World War II through 1953 was nearly $10.5 billion, as compared with the $9.8 billion given in the above table.

The 1953 figure for "military supplies and services" exceeds that given for "military aid" in Table 17, Chapter VII. The reasons are that the above table, but not Table 17, includes United States contributions to the European infrastructure program, and the above figure is a gross one while the latter is net of returns of Lend-Lease shipments and certain other military equipment.

c) Includes grants provided under the Economic Cooperation Act, the Mutual Security Act, the Act for International Development, the Smith-Mundt Act, and the Yugoslav Emergency Food Assistance Act, and by the Institute for Inter-American Affairs.

d) Includes civilian supplies furnished to Korea by the Defense Department, as well as civilian supplies provided under the Government and Relief in Occupied Areas Program. All of the aid in this category in 1953 was to Korea except for $7.8 million which went to the Ryukyu Islands.

e) Includes, for 1953, $2.3 million in Department of Agriculture contributions to help eradicate foot and mouth disease in Mexico and a $12.8 million grant by the State Department for the so-called "Berlin Investment Fund." The 1952 figure includes $2.8 million in contributions to the foot and mouth disease eradication project in Mexico. For the entire postwar period, this includes the above programs plus United States contributions to the International Refugee Organization, the United States contribution to the American Red Cross for foreign war relief, and $120 million of the $500 million 1942 stabilization loan to China.

f) Greece and Turkey are included in Western Europe.

g) The 1953 grant was for food to the residents of the Soviet sector of Germany.

h) Includes $1 million of gross grants in the form of military equipment to Canada in 1952 and $3 million in earlier years, all of which have been offset by reverse grants or returns.

Source: Compiled from data given in U.S. Department of Commerce, *Foreign Grants and Credits by the United States Government*, issue of December 1953, Appendix Table 8.

were pension payments. Probably disvestments by the Alien Property Custodian and the settlement of various claims against the U.S. Government also contributed to the total.

## K. *PRIVATE REMITTANCES*

Net private charity remittances, in cash and in kind, during 1953 were some one-seventh greater than in the previous year and at an estimated $487 million were the highest they had been since 1949. Western Europe, including Greece, received almost exactly half of the total. Although details are not available, it is probable that Israel was the largest single recipient nation.

As a part of its policy of encouraging private gifts in kind, Congress authorized the Economic Cooperation Administration and its successor agencies to use small amounts of appropriated funds to finance the ocean-freight costs of voluntary relief shipments, and on occasion the President has made additional funds available for this purpose. In March 1953 the program of subsidizing the parcel post costs of shipments by individuals was terminated, but the Foreign Operations Administration continued to meet all or part of the ocean-transportation costs of foreign-relief shipments made by American voluntary nonprofit relief agencies. Details on the expenditures in 1953 are not available, but nearly $30 million had been spent under this program in the period from mid-1948 to the end of 1953.

# III · LOANS AND INVESTMENTS

FOLLOWING a short period immediately after World War II, when the U.S. Government made large foreign loans, the emphasis in official aid programs shifted to grants. This shift took place partly because it was felt that the nature of the emergency economic and military needs of the aid recipients was such that the servicing obligations on assistance of these dimensions and for these purposes would create an intolerable burden, and partly because it was believed that aid that could appropriately be extended on a credit basis should be provided by the International Bank and, more importantly, by private American investors. The U.S. Government did, however, continue to grant some loans to foreign borrowers, most of them after 1950 through the Export-Import Bank and for the purposes of facilitating the economic development of underdeveloped areas, encouraging the expansion abroad of facilities for the production of strategic and critical materials, and stimulating the export of certain United States products. The policy of the Eisenhower Administration was to limit even more severely than its predecessors the provision of official long-term loans, and the *net* outflow in 1953 was only about 60 percent of the previous year's figure.

In recent years it has been commonly observed, both here and abroad, that in view of the international economic position of the United States, private American foreign investments have been small; for the postwar period as a whole earnings on United States private investments abroad have exceeded the amount of new investments, a large portion of which represented reinvested earnings. For some time the U.S. Government had been using a variety of devices to encourage an expanded outflow of private funds, especially long-term capital, but these efforts had met with little if any success. The new Administration in Washington made it clear in 1953 that it looked to private investors as the main source for meeting foreign needs for long-term American investments, and it intensified and expanded the previous governmental efforts to create conditions that would entice more private capital exports. These bore no fruit during 1953, however, in the face of the attractive investment outlets in the United States and the continued existence of what were regarded as much greater risks abroad. Indeed, the net capital outflow on private account was the lowest for any year since 1946, as is shown in Table 5.

TABLE 5

*Net United States Capital Outflow, 1946-1953*[a]
(millions of dollars)

| Year | Total as a Percentage of Exports of Goods and Services[b] | Total | GOVERNMENT Long- Term | GOVERNMENT Short- Term | PRIVATE Long- Term[c] | PRIVATE Short- Term |
|---|---|---|---|---|---|---|
| 1946 | 21 | 8881[d] | 8262[d] | —250 | 59 | 810 |
| 1947 | 24 | 7956[d] | 6849[d] | 108 | 810 | 189 |
| 1948 | 10 | 1750 | 978 | —87 | 748 | 116 |
| 1949 | 7 | 1256 | 474 | 173 | 796 | —187 |
| 1950[r] | 10 | 1401 | 127 | 87 | 1088 | 149 |
| 1951[r] | 6 | 1155 | 140 | 28 | 889 | 108 |
| 1952[r] | 7 | 1564 | 409 | 68 | 993 | 94 |
| 1953[p] | 8 | 590 | 231[e] | —10 | 517 | —148 |

r) Revised.
p) Preliminary.
a) Excludes Government grants and unilateral transfers and private remittances.
b) In calculating these percentages, subscriptions by the U.S. Government to the International Bank and Fund have been excluded.
c) Includes net purchases of debentures sold or guarantied by the International Bank.
d) Includes subscriptions to the International Bank and Fund of $828 million in 1946, and $3062 million in 1947.
e) The small discrepancy between this figure and that calculable from Table 7 is mainly due to the inclusion in the latter (but not in the above table) of loans made by agent commercial banks under the guaranty of the Export-Import Bank.
Sources: Department of Commerce, *Balance of Payments of the United States, 1949-1951*, Wash., D.C., 1952, pp. 156 and 160, and Department of Commerce, *Survey of Current Business*, Wash., D.C., June 1953, pp. 4-5; January 1954, pp. 5-10; and March 1954, pp. 22-23.

Taking into account both official and private loans, the net capital outflow during the year under review was equal to less than 3 percent of the nation's exports of goods and services—less than half the proportion registered during the previous two years.

## III. LOANS AND INVESTMENTS

# A. UNITED STATES GOVERNMENT
# LOANS AND CREDITS

## Long-Term

### a. EXPORT-IMPORT BANK LENDING AUTHORITY AND POLICIES

The future role of the Export-Import Bank was being re-formulated by the new Administration during 1953, but apparently firm decisions had not been taken as the year ended. The Bank, whose basic responsibility under the law was to facilitate United States exports and imports, had been used for various other purposes as well and during the preceding few years had made many loans designed to hasten the economic development of some of the so-called underdeveloped areas in support of the Government's Point Four Program.[1] In mid-1953 President Eisenhower, under the provisions of the Reorganization Act of 1949, replaced the Bank's Board of Directors with a Managing Director and transferred to the National Advisory Council on International Monetary and Financial Problems, of which the Secretary of the Treasury is chairman, responsibility for establishing the lending and other financial policies of the Bank. The Bank's representative on the Council was reduced from voting to nonvoting membership.[2]

The National Advisory Council had previously been authorized to "coordinate" the activities of the Bank with those of other agencies engaged in international financial activities, and there was little public evidence that there had been in the past any serious conflicts between the Bank and the Council. Nonetheless, the press commonly interpreted this reorganization as presaging a change in the Bank's lending policy in the direction of making fewer loans than in the past and concentrating on short-term

[1] For a fuller account of the Bank's activities prior to 1953, see *Survey—1952*, pp. 105-112, and the references cited there. See also "Investigations of Export-Import Bank Loan Activities," *Subcommittee Print*, House of Rep., Subcommittees of the Committee on Banking and Currency, 82d Cong., 2d Sess., December 80, 1952, and "Legislative History of the Export-Import Bank of Washington," *Committee Print*, U.S. Senate, Committee on Banking and Currency, 88d Cong., 1st Sess., September 10, 1953.

[2] For the text of the President's proposal, set forth in Reorganization Plan No. 5, and his message transmitting it to Congress, see *Congressional Record* (daily edition), April 80, 1953, pp. 4409-4410. See also *Congressional Record* (daily edition), June 30, 1953, pp. 7889-7892.

credits for financing United States exports, leaving to the International Bank the granting of long-term loans for economic development which were not attractive to private investors.[3] In replying to Congressional queries on this point, Secretary of the Treasury Humphrey stated that the new Administration felt that the Bank should be principally concerned with the short-term financing of American imports and exports and that long-term loans to foreign governments for economic development should "generally" be made by the International Bank. At the same time, he said, in "special cases" where the interests of the United States were particularly strong, the Export-Import Bank would continue to make loans for purposes other than financing current trade.[4]

Congress for years had been generous in its praise of the administration of the Export-Import Bank, being particularly impressed by the low loss ratio on its loans, its substantial operating surpluses, and the exceedingly small staff as compared with other Government agencies.[5] Many expressed some doubts as to the wisdom of the reorganization, which would probably increase the influence on the Bank's operations of the Departments of State and the Treasury. For this reason, and also because of complaints of duplication and competition between the Export-Import Bank and the International Bank and because of fears that these institutions discouraged private international investment, the Senate passed a resolution directing its Committee on Banking and Currency to study the operations of both banks. This Committee had not completed its investigation by the end of the year.[6]

[3] See, for example, *Journal of Commerce*, June 15, 1953, pp. 1 and 17, and *New York Times*, September 15, 1953, pp. 45 and 49. For some comments on this issue by a former chairman of the Export-Import Bank, see *New York Times*, October 11, 1953, p. E-8.

[4] See Commission on Foreign Economic Policy, *Staff Papers*, Wash., D.C., February 1954, pp. 134-147 for a statement of many of the issues involved in the future role of the Bank.

[5] For 1953 the total revenue of the Bank from interest on loans amounted to $80.5 million, as compared with only $26.3 million of expenses, $25.2 million of which were paid as interest on funds borrowed from the U.S. Treasury and only $1.1 million of which were operating expenses. At the end of June 1953 the Bank paid $22.5 million as a dividend to the U.S. Treasury, representing 2¼ percent on the $1 billion of capital stock of the Bank, all of which is held by the Treasury. At the end of 1953 the Bank's accumulated reserve against possible losses totalled $324.1 million. As against total disbursements from its inception in early 1934 through 1953 of $4,560,000,000, less than $500,000 had been declared in default.

[6] For some editorial discussion of what it was thought Congress wanted to

The Randall Commission, which was also charged with studying the roles of these two banks, strongly recommended that public
lending should not compete with or displace private foreign investment, but recognized that loans by these banks are often necessary prerequisites to increases in private foreign investments in
underdeveloped countries. The Randall Commission found no evidence that there had been harmful competition or duplication in
the operations of the two banks and concluded that the national
interest of the United States might require the making of certain
loans by the Export-Import Bank which the International Bank
for various reasons could not make. The Commission recommended that the Export-Import Bank should continue to make
loans which were in the "special interest" of the United States
but should use its own funds only for loans which meet "reasonable
standards of bankability." It believed that if there were "urgent
political need" for especially risky ("fuzzy") loans, Congress
should provide special funds.[7] These recommendations appeared
to call for little change in the past policies of the Bank. Furthermore, at the Tenth Inter-American Congress, held in Caracas in
early March 1954, Secretary of State Dulles took note of the
speculation that the Export-Import Bank had withdrawn from
the field of economic development and assured the conference that
the Bank would continue to consider applications for the financing
of "economically sound" development projects abroad.[8]

In keeping with the Bank's primary purpose of facilitating
United States exports, Congress in 1953 authorized it to commit
up to $100 million of its existing lending authority to provide
insurance against loss or damage to United States-owned tangible
property located abroad resulting from hostile or warlike action,
including expropriation. This legislation was especially sought

accomplish by this study, see *Commercial and Financial Chronicle*, September 3,
1953, p. 36. See also "Meeting . . . on a Study of the Export-Import Bank . . . ,"
*Committee Print*, U.S. Senate, Committee on Banking and Currency, 83d Cong.,
1st Sess., September 15, 1953; *H. Rpt. No. 847*, 83d Cong.; and "Study of Export-
Import Bank and World Bank," *Hearings on S. Res. 25*, Part I, U.S. Senate,
Committee on Banking and Currency, 83d Cong., 2nd Sess., January 25 to February 2, 1954.

[7] Commission on Foreign Economic Policy, *Report to the President and the
Congress*, Wash., D.C., January 1954, pp. 23-25.

[8] Department of State *Bulletin*, March 15, 1954, p. 882.

by cotton exporters, but exports of other commodities were also expected to benefit. The proposal's supporters said that exports would be increased if American suppliers could offer better service by maintaining stocks abroad and shipping on consignment, especially in view of the fact that foreign importers were carrying much smaller inventories than had been their practice before the war. Most exporters could not carry stocks abroad because commercial banks were not willing to finance their retained interest in goods located in foreign countries without this sort of insurance, which was not otherwise available.

Spokesmen of the Export-Import Bank were not more than lukewarm toward the proposal, pointing out that actuarily sound premiums might be so high as to defeat the purpose of the proposals and that difficult issues might arise if the premium rates charged varied as between countries according to the differences in risk; they stated that the Bank had not had the opportunity to assess the need for such insurance; and they suggested that if it were authorized, its administration might be better placed under the Secretary of Commerce, who already had authority to issue war-risk insurance in time of war.[9] They did not, however, say they were opposed to having authority given to the Bank, and Congress approved the law without significant opposition.[1] In mid-November the Bank announced it was ready to issue policies insuring exports of raw cotton and cotton-mill waste under the new authority. At the same time it allocated $50 million of the authority to these commodities but limited to $10 million the insurance that could be outstanding at any one time in any one of the sixteen countries initially declared eligible. By the end of the year no insurance had been written under the new authority, the cotton export trade being slack because of the high price of the American product in relation to other cotton in world markets. The Bank, however, had engaged a large number of private insurance companies to handle on an agency basis any insurance that might be issued.

[9] Under P.L. 768, 81st Cong., September 7, 1950.

[1] For more details, see P.L. 80, 88d Cong., May 21, 1953; "Amendment to the Export-Import Bank Act of 1945," *Hearings on H.R. 4465*, House of Rep., Committee on Banking and Currency, 88d Cong., 1st Sess., April 20 and 21, 1953; *H. Rpt. No. 320*, 88d Cong.; and *S. Rpt. No. 169*, 88d Cong.

## b. EXPORT-IMPORT BANK LOANS: FOR OWN ACCOUNT

During 1953 the Export-Import Bank authorized a total of some $561 million in new loans for its own account, slightly less than during the previous year, and disbursements from these and previously authorized credits amounted to $647 million, the largest amount paid out by the Bank in any year since 1947.[2] However, $300 million of these authorizations and payments represented a funding of previous private credits. Both principal repayments, $311 million, and interest receipts from outstanding loans, $80 million, were the largest in the Bank's history. At the end of the year the Bank had a total of $2.8 billion in outstanding loans, involving forty-six foreign countries.[3]

As compared with the immediately preceding years, there was a definite shift in the Bank's lending policy away from long-term loans for economic development purposes toward short- or medium-term loans specifically designed to facilitate United States exports. The largest new loan authorized was the two-year, $300 million credit to Brazil to assist that country in paying off accumulated debts to American exporters. This credit, together with a loan of approximately $50 million from United States commercial banks, supplemented by the use of some of Brazil's own resources, permitted Brazil to clear up its overdue dollar commercial debts by the end of the year.[4]

Japan obtained two short-term loans totalling $100 million from the Export-Import Bank during 1953 to finance the importation of cotton from the United States. The first loan, of $40 million, was made in April and was financed almost entirely with the Bank's own funds.[5] In contrast, the funds for the second credit, $60 million granted in October, were furnished by a group of

[2] In addition, the Bank allocated $42 million of existing credits to specific projects.

[3] As of December 31, 1953, the Bank had authorized but unutilized commitments of $519 million and an uncommitted lending authority of $1148 million.

[4] Brazil also obtained a loan in sterling equivalent to $28 million from the International Monetary Fund to apply on arrearages to British exporters. (See *New York Times*, September 21, 1953, p. 9.) Placing its imports on a current-payments basis had necessitated a sharp decline in Brazil's dollar imports, the value during the first half of 1953 being only about one-third that of the first half of 1952.

[5] The United States commercial banks provided slightly less than $1 million under an agreement whereby the Export-Import Bank would take the private banks out at any time.

## III. LOANS AND INVESTMENTS

### TABLE 6

*Export-Import Bank Operations for Own Account, 1934-1953*
(millions of dollars)

| | New Credits Authorized[a] | Cancellations & Participations without Recourse to EIB | Loans Disbursed by EIB & Its Agent Banks | Principal Collected by EIB & Its Agent Banks | Interest and Commissions Collected | Credits Outstanding Dec. 31 |
|---|---|---|---|---|---|---|
| **By Area—1953** | | | | | | |
| Western Europe and Dependencies[b] | 112.2 | 18.0 | 188.0 | 206.4 | 46.5 | 1583.9 |
| Eastern Europe | 0 | 0 | 0 | 2.2c | 1.2c | 39.0c |
| Latin America | 317.8 | 14.0 | 397.5 | 48.1 | 22.6 | 857.8 |
| Near East | 0 | 35.2 | 12.0d | 8.6 | 4.7 | 129.7 |
| Africa | 31.6 | 0.9 | 86.8 | 8.8 | 1.7 | 71.6 |
| Asia and the Pacific | 100.0 | 0.1 | 62.8 | 40.8 | 3.0 | 145.6 |
| Canada | 0 | 0 | 0 | 0 | 0.3 | 5.7 |
| 1953 Total | 561.2 | 68.2 | 647.1 | 311.0 | 80.5e | 2833.3 |
| **By Period** | | | | | | |
| 1952 | 596.6 | 204.6 | 478.1 | 270.6 | 72.2 | 2496.1 |
| 1951 | 244.2 | 29.6 | 204.1 | 184.5 | 68.2 | 2289.0 |
| 1950 | 565.8 | 48.0 | 199.9 | 160.0 | 64.4 | 2219.5 |
| 1949 | 241.0 | 19.4 | 184.8 | 143.7 | 60.9 | 2179.6 |
| 1948 | 138.3 | 347.0 | 428.9 | 261.2 | 57.3 | 2138.5 |
| 1947 | 614.1 | 97.0 | 824.5 | 95.5 | ⎫ | 1970.7 |
| 1946 | 1211.0 | 149.3 | 1029.8 | 40.3 | ⎬85.8 | 1241.7 |
| 1934-1945 | 2308.5 | 438.5 | 562.4 | 310.3 | ⎭ | 252.1 |
| Cumulative Total, 1934-1953 | 6480.4 | 1401.6 | 4559.7 | 1726.4 | 489.3 | |

Details may not add to totals because of rounding.

a) Includes credits authorized by participants without recourse to the Export-Import Bank. Such participations—which have totalled $190.6 million since the founding of the Bank—were not included in a similar table presented on page 107 of the *Survey—1952*.

b) The Organization for European Economic Cooperation countries (and their dependencies), including Greece and Turkey, plus Finland, Spain, and Yugoslavia.

c) Poland only.

d) Israel only.

e) The available data on area breakdown total only $80.0 million, but the grand total as reported by the Export-Import Bank is $80.5 million.

Sources: Export-Import Bank of Washington, *Sixteenth* and *Seventeenth Semi-annual Report to Congress*, Wash., D.C., 1953, and Department of Commerce, *Foreign Grants and Credits by the United States Government*, December 1953 quarter, Wash., D.C., Appendix Tables 5, 6, 7, and 8.

private commercial banks, with repayment guaranteed by the Export-Import Bank. This shift reflected a policy decision by the new Administration to use more extensively than in the recent past funds from private sources rather than from the U.S. Treasury. Since World War II Japan has been the largest single foreign market for United States cotton, and the Bank reported that had it not been for this financing cotton exports would have declined "significantly" in 1953, inasmuch as lower prices prevailed in the world markets for cotton from other countries.[6] The Bank also authorized a loan of $12 million to Spanish banks to purchase United States cotton. This credit, approved in April, was made with the Bank's own funds.

Repeating a type of loan inaugurated in 1952,[7] the Bank authorized in July a two-year loan of $100 million to France permitting that country to receive immediately the dollar proceeds of offshore procurement contracts placed there by the United States Department of Defense under the military assistance program. This loan specified that repayment would be made as deliveries were accepted, and paid for, by the Defense Department.[8]

The Export-Import Bank continued in 1953 to make some loans out of its own funds to expand the production abroad of strategic materials, but the amounts were less than one-third those authorized in 1952. In June the Bank increased by about $30 million a line of credit to several South African gold-mining companies for the construction of facilities for producing uranium. This was the second increase in the line of credit first opened in 1951 at the request of the Atomic Energy Commission, which had contracted to buy uranium produced by these facilities, and it brought the total Bank commitments to more than $90 million. A $2.5 million loan was made to a United States-owned corporation in Peru for the production of iron ore. Two credits to Mexican sulphur and manganese companies were increased during the year by small amounts; the General Services Administration had a contract to purchase a portion of the output of the manganese mining company.

Loan authorizations by the Bank for what are usually called

[6] For a mild criticism in the foreign press of "tied" loans by the Export-Import Bank, see *The Statist*, July 4, 1953, pp. 17-18. The second 1953 cotton loan to Japan also provided that the cotton could be transported only in vessels of Japanese or American registry.

[7] See *Survey—1952*, p. 109.

[8] In order to decrease interest costs, the French repaid the loan more quickly than required, half of it having been repaid by March 1954. As of the end of March 1954, only $24 million of the 1952 loan was still outstanding.

economic development purposes totalled only about $13.5 million in 1953, as compared with over $137 million in 1952. Of this total, less than $5 million were long-term loans to foreign governments and were in the form of increases in previous credits for highway construction. The remaining $7.5 million were a series of small loans, usually of medium term, specifically tied to industrial equipment exports by American firms. In each of these cases the American exporter sold a portion of the notes of foreign buyers to the Bank without recourse and retained a portion (frequently small) of the credit on his own books. The Bank reported it was receiving an increasing number of applications for loans of this type as American exporters began to face heavier competition abroad.

c. EXPORT-IMPORT BANK LOANS: FOR OTHER AGENCIES

Under the Economic Cooperation Act of 1948 and the Mutual Security Acts of 1951 and 1952, the Export-Import Bank was made the agent for that portion of economic aid under the European Recovery–Mutual Security Program that was extended in the form of loans rather than grants. No new authority for extending such aid to Europe on a credit basis was made in 1953, the Executive Branch having convinced Congress of the inadvisability of such lending,[9] but $18.3 million was disbursed during the year under previous authorizations. Over two thirds of these actual disbursements were for the benefit of Spain. Repayment on most of these loans to Europe was not scheduled to begin until 1956, but interest became payable in 1952; in 1953, $34.3 million in interest payments were received from the European nations by the U.S. Government. At year's end, credits of this type outstanding totalled $1347 million.

A large accounting change that did not affect the aid program in 1953 occurred following the ratification in July of the agreements on Germany's external debt.[1] At the time of the negotiation of these agreements, Western Germany had received from the U.S. Government more than $3 billion in postwar aid, all of it provisionally classified as grants. Under terms of the debt settlement, $1 billion of this aid was reclassified to a loan basis, and the Federal Republic agreed to repay that amount over a thirty-year period

[9] See Chapter I, Section A.
[1] For the terms of the German debt settlement, see *Survey—1952*, pp. 128-129.

beginning in mid-1958. The Export-Import Bank was to act as collection agent, and the first interest payment, $13 million, was received during the latter part of the year.

In September 1952 the Administration authorized a $15 million loan to Pakistan for the purchase of cereals, and in January 1953 a $1.5 million credit to Afghanistan for the same purpose. The funds for these loans were taken from the Mutual Security Program appropriations, but the Export-Import Bank's facilities were used in handling the loans. During 1953 the balance of the Pakistan credit—$8.4 million—was disbursed, and $1.4 million was paid out on the credit to Afghanistan. No repayments or interest were received on these loans, but nearly $1 million was received on the 1951 loan to India for wheat. As of the end of 1953, loans outstanding to Asia under the Mutual Security Program totalled $206 million.

As noted above, the Bank makes loans under the authority of its basic act for expanding the production abroad of strategic and critical materials. Some loans deemed desirable for this purpose, however, were found to be so risky as to fall outside the Bank's normal lending policy, and in 1951, under terms of the Defense Production Act, the Bank was specifically authorized and directed to make, or to participate in, such loans provided "certificates of essentiality" were obtained from certain other Government agencies.[2] Three new credits, totalling $28.4 million, were authorized under this procedure during 1953—all in the first six months—but two previous credits amounting to $28.5 million were cancelled, leaving total net credits authorized since the beginning of the program of approximately $44 million.[3] Of the new credits, $22 million were to help expand the electric power generating facilities of a firm serving the four principal mining companies operating in the Northern Rhodesia copper belt. The

---

[2] In 1953 the authority was slightly broadened by giving the Bank power to guaranty private loans for these purposes. No such guaranties were made during the year. (The Bank's authority, as revised, is contained in Section 811, *Executive Order No. 10480*, August 14, 1953, subject to Section 302 of the Defense Production Act of 1950, as amended.)

[3] One of the loans was cancelled at the request of the applicant, who found that rising construction costs threatened to make his operations uneconomical. The other cancellation followed revocation of the "certificate of essentiality" by the General Services Administration, successor to the Defense Materials Procurement Agency. Both of these applicants were producers of copper and cobalt, one in Northern Rhodesia and the other in British East Africa.

Defense Materials Procurement Agency contracted for purchases of copper and cobalt in amounts sufficient to liquidate the loan without recourse to the sterling area's dollar pool. The remaining credits were granted to Canadian companies for producing copper, molybdenum, and bismuth. The Defense Materials Procurement Agency had purchase contracts with these borrowers. Disbursements by the Bank under these loans amounted to $7.7 million in 1953, almost all of them being made in the latter half of the year; they raised the total to $7.9 million. No repayments were received during the year and a small sum which fell due became delinquent. Every loan guarantied under this authority had been in participation with private capital—investors from the recipient nation—and the total of private participations was more than half the sum of the Bank's loans. The Bank estimated that once the facilities financed by these loans came into production, they would increase by more than $20 million per year the value of critical materials available for purchase by the United States.

d. OTHER

The Economic Cooperation Administration initiated in 1949 a small program of lending dollars and United States-owned counterpart funds to facilitate exploration for and production of strategic materials in various European countries and their overseas dependencies. These loans were to be serviced through the sale of commodities produced to the General Services Administration for the official stockpile. Subsequently, the responsibility for administering this program was transferred to the General Services Administration and was expanded to cover Canada and Latin America. At the equivalent of $25 million in dollars and counterpart funds, disbursements under this program during 1953 were about half those of 1952, and the total outlay since the program was initiated amounted to about $113 million by the end of the year under review. Nearly 40 percent of the disbursements in 1953 were in Norway, with Canada, Northern Rhodesia, British East Africa, Morocco, and Germany accounting for most of the balance. Principal repayments under the program totalled nearly $15 million during the year, as compared with approximately $1 million in 1952; $3 million of interest was also received in 1953.

Most of the repayments were against loans granted in earlier years to enterprises in French Morocco, West Germany, Jamaica, Greece, and the Belgian Congo.

As noted in Chapter II, Congress in 1953 earmarked $19 million of dollars and counterpart funds reserved for United States use for a "basic-materials development" program, comparable, apparently, to the program noted in the previous paragraph although it was to be administered by the Foreign Operations Administration. Most of the projects under this authority were still in the "planning" stage as the year ended, but the equivalent of $3.7 million was disbursed in France and Germany during the last quarter of the year.

No other long-term credits were utilized during 1953, but the U.S. Government received $113 million in principal repayments and interest on previously granted surplus-property and Lend-Lease credits. The British Government made the scheduled payment of $119 million on the 1946 loan, the Maritime Administration received $25 million from its earlier sales on credit of merchant ships, the Philippine Government paid the United States Treasury $5 million on the 1950 funding loan, the Reconstruction Finance Corporation received $8 million in servicing payments on its outstanding foreign loans, and the United Nations repaid $1.5 million of the interest-free loan granted by the U.S. Government for helping to build the headquarters building in New York City.

e. TOTAL GOVERNMENT LONG-TERM

Summary data of total U.S. Government loans and credits utilized, together with principal repayments and interest collections, are given in Table 7. Excluding World War I debts, the U.S. Government had $11.9 million of outstanding long-term foreign loans at the end of 1953.

### Short-Term

The U.S. Government short-term assets abroad declined by $10 million during 1953, this being the first year since 1948 during which there was a net inflow of such loans. Details of the Government's short-term lending activities are not available, but presumably the decline was the result of an excess of expenditure

# III. LOANS AND INVESTMENTS

## TABLE 7

*Long-Term Foreign Loans and Credits of the United States Government,*
*by Program and by Area, 1953*
(millions of dollars)

| | Utilized[a] | Principal Collected[b] | Interest & Commissions Collected[c] | Outstanding Indebtedness Dec. 31, 1953[d] |
|---|---|---|---|---|
| **By Program** | | | | |
| Export-Import Bank: | | | | |
| For own account[e] | 647 | 310 | 80 | 2889 |
| For Foreign Operations Administration | 28 | * | 85 | 1553 |
| For Office of Defense Mobilization | 8 | — | * | 8 |
| (German grants converted into credits) | (1000) | — | 18 | 1000 |
| Foreign Operations Administration | | | | |
| Basic-materials development | 4 | — | — | 4 |
| General Services Administration | | | | |
| Deficiency materials | 25 | 15 | 8 | 97 |
| Surplus property | — | 1 | * | 11 |
| Treasury Department | | | | |
| Surplus property | * | 50 | 19 | 995 |
| British loan | — | 46 | 78 | 8614 |
| Lend-Lease credits[f] | — | 22 | 21 | 1504 |
| Philippine funding | — | 4 | 1 | 27 |
| Defense Department | | | | |
| Surplus property | — | — | — | 20 |
| State Department | | | | |
| United Nations Building | — | 2 | — | 62 |
| Maritime Administration (Ships) | — | 20 | 5 | 117 |
| Reconstruction Finance Corporation | — | 6 | 2 | 58 |
| Total | 712 (1712) | 477 | 251 | 11904 |
| **By Area** | | | | |
| Western Europe[g] and Dependencies | 186 | 841 | 204 | 9512 |
| Including conversion of German grants into credits | (1186) | | | |
| Eastern Europe[h] | — | 4 | 5 | 812 |
| Near East and Africa[i] | 47 | 18 | 6 | 262 |
| Asia and the Pacific | 74 | 59 | 12 | 847 |
| Latin America | 399 | 57 | 23 | 891 |
| Canada | 5 | 1 | 1 | 18 |
| United Nations | — | 2 | — | 62 |
| Total | 712 (1712) | 477 | 251 | 11904 |

*(Notes on next page)*

118

from counterpart funds reserved for United States use over new accumulations.

## B. *PRIVATE FOREIGN INVESTMENT*

### *Government Encouragement of Private Investment*

Since World War II the Executive Branch and Congress, supported by most of the vocal business community, have repeatedly stressed the desirability of a greater outflow of private foreign investment.[4] The new Administration gave even greater emphasis than its predecessor to the role of such investment, seeing it as the main channel through which future foreign needs for long-term capital from America should be satisfied.[5]

---

Details may not add to totals because of rounding.

\* Less than $500,000.

a) "Utilized" means cash disbursements for loans and value of goods delivered under the various property credits, or principal amount of mortgages received for sales contracts or billings.

b) "Principal collected" represents the payments received and applied to the reduction of outstanding indebtedness, including payments received through agent banks of the Export-Import Bank.

c) "Interest and commissions collected" represents payments actually received.

d) "Outstanding indebtedness" represents utilizations from the beginning of the program through 1953 less principal repayments.

e) Includes loans utilized and principal collected by agent banks at Export-Import Bank risk. The total outstanding includes a participation of $7 million by another (unspecified) agency.

f) Includes Lend-Lease current credits, Lend-Lease credit offsets to grants, and Lend-Lease silver credits.

g) Including Greece, Turkey, Yugoslavia, and Finland.

h) The principal collections from Eastern Europe included $0.45 million from Hungary and $8.6 million from Poland. Interest was received from Hungary, Poland, and Russia.

i) Greece and Turkey are included in Western Europe.

Source: Department of Commerce, *Foreign Grants and Credits by the United States Government*, December 1953, Wash., D.C., Appendix Tables 5, 6, 7, and 8.

---

[4] See *Survey—1952*, pp. 114-123, and the references cited there for policies and activities in 1952 and the immediately preceding years.

[5] See, for example, excerpts from President Eisenhower's State of the Union message, in Department of State *Bulletin*, February 9, 1953, p. 208. For a more thorough discussion by a senior Administration official, see Stassen, H. E., "The Case for Private Investment Abroad," *Foreign Affairs*, April 1954, pp. 402-418.

An extended and balanced treatment of many of the aspects of private foreign investment may be found in Commission on Foreign Economic Policy, *Staff Papers*, Wash., D.C., February 1954, pp. 78-147. See also International Bank for Reconstruction and Development, *Summary Proceedings, Eighth Annual Meeting of the Board of Governors*, Wash., D.C., October 1953, pp. 27-45; *Foreign Policy Bulletin*, June 15, 1953, pp. 4-7; and International Chamber of Commerce

The reasons given by the new Administration for favoring larger and more diversified private foreign investment were essentially the same as those put forward in earlier years. It was believed that this type of investment would speed economic development and industrial diversification in the so-called underdeveloped areas; provide technical skills in their most useful form; help solve the balance-of-payments problems of the recipients through increasing the production of goods which would save foreign exchange and increase exports; help offset the adverse political and economic effects, both at home and abroad, of reductions in the amounts of official foreign aid from the United States; increase the production of goods, especially critical raw materials, needed in the United States and the rest of the free world; and encourage and support private enterprise in other countries. Similarly, the major devices relied upon by the Government to encourage private foreign investment were the same as had been used in earlier years, but the new Administration did look more favorably than had its predecessors on granting tax relief for foreign investment income.[6]

*Economic Development and Private Investments*, Brochure 165, Paris, 1953.

For an article stressing the many-sided benefits of private foreign investment, see Hunter, J. M., "Long-Term Foreign Investment and Underdeveloped Countries," *Journal of Political Economy*, February 1953, pp. 15-24. For a view that such benefits may be small in some cases, see Mears, L. A., "Private Foreign Investment and Economic Development: Venezuela, Saudi Arabia, and Puerto Rico," *Inter-American Economic Affairs*, Summer 1953, pp. 8-19. See also the articles by Pelissier, R. F., in *Inter-American Economic Affairs*, Autumn 1953, pp. 80-91, and Winter 1953, pp. 78-80. For a general discussion of private investment, see Feis, H., "Private Investment Abroad," *Proceedings of the Academy of Political Science*, May 1953, pp. 49-60.

For findings that United States foreign investment since World War II has not given much aid to countries having the greatest problems in meeting international payments and doubts that such investment will ever flow in substantial amounts to soft-currency countries, see Bloch, E., "United States Foreign Investment and Dollar Shortage," *The Review of Economics and Statistics*, May 1953, pp. 154-160.

[6] Spokesmen for both the Truman and Eisenhower administrations repeatedly stated that most of the action to encourage a greater outflow of American investment must come from countries wishing to receive such capital. Available data suggest that, by and large, United States private investors found little change during the year in the economic climate abroad. A number of countries, including Turkey and several in Latin America and in Southern and Southeast Asia, took actions in 1953 designed to attract foreign capital. Among the more important measures were certain tax exemptions and concessions, as well as liberalization of laws regulating transfer of earnings and repatriation of capital. However, some of the countries which offered such positive attractions also took other actions that tended to limit or discourage American investors; an example

The Mutual Security Act of 1952 had directed the Administration to study impediments to private investment abroad and to suggest means for removing or decreasing them. The Department of Commerce published the first installment of this study during 1953 and tentatively concluded that the obstacles were so great and so varied in many areas, especially the Near East and Africa, that it was unlikely the next few years would witness a substantial increase in investments by private Americans; the report was somewhat more optimistic for the longer run.[7] Mr. Lewis Douglas, in a special report requested by the President, also concluded that American private investments abroad—he was particularly concerned with the sterling area—were not likely to increase "in adequate amounts" in the near future.[8]

The Randall Commission was more optimistic as to the possibilities for an enlarged outflow of private capital, although it did not attempt to make any estimates as to its future size. The Commission recommended that the United States "make clear" that primary reliance for assisting economic development abroad should be placed on private investors, and it urged the Government to give "full diplomatic support" to improving the climate abroad for such private investment. The Commission also urged that the Administration continue to negotiate treaties establish-

---

was the move in some countries to reduce the types of operation in which investment by foreigners was permitted and to subject the operations of foreign-owned firms to additional governmental controls. (See "Proud Borrower and Shy Investor," *The Economist*, November 7, 1953, pp. 402-404.) Against the favorable prospect of reaching a settlement in the Anglo-Iranian Oil Company dispute had to be set Brazil's decision making all phases of the petroleum industry within its borders a state monopoly and Guatemala's action confiscating additional holdings of the United Fruit Company.

[7] Department of Commerce, "Survey of Factors in Foreign Countries," *Factors Limiting U.S. Investment Abroad*, Part I, Wash., D.C., 1953. The 1952 Mutual Security Act had also directed the Administration to find and draw to the attention of private enterprises foreign investment opportunities; accordingly, the Department of Commerce began publication in 1953 of a series of "investment guides," giving considerable detail on the investment problems and general possibilities in individual foreign countries. Volumes covering Colombia, India, and Venezuela were published during 1953.

The National Planning Association, a private organization, published during the year the first of a projected series of case studies designed to demonstrate instances where the operation of private American business enterprise abroad had contributed to the economic development of the recipient areas. See its *United States Business Performance Abroad: The Case Study of Sears, Roebuck de Mexico, S.A.*, Wash., D.C., 1953.

[8] See Department of State *Bulletin*, August 31, 1953, p. 278.

ing rules of fair treatment for foreign investment, that Congress extend and enlarge the tax concessions for income earned abroad, and that "a further period of trial," together with an expansion of coverage, be given the investment guaranty device.[9]

### a. INVESTMENT TREATIES

Since the early part of the nineteenth century, the U.S. Government has sought to facilitate international trade and investment by entering into treaties of friendship, commerce, and navigation, commonly called "investment treaties" in recent years as more emphasis has been placed in them on attempting to establish standards of treatment which would create conditions more favorable to private foreign investment. Spokesmen for the business community have consistently urged the Government to negotiate such treaties, and the Mutual Security Act of 1952 directed the Department of State to "accelerate" this treaty program. Major negotiations were conducted during 1953 with Japan, West Germany, India, and Pakistan.[1] The only new treaty signed, however, was with Japan; negotiations for it had started in 1952. An agreement was reached with the Federal Republic of Germany whereby the 1923 treaty, suspended during World War II, was put back in force and commitments were made to negotiate without delay a new treaty, presumably providing greater protection than the existing one does to private foreign investors.[2]

On July 21 the Senate, virtually without opposition among its members, gave its advice and consent to the ratification of both these agreements and to ones which had been signed by the Administration in 1951 with Denmark, Greece, Israel, and Ethiopia. Senate approval was also given to certain amendments in the existing treaties with Italy and Finland, which had been negotiated in 1951 and 1952, respectively. Ratification of the treaties involving them was completed by Japan and Ethiopia before the

[9] Commission on Foreign Economic Policy, *Report to the President and the Congress*, Wash., D.C., January 1954, pp. 16-27.

[1] The United States Ambassador to Pakistan felt called upon publicly to deny that the United States was putting "pressure" on Pakistan to sign a treaty favorable to the United States. *New York Herald Tribune*, Monthly Economic Review, Paris, September 7, 1953, p. 9.

[2] A treaty signed with Colombia in 1951, replacing one in effect since 1848, was withdrawn from consideration by the Senate at the request of the President, who stated that further negotiations would be undertaken on it.

end of the year and these pacts therefore entered into effect, as did the one with Israel early in 1954.[3]

## b. TAX REFORMS AND CONVENTIONS

For several years the U.S. Government also has been seeking to promote private international investment by negotiating treaties designed to avoid double taxation of income earned in one country by nationals or corporations of another and, to a lesser extent, by granting certain tax concessions on foreign investment income.

Tax conventions, which apply only to federal taxes in the United States, seek to avoid double taxation by granting credits against domestic taxes for taxes paid to foreign governments and to prevent fiscal evasions through reciprocal administrative assistance. Usually two conventions are signed, one relating to income taxes and the other to taxes on estates and inheritances. At the beginning of 1953 conventions with respect to income taxes had been signed with fourteen nations and treaties dealing with estate and inheritance taxes had been signed with nine.

Spokesmen for the new Administration asserted that they supported the objectives and principles of tax conventions, which had long been encouraged by various business groups. During the year under review, tax convention negotiations of one kind or another were held with Australia, Belgium, West Germany, Italy, and Japan. The only conventions signed, however, were with Australia, but included were not only the two usual conventions but also, for the first time, one on gift taxes; the terms of the latter paralleled the usual agreement on estates and inheritances. The advice and consent of the Senate were given on July 9, without debate, to the ratification of these conventions and of the convention and supplemental agreement with Belgium for the avoidance of double taxation with respect to income taxes, which had been signed in 1948 and 1952, respectively. Ratification pro-

[3] For the texts of, and some supporting documents for, all the agreements ratified by the Senate in 1953, see *Congressional Record* (daily edition), July 21, 1953, pp. 9618-9645. For some general discussion of treaties of friendship, commerce, and navigation, see Commission on Foreign Economic Policy, *Staff Papers* op.cit., pp. 94-98.

A calendar of treaties of friendship, commerce, and navigation in effect at the beginning of 1953 may be found in *Survey—1951*, Appendix Table X, p. 309.

cedures were completed by both of the other countries involved, and the conventions with Australia and Belgium therefore entered into effect during 1953, as did those with Finland and Greece, which had earlier been approved by the United States. Thus all the tax conventions that had been signed by the United States had come into effect by the end of 1953.[4]

It is to be noted that all fifteen countries with whom the United States had one or more tax conventions by the end of 1953 were located in Western Europe or were members of the British Commonwealth. Few if any of these countries were usually included in the category "underdeveloped areas," in which the need for foreign investment was so frequently emphasized by the Administration. Several private groups urged the negotiation of conventions with such countries, especially those in Latin America, but it was reported that tax treaties with these countries were especially difficult to negotiate because, among other things, their governments frequently maintained complex systems of "near-income" taxes, rather than income taxes in the more generally accepted sense. Moreover, many of the officials in these countries doubted that the removal of double taxation would provide an important incentive to United States investors so long as United States corporate income taxes were so high.

The tax issue was discussed in the Economic and Social Council of the United Nations when that body again considered the question of providing fiscal incentives to international private investment.[5] As in the previous year, the Cuban spokesman, supported by many of those from so-called underdeveloped countries, sought to obtain approval of a resolution declaring that earnings from foreign investments should be taxed *only* in the countries where they were earned. The delegate from the United States, backed

[4] For more information on tax conventions, including the texts of those approved by the Senate in 1953, see "Double Taxation Conventions with Belgium and Australia," *Hearing*, U.S. Senate, Subcommittee of the Committee on Foreign Relations, 83d Cong., 1st Sess., June 29, 1953, and *Congressional Record* (daily edition), July 9, 1953, pp. 8608-8617.

For a calendar of the tax conventions in effect at the end of 1951, see *Survey—1951*, Appendix Table IX, p. 308. This calendar may be corrected up to the end of 1953 by adding the changes discussed in the text above as well as the ratification of all the conventions with South Africa and the estate tax convention with Switzerland, which took place in 1952.

[5] See *Survey—1952*, p. 120, and the references cited there for a summary statement of debates on this issue in the United Nations in 1952.

by delegates from most of the other large capital-exporting countries, opposed this resolution. He argued that the loss of revenue would be a serious problem for the United States and pointed out that his Government, as well as those of other countries, had already provided some tax incentives to foreign investments and that others were under consideration. He asserted that each nation should develop its own tax practices on the basis of its particular political and economic objectives and that differential treatment of income earned abroad would involve discrimination in the application of these internal standards. In the end the Council passed another compromise resolution, recognizing the need for finding means to expand the flow of private investment to underdeveloped countries, recognizing that lower taxes in these countries are an important attraction to foreign capital but that this incentive is less effective if the capital-exporting countries also tax the income from these investments, recommending the continued study of the problem, and requesting the more highly developed countries to take action insuring that income from foreign investment be taxed "only or primarily" in the country where produced.[6]

For several years various business groups in the United States had joined representatives of underdeveloped countries in urging the U.S. Government to grant special tax concessions to income from private foreign investments. Some concessions had already been granted, the more important being the postponement of taxation of income from subsidiaries (but not branches) operating

[6] UN Economic and Social Council Resolution 486 B (XVI), July 9, 1953. For a discussion on this issue, see UN Economic and Social Council, *Official Records:* Sixteenth Session, 710th-712th and 719th Meetings, July 3-4 and 9, 1953. See also "Fiscal Commission: Report of the Fourth Session," UN Economic and Social Council, *Official Records*: Sixteenth Session, Supplement No. 5, and UN Doc. E/CN. 8/L.6.

For the full statement to the Fiscal Commission by Dan Throop Smith, Assistant to the U.S. Secretary of the Treasury, giving the United States position on this matter, see United States Mission to the United Nations, *Press Release* No. 1711, New York, April 28, 1953.

In partial completion of a study that had been requested in 1952 in Economic and Social Council Resolution 416 D (XIV), the United Nations Department of Economic Affairs published *United States Income Taxation of Private United States Investment in Latin America*, UN Publication Sales No.: 1953.XVII. This study concluded that while existing taxation practices were a barrier to foreign investment, they were not the most important deterrent. It suggested, however, that tax incentives might be used more extensively to overcome the nontax barriers. For a short summary of this study, see UN Doc. E/Cn.12/352.

abroad until this income was brought home and lower corporate income tax rates for firms that qualified as "Western Hemisphere Trading Corporations." A proposal by the Truman Administration that branches be given the same treatment as subsidiaries died in Congress in 1952.

No significant changes were made during 1953 on taxes affecting foreign investment.[7] The new Administration, however, was more receptive than its predecessors to the requests of the business community and was more optimistic as to the effects tax incentives would have in encouraging private foreign investment. In his 1954 Budget message President Eisenhower therefore asked Congress to approve a series of changes in the tax laws that would reduce the rates of taxation to be applied on income earned on private foreign investments. Included in the suggested changes were a proposal that foreign branches of American corporations be treated the same for tax purposes as foreign subsidiaries and a recommendation to extend to all foreign investments the reductions in the corporate income tax presently available only to "Western Hemisphere Trading Corporations." These and other tax proposals designed to increase the attractiveness of foreign investment were also made by the Randall Commission in its January 1954 Report.[8]

[7] Congress did place a limit of $20,000 per year on the amount of income earned abroad which was exempt from the federal income tax of persons living abroad for seventeen out of eighteen consecutive months. This exemption had been created in 1951 to encourage technicians to serve abroad, but abuse of the law by persons going overseas to perform services normally performed in the United States, in order to avoid taxation, raised a clamor for its repeal. Professional entertainers were frequently cited as major offenders. Congress did not wish to remove the incentive for technical experts to go abroad and believed that the limit placed on the exemption would maintain this incentive while preventing large-scale abuses. (For more details, see *S. Rpt. No. 685*, 83d Cong.)

[8] For a discussion of tax incentives as devices for encouraging foreign investment, see Commission on Foreign Economic Policy, *Staff Papers*, op.cit., pp. 98-126. A study of United States practices may be found in Phillips, N. F., *U.S. Taxation of Foreign Entities*, Toronto, 1952. For a brief discussion of tax incentives to foreign investment offered by other industrialized countries, see Carroll, M. B., "Tax Measures to Spur Foreign Trade and Investments," *The Commercial and Financial Chronicle*, November 26, 1953, pp. 12-18.

For a paper urging accelerated amortization as a means of offsetting the greater risks incident upon foreign investment, see Conick, M. C., "Stimulating Private Investment Abroad," *Harvard Business Review*, November-December 1953, pp. 104-112.

# III. LOANS AND INVESTMENTS

## C. INVESTMENT GUARANTIES

Under the investment guaranty program, initiated as part of the European Recovery Program in 1948 and subsequently expanded, the Government makes a commitment, in return for a fee, to *convert* into dollars certain returns on approved foreign investments that cannot be converted through normal channels and to *compensate* in dollars for losses arising from expropriation or confiscation of such investments.[9] The existing law authorizes up to $200 million of commitments at any one time, but the total guaranties outstanding at the beginning of 1953 were less than one-sixth this sum. It was generally acknowledged that this device was not having the effects its advocates anticipated, and several business groups, as well as some Government agencies, called for its abolition. One major objection to it was that the issuance of guaranties by the U.S. Government was alleged to encourage the very acts insured against.

The majority of Congress in 1953 were disappointed that so few private investors had shown interest in the program. However, they were reluctant to abandon the scheme and in an effort to make it more attractive amended the Mutual Security Act so as to increase the number of countries in which investments would be eligible for this insurance and provided that such contracts, which formerly had to expire in or before 1962, could extend for periods up to twenty years from the date of issuance. The authority to enter into new commitments was extended until mid-1957.

An agreement was signed with Haiti during the year authorizing the issuance of guaranties for investments in that country. This agreement, the first with any Latin American country, was hailed by Administration spokesmen, who expressed the hope that other countries in that area would follow Haiti's lead. None did during the year and no private investors took advantage of the arrangements in Haiti.

Twelve new convertibility guaranties were issued in 1953, all for investments in Western Europe, but the total was only $2.8 million. Inasmuch as there were reductions of $6.6 million in previ-

---

[9] Summary accounts of this program in earlier years are given in *Survey 1952*, pp. 117-119. The guaranty agreements provide that if the Government should be called upon to fulfill its commitment, title to the foreign currencies converted and claims for property expropriated go to the U.S. Government.

ous contracts during the year, the total amounts outstanding on December 31 were only $31.1 million, of which $1.8 million were against expropriation or confiscation and the remainder against nonconvertibility of foreign currency earnings. The U.S. Government had not been called on to make any disbursements under these contracts and had collected nearly $1 million in fees.[1]

The Randall Commission found that the program had not "proved itself," but it noted that a number of potential investors continued to show interest in the device and asserted that the mere fact that such guaranties were available had encouraged some investors to look more deeply into investment opportunities, which were then found to be promising enough without the guaranty. The Commission reported that many investors had suggested that the program would be more attractive if it were expanded to cover, in some areas at least, the risks of war, revolution, or insurrection. These risks appeared to the Commission to be especially appropriate for Government insurance, and the majority therefore recommended that the program be given a further period of trial during which coverage would be authorized for such war risks.[2]

## Private Capital Movements[3]

The efforts described above to encourage an increased flow of investment capital from the United States did not bear fruit

[1] For more information on the investment guaranty program, see Export-Import Bank of Washington, *Sixteenth Semiannual Report, op.cit.*, pp. 15-17 and Appendix J, and *Seventeenth Semiannual Report, op.cit.*, pp. 16-17 and Appendix J. (The Export-Import Bank acts as the Government's agent in issuing investment guaranties.)
Authority for making information-media guaranties, which had been transferred from the Mutual Security Agency to the Department of State at the end of 1952, was transferred again, to the United States Information Agency, by *Executive Order No. 10476*, August 1, 1953. Data on the amount of information-media guaranties *issued* during 1953 are not available as this document goes to press.

[2] Commission on Foreign Economic Policy, *Report to the President and the Congress, op.cit.*, pp. 22-23.

[3] For detailed official data on United States investments abroad, see U.S. Department of Commerce, *Foreign Investments of the United States*, Wash., D.C., 1953. This study, based on the extensive census taken in 1950, makes many revisions of earlier-published data, including those given in earlier volumes of this *Survey*. For data covering 1951 and 1952, see Pizer, S., and Cutler, F., "Growth in Private Foreign Investments," *Survey of Current Business*, January 1954, pp. 5-10. These, and the quarterly reports in the *Survey of Current Business* on developments in the United States balance of payments during 1953, are the source of the information given in this section.

during 1953. The net outflow of private investment funds fell from nearly $1100 million in 1952 to an estimated $369 million in the year under review. However, most of the decrease represented a change from an outflow to an inflow of portfolio and short-term private investments. Private direct long-term investments fell from the 1952 level but were above the amounts recorded in 1950 and 1951.[4]

#### a. LONG-TERM

As Table 8 shows, there was a net inflow of $180 million of private portfolio investments during 1953, reversing the movement of several years' duration. The United States continued to

### TABLE 8

*Net Outflow of Private Long-Term United States Capital, 1950-1953*
(millions of dollars: inflow [—])

| Year | Outflow | Direct Investments[a] | Portfolio Investments[b] |
|------|---------|------------------------|---------------------------|
| 1950 | 1088 | 621 | 467 |
| 1951 | 889 | 528 | 861 |
| 1952 | 998 | 850 | 143 |
| 1953p | 517 | 697 | —180 |

p) Preliminary.
a) Direct investments consist of (1) the United States equity in foreign incorporated companies in the management of which United States investors have an important voice and (2) the foreign branches of United States companies, including partnerships and sole proprietorships.
b) Portfolio investments consist of investments in stocks, bonds, real estate, etc. in which United States investors do not have an important voice in management. Included are the net purchases of debentures sold and guarantied by the International Bank for Reconstruction and Development.
Sources: Pizer, S., and Cutler, F., "Growth in Private Foreign Investments," *Survey of Current Business*, January 1954, pp. 8 and 9, and *Survey of Current Business*, March 1954, pp. 22-23.

make relatively large investments in securities guarantied by the International Bank, investing $63 million in this manner during 1953. In 1950 and 1951 Canadian securities of one kind or

---

[4] Virtually no data have been published on the movements of foreign long-term capital into and out of the United States during 1953. It is estimated that for the year the rest of the world sold a net of some $89 million of long-term U.S. Government securities and purchased a net of $194 million of other long-term investments. Canada accounted for most of the sales of U.S. Government securities and the Western European countries for the bulk of the net purchases of other long-term investments.

another had also been popular investments for United States residents, but only small amounts, net, were so invested in 1952 and 1953. There were, however, considerable variations in the flow of funds between Canada and the United States during 1953. In the second quarter there was a large inflow as various Canadian authorities repurchased their bonds, which had fallen below parity as a result of the rise in interest rates in the United States; but with the reversal in United States interest-rate policy during the last part of the year, the American market was again favorable to Canadian borrowing and substantial amounts of Canadian securities were floated in it.

The Western European countries, and to a lesser extent the nations of Latin America, accounted for the net inflow of private portfolio investments as these areas reduced their portfolio obligations to the United States during each quarter. Most of the decline represented the repayment of bank loans, made feasible by the continued accumulation of gold and dollar reserves abroad, plus, in Europe at least, the greater availability of domestic capital.

At nearly $700 million, the *net* outflow of private direct investments was well below that of the preceding year but exceeded by sizable amounts the outflows in 1950 and 1951. Canada, as in the immediately preceding years, received nearly half the total. The share of Latin America, however, dropped from nearly a third of the total in 1952 to one sixth in 1953, as petroleum investments out of new funds declined and as the Guatemalan and Bolivian nationalization operations made their countries less attractive to American investors. In contrast, Western Europe and its dependencies received a net influx of long-term United States direct investments of nearly $100 million, compared with some $13 million in 1952. Although data are not yet available, presumably a large part of the investments in the dependencies were in connection with various mining operations.

Information on the industries receiving United States direct investments during 1953 has not yet been published, but revised data for 1951 and 1952 show that for those two years manufacturing held first place. Mining and smelting were increasingly important, exceeding petroleum for both years (see Table 9).

The value of private direct long-term investments abroad was

## TABLE 9

*Factors Affecting Value of United States Private Direct Investments Abroad,*
*1951 and 1952*
(millions of dollars; reduction [—])

| Area and Industry | 1951r | | | 1952 | | |
|---|---|---|---|---|---|---|
| | Net Capital Movements | Reinvested Earnings[a] | Total | Net Capital Movements | Reinvested Earnings[a] | Total |
| *Area* | | | | | | |
| Latin America | 165 | 276 | 441 | 277 | 305 | 582 |
| Canada | 240 | 153 | 393 | 420 | 201 | 621 |
| Western Europe | 62 | 197 | 259 | —8 | 174 | 166 |
| Western European Dependencies | 1 | 9 | 10 | —5 | 27 | 22 |
| All Other | 59 | 139 | 198 | 166 | 172 | 338 |
| Total | 528 | 774 | 1302 | 850 | 880 | 1730 |
| *Industry* | | | | | | |
| Manufacturing | 190 | 331 | 521 | 211 | 357 | 568 |
| Petroleum | 93 | 220 | 313 | 248 | 340 | 588 |
| Mining and Smelting | 100 | 88 | 188 | 278 | 47 | 325 |
| Distribution | 58 | 63 | 121 | 17 | 66 | 88 |
| Agriculture | 24 | 29 | 53 | —8 | 28 | 20 |
| Public Utilities | —8 | 14 | 6 | 23 | 15 | 38 |
| Miscellaneous | 70 | 80 | 100 | 80 | 27 | 107 |
| Total | 528 | 774 | 1302 | 850 | 880 | 1730 |

Details may not add to totals because of rounding.
r) Revised.
a) Includes small amounts for "other changes," chiefly losses on liquidation and adjustment of book values.
Source: Pizer, S., and Cutler, F., "Growth in Private Foreign Investments,"
*Survey of Current Business*, January 1954, p. 6. Many additional details are given in this source.

increased not only by the flow of investment funds from the United States, which often included substantial amounts of previously remitted earnings on foreign investments, but also by the reinvestment of earnings not brought home—defined in the official statistics as the undistributed profits of foreign-incorporated subsidiaries. Although some such undistributed profits were doubtless idle, pending permission for their conversion into dollars, the Department of Commerce has stated that the bulk of them were voluntarily left abroad and were used for additional capital formation. As Table 9 shows, the undistributed earnings of subsidiaries exceeded net new capital movements in 1951 and 1952, as they probably did in 1953. Such reinvested earnings have for years been a major factor in increasing the value of United States investments in foreign manufacturing enterprises, and in recent years they have also been very important in the case of petroleum. Taking into account both new capital movements and the undistributed earnings of subsidiaries, the value of United States direct investments abroad increased from $7.5 billion in 1929, to $6.7 billion in 1936, to $7.9 billion in 1943, to $11.8 billion in 1950, and to $14.8 billion by the end of the 1952. The Commerce Department's preliminary estimate put the total as of the end of 1953 at over $16 billion.

b. SHORT-TERM

In each postwar year, except 1949, the United States had supplied substantial amounts of short-term credits to foreign countries, but in 1953 there was a net inflow of an estimated $148 million. Small additional amounts of short-term credits were supplied the Western European countries and their dependencies, but these were greatly exceeded by repayments from Latin American countries, especially Brazil, which, as noted above, received a $300 million loan from the Export-Import Bank early in the year for the specific purpose of repaying overdue commercial arrearages. Canada also reduced its short-term indebtedness on private account to the United States by a few million dollars, while the other countries of the world continued to borrow small amounts.

# IV · INTERNATIONAL FINANCIAL INSTITUTIONS

THE U.S. Government played an important role in creating the three most important postwar international financial institutions —the International Bank, the International Monetary Fund, and the European Payments Union—and made important financial contributions to each. Almost from the beginning, many of the member nations criticized the Fund for what they regarded as its overly cautious lending policies, but the U.S. Government supported these policies and insisted that the Fund operate according to the principles embodied in its Articles of Agreement. During 1951 and 1952 the Fund, with the approval of the U.S. Government, actively searched for new procedures and practices designed to ease access to its resources and, in 1952, began consultations with many of its members looking toward a relaxation and removal of exchange restrictions. This upsurge in activity was welcomed generally, but many asserted that the Fund had taken only a first step in making itself into an institution that would be of significant service to the world.

In part because of the inability of the Fund to provide large amounts of short-term credits to the Western European nations, but more importantly because many became convinced that an acceptable solution to Western Europe's economic problems required those countries to "integrate" their economies, the European Payments Union was set up in 1950 with the immediate objective of creating a multilateral system of payments providing for the transferability *within* Europe of various European currencies. This was accompanied by commitments of the members to reduce their quantitative restrictions on trade among themselves. Although the agreement establishing the Union provided that it was to be only a temporary organization and that its goal was to facilitate a return to full multilateral trade and the general convertibility of currencies, some in the United States and elsewhere feared this regional approach would operate to make these goals more difficult of attainment.

The discussions by the authorities of the sterling area countries in late 1952 on the possibilities and techniques of making the pound sterling again convertible promised to bring to the fore during 1953 not only the questions of the role to be played in such a move by the Fund and the Union and the relationships between them, but also the question of what the U.S. Government was prepared to do to facilitate the achievement of what for years has been one of its major international financial policy goals.

The International Bank had been subject to less criticism than its Bretton Woods sister, primarily because the scale of its operations was increasing year by year. The U.S. Government expressed satisfaction with the general policies of the Bank, the level of its operations, and its concentration on making so-called development loans to the poorer areas of the world. Most of the members were more restrained in their approval, and spokesmen for the underdeveloped countries repeatedly urged the Bank greatly to expand its level of operations and, in the United Nations, pressed for the establishment of a new international development fund that would extend grants and long-term loans at low interest rates for basic development projects. The U.S. Government, supported by the other historically capital-exporting nations, vigorously opposed creating such a new institution but reluctantly agreed that the proposal be studied further and discussed again in 1953. Official representatives from neither the potentially capital-exporting nor the potentially capital-receiving nations were enthusiastic over the proposal that an international finance corporation be created to make, and to encourage private investors to make, equity investments in enterprises located in underdeveloped countries. This too was remanded for further study and was slated to be discussed again in 1953.

## A. EUROPEAN PAYMENTS UNION[1]

For several years both the United States Congress and the Administration had urged the Western European nations to

[1] The major sources of information for this section are the following: Organization for European Economic Cooperation, *European Payments Union, Third Annual Report of the Managing Board,* Paris, 1953; Organization for European

"integrate" (or to "unify") their economies, and the U.S. Government played a major part in the establishment of the European Payments Union (EPU) and related trade liberalization measures as well as in the formation of the European Coal and Steel Community.[2] The new Administration in Washington was on record as wholeheartedly supporting these institutions and the general policy of encouraging the economic unification of Europe. So far as could be determined from the public record, the U.S. Government did not during 1953 play an important role in the development of the European Coal and Steel Community, and therefore no attempt will be made here to summarize that institution's operations, problems, and accomplishments.[3] The United States apparently was less active in the European Payments Union than in earlier years, but some financial assistance was given it and the institution was of continuing major concern to the United States, in part because of its relationship to the problem of convertibility, discussed in Section C, below.

---

Economic Cooperation, *European Economic Cooperation*, Paris, September 1953; Organization for European Economic Cooperation, *Progress and Problems of the European Economy*, Paris, January 1954; Economic Commission for Europe, *Economic Survey of Europe in 1953*, Geneva, 1954; and Marjolin, R., "The European Trade and Payments System," *Lloyds Bank Review*, January 1954, pp. 1-15.

[2] See the chapters entitled "European Economic Cooperation" in the previous volumes of this *Survey* for a brief account of the accomplishments and problems of these institutions during the period 1949-1952.

[3] In late April 1954 the U.S. Government announced that it had signed a $100 million loan agreement with the Community. The twenty-five-year loan, to be administered by the Export-Import Bank, is to be drawn from Foreign Operations Administration funds and is to be used to make loans to individual enterprises in the Community.

The reader interested in the activities and problems of the Coal and Steel Community during 1953 is referred to the periodic *Journal Officiel* of the Community and, especially, to the following 1953 publications by the High Authority, published in Luxembourg: *Rapport Général sur l'Activité de la Communauté (10 août 1952-12 avril 1953)*, *Exposé sur la Situation de la Communauté au début de 1954*, and *Rapport sur les Problèmes Posés par les Taxes sur le Chiffre d'affaires dans le Marché Commun*.

See also "European Coal and Steel Community," *Hearings*, U.S. Senate, Committee on Foreign Relations, 83d Cong., 1st Sess., June 4 and 5, 1953; Mendershausen, H., "First Tests of the Schuman Plan," *The Review of Economics and Statistics*, November 1953, pp. 269-288; Zawadzki, K. K. F., "The Economics of the Schuman Plan," *Oxford Economic Papers*, June 1953, pp. 157-189; Economic Commission for Europe, *Economic Survey of Europe in 1953*, Geneva, 1954, pp. 12-14; and Aron, R., "Problems of European Integration," *Lloyds Bank Review*, April 1953, pp. 1-17.

## Operations and Adjustments in Mechanism during 1953

The Union—through which each member's[4] surpluses or deficits with every other member are set off against one another monthly and the resulting cumulative net position then settled by a predetermined combination of credits and gold or dollar payments—can only operate smoothly if the debtor or creditor position of individual members does not become excessive and if the disequilibrium of individual members does not persist over too long a period. Otherwise, countries in extreme debtor positions may have great difficulty making the gold payments required—especially if they have exceeded their EPU quotas and so must pay any excess above the quota entirely in gold—and thus may be tempted to reimpose quotas on imports. Excessive creditors, on the other hand, may find it difficult to receive only partial payment for their export surplus in gold—especially if they do not also have a surplus position with non-EPU countries. These problems are at least in part inherent in any regional system, and in practice several EPU countries had found themselves in extreme positions during the years prior to 1953 and some, but not all, had been in such positions persistently.

During 1953 the pressure on the Union from these sources was reduced somewhat as the cumulative debtor position of the United Kingdom was reduced and the extreme creditor positions of Belgium-Luxembourg and Portugal also declined moderately. (See Table 10.) Moreover, Italy switched from a net creditor to a net debtor position and the rate of increase in the net cumulative positions of several other members increased at a slower rate than in previous years. In general, these developments reflected the greater degree of internal monetary stability in many of the countries, together with increases in production. Although the immediate strains on the Union were less than in the preceding year, the institution's position remained precarious inasmuch as the noted reductions in the accumulated surpluses of several of the big creditors were only modest; those of Germany, the Netherlands, and Switzerland rose substantially; and the debtor position of France increased. That is, the position of the Union was such

[4] Including its associated monetary areas.

## TABLE 10

*Cumulative Position of Member Countries with the European Payments Union, 1952-1953*

(millions of dollar equivalents)

| Member Country | Quota | Cumulative Net Position:a Surplus (+) or Deficit (—) | | Cumulative Net Accounting Position:b Surplus (+) or Deficit (—) | |
|---|---|---|---|---|---|
| | | Dec. 31, 1952 | Dec. 31, 1953 | Dec. 31, 1952 | Dec. 31, 1953 |
| Austria | 70 | —108.8 | —28.9 | +16.8 | +96.1 |
| Belgium-Luxembourgᶜ | 860 | +761.8 | +726.7 | +424.8 | +400.2 |
| Denmark | 195 | —27.8 | —78.1 | —82.8 | —78.1 |
| Franceᶜ | 520 | —625.7 | —934.1 | —612.8 | —832.1 |
| Germany | 500 | +866.0 | +809.8 | +377.9 | +821.2 |
| Greece | 45 | —229.0 | —256.5 | — | —1.0 |
| Iceland | 15 | —12.5 | —19.2 | —1.6 | —4.0 |
| Italy and Trieste | 205 | +104.9 | —155.0 | +147.4 | —112.5 |
| Netherlands | 855 | +266.8 | +840.2 | +296.8 | +870.2 |
| Norway | 200 | —76.9 | —166.8 | —16.5 | —106.4 |
| Portugalᶜ | 70 | +66.7 | +56.0 | +68.7 | +58.0 |
| Sweden | 260 | +208.8 | +215.5 | +214.4 | +221.8 |
| Switzerland | 250 | +185.6 | +814.9 | +185.6 | +815.0 |
| Turkey | 50 | —218.1 | —251.1 | —147.5 | —159.1 |
| United Kingdom and Irelandᶜ,ᵈ | 1060 | —662.2 | —578.8 | —905.8 | —822.0 |

a) After adjustment for interest paid to or received from the Union on credits received from or granted to the Union.

b) To arrive at the "cumulative net *accounting* position" of each member—the basis for calculating gold payments and/or credit extended to or by the Union—the "cumulative net position" is adjusted by taking account of "initial positions" (for the first year of the Union's operations, certain debtors were allocated "initial credit balances" with the Union to facilitate the settlement of their deficits, and certain prospective creditors were assigned "initial debit balances" for which they received an equivalent amount of ECA conditional aid), "existing resources" (bilateral debts—mostly sterling—outstanding on June 80, 1950, for which no specific amortization plans had been agreed on bilaterally and which go through the Union mechanism), and "special resources" (dollars provided by the U.S. Government to cover in whole or in part the deficits of Austria, France, Greece, Iceland, and Turkey).

c) The cumulative net position of Belgium was reduced on July 1, 1952, by $50 million, while, correspondingly, the positions of France and the United Kingdom were increased by $25 million each. At the same time, the cumulative net accounting position of Belgium was reduced by $872.9 million and that of Portugal by $8 million, and those of France and the United Kingdom were increased by $25 million each. (See *Survey—1952*, pp. 248-244 for a brief account of the reasons for and the methods of this operation.)

d) Includes the dependent overseas territories and the nonparticipating portion of the sterling area.

Sources: International Monetary Fund, *International Financial Statistics*, Wash. D.C., February 1958, p. 11, and February 1954, p. 11.

that any revival of the pattern of surpluses and deficits that had occurred in 1951 would create anew great operating problems.

The financial commitments of the members to the Union expired in mid-1953 and only minor changes were made in the agreement when it was renewed for one more year. Decisions on major amendments designed to facilitate the transition to a wider multilateral system of trade and payments and credits were postponed pending further study and, presumably, the formulation of policy regarding convertibility in Washington. In a move to more nearly balance the Union's receipts and expenditures on account of interest payments and to increase the influence of interest rates on the members' economic and financial policies, it was decided to raise slightly the interest rates applicable to credits granted to or by the Union and to step up the progression of interest rates in proportion to the time credits had been outstanding to the Union's debtors. To meet temporarily the problems created by extreme creditors, provision was also made that postquota surpluses—up to specified amounts, later increased in Germany's case—would be settled half in gold payments by the Union to the creditors and half in credit extended to the Union by the creditors. These extensions beyond the quota were commonly referred to as *rolanges* and were agreed to by Belgium-Luxembourg, Germany, the Netherlands, Portugal, and Switzerland.[5] In the event, only Germany, the Netherlands, and Switzerland recorded surpluses of significant dimensions during the last half of the year, but officials of both Germany and Switzerland made clear their reluctance to continue granting what in effect were long-term, low-interest loans via the EPU. This problem promised to be a major hurdle in seeking accord for further extension of the agreement in mid-1954.[6]

During 1952 the Managing Board had urged that the gold

[5] As from July 1, 1953, Austria was permitted to make use of her debtor quota, that is, to receive specified amounts of credit from the Union. Greece's debtor quota, however, remained frozen.

[6] As of the end of October 1953, approximately 60 percent of the claims of the creditors against the Union had been outstanding for over eighteen months, and some 85 percent of the credits granted by the EPU to debtors at that time had been frozen for over eighteen months. It had not been anticipated when the Union was established that it would be the vehicle for such long-term capital movements. See Economic Commission for Europe, *Economic Survey of Europe in 1953*, op.cit., p. 9, n. 4.

See also *The Statist*, June 27, 1953, pp. 920-921.

and dollar assets of the Union be increased and, reportedly, had unsuccessfully sought additional contributions to the capital fund from the U.S. Government.[7] The central fund position of the Union was found not to be a serious problem during 1953, and the convertible assets of the Union increased from $373 million at the beginning of the year to nearly $475 million at year's end. This improvement resulted in large part from the facts noted above: some members, most notably France, had exhausted their quotas and so were required to settle their deficits entirely in gold while the extreme creditors agreed to settle half of their surpluses in excess of their quotas by granting credit to the Union.[8] The U.S. Government contributed indirectly to the Union's convertible assets by paying a total of $141.1 million out of Mutual Security Program funds to the EPU to help cover a part of the deficits incurred by France, Greece, Iceland, and Turkey. Virtually all of these payments were made during the first half of the year.

The Organization for European Economic Cooperation (OEEC) from the beginning recognized that if the reduction of monetary barriers were to have great significance it must be accompanied by a relaxation of trade barriers. The organization therefore fostered a trade liberalization program, also supported by the U.S. Government, the core of which was a concerted move to get each member to remove import quotas on *private-account* imports from other members as a group for a specified percentage of imports from them in a base year—usually 1948.[9] This linking of financial and commercial liberalization, more intimate than that

[7] See *Survey—1952*, p. 246.

[8] The 1952 changes in the gold-credit ratios applicable to debtors, whereby the percentage of gold payable to the Union in the early tranches of their quotas was increased and that in the later tranches decreased, also operated to increase reserves of the Union. Provision had also been made in 1952 for members to make temporary gold loans to the Union, but no such contributions were requested in 1953. (See *Survey—1952*, p. 247.)

[9] The liberalization percentages represent the share of commodities privately imported in the base year which are free of quota restrictions in the given year. That is, a 75 percent liberalization percentage for country X means that quantitative restrictions have been removed from imports that accounted for 75 percent of the value of X's private-account imports from other members in the base year. For reasons cited in earlier volumes of this *Survey*, these percentages tend to overstate the proportion of current trade which is free of quantitative restrictions. The overstatement has tended to decline, however, as the amount of state trading in the various member countries, especially the United Kingdom, has decreased.

between the International Monetary Fund and the GATT, was commonly regarded as one of the more important developments in postwar international economic relationships.

As of the end of 1952 it was reported that the average liberalization percentage achieved for all the member countries as a group was about 67 percent. Although there had been virtually no retaliatory reimposition of restrictions, the OEEC Steering Board for Trade in early 1953 reported that the whole trade liberalization program was being endangered as a result of the deliberalization measures taken by the United Kingdom and France in 1952.[1] So long as the degrees of liberalization differed greatly as among the various members, those applying a high percentage of liberalization, it was averred, not only risked running big deficits in the EPU but deprived themselves of bargaining counters with other members. Moreover, it was argued, those who had removed most of their restrictions might find themselves at a disadvantage, as compared with other members, in trading with nonmember countries; if such nonmembers carried on their trade on the basis of bilateral agreements, members with a lower percentage of liberalization might be tempted to favor imports from such bilateral agreement countries rather than from OEEC members who had removed most of their import restrictions. The OEEC Council in March therefore welcomed the British decision to remove some of the quotas which had been reimposed during the previous year. It also recommended that the French Government take "appropriate measures to ensure the progressive liberalisation of imports" and that all others, especially those in strong creditor positions, make special efforts to extend further their liberalization measures.[2]

Details as to subsequent action by each of the members are not available, but the over-all percentage of liberalization for the member countries as a group was reported to have risen to just over 75 percent by the end of 1953.[3] The most important advances

[1] See *Survey—1952*, p. 255.
[2] See Organization for European Economic Cooperation, *Press Release* A(53)16, Paris, March 24, 1953.
[3] As might be expected, the extent to which import quotas had been removed was highest for raw materials—100 percent in some countries. Progress toward liberalization had been slowest in the agricultural and food products sector, where political and social factors rather than balance-of-payments difficulties were the

were the increase in the United Kingdom's liberalization percentage from some 46 percent at the beginning of the year to 75 percent at the year's end and the October action by France (which had suspended all its earlier liberalization measures in 1952) freeing from quotas 19 percent of her private-account imports from other members. Germany and the Netherlands also increased their liberalization percentages, and Greece, for the first time, removed most of her import quotas. On the other hand, Turkey and Iceland completely suspended their earlier relaxations in the face of heavy deficits in the European Payments Union.

In its year-end report the OEEC was more optimistic than it had been earlier in the year and expressed the opinion that, in view of the greater degree of internal financial stability and the improvement in the over-all balance-of-payments position of most members, further removal of import quotas should be possible. The Organization also declared that the time had come when greater emphasis than in the recent past should be put on lowering such other obstacles to the expansion of intra-European trade as tariffs and state trading practices.[4]

## Accomplishments and Problems

The European Payments Union continued during 1953 to permit virtually all transactions within the area to be on a multilateral, nondiscriminatory basis—generally recognized as a vast improvement over the network of bilateral agreements which had characterized much of this trade before the Union was created in 1950. The multilateral clearing and settlement mechanism worked well, enabling members to settle transactions among themselves with relatively small movements of gold and dollars. As in previous years, approximately 80 percent of the total monthly bilateral surpluses and deficits ($4.5 billion) were settled by the multilateral compensation process and the operation of the cumulative principle—that is, the reversal of various countries' positions

---

overriding considerations in maintaining import quotas. For a discussion of this issue, see Organization for European Economic Cooperation, *European Economic Cooperation* (1953), *op.cit.,* pp. XIV-XVI.

[4] Organization for European Economic Cooperation, *Progress and Problems of the European Economy, op.cit.,* pp. 11-12.

through time within the Union.[5] The remainder were settled by extensions of credit or by gold or dollar payments. The automatic availability of credit—up to specified limits—has been one of the major virtues of the Union from the point of view of actual or potential debtors, but, as noted earlier, some of the large creditors were becoming increasingly restless over the amounts and long-term nature of the credits they were furnishing the Union. During the year a net of $146 million of credit was granted to debtors by the Union, Italy and Norway being the biggest recipients. Members granted a net of $255 million of credits to the Union, Germany being by far the most important creditor, with sizable amounts also being extended by Switzerland and the Netherlands. The Union's creditors received some $295 million in gold or dollars from the institution in 1953, while debtors paid approximately $395 million to the Union, including the $141 million provided by the U.S. Government to help France, Greece, Turkey, and Iceland cover their deficits.

The EPU and the trade liberalization measures commonly have been defended on the grounds that they permit a great expansion of intra-European trade and that the resulting increase in competition promotes cost and price declines and adjustments that facilitate (rather than hamper, as some maintained, by encouraging each member to balance its accounts *within* the region) the restoration by members of world-wide convertibility. Moreover, it has been argued, once debtors reached the position in which their Union deficits had to be paid largely or wholly in gold or dollars and creditors received a large percentage of dollars for their surpluses, there would be less grounds for discrimination against imports from outside areas, especially the United States. Intra-European trade certainly increased substantially after the introduction of the Union—and few if any questioned that this trade was larger than it would have been under a system of

[5] The $4.5 billion of bilateral surpluses and deficits cleared through the Union in 1953 may be compared with the equivalent of $6.8 billion in 1952 and nearly $8 billion in 1951. The reasons for this decline have not been found, but it may have reflected an increasing amount of bilateral balance between pairs of countries. Further, the operations of the day-by-day European currency arbitrage scheme, inaugurated in May 1953, doubtless reduced the amount of surpluses and deficits reported monthly to the Union. Indeed, these arbitrage arrangements, if expanded to cover all members, could perform most of the clearing functions of the Union.

bilateral agreements. But the amount of such trade has followed closely the changes in European production,[6] and the value of intra-European members' trade as a percentage of the members' total trade has fluctuated little since 1950. There was through 1953 virtually no evidence available as to the effect—one way or the other—of the trade and payments arrangements on the productivity of the member countries. While the various liberalization measures had, at least in some cases, exerted a downward pressure on prices, one European observer declared that these measures had "never, or hardly ever, been allowed to modify the existing structure of production."[7]

According to official OEEC statements, the major problems facing both the EPU and the trade liberalization program during 1953 were the ways in which an "orderly transition" could be made toward freer trade and payments throughout the world. A frequently reiterated theme in the official literature was that the scope of trade liberalization must be extended to trade with other areas and that the payments system provided by the Union "will have to be replaced by a wider system."[8] Improvements in the dollar payments position of several Western European countries permitted a number of them to relax somewhat the restrictions on dollar imports during 1953. The OEEC was studying what other actions its members might take in this direction, including extending the scope of the application of the intra-European

[6] See Economic Commission for Europe, *Economic Survey of Europe in 1953*, *op.cit.*, pp. 11-12. This report points out, however, that "it would be too much to conclude that the course of intra-European trade has been governed by the development of production alone."

[7] Aron, R., "Problems of European Integration," *Lloyds Bank Review*, April 1953, p. 8.

[8] Organization for European Economic Cooperation, *Progress and Problems of the European Economy, op.cit.*, p. 13.

Some nonofficial supporters of the Union, however, urged that it be retained as a permanent organization within which the European nations, in the event of a recession in the United States or a reemergence of serious dollar-shortage problems, could retreat; under such circumstances it would be a regional system enabling members to maintain a large area of multilateral trade and agreements while discriminating against the dollar area. (See Knorr, K., and Patterson, G., *A Critique of the Randall Commission Report*, International Finance Section and Center of International Studies, Princeton University, 1954, pp. 50-55, and Mikesell, R. F., "The Emerging Pattern of International Payments," *Essays in International Finance*, No. 18, International Finance Section, Princeton University, April 1954.)

liberalization measures to trade with members' dependent overseas territories and with Latin American countries.[9]

The Managing Board of the EPU stressed again in 1953 that the ability of the European countries to make their currencies generally convertible depended primarily on the individual countries' maintaining internal financial stability, increasing production and productivity, maintaining "proper" exchange rates, increasing their gold and dollar reserves, and removing import restrictions which were unnecessary for balance-of-payments purposes. Furthermore, as before, the OEEC emphasized the importance of the United States' maintaining a high level of economic activity and reducing its import barriers. For most of these problems the Managing Board had little responsibility, but it did study possible ways of changing the mechanism and working of the Union so as to put it in a better position to hasten the transition of its members from a regional to a world-wide system of convertibility. One problem discussed in this connection was changing the size of members' quotas. Some argued that the quotas should be reduced, thus cutting the amount of credit available, with the aim of forcing debtors more quickly to establish equilibrium in their balances of payments. This proposal was countered by the assertions that the relative size of the quotas had already been reduced as a consequence of the increase in the value of intra-European trade and that any cut in their absolute amount would lead debtors to reimpose import restrictions, thus depriving of significance any move toward financial convertibility. In the event, the quotas were not altered during 1953. The Managing Board also examined the problem of repaying at least a portion of the long-outstanding credits that had been extended by the surplus countries, but no decision had been taken on either the consolidation or the amortization of these debts as the year ended. The Managing Board also considered the possibility of "hardening" the EPU by increasing the ratio of gold to credit in settling the net position of members in the Union. Some, including the large

[9] For a discussion of the possibility of extending the operations of the Union to Latin American countries, see Organization for European Economic Cooperation, *European Payments Union* . . . *(1953)*, *op.cit.*, p. 73, and Triffin, R., "Possibility of Effecting Multilateral Compensatory Settlements between Latin America and European Countries through the European Payments Union," UN Doc. E/CN.12/299, March 4, 1953.

creditors, favored such a change on the grounds that it would permit those with EPU surpluses to ease their payment and import restrictions against the dollar area and would force debtors more quickly to establish equilibrium in their balances of payments; but others argued that if those with EPU deficits were faced with the requirement of increasing the gold payments, they would react by increasing their restrictions against imports from other members.[1] This problem, too, was not resolved in 1953 and the Board made no changes in the ratios, although, as noted above, some of the creditors, especially Germany and Switzerland, were increasingly reluctant to provide additional credits.

The future of the Union was closely bound up with the decisions which were still to be taken at year's end on the timing and approach to convertibility, briefly discussed in Section C below.

## B. *INTERNATIONAL MONETARY FUND*[2]

For years the Fund had been strongly criticized by most of its members—but not by the U.S. Government—and by many private observers for being too cautious in its lending policy and for exercising no appreciable influence on members' international financial policies and practices.[3] In contrast, there was in 1953 evidence that the Fund was in the initial stages of greatly expanding its role, and its critics were more restrained than in the past.

### Lending Policies and Operations

The Fund engaged in more exchange transactions during 1953 than in any year since its first (1947), when many loans had been

---

[1] See Organization for European Economic Cooperation, *European Payments Union . . . (1953), op.cit.,* pp. 87-95.

[2] The more important official sources for information on the policies and activities of the Fund are the following publications of the International Monetary Fund, all published in Washington, D.C.: *Annual Report, 1953,* July 1953; *Fourth Annual Report on Exchange Restrictions,* May 1953; *Summary Proceedings of the Eighth Annual Meeting of the Board of Governors,* September 1953; *International Financial News Survey* (weekly); *International Financial Statistics* (monthly); and the various mimeographed *Documents* prepared for the eighth annual meeting of the Board of Governors of the International Monetary Fund, held at Washington, D.C., in September 1953. See also the National Advisory Council on International Monetary and Financial Problems, *Semiannual Report to the President and to the Congress for the Period October 1, 1952–March 31, 1953,* Wash., D.C., July 1953, and *Semiannual Report to the President and to the Congress for the Period April 1–September 30, 1953,* Wash., D.C., March 1954.

[3] See *Survey—1952,* pp. 131-148, and the references cited there.

made to Western European countries in the months preceding the inauguration of the European Recovery Program. This was an acceleration of a trend noticeable in 1952 and it reflected four major developments: the improved international payments position of much of the world—expanding the scope for making short-term advances to meet temporary disequilibria in members' balances of payments; the attempts by the Fund to work out new procedures for easing access to its resources; the fact that sterling was becoming a relatively scarce currency in several countries; and the extensive use made of the Fund by Japan, which had become a member in 1952.

In early 1952 a major policy statement was issued by the Fund's Executive Directors designed to permit and encourage a great short-term use of its resources. This statement, among other things, defined more precisely than before what constituted a "temporary" use of Fund resources—generally three to five years; stated that the ability of members to draw would depend in large part on whether the members proposed policies adequate to overcome the payments problem giving rise to the request; declared that access to the Fund would not be denied a member because it was in payments difficulties; stated that the difficulties warranting access would not be predefined; and assured members that they could virtually automatically draw amounts equal to their gold and dollar contributions to the Fund.[4] In late 1953 the Executive Directors declared that, subject to review from time to time, this decision would continue in effect indefinitely.[5]

Anticipated in the February 1952 decision, and following a similar special arrangement concluded with Belgium in June, the Fund announced in October 1952 what it regarded as an even more important new general policy when it said that it was "prepared to consider requests by members for stand-by arrangements designed to give assurance that, during a fixed period of time, transactions up to a specified amount will be made whenever a member requests and without further consideration of its position, unless the ineligibility provisions of the Fund Agreement have

[4] See *Survey—1952*, pp. 183-184.
[5] International Monetary Fund, *International Financial News Survey*, January 15, 1954, p. 218.

been invoked."⁶ This decision specified that such arrangements would be limited to periods of not more than six months but would be subject to renewal; that in considering such arrangements the Fund would apply the same policies as it applied to requests for immediate drawings; and that, in general, such arrangements would cover only up to 25 percent of a member's quota. In December 1952 Finland entered into such a stand-by arrangement for an amount of $5 million and under it purchased $2 million in January 1953 and the remaining $3 million in May. No stand-by agreements were concluded during the year under review, but Belgium's 1952 arrangement was renewed and was in effect as the year ended.⁷ No drawings had been made under it but it had been used by the Belgian Ministry of Finance as collateral for borrowing from the Central Bank of Belgium.

At the annual meeting of the Governors of the Fund in September no one criticized this stand-by policy and several took occasion to welcome it, seeing it as presaging a period of greater activity by the Fund. United States officials made no comments at the time, in keeping with the general policy of saying nothing on policy matters pending the submission of the Randall Commission's report, but it can be safely assumed that they too approved of it. In December 1953 the Fund liberalized the stand-by arrangement policy. It announced that it would give "sympathetic consideration" to requests for such arrangements for periods longer than six months, it deleted the provision that such arrangements would, in general, be limited to not more than 25 percent of the member's quota, and it provided that a part of the charges for such arrangements would be offset against the service charges imposed if a drawing were made. While not mentioned in the official announcement, these amendments would permit the Fund to be of greater help than before in providing reserves to nations undertaking convertibility.

The Fund gave additional evidence of its desire to become

⁶ For a full text of this decision, see International Monetary Fund, *Annual Report, 1953, op.cit.*, pp. 95-96.

⁷ In early 1954 a three-year stand-by agreement was entered into with Peru for $12.5 million. The U.S. Government simultaneously entered into a $12.5 million stabilization credit agreement with that country and the Chase National Bank extended a $5 million loan to the Government of Peru.

more active in its handling of a request by Turkey. The Fund's Articles of Agreement specify that, as a general rule, a member shall not draw more than 25 percent of its quota in any one year. In August the Fund, for the first time, took advantage of another article of the Agreement and waived this provision, authorizing Turkey to withdraw just over 46 percent of her quota.

Sales of foreign exchange by the Fund during the year totalled the equivalent of $229.5 million, slightly more than the total sales during the preceding four years. In sharp contrast with the earlier years, sales of other currencies during 1953 were considerably larger than sales of dollars. As shown in Table 11, Japan, the par value of whose currency was agreed upon in May 1953, accounted for over 60 percent of the total. Interesting also were the facts that Japan purchased only pounds sterling and that four separate transactions were involved. The Turkish drawing of the equivalent of $20 million in August was noteworthy not only because it involved the waiver on the amount of drawings noted above, but also because it included the equivalent of $5.6 million in pounds sterling and of $4.4 million in German marks, this being the first time the latter currency had been sold by the Fund. Brazil also purchased sterling, as well as dollars. The other purchases, by Bolivia, Chile, and Finland, were all of United States dollars.

Repayments to—that is, repurchases from—the Fund also reached a new high in 1953, totalling the equivalent of $167.5 million. Included here were repurchases of nearly $62 million of yen by Japan, $48 million of guilders by the Netherlands, $37.5 million of cruzeiros by Brazil, $12 million of pounds by Australia, $5.4 million of pesos by Chile, $2 million of markkas by Finland, and $1 million of pounds by Syria. All the repurchases during the year were made with United States dollars, with the result that, as in the preceding three years, receipts of dollars by the Fund exceeded sales of dollars. Of the repayments during the year, only the $48 million by the Netherlands and $0.9 million by Chile were against the approximately $570 million of loans outstanding since before the end of 1948. In early 1953, at about the time of the Dutch repurchase, the U.S. Executive Director of the Fund stated that the time was approaching when the Fund would "have to

## TABLE 11

### International Monetary Fund Exchange Transactions, 1947-1953
#### (millions of dollar equivalents)

| | 1952 | 1953 | Total 1947-1953 |
|---|---|---|---|
| *Currency Sold* | *85.1*[a] | *229.5*[a] | *1126.4*[a] |
| U.S. dollars | 85.1 | 67.5 | 919.0 |
| British pounds | 0 | 157.6 | 191.6 |
| Belgian francs | 0 | 0 | 11.4 |
| German marks | 0 | 4.4 | 4.4 |
| *Currency Bought* | *85.1* | *229.5* | *1126.4* |
| Australian pounds | 30.0 | 0 | 50.0 |
| Belgian francs | 0 | 0[a] | 33.0[a] |
| Bolivian bolivianos | 0 | 2.5 | 2.5 |
| Brazilian cruzeiros | 37.5 | 65.5 | 168.5 |
| British pounds | 0 | 0 | 300.0 |
| Chilean pesos | 0 | 12.5 | 21.8 |
| Costa Rican colones | 0 | 0 | 1.2 |
| Czechoslovakian korunas | 0 | 0 | 6.0 |
| Danish kroner | 0 | 0 | 10.2 |
| Egyptian pounds | 0 | 0 | 8.0 |
| Ethiopian dollars | 0 | 0 | 0.6 |
| Finnish markkas | 4.5 | 5.0 | 9.5[a] |
| French francs | 0 | 0 | 125.0 |
| Indian rupees | 0 | 0 | 100.0 |
| Iranian rials | 2.2 | 0 | 8.8 |
| Japanese yen | 0 | 124.0 | 124.0 |
| Mexican pesos | 0 | 0 | 22.5 |
| Netherlands guilders | 0 | 0 | 75.3 |
| Nicaraguan cordobas | 0 | 0 | 0.5 |
| Norwegian kroner | 0 | 0 | 9.6 |
| Paraguayan guaranies | 0.9 | 0 | 0.9 |
| Turkish liras | 10.0 | 20.0 | 35.0 |
| Union of South Africa pounds | 0 | 0 | 10.0 |
| Yugoslav dinars | 0 | 0 | 9.0 |
| *Currency Repurchased* | *118.0* | *167.5* | *360.2* |
| U.S. dollars and gold | 118.0 | 167.5 | 360.2 |
| Other currencies | 0 | 0 | 0 |
| *Currency Resold*[b] | *118.0* | *167.5* | *360.2* |
| Australian pounds | 0 | 12.0 | 12.0 |
| Belgian francs | 0 | 0 | 21.6 |
| Brazilian cruzeiros | 65.5 | 87.5 | 108.0 |
| Chilean pesos | 8.7 | 5.4 | 12.5 |
| Costa Rican colones | 0 | 0 | 2.1 |
| Egyptian pounds | 0 | 0 | 8.5 |
| Ethiopian dollars | 0 | 0 | 0.6 |
| Finnish markkas | 0 | 2.0 | 2.0 |
| Japanese yen | 0 | 61.6 | 61.6 |
| Lebanese pounds | 0 | 0 | 0.9 |
| Mexican pesos | 0 | 0 | 22.5 |
| Netherlands guilders | 27.3 | 48.0 | 75.3 |
| Nicaraguan cordobas | 0 | 0 | 0.5 |
| Norwegian kroner | 0 | 0 | 9.6 |
| Peruvian soles | 8.1 | 0 | 8.1 |
| Swedish kronor | 8.0 | 0 | 8.0 |
| Syrian pounds | 0.4 | 1.0 | 1.4 |
| Turkish liras | 5.0 | 0 | 5.0 |
| Union of South Africa pounds | 0 | 0 | 10.0 |

*(Notes on next page)*

7

work out some arrangement" with those members whose drawings had in effect become long-term loans.[a]

The question of the Fund's lending policy in the event of a serious recession—especially in the United States—had been discussed for several years.[9] Early in 1953 the U.S. Executive Director of the Fund had testified before a Congressional committee that in the event of a recession, which it was thought was likely to be a "quick turnaround," the Fund would probably greatly increase its operations.[1] The 1953 *Annual Report* of the Fund stated that a decline in United States economic activity would greatly intensify the payments problems of other nations, but, it hastened to add, the maintenance of high levels of employment was a major objective of public policy in the United States. In his statement before the Randall Commission late in the year, the Managing Director of the Fund stated that one of the major tasks of the Fund was to minimize the international impact of business fluctuations by assuring members of funds to supplement their reserves in order to maintain a "tolerable" level of imports. He believed that no change in the Articles of Agreement was necessary for such a purpose but stated that the Fund's resources were not adequate to meet the demands in the event of a "serious" recession. He suggested therefore that the principal members of the Fund would be "well advised to agree beforehand on at least some temporary increase in its [the Fund's] resources whenever

a) There were outstanding on December 81, 1952, commitments on stand-by agreements to buy members' currencies totalling the equivalent of $55 million, consisting of a commitment to purchase amounts up to $50 million of Belgian francs and a commitment to purchase amounts up to $5 million of Finnish markkas. On December 81, 1958, the Belgian commitment was still outstanding.

b) Repurchase obligations of members are not restricted solely to cases where purchases have been made by a member from the Fund but may also arise from an original payment of less than 25 percent of a member's quota in gold, or from other cases where the Fund acquires amounts of a member's currency in excess of its quota. (Article V, Section 7.)

Source: International Monetary Fund, *International Financial Statistics*, Wash., D.C., February 1954, p. iv.

[8] "Foreign Economic Policy," *Hearings*, House of Rep., Subcommittee on Foreign Economic Policy of the Committee on Foreign Affairs, 88d Cong., 1st Sess., March 12 to May 12, 1958, p. 222.

In March 1954 India repurchased with dollars the equivalent of $86.2 million of rupees against a drawing which had been made in 1948.

[9] See *Survey—1952*, pp. 188-189, and the references cited there.

[1] "Nomination of Frank A. Southard, Jr.," *Hearing*, U.S. Senate, Committee on Banking and Currency, 88d Cong., 1st Sess., June 8, 1958, p. 12.

necessary."[2] The Randall Commission made no specific reference to this question in its *Report*, but it appeared that the measures the Commission recommended for providing additional reserves to countries attempting convertibility (see next section) were adequate to furnish some cushion against the repercussions of a mild United States recession.

With the Korean armistice in mid-1953, some looked forward to a decline in the world's military expenditures, and the Economic and Social Council of the United Nations held a general debate on the problem of preventing a recession after the rearmament period.[3] Several delegates stressed the important role of the United States, arguing that even a small drop in United States national income would result in a decline in imports which would be catastrophic for other countries. The United States delegate, observing that his country was blamed alternately and sometimes simultaneously for taking too much and too little of the world's goods, pledged the United States to do "everything necessary" to maintain high levels of employment and rising standards of living. He pointed out that the American economy had adjusted itself rapidly to the gigantic reconversion task after World War II, said that with its rapidly increasing population there was a constantly growing demand for goods and services and so for investments, and promised that if the market forces of adjustment faltered there were "regular techniques" for maintaining employment at high levels which would be applied. He declared that the United States was "not afraid of peace" and that a reduction in defense expenditures would free resources for civilian needs at home and abroad—including the needs of the underdeveloped countries for capital equipment and manufactured goods.

## Foreign-Exchange Rate Policy

### a. EXCHANGE RESTRICTIONS

A basic objective of the Fund is that its members should not

[2] International Monetary Fund, *International Financial News Survey*, December 4, 1953, p. 188.

For an account of a 1947 proposal by Harry D. White designed to supplement the Fund's resources, see Behrman, J. N., "A Suggested Amendment to the International Monetary Fund Charter," *The Economic Journal*, June 1953, pp. 471–477.

[3] See UN Economic and Social Council, *Official Records*: Sixteenth Session, 720th–724th Meetings, July 10–13, 1953.

impose restrictions or engage in discrimination in their foreign-exchange practices. The U.S. Government has consistently supported this goal. The Fund Agreement provides that any member maintaining specified types of restrictions or discriminations after March 1952 must consult annually with the Fund as to their retention. The discussions in 1952 and early 1953 had led to a few simplifications and some minor relaxations in these controls, but there were no major changes in the restrictive systems.[4] The Fund reported that it had not recommended any large-scale removal of restrictions and that the most important aspect of the consultations had been the exchange of views as to economic policies that might be conducive to future relaxation.[5] Although there was general agreement as to the desirability of reducing restrictions and as to the kind of policies that would lead in this direction, most members took a more cautious attitude than the Fund as to the speed with which reductions could be expected to take place.

In its mid-1953 report the Fund cited as the key obstacles to a rapid relaxation of restrictions the pressure of inflation in certain countries, the overvaluation of certain currencies, the continued inconvertibility of some major international currencies, and the inadequate flow of private capital. It particularly stressed that import as well as payment restrictions in one country—and especially in one whose economic position was dominant and whose share in world trade was large—tended to create the need for restrictions in other countries, and gave its opinion that the point had been reached where actions by surplus countries—the United States was clearly implied—could have a decisive effect in permitting others to relax their restrictions.[6] This conclusion was widely supported at the annual meetings in September, but perhaps more significant was the evidence of a growing belief among officials of many nations that continued dependence on exchange

---

[4] Of all the Fund's members, only Canada, El Salvador, Guatemala, Honduras, Mexico, Panama, and the United States were not maintaining restrictions inconsistent with Article VIII of the Fund Agreement.

[5] International Monetary Fund, *Annual Report, 1953, op.cit.*, p. 47. For details of the 1952 discussions, see International Monetary Fund, *Fourth Annual Report on Exchange Restrictions, op.cit.* This report also gives considerable detail on the exchange control systems in force in the various member countries.

[6] See International Monetary Fund, *Fourth Annual Report on Exchange Restrictions, op.cit.*, p. 26.

restrictions was an increasingly unsatisfactory way of dealing with balance-of-payments difficulties and was not likely to lead to a lasting international payments equilibrium.

Much of the Fund's energy in 1953 was devoted to the second round of these consultations. The talks were confidential and no report on their results has been released as this document goes to press. From the scanty data available it appears that there was some relaxation of restrictions by several members but that there certainly was no wholesale dismantling of them. The Managing Director reported late in the year that the Fund had never expected the consultations to result promptly in large-scale relaxations but stated that some countries had taken the occasion of the consultations to announce more liberal practices and that in some of the discussions the Fund's staff had persuaded the officials not to adopt new restrictive measures then being contemplated. He also regarded as important the technical services the Fund had been able to supply members as an outgrowth of the talks and reported that the consultations had in some cases resulted in members making drawings from the Fund.[7]

[7] See International Monetary Fund, *Summary Proceedings, 1953, op.cit.,* pp. 104-105, and International Monetary Fund, *International Financial News Survey,* December 4, 1953, p. 181.

Several of the Fund members had in recent years instituted retention quotas of one kind or another—the practice of granting advantages or privileges to particular categories of exports in the form of special facilities for retaining or obtaining foreign exchange—as a device for increasing the earnings of specific currencies, frequently dollars. At the annual meetings in September 1952, the Board of Governors approved a resolution asking the Executive Directors to make a special study of this practice and to make appropriate recommendations. In May 1953, the Executive Directors wrote all Fund members that they had found that what were referred to as retention quotas covered a wide variety of exchange measures, some of which were unobjectionable to the Fund while others should be removed since they appeared to result in exchange instability, to cause unnecessary damage to others by forcing shifts of trade, and to result in retaliatory measures. They concluded, therefore, that it was not practicable to deal with all these practices on a general basis and proposed to proceed on a case-by-case basis. No report on the results of the subsequent consultations has yet been issued, but in September Managing Director Rooth stated that, while these practices had seemed to be spreading a year earlier, during 1953 several countries had abolished them altogether, or reduced them, or were at least planning to reduce them. (International Monetary Fund, *Annual Report, 1953, op.cit.,* pp. 79-81 and 97-98, and International Monetary Fund, *Summary Proceedings, 1953, op.cit.,* pp. 105-107. See also International Monetary Fund, *Fourth Annual Report on Exchange Restrictions, op.cit.,* pp. 14-16 for a description of retention quotas and similar practices.)

b. PAR VALUES AND EXCHANGE RATES

Germany, Japan, Austria, Jordan, and Burma established, in agreement with the Fund, initial par values for their currencies during 1953. The German, Japanese, Burmese, and Jordanian rates were identical with those in effect for some time and involved no important policy issues, all of these nations having only recently joined the Fund. The action by Austria was more significant in that it was associated with the abandonment of some (but not all) of her multiple-currency practices; moreover, the new rate represented a devaluation of about 20 percent for many commercial transactions.

Three South American countries—Bolivia, Chile, and Paraguay —obtained Fund concurrence during the year to a change (devaluation) in the par values of their currencies. The Bolivian and Chilean actions also involved a simplification of their multiple-exchange rate structures and the taking of steps toward unification of their exchange systems.[8] Following what the U.S. Executive Director referred to as "very effective" consultations with the Fund, Greece eliminated all multiple-currency practices early in the year and cut the official foreign-exchange value of the drachma in half.[9] The role of the Fund in these devaluations and the degree to which, if at all, it had urged others to devalue were not public information; but it was noteworthy that the Fund had publicly stated that one of the obstacles to further relaxation of exchange restrictions was the overvaluation of certain currencies.[1]

On May 30 the Czechoslovakian National Assembly appreciated the par value of the koruna from 50 to 7.2 korunas to the dollar. This change was made without consulting the Fund, the Czechoslovakian authorities arguing that the Fund's concurrence was not necessary inasmuch as the action did not affect the international transactions of the Fund's members.[2] The Fund did not accept this position and therefore does not recognize the new par

[8] For an unofficial criticism of the Fund's policy vis-à-vis Venezuela, see Schmidt, W., "Venezuela, the International Monetary Fund and Multiple Exchange Rates," *Inter-American Economic Affairs*, Summer 1953, pp. 48-68.

[9] By the end of 1953 Greece, China, Haiti, Italy, Thailand, and Uruguay had not established initial par values for their currencies.

[1] See International Monetary Fund, *Fourth Annual Report on Exchange Restrictions, op.cit.*, p. 26.

[2] That is, it was argued that the change came under Article IV, Section 5(e) of the Fund Agreement.

value. Little publicity was given this action, but the issue could become a serious one.

In previous years three members of the Fund—Canada, France, and Peru—had, with varying degrees of "acceptance" by the Fund, abandoned earlier par values and established fluctuating rates; the French franc rate had, however, been held stable for several years. In early 1953 the Fund agreed to Brazil's establishing a free market for most capital and invisible transactions, as well as for some trade items.[3] In its *Annual Report* the Fund acknowledged that the fluctuating rate had worked well for Canada but emphasized that Canada's position was unique.[4] The *Report* made no adverse comments on the fluctuating rate policies of other countries, including those which had never established a par value, and stated that the moderate widening of the limits of exchange movements initiated as a part of the European currency arbitrage scheme could help to deter speculation and perhaps even induce equilibrating capital movements.[5] The Fund did not, however, modify its 1951 conclusion that a fluctuating rate system was not a "satisfactory alternative" to the par-value system—except in "occasional exceptional circumstances."[6]

The new United States Administration took no official position during the year on the issue of fixed versus fluctuating rates. However, the Randall Commission, in its early 1954 report, said that while it did not favor letting a currency "find its own level" inasmuch as this might result in a vicious circle of inflation, it was "sympathetic to the concept of 'floating rate,' " provided a country were strong enough to administer such a system effectively.[7] The Commission also recommended "reasonable relaxations" by the Fund in its provisions for maintaining fixed parities. These recommendations, however, were so cryptic that it was not clear whether or not they were intended to call for

[3] International Monetary Fund, *International Financial News Survey*, February 27, 1953, p. 261, and November 6, 1953, pp. 154–155.
[4] International Monetary Fund, *Annual Report, 1953, op.cit.*, pp. 68–70.
[5] International Monetary Fund, *Annual Report, 1953, op.cit.*, pp. 66–67. The spread allowed in the European currency arbitrage scheme was within the 1 per cent margin on each side of the par values permitted in the Fund Agreement for the countries concerned.
[6] See International Monetary Fund, *Annual Report, 1951*, Wash., D.C., pp. 36–4.
[7] Commission on Foreign Economic Policy, *Report to the President and to Congress, op.cit.*, p. 73.

important changes in the exchange rate policies of the Fund and the U.S. Government.[8]

## Gold Policy

There was no change during 1953 in the gold policy of the Fund and the U.S. Government. That policy, as modified in 1951, supported the existing dollar price for gold, discouraged premium sales, and held that, except for bona fide industrial, professional, or artistic purposes, gold should be directed into official reserves.[9] There were but few changes during the year in the policies of gold-mining countries on sales in premium markets.[1] South Africa and Canada relaxed their requirements somewhat by discontinuing the costly artifice of "processing" gold before selling it in the premium market, joining most of the British Commonwealth and colonial gold producers, who already were permitted to sell gold in the form of bars.[2] Japanese producers were officially permitted for the first time to sell two thirds of their output on the open market, and free-market gold trading was reestablished in Colombia, the largest South American producer.[3]

Gold production outside Russia during 1953 was estimated at about 25 million ounces ($870 million at the official United States price), the highest for any postwar year but some 30 percent below the 1940 peak level. As in the preceding year, it was estimated that approximately two thirds of the free world's production went into private hoards or was consumed in industry and

[8] The Commission did not define its concepts, but some interpreted letting a rate "find its own level" as meaning that the exchange rate would be set in the market without government intervention of any sort while a "floating rate" would permit the authorities to prevent the rate from moving beyond certain limits by buying and selling in the market and by increasing or decreasing import restrictions. (See Knorr, K., and Patterson, G., *A Critique of the Randall Commission Report*, op.cit., pp. 55-58.)

[9] See *Survey—1951*, pp. 187-189.

[1] See *Survey—1952*, p. 144, and the references cited there for a statement of their policies during that and earlier years.

[2] Canadian producers selling gold in the premium market were disqualified from receiving the subsidy paid by the Canadian Government for newly mined gold. It was reported that during 1953 an increasing number of gold-mining companies in Canada elected to sell their output to the Canadian Mint and receive the subsidy rather than to sell in the free market.

[3] Much of the material in this section was taken from Kriz, M. A., "Gold in 1953," *Engineering and Mining Journal*, February 1954.

the arts; about four fifths went into such channels in 1951. During the last few months of 1953 Russia was reported to be selling some gold in the free markets of Western Europe and to the Bank of England. Details on these transactions were not available, but the press estimated that all such sales totalled about the equivalent of $100 million.[4]

After fluctuating around $37 per ounce during much of 1952 and early 1953, the free-market gold price slumped to $35 per ounce by year's end, the lowest figure since the beginning of World War II.[5] This fall was attributed to the continued large supplies—including the Russian sales—at a time when demand was falling in many areas as a result of the Korean armistice, the fall in prices of primary commodities, the closing of certain markets in China, and the maintenance of internal financial stability in France.[6]

Although there was no official confirmation, the press reported that British officials "pressed the case" for a higher official gold price in discussions with American officials and that similar requests were put forward by other nations.[7] At the annual meeting of the Fund in September the price of gold was debated less than in previous years, but the spokesman for South Africa insisted that it was still a "live issue." He cited the increase in world prices, public debts, money supplies, and volume of international trade as pointing toward the need and justification for a higher gold price. He argued that a prerequisite for convertibility of sterling and other currencies was an increase in international liquidity. While recognizing that a higher dollar price for gold would not by itself be sufficient to achieve an adequacy of reserves, and that it would not result in benefits to all countries proportional to needs, he insisted that it would make the other

[4] See International Monetary Fund, *International Financial News Survey* January 8, 1954, p. 208. These Russian sales were reportedly occasioned largely by Russia's need for sterling to make down payments on orders placed in British shipyards at a time when British purchases of Russian grain were declining.

[5] Some sales in the free market were reported to have taken place at just below $85 per ounce. Sales at such prices can be explained by the fact that producers receive on sales to the U.S. Treasury a price of $85 an ounce less insurance, freight, and handling charges. In the case of South African producers, this means a net price to the producer of around $84.77 per ounce.

[6] See *The Economist*, November 14, 1953, pp. 545-546.

[7] See *The Economist*, April 4, 1953, p. 48.

steps necessary for achieving convertibility more effective and less burdensome than they would otherwise be.[8] This was one of the few issues at the annual meetings on which United States officials publicly took a firm position. The Deputy to the Secretary of Treasury, W. Randolph Burgess, stated categorically that the new Administration could not approve "tampering" with the price of gold. He maintained that such action would be inflationary, would undermine the Administration's "sound-money" program, would disrupt the efforts of other countries to restore stable currencies, and would not "go to the root of our problem."[9] The Randall Commission made no mention of the gold price, presumably on the ground that it saw no reason for a change in United States policy.

The net outflow of gold from the United States which began in the summer of 1952 continued throughout 1953 as the rest of the world tended toward a closer balance in its current accounts with the United States and as large amounts of foreign aid continued to be provided by the U.S. Government. Net gold sales were recorded to every major area except Canada, from whom small purchases were made. The United Kingdom was the biggest single purchaser, taking $480 million from the United States reserves, as is shown in Table 12. The Federal Republic of Germany was the second biggest buyer, purchasing $130 million, followed by the Bank for International Settlements and Belgium–Belgian Congo, which bought approximately $95 million each. Net gold sales were recorded in each quarter of the year, but over half the year's total sales were made during the first three months. Total sales during 1953 were approximately $1.2 billion, and inasmuch as industrial consumption in this country approximately matched domestic production, the monetary gold stock of the United States declined by the amount of sales to foreign countries, leaving $22.1 billion in United States official reserves

[8] International Monetary Fund, *Summary Proceedings, 1953*, op.cit., pp. 65-67.
For some nonofficial arguments for raising the price of gold, see Harrod, R. F., "Imbalance of International Payments," International Monetary Fund *Staff Papers*, April 1953, pp. 1-46; Copland, Sir Douglas, "Problems of the Sterling Area," *Essays in International Finance*, No. 17, International Finance Section, Princeton University, September 1953; and Baffi, P., "The Dollar and Gold," Banca Nazionale del Lavoro *Quarterly Review*, Rome, July-September 1953, pp. 181-195.
[9] International Monetary Fund, *Summary Proceedings, 1953*, op.cit., pp. 70-71.

## TABLE 12

*Net Foreign Gold Transactions by the United States, 1953*
(net purchases [+]; net sales [—])
(millions of dollars)

| Country or Area | First Half | Second Half | Year |
|---|---|---|---|
| Continental Western Europe | —211 | —241 | —452 |
| United Kingdom | —860 | —120 | —480 |
| Latin America | —122 | —10 | —182 |
| Asia and other | —2 | —4 | —6 |
| Bank for International Settlements | —82 | —62 | —94 |
| Total | —727 | —487 | —1164 |

Source: Board of Governors of the Federal Reserve System, *Federal Reserve Bulletin*, March 1954, p. 239.

at year's end. This was about 60 percent of the known world gold reserves (excluding Russia), approximately the same percentage as at the end of World War II but larger than the 38 percent recorded in 1928 and the 56 percent in 1938.

### The Fund and the European Payments Union

Fund spokesmen had in previous years been critical of the European Payments Union, fourteen of whose members are also members of the Fund, on the ground, among others, that it might operate to retard rather than to hasten the ultimate convertibility of the participants' currencies. Nonetheless, in 1952 the Fund had entered into a stand-by credit arrangement with Belgium, the absence of which, Fund officials believed, would have made it most difficult to reach an agreement on the terms for extending the Union.[1]

During 1953 officials of the two institutions confidentially discussed problems of mutual interest, especially ways in which the two institutions could achieve more effective cooperation. In discussing the work and some of the problems of the Union, the Fund's 1953 *Annual Report* did not, as had earlier reports, make adversely critical remarks about the Union. And in their midyear report the Managing Board of the Union, pointing out that their institution was intended only as a temporary system designed to help European countries until they were able to take their full place in a world-wide system, stated that it seemed likely that it

[1] See statement of Frank A. Southard, Jr., in "Foreign Economic Policy Hearings, *op.cit.*, p. 224.

the year ahead close cooperation between the two institutions would be both more necessary and easier than in the past: more necessary because Union members might need additional reserves as they made fresh progress toward trade and payments liberalization; easier because as the Union members' balance-of-payments positions improved the Fund would find it possible to help them within the terms and intentions of its Articles of Agreement.[2] By year's end, however, there had been no public indication that any specific new relationships had yet been worked out.[3]

## C. THE QUESTION OF CONVERTIBILITY

For many years the return of the rest of the world to a system of fully convertible currencies has been a major objective of United States foreign economic policy. This is also one of the chief goals of the International Monetary Fund, and officials of the European Payments Union have insisted that a primary task of that organization is to facilitate a return to general convertibility of its members' currencies.

During 1953 there was much discussion of this topic as many countries improved their balance-of-payments positions—especially via-à-vis the United States—as inflationary forces subsided, and as increasing numbers of peoples concluded that direct control and restraints over trade and payments were not providing solutions to the problems of international imbalance. The term "convertibility" was used in many different senses, but it appears that what was usually envisaged for the near future was not the complete removal of all exchange controls and quantitative trade restrictions, but rather the giving to nonresidents of any country whose currency was to be made convertible the right to convert their current earnings of such currency into any other currency, especially United States dollars, and—on the trade side—the elimination of discriminatory import restrictions,

[2] Organization for European Economic Cooperation, *European Payments Union, Third Annual Report of the Managing Board*, Paris, 1953, pp. 94-95.

[3] At the annual meeting of the Fund in September, the Governor for Uruguay, speaking for the Governors of all the Latin American countries, spoke favorably of the work of the European Payments Union and asked the Fund to continue to study the problem of whether some of the "instruments" of the Union could not usefully be applied to Latin America. (International Monetary Fund, *Summary Proceedings, 1953, op.cit.*, p. 151.)

*again* especially against the United States, imposed on the residents of the country attempting convertibility.[4]

Much of the discussion on convertibility centered around the questions of the adequacy of the reserves of the European countries, the ability of those countries and the sterling area to continue to improve their balance-of-payments positions, and the trade and investment policies to be pursued by the United States. However, questions as to the route by which convertibility should be achieved were also debated at length. The two most important issues here were: Should financial convertibility precede, follow, or accompany relaxations in discriminatory trade restrictions? and Should the approach to convertibility by the OEEC countries be within the framework of a modified European Payments Union or should it be by individual nations, perhaps acting in concert, withdrawing from the Union when they were in a position to make their own currencies convertible?

At the conference of Commonwealth Prime Ministers, held in London in late 1952, the problem and prospects of restoring the convertibility of sterling were discussed. The communiqué issued at the end of that conference stated that the achievement of convertibility would depend, in part, on the lowering of trade barriers by other countries—implying in particular the United States —and on the availability of "adequate financial support through the International Monetary Fund or otherwise." Shortly after the conference ended, arrangements were made for a visit to Washington by senior British officials to discuss convertibility and related economic problems.[5] Apparently, the British at that time envisaged making sterling convertible—in concert with a few of the major Continental currencies—outside the framework of the European Payments Union.[6]

[4] For a discussion of the definitions and objectives of currency convertibility and of various approaches to convertibility, see Commission on Foreign Economic Policy, *Staff Papers*, Wash., D.C., February 1954, pp. 465-491.

[5] For a text of the communiqué, see Department of State *Bulletin*, March 16, 1958, pp. 897-899.

[6] The details of the British plans on convertibility and the discussions with the U.S. Government, the Fund, and the Organization for European Economic Cooperation were not made available to the public. For some unofficial discussion of the nature of the "plan" for sterling convertibility, as well as changes in it during the year, and for discussion of some of the problems and prospects, see Day, A. C. L., "What Kind of Convertibility?" *Lloyds Bank Review*, April 1954, pp. 83-44; Robbins, L., "The International Economic Problem," *Lloyds Bank Re-*

The new Administration in Washington, having just taken office, stated that it was prepared only to listen to the British ideas, and there was agreement in advance that no commitments would be made. Secrecy surrounded the meetings, held in early March, but the press stated that the British spokesmen asked the United States to reduce its tariffs, repeal the "Buy American" Act, simplify its customs administration, remove existing discrimination in favor of United States shipping, and—on the financial side—to foster steps to increase United States foreign investments, support a liberalization in the lending policy of the International Monetary Fund, raise the price of gold, and stabilize American purchases of raw materials.[7] The official communiqué issued at the end of the talks was not communicative. After repeating the usual well-polished generalities as to agreement being reached on the need for "sound internal policies" and "freer trade and currencies," the communiqué stated that the nature, scope, and timing of specific measures which might be taken to restore a multilateral system of trade and payments would require further study by the two governments and by other governments and international organizations.[8] In subsequent months

---

view, January 1953, pp. 1-24; Leith-Ross, F., "Sterling Convertibility," South African Journal of Economics, March 1953, pp. 1-10; Day, A. C. L., "Convertibility and the European Payments Union," Bulletin of the Oxford University Institute of Statistics, May 1953, pp. 151-162; Brown, W. A., Jr., "Sterling Convertibility and Some Related Problems," Papers and Proceedings, American Economic Review, May 1953, pp. 71-80; Haberler, G., "Reflections on the Future of the Bretton Woods System," Papers and Proceedings, American Economic Review, May 1953, pp. 81-95; Meade, J. E., "The Convertibility of Sterling," The Three Banks Review, September 1953, pp. 8-26; Paish, F. W., "Aspects of the British Economy and Some Current Economic Problems," South African Journal of Economics, June 1953, pp. 147-161; Robertson, D. H., Britain in the World Economy, London, 1954; Day, A. C. L., The Future of Sterling, Oxford, 1954; Hawtrey, R. G., "Confidence and Convertibility," International Affairs, October 1953, pp. 429-488; Nurkse, R., "The Problem of Currency Convertibility Today," Proceedings of the Academy of Political Science, May 1953, pp. 61-78; Fleming, J. M., "Britain's Balance of Payments Problem," Proceedings of the Academy of Political Science, May 1953, pp. 14-29; International Chamber of Commerce, Steps to Convertibility (Brochure 168), Paris, 1953; and the following issues of The Banker (London): March 1953, pp. 130-133; June 1953, pp. 326-330; September 1953, pp. 183-189; October 1953, pp. 224-280; December 1953, pp. 385-340; and January 1954, pp. 7-12. See also the index of The Economist, which throughout the year carried many articles on this problem, as did The Statist.

[7] See The Economist, March 21, 1953, p. 828, and April 4, 1953, p. 48.

[8] For a text of the communiqué, see National Advisory Council on International Monetary and Financial Problems, Semiannual Report to the President and to

British officials confidentially discussed their plans with the Organization for European Economic Cooperation, and, as noted in Section A above, the Managing Board of the EPU did consider various ways by which the Union could be the vehicle for achieving a wider system of convertibility.

United States officials also held confidential talks on the convertibility problem with representatives of several European governments and with a mission from the OEEC. Spokesmen for the Continental countries urged the United States to pursue international economic policies similar to those suggested by the British delegation and received the same reply: the United States agreed with the objectives of freer and expanded world trade and payments, but specific action by the United States to facilitate these would have to await further study.[9] Several of the Continental countries, in their talks with both British and American officials, opposed action to make sterling convertible in advance of other major European currencies lest it result in new restrictions by the sterling area against imports from Europe and also result in the sterling area's withdrawing from the European Payments Union and so threatening to wreck that institution, which event, they said, would raise the possibility of a revival within Europe of *bilateral* bargaining and settlement.[1]

In late March President Eisenhower appointed Lewis W. Douglas to make a special study of the problems raised in the discussions with the British. In his brief report, completed in mid-July, Mr. Douglas stated that the convertibility of sterling (together with the removal of restrictions on trade) would greatly benefit the United States and "would have favorable and marked effects on the international economic environment," even if other currencies remained inconvertible.[2] He noted with approval the

---

*the Congress for the Period October 1, 1952–March 31, 1953,* Wash., D.C., July 1953, pp. 64–65.

[9] For the official communiqué issued after the meeting with the OEEC mission, see *New York Herald Tribune,* Monthly Economic Review, Paris, May 4, 1953, p. 8. See also *The Economist,* April 25, 1953, p. 242, and *New York Times,* April 18, 1953, p. 1.

[1] For a discussion of the differences in approach, see Aschinger, F. E., "Convertibility: The Status of Talks and Measures," *Swiss Review of World Affairs* (Zurich), July 1953, pp. 3–8.

[2] For the text of Mr. Douglas's report, see Department of State *Bulletin,* August 31, 1953, pp. 275–279.

internal fiscal and monetary reforms of the British Government during the previous year or two, the derationing and decontrolling of many internal transactions, the reopening of many international commodity markets, the resumption of currency arbitrage transactions among sterling and several European currencies, the return to private traders of many foreign-exchange transactions, and the improvement in the British foreign-exchange reserve position.[3] Nonetheless, he concluded, the imbalance between the sterling area and the dollar area was deep-seated, and more remained to be done if sterling were to be able to stand the strain of convertibility. Although he believed that many of the additional measures could be taken only by the British Government, Mr. Douglas stated that it was also necessary for the United States to remove "as soon as possible" its own impediments to freer trade; he offered no detailed prescription for United States policy. While making clear that he had no hopes for a successful "dash" toward convertibility, an important theme running throughout Mr. Douglas's report was that "time . . . is of the essence." He emphasized the importance of not arresting the recent progress in the sterling area toward "economic liberty" and of not allowing the existing enthusiasm for convertibility to subside. He therefore urged the U.S. Government to make a prompt announcement that it was its determined policy to work toward a consistent relaxation of United States "restrictive foreign trade legislation." President Eisenhower wrote Mr. Douglas that his report was a "most valuable contribution" and sent it on to the Randall Commission, commending it to the latter's earnest attention.

A few weeks later the annual meeting of the Board of Governors of the Fund was held, and convertibility was a major topic of discussion. The Fund's *Annual Report*, approved by the U.S. Executive Director following consultation with other U.S. Government officials, gave much attention to the improvement which

---

[3] For an account of the European currency arbitrage arrangements and a statement of the importance of the reopening of the foreign-exchange markets as a preliminary step toward introducing convertibility, see Bank for International Settlements, *Twenty-third Annual Report*, Basle, June 1953, pp. 131-140.

For an early 1954 statement of Britain's relaxation of controls over international transactions, see Federal Reserve Bank of New York, *Monthly Review*, January 1954, pp. 4-9.

had taken place in the preceding year and a half in the world's balance-of-payments situation and stated that the determination of many countries to move toward convertibility "deserves the utmost encouragement."[4] The *Report* warned, however, that there was still an important "residual" dollar problem and that some of the recent improvements were the result of special and non-recurring circumstances. In an opening speech at the meeting, Fund Managing Director Rooth was more optimistic than the *Report*, prepared some two months earlier, as to the improvement in the world's payments situation and stated that in his opinion convertibility could be undertaken when a nation had established a strong payments position. He warned that if individual countries put off convertibility until others were able to take similar action, inconvertibility would be the rule for some time to come. He stressed the importance of countries' not restricting their imports from nations attempting convertibility in an effort to get third currencies and asserted that the creditor countries, especially the United States, had an especially great responsibility to ease the access to their markets. He also recognized the responsibility of the Fund to help its members move toward convertibility by providing them with secondary reserves and mentioned the various measures, noted in Section B above, which had been taken by the Fund to make its resources available.[5]

The Governor for the United Kingdom said that his Government was "convinced that the time is ripe for a courageous and a concerted move to a freer system of multilateral trade and payments" and that it had explained its ideas "to our American friends" and to others and "now await their reactions." He went on to say that his Government welcomed the Douglas report and the creation of the Randall Commission but warned that "time presses upon us" and that if the chance of moving forward were not seized "we may find that we shall be forced inevitably back upon the course along which we have already progressed."[6] He also said his Government believed the Fund's resources were not likely to be large enough to meet the requirements of a convertibility move by several countries. Subsequently, the Fund's Manag-

[4] International Monetary Fund, *Annual Report, 1953, op.cit.,* p. 42.
[5] International Monetary Fund, *Summary Proceedings, 1953, op.cit.,* pp. 10-11
[6] *ibid.,* pp. 86-87.

ing Director told the Randall Commission that the Fund's resources were probably not adequate if "standby arrangements" should be necessary to support convertibility attempts by all the leading countries and that it would therefore be desirable for the Fund's major members to agree beforehand that more money would be available if needed.[7]

Several of the other Governors also stressed the responsibility of the United States to make it easier for their countries to earn dollars and many stated that further movement toward convertibility awaited the formulation of policy in Washington. Although there was virtually nothing in the way of precise official documentation, it was apparent from the speeches of many foreign officials, at the annual meeting of the Fund and elsewhere, that the governments of many European countries were preoccupied with the possibility of an American recession and probably would take no important step toward convertibility until the prospects for a continued high level of economic activity in the United States were brighter than they felt them to be in the latter part of 1953.

The spokesman for the United States had little to say on

[7] Pursuant to a resolution by the UN Economic and Social Council in 1952 (Resolution 427 [XIV], July 10, 1952), the Fund prepared a report on the adequacy of international reserves. (For the text of this report, see International Monetary Fund, *Staff Papers*, October 1953, pp. 181-227.) The report dealt in some detail with the nature of monetary reserves, gave statistical data on the reserves of various countries, and emphasized that "adequacy" depended on many factors which changed over time. It explained that no final or absolute determination of adequacy could be given in advance for any specific country or area and pointed out that no amount of reserves was sufficient to finance a permanent disequilibrium in a country's balance of payments. The report drew no explicit conclusions as to the adequacy of the world's reserves; it declared, however, that if the monetary reserves of the world were redistributed in accordance with apparent need they would soon be redistributed with the wealthy or less "dynamic" countries reacquiring many of them, inasmuch as the holding of reserves was lower in the scale of preferences for many countries than the goods and services for which the reserves could be exchanged. In discussing this report the United Kingdom delegate to ECOSOC said that he was glad to note the "indications" in the report that the Fund would be prepared to consider the desirability of additions to its reserves and to changes in its methods of operation, for his Government believed present reserves were inadequate to finance a free flow of international trade. The United States delegate said only that while his Government was in broad agreement with the Fund's findings, it was not prepared to endorse the report in its entirety. (United Nations Economic and Social Council, *Official Records*: Sixteenth Session, 724th Meeting, July 13, 1953, p. 184.)

For a statement arguing that the reserves held by the sterling area, at least, as of late 1953 were not adequate to underwrite the risks of sterling convertibility, see Commission on Foreign Economic Policy, *Staff Papers, op.cit.*, pp. 476-485.

these matters. He stated that the new Administration had as one of its major objectives the creation and maintenance of "sound, honest money"—an oft-repeated phrase—both at home and abroad and that it believed the path toward convertibility would not be an easy one but that the goal was worth achieving. He said the U.S. Government welcomed the suggestions that had been made by others as to the conduct of affairs in the United States and that these suggestions would be placed before the Randall Commission.

In late January 1954 the Randall Commission issued its *Report*, including a short chapter on convertibility.[8] It spoke in favor of other countries' making their currencies convertible, adhered to the view that the restoration of convertibility was a most complex problem and not just one of curbing inflation, and stated that the decisions on methods and timing and the responsibility for taking action must rest with the countries concerned. It recognized, however, that United States policies were an important factor and declared that the other recommendations of the Commission, if carried out, would encourage and assist foreign countries in removing restrictions on trade and payments. The Commission emphasized that it believed the removal of restrictions on trade and on payments should go hand in hand and stressed that it favored *gradual* progress and not a "dash" toward convertibility. It also said that while it did not favor letting a foreign currency "find its own level," it was sympathetic to the concept of a "floating rate," which would provide alternative methods of meeting trade and speculative pressures.

The Commission stressed that sterling was a "key" currency—widely used to finance the trade of other nations—and that it was therefore especially desirable that it become convertible. It noted that the effect which sterling convertibility might have on the European Payments Union raised important questions and stated that, while the Union was a temporary mechanism, it had achieved an impressive measure of success. The Commission felt, therefore, that its *Report* should not sponsor any measures which might wreck the Union before there was something better to put in its place. Although these statements admitted of more than one

[8] Commission on Foreign Economic Policy, *Report to the President and the Congress*, op.cit., pp. 72-75.

interpretation, it was commonly believed that the Commission favored moves toward convertibility by individual countries, and particularly by the United Kingdom, over the regional approach exemplified by an extension of the European Payments Union and a strengthening of the Union's settlement provisions.

On the question of reserves, the Commission believed some additional reserves to be needed—especially by Britain—if convertibility were to be maintained successfully. The Commission took the position, however, that adequate reserves could be found for a *gradual* approach to convertibility through a more active utilization of the International Monetary Fund's holding of gold and dollars, which currently totalled $3.3 billion. It therefore favored some relaxation of Fund policies, especially with regard to the time schedule for utilizing quotas and the provisions for maintaining fixed parities. In addition, as a second method of strengthening foreign reserves, the Commission recommended that the Federal Reserve System explore with foreign central banks the possibility of extending stand-by credits or line-of-credit arrangements.[9] No action had been taken by the U.S. Government on these recommendations, so far as the public could tell, as this document went to press.

## D. *THE INTERNATIONAL BANK*[1]

### *Lending Policies and Operations*

The International Bank has from the beginning been a less controversial organization than the International Monetary Fund.

---

[9] For an appraisal of these recommendations by a group of economists, see the report prepared by K. Knorr and G. Patterson, *A Critique of the Randall Commission Report, op.cit.*, pp. 46-62.

[1] The more important official sources of information on the activities and policies of the Bank during 1953, and the sources of much of the material in this section, are International Bank for Reconstruction and Development, *Eighth Annual Report, 1952-1953*, Wash., D.C., 1953; International Bank for Reconstruction and Development, *Summary Proceedings, Eighth Annual Meeting of the Board of Governors*, Wash., D.C., 1953; Black, E. R., "Policies and Operations of the World Bank," *Lloyds Bank Review*, July 1953, pp. 17-32; International Monetary Fund, *International Financial News Survey* (various issues); International Monetary Fund, *International Financial Statistics* (various issues); National Advisory Council on International Monetary and Financial Problems, *Semiannual Report to the President and to the Congress for the Period October 1, 1952–March 31, 1953*, Wash., D.C., July 1953; and National Advisory Council on International Monetary and Financial Problems, *Semiannual Report to the President and to the Congress for the Period April 1, 1953–September 30, 1953*, Wash., D.C., March 1954.

In 1953, as in earlier years, the United States Administration expressed general approval of its policies and operations. Officials of most other member governments also believed the Bank was doing commendable work, but many of them, especially from the poorer countries, continued to urge the Bank to expand its lending activities.[2] In late 1952 the President of the Bank had stated that if both it and its members took advantage of all their opportunities, the coming year would see a significant increase in the Bank's operations. But, in the event, loans agreed to during 1953 totalled the equivalent of only $257 million, as compared with $292.5 million during 1952, raising the total since the Bank began operations to $1749.9 million, as Table 13 shows. Actual disbursements during the year under review were approximately $240 million, slightly above those of the previous year and exceeded only by those in the first year of the Bank's operations, when large crisis loans were made to France, the Netherlands, Luxembourg, and Denmark, during the period just preceding the inauguration of the European Recovery Program. Principal repayments to the Bank during the year totalled the equivalent of only $3.9 million, were made by eight different borrowers, and raised the total of repayments to the Bank since it began operations in 1947 to just under $15 million.[3] None of the Bank's loans was in default and some of these repayments were in advance of maturity.

A notable feature of the Bank's disbursements during 1953 was that only 70 percent of them were in United States dollars, as compared with 85 percent in 1952 and 93 percent for the

[2] Czechoslovakia, which had never received a loan from the Bank and which had concentrated its efforts at the annual meetings in recent years on preventing the representative of Nationalist China from taking part in the Fund and Bank, was suspended from membership in the Bank, but not the Fund, as of December 31, 1953. This action was taken because Czechoslovakia had failed to remit the balance due on its 2 percent capital subscription to the Bank, payable in gold or dollars. Czechoslovakia had paid three fourths of this amount but had been in default on the remaining one fourth for over two years. China was similarly in default, but it made several token payments in 1951, 1952, and 1953, formally recognized its obligation, and had assured the Bank that payments would be made as soon as the Government was in a position to do so.

[3] These repayment figures do not include repayments on loans which the Bank had resold to private investors. Details on such repayments are not at hand, but it is known that four Dutch shipping companies repaid in 1953, five years before maturity, $12 million which they had borrowed from the Bank in 1948-1949, the paper having been sold to private banks in the United States and elsewhere.

## TABLE 13

*International Bank: Loans Authorized and Disbursed, 1947-1953*
(millions of dollar equivalents)

| Country[a] | Loans Authorized | | | Loans Disbursed | | |
|---|---|---|---|---|---|---|
| | 1952 | 1953 | 1947-1953[b] | 1952 | 1953 | 1947-1953 |
| Australia | 50.0 | 0 | 150.0 | 43.2 | 44.7 | 124.8 |
| Belgium– | | | | | | |
| Belgian Congo | 0 | 0 | 86.0 | 25.6 | 32.2 | 70.6 |
| Brazil | 37.5 | 32.8c | 175.3 | 20.4 | 7.5 | 103.4 |
| Chile | 0 | 20.0 | 37.3 | 5.1 | 2.6 | 15.2 |
| Colombia | 25.0 | 14.4c | 69.3 | 12.3 | 9.1 | 81.8 |
| Denmark | 0 | 0 | 40.0 | 0 | 0 | 40.0 |
| El Salvador | 0 | 0 | 12.5 | 4.2 | 4.3 | 11.9 |
| Ethiopia | 0 | 0 | 8.5c | 2.6 | 0.8 | 5.4 |
| Finland | 23.5 | 0 | 38.1 | 7.1 | 9.0 | 26.7 |
| France | 0 | 0 | 250.0 | 0 | 0 | 250.0 |
| Iceland | 0.9 | 1.6c | 5.9c | 1.7 | 2.1 | 4.5 |
| India | 31.5c | 19.5c | 109.8c | 5.7 | 3.6 | 54.3 |
| Iraq | 0 | 0 | 12.8 | 4.6 | 1.2 | 5.9 |
| Italy | 0 | 10.0c | 20.0c | 5.1 | 4.9 | 10.0 |
| Japan | 0 | 40.2 | 40.2 | 0 | 0 | 0 |
| Luxembourg | 0 | 0 | 11.8 | 0 | 0 | 11.8 |
| Mexico | 29.7 | 0 | 80.3 | 17.1 | 11.6 | 59.4 |
| Netherlands | 7.0 | 0 | 221.5 | 5.6 | 4.5 | 221.5 |
| Nicaragua | 0 | 4.0 | 9.2 | 2.7 | 0.6 | 8.4 |
| Pakistan | 30.4c | 0 | 30.4c | 5.7 | 4.8 | 10.5 |
| Panama | 0 | 1.5c | 1.5c | 0 | 0 | 0 |
| Paraguay | 0 | 0 | 5.0 | 0 | 1.5 | 1.5 |
| Peru | 3.8 | 0 | 3.8 | 0.7 | 1.7 | 2.4 |
| Thailand | 0 | 0 | 25.4 | 9.0 | 8.2 | 20.9 |
| Turkey | 25.2 | 9.0c | 59.6c | 3.7 | 9.5 | 18.9 |
| Union of South | | | | | | |
| Africa | 0 | 60.0c | 110.0c | 22.0 | 24.9 | 57.7 |
| United Kingdom | | | | | | |
| (N. Rhodesia) | 0 | 14.0 | 14.0 | 0 | 8.6 | 8.6 |
| (S. Rhodesia) | 28.0 | 0 | 28.0 | 6.5 | 7.5 | 14.0 |
| Uruguay | 0 | 0 | 33.0 | 8.4 | 11.0 | 18.4 |
| Yugoslavia | 0 | 30.0 | 60.7 | 11.7 | 23.4 | 37.8 |
| Total | 292.5 | 257.0 | 1749.9 | 225.7 | 239.8 | 1236.3 |

a) For details of individual loans—principal amounts, dates of agreement, maturities, interest rates—see: for loans made prior to July 1, 1951, International Monetary Fund, *International Financial Statistics*, September 1951, p. xv, and October 1951, p. xv; for loans made after June 30, 1951, *ibid.*, February 1953, p. 9, and February 1954, p. 9.

b) The total amount of loans granted prior to cancellations was the equivalent of $1781.2 million.

c) As of December 31, 1953, part or all of these loans still required action by the borrower and/or member government before becoming effective.

Source: International Monetary Fund, *International Financial Statistics*, Wash., D.C., January 1952, p. xv; February 1953, p. 9; and February 1954, p. 9.

entire period prior to 1953.[4] This shift reflected both the improved credit and production situation in the nondollar world and the Bank's policy of encouraging purchases from sources most favorable to the borrower.

The purposes and distribution of the loans authorized in 1953 were somewhat more varied than in the preceding year, but they were still heavily concentrated on basic (frequently public utility) projects in the so-called underdeveloped countries.[5] The continued interest of the Bank in the poorer areas of the world was further attested by the decision to maintain representatives of the Bank in the Middle East (in Lebanon) and Latin America (in Brazil). Loans totalling $107.5 million were agreed to for electric power development projects in Brazil, India, South Africa, Nicaragua, and Japan. The Japanese loan was noteworthy, not only because it was the first Bank credit to this country but also because the two United States companies which were the prime contractors for the supply of equipment and services entered into arrangements with the Bank to participate in the loan with a commitment that they would be paid out of the early maturities. Loans for expanding and improving railroads totalled $56.5 million and were made to Northern Rhodesia, South Africa, and Brazil.[6] The loans to Northern Rhodesia and South Africa were mainly in dollars, but it was understood that most of these would be spent in the United Kingdom. Road development loans totalled nearly $21 million and were made to Colombia, Nicaragua, and Brazil. Loans for improving agricultural production were small, totalling only $2.8 million, and were divided between Iceland and Panama. The Icelandic loan was noteworthy in that it was

[4] These calculations include both dollars disbursed by the Bank to borrowers and dollars used by the Bank to purchase other currencies required by borrowers. Borrowers are required to repay in the currency used by the Bank.

[5] The President of the Bank had suggested in 1952 that loans to Western Europe might increase in the future and that credits might be available to assist the European Coal and Steel Community. (See *Survey—1952*, p. 150.) In the event, however, loans were authorized in Europe only to Yugoslavia and to Italy. A Bank mission visited Germany during the year to discuss the possibility of a loan (reportedly to assist German steel concerns), but no action had been taken at year's end. (See *United States News and World Report*, October 16, 1953, p. 110.)

[6] The Rhodesian railway loan complemented a 1952 loan for similar purposes by the Export-Import Bank to Portuguese East Africa. The two loans were helping to finance a new railway line from the Rhodesias to the coast.

in various European currencies, and a smaller loan to that country for improving radio facilities was in sterling. In a transaction similar to one entered into in 1951, the Bank agreed to lend the equivalent of $30 million to Yugoslavia for the purpose of helping that country in a wide variety of projects, ranging from public utilities to various manufacturing undertakings.[7] As in 1951, this loan was entirely in European currencies, although it was anticipated that some of the Swiss francs would be spent for purchases in the United States.[8]

Chile was the first Western Hemisphere country to receive a loan for manufacturing purposes from the Bank: $20 million to help finance the construction of a pulp mill and a newsprint-paper mill. A $10 million loan to Italy was designed to support the next phase in the Italian Government's ten-year development program in southern Italy, for which the Bank had lent a similar amount in 1951. It was agreed that these funds could be used not only to pay for imports directly used in this program, but also for additional imports demanded as a result of the greater activity and employment resulting from the development program. At the annual meetings several of the Governors, but not the United States spokesman, urged the Bank to make more loans which were not tied to specific projects and which could be used to cover the *indirect* foreign-exchange costs of investments. There was no evidence, however, that the Bank intended to make such loans the rule rather than the exception. In 1950 the Bank had helped Turkey set up an Industrial Development Bank and had loaned it $9 million in an experiment designed to permit small borrowers to have access to the World Bank.[9] Most of these funds had been used by mid-1953, and the International Bank, finding that the Turkish bank had encouraged private domestic investment in Turkish industry, agreed to advance another $9 million to replenish the Turkish bank's foreign exchange. The general purposes of the Bank's loans and the areas receiving them for the entire period of the institution's operations are shown in Table 14.

[7] The press reported that a substantial portion of this loan would be used in exploiting uranium mines. See *United Nations World*, April 1953, p. 7.
[8] Black, E. R., "Policies and Operation of the World Bank," *op.cit.*, p. 25.
[9] See *Survey—1950*, pp. 143-144.

TABLE 14

*International Bank: Loans Authorized, by Purpose and Area, 1947-1953*[a]
(millions of dollar equivalents)

| Purpose | Total | Asia and Middle East | Africa | Australia | Europe | Latin America |
|---|---|---|---|---|---|---|
| European reconstruction[b] | 497[b] | — | — | — | 497[b] | — |
| Electric power | 492 | 68 | 88 | 80 | 85 | 271 |
| Transportation | 802 | 72 | 64 | 89 | 85 | 92 |
| Telephone and telegraph | 26 | 2 | — | — | — | 24 |
| Agriculture and forestry | 158 | 51 | — | 54 | 29 | 19 |
| Mining | 28 | — | — | 7 | 16 | — |
| Manufacturing | 146 | 82 | — | 20 | 74 | 20 |
| General development | 111 | 2 | 40 | — | 68 | 1 |
| Total | 1750 | 227 | 192 | 150 | 754 | 427 |

a) Net of cancellations. Prior to cancellations the total was $1781.2 million. The data include a few loans still requiring action by the borrowers before becoming effective.
b) All these loans were made in 1947 or early 1948, prior to the beginning of the European Recovery Program, and were to France, the Netherlands, Luxembourg, and Denmark.
Sources: International Bank for Reconstruction and Development, *Eighth Annual Report 1952-1953*, Wash., D.C., 1953, p. 15, and various press releases of the Bank during the last half of 1953.

The interest rate charged on loans during 1953, including the 1 percent commission charge, varied between 4¼ and 5 percent.[1] Some of the actual and potential borrowers suggested that inasmuch as the Bank was making rather large profits, it should consider reducing the commission charge. Although the Bank's gross income exceeded its gross expenses during 1953 by nearly $32 million, apparently no serious consideration was given to this request.

Officials of the Bank stressed in their public statements that private foreign investment was an indispensable element in the economic development of the so-called underdeveloped countries and held that the Bank's operations paved the way for private flows by financing basic projects which were a prerequisite to private investments and by providing a channel—via the sale of its own bonds and of securities from its portfolio—for private investors to participate in foreign loans.[2] United States officials

[1] The general policy of the Bank has been to charge its borrowers what it cost (or what the Bank estimated it would cost) the Bank to borrow, plus 1 percent commission, plus about ¼ of 1 percent for administrative expenses.
[2] At Bretton Woods it was thought that a great deal of the Bank's business

emphasized that the Bank must not be regarded as a substitute for private direct investment and urged the Bank to use its good offices to assist its members in pursuing policies which would attract private capital. Spokesmen for some of the poorer countries, on the other hand, again argued that the United States and the Bank were overly optimistic as to the amount of private capital that could be enticed into their countries. Some implied that capital movements through governments or international institutions were in fact preferable from their point of view to private investment, in part because private capital was not interested in many of the investments regarded as most important by the underdeveloped countries, in part because of fears of "exploitation" and "interference" by private foreign investors, and in part because capital supplied through governments or their agencies was often less costly.[3]

In its *Annual Report* the Bank again dealt at length with the problems of the so-called underdeveloped areas. It repeated earlier statements that the resources of these areas, if effectively used, were adequate to support a substantially higher level of production and investment; and, as before, spokesmen for these areas replied that the Bank overestimated what the poor countries could do to help themselves. The Bank cited as major obstacles to economic growth in these areas the lack of traditions of political responsibility, the weakness of incentives for material advance, the low standards of education and training, the poverty of resources in some instances, and inadequate appreciation by the peoples that economic progress required patience, great effort, and much self-denial. The Bank went on to emphasize that its experiences had shown that governmental investment-programming units could do much to reduce the misdirection of investment which had been an important feature of the poorer countries' economic his-

---

would consist of giving its guaranty to loans raised in private capital markets. No such operations had been carried out through 1953, and the Bank's President explained that only a couple of proposals for such action had been received and that in these cases it was clearly not a suitable technique. He pointed out also that this type of operation was hampered by its unfamiliarity to United States investors. (Black, E. R., "Policies and Operations of the World Bank," *op.cit.,* p. 30.)

[3] See the record of the panel discussion on "Private International Investment in Underdeveloped Countries," in International Bank for Reconstruction and Development, *Summary Proceedings . . . ,* 1953, *op.cit.,* pp. 27-45.

tory. It stressed that such organizations should be charged with "programming" and not with making detailed blueprints for the economy or with exercising close and coercive economic controls. That is, the Bank recommended that such organizations be charged with formulating broad and flexible development programs which looked ahead for many years; with setting out major investment and production goals; and with providing advice to governments on economic policy measures that affect the amounts and direction of private investment, on appropriate magnitudes and types of public investment, and on the timing of individual projects. The Bank spoke with approval of the governmental programming units which had been set up in several countries, sometimes with the advice and help of the Bank.[4] Spokesmen for some of the underdeveloped countries welcomed this statement by the Bank, asserting that it gave support to the conclusion that such programming was possible without the imposition of totalitarian political regimes. United States officials made no public comment on this section of the Bank's *Report* during the meeting, but it was approved by the United States Executive Director, who is an official of the American Government.

In his July report to President Eisenhower, Mr. Lewis Douglas suggested in general terms that the International Bank should work in closer association with private management and capital and implied that the Bank might, by the terms of its loans, do more to improve the climate abroad for private capital.[5] There were no public indications that the Bank was contemplating changes in its policies and operations as a result of these suggestions. The Randall Commission *Report*, published in January 1954, laid great emphasis on measures to increase private foreign investment but stated that the Bank had performed a useful role and implied that it should continue to operate much as it had in the past.[6]

### Marketing Operations and Financial Resources

Of the equivalent of $1556 million of funds available to the

[4] See International Bank for Reconstruction and Development, *Eighth Annual Report, 1952-1953, op.cit.,* pp. 9-13.

[5] Department of State *Bulletin,* August 31, 1953, p. 278.

[6] Commission on Foreign Economic Policy, *Report to the President and the Congress, op.cit.,* pp. 24-25.

Bank for lending up to the beginning of 1953, nearly $1500 million had been committed and nearly $1 billion had been disbursed.[7] To meet the need for additional funds, the Bank floated three issues of its own bonds during the year, sold a small amount of its portfolio, and obtained consent from some of its members for the use of their 18 percent local-currency subscription to the Bank's capital stock.

Early in the year the Bank paid at maturity $10 million of its serial dollar bonds and 5 million Swiss francs ($1.2 million) of its Swiss franc serial bonds sold in 1950. Switzerland is not a member of the Bank, but Swiss francs continued to be in demand by the Bank's borrowers and two more fifteen-year issues of Swiss franc bonds, totalling 100 million Swiss francs ($23.1 million), were offered publicly in Switzerland by a syndicate of Swiss banks. Both flotations were regarded as successful by the Bank, raising to six the number of issues sold in Switzerland since the Bank began operations. The total of its outstanding Swiss franc bonds at the end of the year was the equivalent of $51.8 million.

The Bank pointed out in its *Annual Report* that the sharp rise in interest rates during the first part of 1953, which accompanied the return of freer money-market conditions in the United States, had "created difficulties." Nonetheless, in late September the Bank marketed its seventh dollar issue: $75 million of three-year, 3 percent bonds. This was a shorter maturity than that of any previous issue and was designed to meet the demand from institutional investors and commercial banks in the United States and abroad for high-grade, short-term bonds. Member governments in eleven foreign countries had asked to buy approximately $20 million of these bonds, and the Bank planned to sell another $20 million in five Western European countries.[8] Prior to the above

[7] The figure of funds available for lending is composed of payments by members on their capital subscription (the 2 percent paid in gold and dollars and that portion of the 18 percent subscription which had been released for use by the Bank), profits from operations, net proceeds of bond sales, proceeds from portfolio sales, and principal repayments.

For a statement of the source and disposition of the funds of the International Bank at the end of each year since it began operations, see International Monetary Fund, *International Financial Statistics*, February 1954, p. 8.

[8] For details, see International Monetary Fund, *International Financial News Survey*, October 2, 1953, p. 109. In early 1954, after interest rates had been permitted to fall in the United States, the Bank floated a $100 million issue of fifteen-year United States dollar bonds.

issue, some 71 percent of the Bank's outstanding *dollar* securities were held in the United States, distributed as follows: 22 percent by insurance companies, 20 percent by mutual savings banks, 20 percent by pension and trust funds, and 9 percent by commercial banks and others.[9]

The Bank also added to its liquid resources by selling the equivalent of some $18.4 million from its portfolio during the year. This was only about half as much as had been sold in 1952 and raised the total since the Bank began operations to the equivalent of $84 million. United States spokesmen at the annual meeting took occasion to note that while these sales were small they were "encouraging" in that they were helping to reestablish the private market for international lending.[1]

Strongly supported by the United States, the Bank continued during 1953 to urge members who had not already done so to permit the use of that part of their subscription to the Bank's capital represented by their 18 percent local-currency contribution. As the supply position in Western Europe improved, a growing number of borrowers expressed interest in buying there rather than in the United States or Canada. The Bank pointed out, however, that if it had to use dollars or Swiss francs to buy the European currencies, then its borrowers had to repay the Bank in dollars or Swiss francs. Since borrowers often found this more difficult than repaying in other currencies, the Bank's operations were restricted and Europe lost export markets. A spokesman for the United Kingdom said his Government could appreciate all this, but that it was also necessary for the Bank and its members to understand the importance of maintaining an outflow of dollars which not only permitted the borrowers to carry on their development programs but also enabled countries selling to them to increase their dollar reserves. Details on releases of the 18 percent local-currency contributions are not available, but several countries made only conditional releases, specifying that the funds were not convertible into other currencies, could be used only for loans to specified countries, and were available only to finance

[9] See International Bank for Reconstruction and Development, *Summary Proceedings* . . . , 1953, *op.cit.*, p. 22.

[1] International Monetary Fund and International Bank for Reconstruction and Development, *Press Release* No. 5, Wash., D.C., September 9, 1953.

purchases of specified goods. Bank officials stated that such releases were preferable to no releases but that they did not adequately meet the requirements of the Bank or of its borrowers.[2]

## E. *PROPOSED NEW INTERNATIONAL FINANCIAL INSTITUTIONS*

Spokesmen for many of the so-called underdeveloped countries of the world had been insisting for years that their economic development "required" larger amounts of foreign capital assistance than existing public institutions, notably the International Bank and the Export-Import Bank, were able or willing to furnish or than private sources could be enticed to provide under conditions acceptable to the recipients. They therefore repeatedly urged that new international financial institutions be created. Taking encouragement from the 1951 report of the United States International Development Advisory Board (*Partners in Progress*, commonly known as the Rockefeller Report), they concentrated on trying to get the United Nations to create an international development fund to make long-term, low-interest loans or grants and to establish an international finance corporation that would make loans to private enterprises without government guaranties and also make equity investments in participation with private foreign and domestic investors. These proposals were debated at length in the United Nations in 1951 and 1952. The United States—supported by many of the other potential large contributors to these institutions—vigorously opposed any action to create a new development fund but reluctantly agreed that the matter be explored further, and found the idea of an international finance corporation interesting but also needing further study.[3]

---

[2] For a discussion of this issue, see International Bank for Reconstruction and Development, *Summary Proceedings* . . . , 1953, *op.cit.*, p. 6, and International Bank for Reconstruction and Development, *Annual Report, 1953, op.cit.*, pp. 39-40. For an example of the sorts of restrictions placed on some of the releases, see International Monetary Fund, *International Financial News Survey*, September 4, 1953, p. 76.

A calculation based on a summary statement of the Bank's sources of funds indicates that only some $25 million of 18 percent funds had been made available during the year. This figure apparently does not include conditional releases which had not been used. (See International Monetary Fund, *International Financial Statistics*, Wash., D.C., February 1954, p. 8.)

[3] See *Survey—1952*, pp. 158-166, and the references cited there for a summary of the discussions on these institutions in 1952 and earlier years.

## Special United Nations Fund for Economic Development

The sharp differences between the potential contributors to and the potential recipients of aid from the proposed new international development fund were compromised in 1952 in a United Nations resolution establishing a group of experts to work out a detailed plan for the proposed authority.[4] This Committee's *Report on a Special United Nations Fund for Economic Development* was completed in March 1953 and was placed before the Economic and Social Council at its Sixteenth Meeting, held in Geneva in July and August.[5] The *Report* was based on the following premises: (a) A cardinal feature of any scheme for economic development must be that the primary responsibility for development rests with the underdeveloped country itself. (b) The continued existence of the grave economic and social consequences of the underdevelopment of many countries constitutes a threat to international peace and to economic stability throughout the world. (c) The existing flow of international capital and technical assistance is not sufficient in many cases to solve these problems. And (d) the economic development of underdeveloped countries is therefore a matter of concern to all United Nations members. The *Report* did not discuss whether a new fund was justified, and it did not deal with the question of whether it was possible or feasible to create such a fund. Rather, it was concerned with the technical problems of how such a fund could be organized and could operate, should its establishment be decided upon. Inasmuch as the debates centered on the issue of whether or not a fund should be created and specific provisions of the *Report* were but little discussed, there is no need to attempt here a summarization of its various provisions.

At the beginning of the debate, a resolution was submitted by some of the poorer countries asking the Economic and Social Council to recommend to the General Assembly that it establish "as soon as possible" a Special United Nations Fund for Economic Development (SUNFED) along the lines suggested by the experts. The United States delegate countered by introducing a draft resolution calling upon the government of each United Nations member, when genuine progress had been made in inter-

---

[4] UN Economic and Social Council Resolution 416 A (XIV), June 23, 1952, and UN General Assembly Resolution 622 A (VII), December 21, 1952.
[5] UN Publication Sales No.: 1953.II.B.1.

nationally supervised world-wide disarmament, to ask its people to devote a portion of the savings achieved by the disarmament to an international fund for development and reconstruction.[6] The United States resolution disposed of the SUNFED *Report* by proposing that the Council state that further refinement of the scheme would be premature and that the *Report* merely be transmitted to the General Assembly for its information.[7]

The discussion followed lines similar to those in 1951 and 1952. The United States delegates, usually supported by those from such other relatively wealthy countries as Canada, France, and the United Kingdom, stated again that the responsibility for economic development was primarily one for the peoples of the underdeveloped areas themselves but recognized, as they had before, that in some cases external aid might be of crucial importance. United States spokesmen stressed somewhat more than had those of the previous Administration the advantages to the rest of the world of receiving foreign investment from private sources and said that such capital investment would be much larger if only the underdeveloped countries were more hospitable to it. They repeatedly reminded the underdeveloped countries that the United States had been and was making large contributions to the poor areas of the world and planned to continue to do so. But, the United States delegates stated, their nation's ability to help the poor areas of the world was limited by circumstances over which it had no control—aggression and threats of aggression by the Soviet-bloc countries. Given the necessity of rearming, the American people were said to be unwilling at that time to accept new financial commitments and, indeed, were most anxious for

[6] This was in keeping with President Eisenhower's widely publicized speech in April. See *New York Times*, April 17, 1953, p. 4.

[7] For a text of the United States draft resolution, see UN Doc. E/AC.6/SR.188. The debate on these and related resolutions continued off and on throughout the last half of the year, taking place in the Economic and Social Council, the Council's Economic Committee, the Second Committee of the General Assembly, and, finally, in the General Assembly itself. Most of what follows was taken from these official sources: UN Economic and Social Council, *Official Records*: Sixteenth Session, 725th-731st Meetings, July 15-18, 1953; UN Docs. E/AC.6/SR.-188 and 189; UN General Assembly, *Official Records*: Eighth Session, Second Committee, 257th-268th Meetings, October 18-29, 1953, and 277th-279th Meetings, November 25-27, 1953; and UN General Assembly, *Official Records*: Eighth Session, 468th Meeting, December 7, 1953. See also *United Nations Bulletin*, August 15, 1953, pp. 143ff.; September 15, 1953, p. 215; November 15, 1953, pp. 465-466; and December 15, 1953, p. 591.

relief from existing tax burdens. American officials argued that since the United States and several of the other countries did not at that time find it possible to contribute to a new fund, it would be a sham to create it; furthermore, they warned, even to raise the question in the United States Congress at that time might jeopardize the continuation of existing aid programs.

United States spokesmen repeatedly emphasized that the new Administration in Washington was sympathetic to the economic-development aspirations of the poorer countries and looked forward to the day when it could do more to help, citing the resolution to so use some of the savings from disarmament as evidence of America's concern and interest. It was apparent, however, from the American statements that virtually no plans had yet been made by the Administration as to what, and how much, would be done in the event of "genuine progress" in internationally super-vised world-wide disarmament.[8]

Spokesmen for many of the underdeveloped nations formally welcomed the United States proposal on disarmament savings, but some of them clearly regarded it as a dilatory tactic. Most of them stated they could not accept the proposition that the creation of the fund should await disarmament for this would mean in-definitely postponing it. They argued that savings from disarma-ment should be regarded as *additional* sources of finance, and many professed not to understand why the United States and the Western European nations, which were spending billions of dol-lars on defense, could not find a few hundred million dollars for facilitating economic development in other areas. None questioned that the Western countries had to look to their defenses, but many insisted that most underdeveloped countries had to defend them-selves against internal unrest and warned that such disturbances—which it was assumed more rapid economic development would help forestall—would endanger world peace. A recurring theme was that economic development should be regarded as a contribution to, and not a result of, disarmament.

[8] Several of those who supported the American resolution on disarmament savings specified that their support was given on the understanding that it did not commit their governments to any future arrangements, and some, for ex-ample New Zealand, noted that while they supported the resolution, any dis-armament savings their nations could achieve would have to go entirely to internal investment.

Russian delegates, together with those from other Soviet-bloc countries, denied the United States charge that they were responsible for rearmament. They did not oppose creating a new international development fund, provided it was not placed under the domination of the U.S. Government or the International Bank (which they regarded merely as a tool of "capitalist monopolies"), but stated that they did not believe it would be of much help to the poorer countries. More effective help, they said, would be given by the rich industrialized countries' lowering their barriers to imports, taking action to stabilize the prices of raw materials, and ceasing the practice of restricting East-West trade. Spokesmen for most of the underdeveloped countries agreed that the policies proposed by Russia and her satellites would be helpful, but there was virtually no support among them for the general position of the Soviet bloc.

Finally, on December 7, the General Assembly of the United Nations approved a resolution on these matters.[9] The first part followed closely the original American draft and stated that the members declared themselves ready, when "sufficient" progress had been made with internationally supervised world-wide disarmament, to ask their peoples to devote a portion of the savings to an international fund for economic development, such fund to be within the framework of the United Nations. No members voted against this resolution, but a few countries abstained on the ground that a "yes" vote would mean acceptance of the proposition that the development of underdeveloped areas was to be conditional on disarmament. Some voting for the resolution insisted, however, that this interpretation could not be placed on a "yes" vote inasmuch as the preamble referred, as the original American draft did not, to these savings as "additional resources."

Given the strong statements by the United States and the other potential large contributors that they were not in the position to make any contributions to a new fund, most of the spokesmen for the underdeveloped countries agreed there was little point in creating a fund without funds. They did, however, insist that the issue be kept alive. The second part of the General Assembly resolution, characterized by one as "more a concession to realism than a stimulus to the imagination," called for further examination of

[9] UN General Assembly Resolution 724 A and B (VIII), December 7, 1953.

the SUNFED proposal in 1954, and the preamble expressed the hope that it would be possible to create such a fund in the near future. This part of the resolution also stated that the members believed that the economic and social advancement of under-developed countries would help to achieve international peace and security. Members of the United Nations and the specialized agencies were therefore invited to comment before the summer of 1954 on the SUNFED proposal and on the degree of material and moral support they could be expected to give such a fund. Presumably this part of the resolution went further than the United States delegates would have preferred, inasmuch as they had stated toward the close of the debate that they could not at that time foresee any conditions under which the U.S. Government would be ready to make contributions to such a fund apart from genuine progress toward international disarmament; and they were not prepared to forecast when such progress might be made.

### International Finance Corporation

Mingled with the debates on the SUNFED was the issue of establishing an international finance corporation to stimulate private foreign investment in underdeveloped areas by helping to finance private undertakings through equity investments and by making loans without government guaranties.

In response to Economic and Social Council and General Assembly resolutions in 1952,[1] the International Bank continued to study the finance corporation proposal and to seek the views of its member governments and business groups on the desirability of establishing such a corporation.[2] The Bank's report, submitted in May 1953, stated that almost without exception the official representatives of the less developed nations supported the creation of such a corporation while most of the spokesmen for more highly developed countries, although showing a sympathetic interest in the idea, were reserving judgment and had not yet formulated definite views.[3] The Bank reported that the views of business

[1] UN Economic and Social Council Resolution No. 416 C (XIV), June 23, 1952, and UN General Assembly Resolution No. 622 A (VII), December 21, 1952.

[2] See *Survey—1952*, pp. 159-162, for a brief statement of the substance of the proposal and of the discussion of it during that year.

[3] For a text of the report, see International Bank for Reconstruction and De-

and financial communities were mixed, but it was implied that the majority of the private business community in the United States was hostile to it, on the grounds, among others, that it was wrong in principle to use public funds for investment in private enterprises and that the establishment of such a corporation would weaken rather than strengthen the incentive of underdeveloped countries to improve the climate for private investors.[4] The Bank concluded that the most significant present fact was that the countries on which the corporation would have to depend for most of its funds had not yet indicated a willingness to commit themselves to contributions and that therefore no useful purpose would be served by a further formalization of the project. Some of the spokesmen for the underdeveloped countries expressed disappointment over what they interpreted as a weakening of support for the corporation by the Bank itself.[5]

Many of the spokesmen for the underdeveloped countries in the United Nations again spoke in favor of setting up the corporation forthwith, although none of them believed it would satisfy more than a small part of their needs and all were much more interested in the SUNFED proposal. As compared with the previous years, more of these spokesmen gave lip service to the benefits their nations would receive from an enlarged inflow of private foreign capital and some stated that their countries must do more to encourage such investments. At the same time, none of these spokesmen dissociated himself from the views of the Yugoslav delegate that private foreign capital was an "outmoded" form of international investment that could not be "resurrected": outmoded because the private profit motive did not produce investment in those sectors of the economy where investments were regarded as most needed by the recipient nations, and impossible to resurrect because many of the so-called underdeveloped coun-

velopment, *Report on the Status of the Proposal for an International Finance Corporation*, Wash., D.C., May 1953.

[4] See, for example, the statement in National Foreign Trade Council, *Final Declaration of the Fortieth National Foreign Trade Convention*, November 16, 17, and 18, 1953, pp. 17-18.

[5] Earlier in the year a State Department official had said that, inasmuch as the International Bank was forced to go to the private banking community in the United States for much of its funds, the Bank could not fail to take "serious account" of the opposition of that community to the international finance corporation. ("Foreign Economic Policy," *Hearings*, op.cit., p. 21.)

tries were newly independent or intended to become so and usually felt it necessary to impose restrictions and controls that discouraged private foreign investors.

The views of the spokesmen for the richer countries on the international finance corporation were, in general, the same as in the past: the idea was an interesting one that needed further study, the primary responsibility for encouraging private capital rested with the underdeveloped countries, and the richer countries were not able to subscribe to the capital of a new international institution at that time.

Early in the year the Assistant Secretary of State for Economic Affairs, a carryover from the Truman Administration who was later replaced, told a Congressional committee that the State Department was "sympathetic" to the creation of such a corporation;[6] but subsequently, in the United Nations, newly appointed officials stated that the Eisenhower Administration had not reached a definite conclusion about the merits of the proposal. The U.S. Government was not, they said, in a position to commit itself to making contributions to such an institution and would not at that time support any resolution which explicitly or implicitly approved taking steps toward its establishment.

When it passed the resolution noted above on the SUNFED, the General Assembly also approved, with United States support, a resolution "recognizing" that, while the economic development of the underdeveloped areas depended primarily on their own efforts and resources, the internal financial resources available to many of them were inadequate to finance the "desired" rate of economic development and that additional external resources, both public and private, would greatly aid these countries.[7]

The resolution requested the International Bank to continue its studies, and governments were urged to give early consideration to the merits of establishing an international finance corporation and to make known their views on the possibility of their giving financial support to it. Those, including the United States, who had stressed the importance of private investment during the discussions were pleased at a second part of the resolution, which "recognized" the "importance of finding means to stimulate the

6 "Foreign Economic Policy," *Hearings, op.cit.*, p. 21.
7 UN General Assembly Resolution 724 C (VIII), December 7, 1953.

flow of external private capital to the underdeveloped countries in order to accelerate their development" and requested the Economic and Social Council to examine the question of the general role of private foreign investments with a view to ascertaining under what conditions such capital flows could contribute to the economic and social development of the underdeveloped countries.[8]

The Randall Commission made no specific references to either the SUNFED proposal or the international finance corporation proposal, but it noted that in the United Nations some of the underdeveloped countries were "claiming a right to economic aid from the United States . . ." and went on to say that "we recognize no such right." Furthermore, the Commission's approval of continuing the technical assistance programs was conditional on their not involving capital investments, and the general tenor of the *Report* was that, except for special circumstances, capital outflows from the United States should come from private rather than official sources.[9]

[8] Another part of this resolution recognized the importance of fluctuations in the terms of trade for the financing of economic development and asked the Economic and Social Council to consider this problem and to make such recommendations as it might find desirable for consideration by the General Assembly.

[9] Commission on Foreign Economic Policy, *Report to the President and to the Congress, op.cit.,* pp. 9 and 12.

# V · TRADE AGREEMENTS PROGRAM

THE Reciprocal Trade Agreements Program, the center of United States commercial policy since 1934, seemed to many observers to be more or less on dead center in 1952. Despite the widespread verbal support in both official and private circles for the principle of "trade, not aid," there was no evidence that those—especially in Congress—who had in the past favored relatively high protection had become less determined in their opposition to a more liberal trade policy even though they were less vocal than those favoring lower import barriers.

Authority to make substantial changes in the nation's trade policies is in the hands of Congress. That body had renewed the Trade Agreements Act for two years in 1951, and, since it was not a pressing legislative issue in 1952, no thorough reexamination of the problem was undertaken by Congress during that year. Such action as Congress did take, or did not take, however, seemed to strengthen the fears of many that the United States was veering in the direction of providing greater protection to domestic producers and of intensifying the conflicts between trade policy and the other international economic policies of the nation.[1]

The victorious Presidential candidate, Dwight D. Eisenhower, had in the campaign given general but qualified endorsement to a national policy of enlarging and liberalizing foreign trade, but he had given virtually no indication of what his position would be on the many specific issues involved. He had promised that the new Administration, composed of members of a political party long regarded as favoring relatively high import barriers, would undertake a thorough reevaluation and reformulation of the nation's commercial practices.

The future trade policy of the United States was the subject of much public discussion in 1953, and a brief summary of some

[1] See *Survey—1952*, Chap. VI, for details on activities in this field in 1952. See also U.S. Tariff Commission, *Effect of Trade Agreement Concessions on United States Tariff Levels Based on Imports in 1952*, Wash., D.C., September 1953.

of the more widely publicized views and statements may serve as the background for the discussion in the following sections of the specific activities during the year of Congress and the Administration.[2] Early in the year the Public Advisory Board for Mutual Security transmitted to the new President a special report on United States trade and tariff policy—undertaken at the request of President Truman some six months earlier.[3] This study, commonly referred to as the Bell Report, concluded that there was urgent need for a drastic revision and liberalization of United States trading regulations, made many specific recommendations for reform, and warned that "if this country does not soon take measures to facilitate an increase in imports, United States exports will fall and American industry and agriculture will be seriously affected."[4] Although this Report received virtually no public recognition from the new Administration, many of the principles and recommendations contained in it were supported by several national private organizations. Such business groups as the United States and International Chambers of Commerce, the Committee for Economic Development, the National Foreign Trade Council, and the National Association of Manufacturers all went on record as favoring a reduction in United States trade barriers.[5]

[2] For one statement of the problems involved, see Foreign Commerce Department of the United States Chamber of Commerce, *International Trade Policy Issues*, Wash., D.C., 1953. See also "The Question of U.S. Foreign Trade Policy," *Congressional Digest*, Wash., D.C., January 1954.

[3] Public Advisory Board for Mutual Security, *A Trade and Tariff Policy in the National Interest*, Wash., D.C., 1953.

[4] *ibid.*, p. 7.

[5] For the views of the groups referred to above, see Foreign Commerce Department of the United States Chamber of Commerce, *International Economic Policy*, Wash., D.C., June 1953; United States Council of the International Chamber of Commerce, *The Expansion of Trade*, New York, April 1953; Committee for Economic Development, *Britain's Economic Problem and Its Meaning for America*, New York, March 1953; National Foreign Trade Council, *Final Declaration of the Fortieth National Foreign Trade Convention*, New York, November 16, 17, and 18, 1953; and National Association of Manufacturers, *Topics of Current Interest in International Economic Relations*, Economic Series, No. 63, New York, September 1953.

The National Association of Manufacturers' stand in favor of a gradual cut in tariffs, quotas, and customs duties, coupled with the suggestion that European businessmen should stop complaining about such impediments and start studying ways to break into the American market, was more moderate than that of many other groups. Nevertheless, the Monsanto Chemical Company—sixth largest chemical manufacturer in the United States and a member of the National As-

These general views were shared by many prominent individuals as well. A survey by the Council on Foreign Relations of the views of 825 "leading citizens" in various occupations throughout the country revealed that 98 percent felt the United States should continue the reciprocal reduction of tariffs; it was also noteworthy that over two thirds of those questioned said they knew of no United States producer whose postwar domestic market had been "damaged" by foreign competition.[6] Perhaps more significant were two surveys, conducted by another private organization, which showed that in 1951 most of the small group of manufacturers polled "were unfavorably disposed toward lowering tariffs to bridge the dollar gap," while in 1953 the same producers, "including even those facing foreign competition," wanted gradually lower tariffs, provided that temporary federal aid were available to those hurt and that protection were granted to certain defense industries.[7] It was also noteworthy that wide publicity was given in the press to the estimate by Howard Piquet that the complete suspension of all United States tariffs (for a limited period and under 1951 conditions) would result in an increase in the value of imports of only between $845 million and $1800 million.[8] This calculation—as well as a statement before the

---

sociation of Manufacturers for over twenty years—resigned from the organization on the ground that the "trend" toward tariff reduction contained in official NAM statements was "detrimental" to the interests of the domestic chemical industry. (*New York Times*, November 15, 1953, p. 86.) It should also be noted, however, that the President of the Dow Chemical Company, while opposing immediate abolition of tariffs, approved of some tariff changes so long as they were slow, judicious, and selective. (*New York Times*, August 27, 1953, p. 41.)

[6] Council on Foreign Relations, *Foreign Trade and U.S. Tariff Policy: A Report on the Views of Leading Citizens in Twenty-five Cities*, New York, March 1953.

[7] *New York Times*, June 18, 1953, p. 45, and *Congressional Record* (daily edition), June 28, 1953, pp. A8921-A8922.

The majority of the Randall Commission, in January 1954, was in sympathy with a proposal presented to the Commission for Government assistance to communities, employers, and workers to facilitate adjustment in case injury should be caused by tariff changes, but said it could not recommend it because this was but a phase of a much broader problem. The Commission did recommend that if it were found necessary on solely military grounds to assure a domestic supply of raw materials this should be accomplished by direct subsidies and not by import restrictions. (See Commission on Foreign Economic Policy, *Report to the President and the Congress*, January 1954, pp. 54-61 and 89-41.) For some comment on these questions, see Knorr, K., and Patterson, G., *A Critique of the Randall Commission Report*, International Finance Section and Center of International Studies, Princeton University, 1954, pp. 29-88.

[8] Piquet, H., *Aid, Trade and the Tariff*, New York, 1953, p. 85.

Randall Commission by a representative of the American Federation of Labor which characterized as "sheer nonsense" an estimate that four to five million workers would be displaced by increased imports if trade barriers were greatly reduced, maintaining that even 45,000 unemployed could be avoided—was often cited in answer to those who forecast dire damage to domestic producers and workers if a more liberal trade policy were pursued.

Those favoring greater protection also tightened their ranks and became more vocal in 1953. Under the leadership of Mr. O. R. Strackbein the Nation-wide Committee of Industry, Agriculture and Labor on Import-Export Policy, representing mostly small industries and firms, was formed for the purpose of counteracting "ruinous free trade proposals."[9] This organization gave wide publicity to its views that lower tariffs would cause great unemployment in the United States, which in turn would lead to "world-wide economic disruption and dislocation"; that the restoration of balanced international trade through the elimination of the dollar gap was not dependent upon further reductions in United States tariffs; that protective tariffs were necessary to maintain adequate defense capacity in many fields; and that freer trade would result in such specialization that the nation would be "dominated" by a few gigantic industries.[1]

As noted in various other sections of this volume, spokesmen—both official and private—for many foreign nations expressed fears over what they often regarded as a new wave of protectionism in the United States and emphasized that important actions by them must await the formulation of policy in Washington.[2] Uneasiness over present and prospective United States

[9] See *New York Times*, March 23, 1953, p. 33, and March 29, 1953, pp. F-1 and -8.

[1] For a more detailed statement of the views of this new organization, see Strackbein, O. R., *Free Trade: A Form of Economic Pacifism*, Wash., D.C., December 1953. In an effort to counter the influence of this organization, a Committee for a National Trade Policy was formed in the summer of 1953 for the purpose of carrying out an "information" campaign to show the importance of larger international trade to world prosperity and to stress the importance of United States export industries. (See *New York Times*, August 6, 1953, p. 29; November 6, 1953, p. 35; and December 20, 1953, pp. F-1 and -6.)

[2] The commercial policy of the United States was a much discussed issue at the annual meetings of the International Monetary Fund and the International Bank. The *Annual Report* of the Fund stressed that more liberal United States commercial policies would contribute greatly to a continued improvement in the

policies was especially noticeable in Canada—the most important single market and source of goods for the United States. An attempt to lessen this concern was made in November, when President Eisenhower announced the establishment of a Joint Committee on Trade and Economic Affairs. This Committee, which would have cabinet stature in both countries, was to "meet periodically to discuss in broad terms economic and trade problems and the means for their equitable solution."[3] So far as the public could tell, however, no matter of substance had been dealt with by the group by the end of the year.

As in many previous years, United States–United Kingdom relations were the subject of special study. In 1953, discussions revolved around the question of sterling convertibility, as described in Chapter IV, Section C, above. It was generally agreed that United States commercial policy was a crucial element in any convertibility attempts by Britain. In the spring the President asked Mr. Lewis W. Douglas to study and report on United

payments position of the rest of the world and would enhance the prospects of reducing or eliminating restrictions on imports from the United States by other countries. (See International Monetary Fund, *Annual Report, 1953*, Wash., D.C., 1953, pp. 24-27.) This view was repeated by the Fund's Managing Director, and the President of the International Bank, presenting his institution's *Annual Report*, stated that the United States "can hardly reconcile her position as the giant of the world economy with the fear of foreign competition, which is implied, and is indeed expressed, in the maintenance of high trade barriers and other restrictions against foreign goods." (International Bank for Reconstruction and Development, *Summary Proceedings, Eighth Annual Meeting of the Board of Governors*, Wash., D.C., October 1953, p. 10.) He went on to give as his opinion that for the United States merely to refrain from reversing the downward trend of United States tariffs would not be enough to put international trade "on an even keel" and much more remained to be done if the United States were to make a durable contribution to the solution of the periodic crises which much of the world had suffered since the war. The Fund Governors for several countries lent their support to these views. United States officials assured the meeting that they were fully aware that American policies had an important bearing on the welfare of other countries, that they welcomed the various suggestions made that the United States liberalize its import policies, and that they would put these suggestions before the Randall Commission but would not attempt at that time to anticipate the recommendations and conclusions of that group. (For the statements on these questions by United States and foreign officials, see International Monetary Fund, *Summary Proceedings, Annual Meeting, 1953*, Wash., D.C., September 1953, pp. 21-80 and 128-130.)

For some press accounts of the discussion on this subject at the Fourteenth Congress of the International Chamber of Commerce, held in Vienna in May, see *New York Times*, May 18, 1953, p. 9; May 19, 1953, p. 12; May 20, 1953, p. 9; and May 22, 1953, p. 38.

[3] Department of State *Bulletin*, November 30, 1953, p. 737.

States–United Kingdom trade and financial relations.[4] In his mid-July report Mr. Douglas said that, as "the world's greatest creditor" nation, the United States could no longer practice with impunity "the protectionist policies of a debtor nation" which for thirty years had "been incompatible with and . . . operated against the reestablishment of international economic and financial health and equilibrium."[5] He therefore urged the United States to start "as soon as possible" to rid its policies of "impediments to freer trade and currencies." As expected, these views were welcomed by those at home and abroad who favored more liberal policies.[6] More important, in the eyes of many, was the fact that President Eisenhower greeted the report warmly, speaking of it as a "most valuable contribution" to thinking on these matters.[7]

Those, both in this country and abroad, who were interested in United States international economic policies focussed their attention during 1953 on the work of the Commission on Foreign Economic Policy—commonly called the Randall Commission after the name of its Chairman—composed of members of Congress and private citizens. The conditions surrounding the creation of this group—charged with examining and making recommendations on the whole field of international economic policy—are discussed briefly in the following section, while the specific recommendations and findings are cited at the appropriate places throughout this document and will not be repeated here. One of the major duties given the Commission by Congress was to study and make recommendations on the subjects of "international trade and its enlargement consistent with a sound domestic economy," and at the first

[4] See Department of State *Bulletin*, April 6, 1953, p. 498, and *New York Times*, March 20, 1953, p. 13, and April 24, 1953, pp. 1 and 18. Mr. Douglas was originally asked to study a much broader range of problems, but his terms of reference were reduced when the Administration decided to create the Randall Commission.

See *Survey—1950*, "Gray Report" in index, and *Survey—1951*, "Rockefeller Report" in index, for references to brief accounts of the reports of two other groups which had been directed in recent years to make official inquiries into the whole range of international economic problems of the United States.

[5] See Department of State *Bulletin*, August 31, 1953, p. 277. For a text of the report and letters concerning it, see *ibid.*, pp. 275-279.

[6] See, for example, *New York Times*, August 30, 1953, pp. F-1 and -5; *The Economist*, August 29, 1953, pp. 554 and 588; *Commercial and Financial Chronicle*, September 10, 1953, p. 19.

[7] Department of State *Bulletin*, August 31, 1953, p. 275. See also *New York Times*, August 26, 1953, p. 26.

meeting of the group President Eisenhower asked it to be "realistic and bold" and, above all, to follow the principle of "what is best in the national interest."[8] The Chairman, along with some other members, was on record as favoring a lowering of United States import barriers, but several members, including the Chairmen of the powerful House Ways and Means Committee and Senate Finance Committee, were commonly regarded as "protectionists." The Commission had the help of a large professional staff and received written and oral statements both in the United States and abroad. It stated that the subject of tariff and trade policy produced more directly divergent statements of alleged fact, more shades of opinion, and more diverse recommendations than any other subject it considered. The Commission's *Report* was published in late January 1954 and the specific recommendations were ridden with dissents; in addition, a strongly worded *Minority Report* by two of the Congressional members was issued and a third member appended to the majority *Report* a long statement dissociating himself from the majority's views on many issues, particularly from its recommendations on tariffs and trade.[9]

The majority *Report* on tariffs and trade policy stated that United States trade restrictions were but one of many groups of factors—both at home and abroad—which were responsible for the world's balance-of-payments difficulties, that the United States was no longer among the high-tariff countries of the world, that many Americans and foreigners had overemphasized the importance of United States import barriers in restricting the flow of international trade. The majority also stated that it did not wish wage levels in the United States to be determined or seriously affected by wage levels in competing industries abroad. Nonetheless, it asserted that neither low foreign wages nor low unit labor costs per se constituted "unfair competition" and agreed that the nations of the free world would be stronger and more cohesive if many of the United States import barriers were reduced, and it made a series of specific recommendations aimed at this objective. In general, the changes proposed were modest and, most observers

[8] Department of State *Bulletin*, October 5, 1953, p. 450.

[9] Commission on Foreign Economic Policy, *Report to the President and the Congress, op.cit.*, and Commission on Foreign Economic Policy, *Minority Report*, Wash., D.C., January 1954.

agreed, represented a compromise designed to get the maximum bipartisan support in Congress for trade liberalization during 1954 rather than to formulate a long-range commercial policy for the nation. Many of those favoring more liberal trade policies by the United States agreed that if all of the specific recommendations of the Commission were favorably acted upon in the next year or two the result would be the biggest single step toward a more liberal international economic policy that had been taken since the Trade Agreements Act of 1934. Still, in view of the violent dissents to the recommendations by some of the more influential Congressional members, not many expected that the Eighty-third Congress would give legislative sanction to more than a few of the proposals. Foreign reception of the *Report*, as indicated in the press, appeared to vary from deep disappointment to cautious and restrained optimism that these recommendations, if in large part implemented, would constitute a first step by the United States toward acceptance of responsibilities commensurate with its influence.

## A. *EXTENSION OF THE TRADE AGREEMENTS ACT*

From 1933, when it was first presented to Congress by Cordell Hull, through 1952 the Reciprocal Trade Agreements Program had been labeled "must" legislation by the Administration, and the Secretary of State had led the fight for its periodic extension by Congress. The Act under which the Program was carried on was due to expire in June 1953, and for the first time in twenty years the question of its extension was to be argued before a Republican Congress by a Republican Administration. There was therefore much speculation as 1952 ended as to the fate of this Program, traditionally associated with a Democratic regime, at the hands of the Republican Party, which had emphasized in its Presidential campaign the general theme "It's time for a change" and the majority of whose representatives in Congress had in the past usually voted against renewal of the Act.

The Trade Program itself had not been an important issue in the election campaign. The 1952 Republican Party platform had favored "the expansion of mutually advantageous world trade" but had also emphasized that the Trade Agreements Program would be carried out on a basis of "true reciprocity" and would be so administered as to protect both American industry and labor against "unfair import competition."[1] Mr. Eisenhower during the campaign had in general aligned himself with the economic internationalists, but his support of the Trade Program was in such qualified terms as these: "While maintaining tariff policies that operate in the interest of our agriculture and industry, we should seek . . . to increase imports . . . which will improve our own economy and help make our Allies self-supporting."[2]

Advocates of more liberal trade policies could find some encouragement in the new President's Inauguration address on January 20, when he said that "we shall strive to foster everywhere, and to practice ourselves, policies that encourage productivity and profitable trade."[3] Some also anticipated that inasmuch as Mr. Eisenhower and his Cabinet were commonly regarded as belonging to the liberal wing of the Republican Party, the new Administration would take the lead in favor of lowering barriers to international trade. It soon became apparent, however, that whatever his personal views on this question, the President did not choose at that time to press for any significant changes in the policies of his predecessor. In his State of the Union message on February 2, after some vague and qualified references to the importance of "profitable and equitable world trade" to the United States, he recommended only that Congress take the Trade Agreements Act "under immediate study and extend it by appropriate legislation."[4] Two months later, on April 7, the President formally requested Congress only to approve a one-year renewal of the Act, "pending completion of a thorough and comprehensive reexamination" of United States foreign economic policy.[5] In this message Mr. Eisenhower made his strongest public plea up to that time for a liberal trade policy: "Our own trade policy as well as that of other countries should contribute to the highest possible level of trade on a basis that is profitable and equitable for all. . . .

[1] *New York Times*, July 11, 1952, p. 8.
[2] Address before the Herald Tribune Forum, October 21, 1952.
[3] Department of State *Bulletin*, February 2, 1953, p. 169.
[4] Department of State *Bulletin*, February 9, 1953, p. 208.
[5] As noted in the first part of this chapter, no less than three such "reexaminations" had been made during the preceding four years.

The solution of the free world's economic problem is a cooperative task. It is not one which the United States, . . . however firm its dedication to these objectives, can effectively attack alone. But two truths are clear: the United States share in this undertaking is so large as to be crucially important to its success—and its success is crucially important to the United States."[6]

Several bills were filed in Congress which embodied the President's request for a simple one-year extension of the Trade Agreements Act, but the Ways and Means Committee of the House decided at the outset to disregard them all and held hearings on the so-called Simpson Bill (H.R. 4294), which was frankly and highly protectionist. Although this measure did grant the President the desired one-year extension, it effectively nullified this gesture by a series of other provisions which, most observers agreed, would have operated to produce a marked increase in the restrictiveness of United States import barriers and would have reversed the policy followed since 1934. One of the more important provisions was that the Tariff Commission recommendations on such things as, among others, invoking the escape clause, setting peril points, proposing special restrictions on agricultural imports, and taking measures to combat "unfair" practices in import trade were to be binding upon the President, instead of merely advisory as in the past. This deprivation of the President's "statutory discretion" was favored by the protectionists because the Tariff Commission is directed by law to consider, by and large, only the position of specific industries, whereas the President has historically also taken into account the effect of these decisions on the national interest. Moreover, the Simpson Bill also would have made the Tariff Commission a partisan body by increasing its membership from six (in practice, three Republicans and three Democrats) to seven (of whom "not more than four . . . shall be members of the same political party").

The scope of the peril-point and escape-clause provisions was also greatly widened in the sense of making injury easier to demon-

---

[6] *S. Doc. 38*, 88d Cong. Other official documents which have been used extensively in the preparation of this section are "Trade Agreements Extension Act of 1953," *Hearings on H.R. 4294*, House of Rep., Committee on Ways and Means, 83d Cong., 1st Sess., April 27 to May 19, 1953; *S. Rpt. No. 472*, 83d Cong.; *H. Rpt. No. 521*, 88d Cong.; *H. Rpt. No. 777*, 83d Cong.; and *H. Rpt. No. 1089*, 88d Cong.

strate. This was done by changing the criterion for invoking the provisions from an increase in imports resulting from concessions which caused "serious injury [in fact or threatened] to the domestic industry producing like or directly competitive articles," as in the existing Act, to an increase in such imports which caused or threatened to cause "unemployment of or injury to American workers, miners, farmers, or producers, producing like or competitive articles, or impairment of the national security."[7] That is, any injury or unemployment to anyone resulting from imports (which need not be "directly" competitive) was to be considered a justification for peril-point or escape-clause action. Furthermore, the proposed Bill would have required that no trade agreement concession entered into in the *past* be permitted to continue in effect if a product on which such a concession had been granted was being imported into the United States under such conditions as to cause or threaten "unemployment of or injury to . . . , etc." Inasmuch as the standard escape clause in existing United States trade agreements, including the General Agreement on Tariffs and Trade, does not provide for the withdrawal of concessions under all these conditions, the results of this and other proposed changes was seen by many as likely to result in a "disruption" or "unraveling" of virtually all the trade agreements which were then in effect.[8]

The Bill reduced the time allowed for investigations by the Tariff Commission on applications for relief under the escape clause and under Section 22 of the Agricultural Adjustment Act —which provides for the imposition of import fees or quotas on agricultural products if imports are found to be (or are likely to be) materially interfering with, or reducing the effectiveness of, any domestic agricultural program of the Department of Agriculture. It was also proposed to amend the Anti-dumping Act of 1921 by eliminating the existing provision that the imposition of duties to prevent dumping be contingent upon a finding that such imports were injurious to domestic industries or were preventing the establishment of domestic industries, in favor of a

[7] The Tariff Commission declared that it had never considered the existing law as authorizing it to consider national defense or security interests in arriving at its findings or recommendations on peril points and escape-clause determinations.

[8] See "Trade Agreements Extension Act of 1953," *Hearings, op.cit.*, p. 1957.

provision applying these duties to "any foreign merchandise [which] is being or is likely to be sold in the United States or elsewhere at less than its fair value. . . ." The Simpson Bill also proposed to recapture for Congress details of tariff making by providing for certain specific new import restrictions. Most importantly, it would have imposed an over-all calendar-quarter import quota on crude petroleum and all products derived therefrom equal to no more than 10 percent of domestic demand for all petroleum oils for the corresponding quarter of the previous year. Within the 10 percent quota, residual fuel oils were singled out for separate treatment and a 5 percent import quota imposed.[9] There was also a provision for imposing on top of existing duties a sliding-scale duty on imports of lead and zinc, the additional duty to vary inversely with the domestic market prices.[1]

Private organizations and individuals appearing before the Committee lined up for or against the Simpson Bill much as they had in past years on the question of extending the Trade Agreements Act. The majority of the spokesmen in favor of the Bill represented such relatively small industries as hats, fur and leather products, pottery, clocks and watches, nut growing, and lead and zinc mining. They were, however, joined by the United Mine Workers and coal industry spokesmen, the so-called independent oil producers, spokesmen for the cattle and dairy industry, and such prominent advocates of protection as Mr. O. R. Strackbein. In addition to straightforward considerations of self-interest, the main arguments of these groups were that national defense considerations required domestic industry to be kept strong and healthy, implying that this rested in part on less for-

[9] The Tariff Commission stated that if the 10 percent quota on petroleum products had been in effect in 1952, the United States would have imported 26.8 percent less crude petroleum and products than it did. As for residual fuel oil, the Commission noted that maximum imports under the 5 percent quota would have been only slightly more than one fifth of what they had been in 1952. (See "Trade Agreements Extension Act of 1953," *Hearings, op.cit.*, pp. 1970-1975 and 1986-1993.)

[1] Several other bills having identical provisions for a sliding-scale duty on lead and zinc products had also been introduced in Congress. The Tariff Commission commented that the domestic effect of the duty would depend upon domestic prices, which could not be foreseen, but that the international effect would be a sharp curtailment of United States imports and possibly foreign production, inasmuch as the United States was the leading world market for these commodities. (See *ibid.*, pp. 1975-1984 and 1994-2014.)

eign competition; that United States employment levels and wages should be protected from the effects of low foreign wage rates and living standards; that tariffs were necessary to make agricultural price-support programs effective; that United States exports had been artificially stimulated during the war and post-war periods and should now be allowed to fall to their "natural levels" instead of imports' being stimulated to balance them; that the tariff was the United States answer to other, more severe restrictions laid down by foreign countries and that there had been a minimum of reciprocity under the Trade Agreements Program; that present tariff levels were the lowest in American history (implying that low average tariffs are necessarily less restrictive); and that rather than "free" trade, the policy of the United States should be to see "fair" trade, the exact meaning of which was not spelled out, although it appeared to signify trade between producers with equal costs.[2]

The Simpson Bill was publicly opposed by importers, including the National Council of American Importers, and by such civic organizations as the Friends Committee on National Legislation, the League of Women Voters, and the General Federation of Women's Clubs. Also arguing against the Bill were several nation-wide business, agricultural, and labor organizations, including the United States Chamber of Commerce (as well as many local Chambers of Commerce), the Committee for Economic Development, the Detroit Board of Commerce, the National Grange, the American Farm Bureau Federation, the Congress of Industrial Organizations, and the National Foreign Trade Council. Officials of the oil companies having large foreign investments and markets, as well as those from certain other industries heavily dependent on exports or imports, also testified against it.

These spokesmen based their arguments against the Simpson Bill and in favor of a simple extension of the existing Act primarily on national (as opposed to individual producer) interests and on international considerations.[3] Their main points were that

[2] The author of the Bill himself at one point gave a reverse twist to the popular 1952-1953 slogan of "trade, not aid," when he said that, if it were determined to be in this nation's interest for other countries to continue their huge imports from the United States, then the burden of providing them with these goods should fall on all Americans, not just import-competing industries.

[3] Some of the witnesses expressed reservations about merely continuing the

for security reasons we must facilitate imports, especially of raw materials, in order to keep important American defense industries operating at high levels;[4] that inasmuch as the rest of the world wanted or needed large supplies of United States products it was in the national economic interest of the United States to have "trade, not aid"—and that if necessary to support such a policy, the Government should help industries which could not meet import competition to redirect their activities into other channels; that high United States trade barriers would frustrate the objectives of the European Recovery Program; that liberal trade policies were a necessary part of American economic and political leadership of the free world and would help to reduce East-West trade and to refute Communist attacks on the sincerity of United States intentions. Virtually no attempt was made to argue the case for freer trade from the classical position that it would result in national gain through a more efficient use of resources; perhaps, as has been suggested, this was because "all the numbers are too small to be impressive."[5] Some witnesses did say, however, that although the probable increase in imports would have little effect on the United States economy as a whole, the effect on foreign nations seeking dollars to raise living standards and to pay for defense commitments would be very important.

In previous years private witnesses had of course appeared at Congressional hearings to expound their views, but it was an established practice that the major responsibility for presenting the case for extending the Trade Agreements Program should fall upon the Administration, and in particular upon the Secretary of State. In marked contrast with the past, the new Secretary of State seemed most reluctant to accept responsibility for the Program and, indeed, resisted attempts by Congressional questioners to pin him down as to his detailed views on trade policy, or even

---

Trade Agreements Program in its current form, testifying that in their view the Program should go further toward encouraging imports than it had in the past. There was, however, no concerted or strong effort to convince Congress that it should at that time do more than extend the existing Act.

[4] During the hearings repeated references were made to the President's Materials Policy Commission study, *Resources for Freedom*, Wash., D.C., June 1952. For a brief statement of some of the major conclusions of this so-called Paley Commission Report, see index of *Survey—1952*.

[5] Stein, H., "Next Steps in U.S. Trade Policy," *Lloyds Bank Review*, October 1953, p. 4.

the extent to which he was speaking for the Administration. He
asserted that he had not yet thought through all aspects of the
problem and that in any case his views represented only 50 percent—the international half—of the Administration's position.[6]
He summed up his position in this statement: "I am against the
Simpson Bill at this time. Whether I will be against it a year from
now, I do not know."[7] His colleagues in the Cabinet were also
unprepared to speak in detail of their views other than to say that
they opposed, at least "at this time," the Simpson Bill. The various Administration spokesmen explained that they had been in
office only a few months and were still "feeling their way." The
heart of their testimony, therefore, was an "earnest recommendation for delay," to be accomplished through a simple one-year
extension of the Trade Agreements Act so as to provide time for
a thorough and comprehensive reexamination of the entire foreign
economic policy of the nation. Two major considerations were
presented to support this plea: such interim legislation would give
the Administration a chance to get its bearings, and it would reassure the allies of the United States that the new Administration
would not take precipitate action in matters that gravely af-

[6] Other members of the State Department had not been so cautious earlier in
expressing their opinions. In a speech at New Orleans on April 17, Assistant
Secretary of State Thruston B. Morton denounced the Simpson Bill as one
"which would tear the vitals out of the present Reciprocal Trade Agreements
Act." "Adoption of such a bill," he went on, "would create consternation among
countries of the free world and would lend credence to the Communist theme
that the United States wants to sell but it does not want to buy." (Department
of State *Bulletin*, May 4, 1953, p. 650.)

These general views were reiterated ten days later in Washington by Under
Secretary of State Walter Bedell Smith, who told a group from the United
States Chamber of Commerce that "hearings opened . . . today on a bill which,
though extending the reciprocal-trade-agreements program, would in effect bring
about a sharp reversal of United States policy to lower barriers to trade in the
free world. The bill would change the Trade Agreements Act from a tariff-reduc-
tion program to a tariff-raising program." (Quoted in "Trade Agreements Extension Act of 1953," *Hearings, op.cit.*, p. 601.)

When queried about the sentiments expressed in these speeches, Secretary
Dulles was careful to avoid supporting them without actually repudiating his
associates, saying that they represented "a point of view" which the Administration thought should be presented to the public as one "element" in the final
decision. He added that it was not to be expected that all Administration spokesmen in all their public speeches would take the same position since the United
States was not a "monolithic" state where no disparate statements were allowed.
("Trade Agreements Extension Act of 1953," *Hearings, op.cit.*, pp. 606 and 608.)

[7] "Trade Agreements Extension Act of 1953," *Hearings, op.cit.*, p. 609.

fected them. Secretary Dulles told the House Ways and Means Committee that in his view foreign countries could be persuaded to accept a "reshaping" of United States foreign-trade policy which resulted from a thorough reexamination of the situation, but they could not stand the "great and sudden shocks" to their economies which would result from abrupt and seemingly arbitrary action by the United States Congress. The Secretary of State warned, moreover, that these governments were already "extremely nervous" as to what the trade policies of the Republican Administration would be—having been told for twenty years that the Republicans were protectionist and isolationist in outlook.[8]

There was little in the testimony of the Administration spokesmen to reduce this nervousness. As compared with their predecessors, there was a marked lack of enthusiasm for the principle of freer trade on the part of the senior Cabinet officers. Both Secretary of Commerce Weeks and Secretary of the Interior McKay stated that they were "good tariff men" at heart, and Secretary Dulles volunteered the information that as a member of the Senate in 1949 he had voted for the inclusion of the peril-points clause in the Trade Agreements Act. Furthermore, Mr. Dulles assured the Committee that if the Act were extended in the form requested by the Administration no attempt would be made to negotiate any new trade agreements during the year, although there might be some minor modifications made in existing agreements. Along with other Cabinet members, he asserted that he would do everything in his power to "speed up" the application of such existing provisions as the escape clause, countervailing duties, and emergency restrictions on imports of perishable agricultural products, designed to "correct" serious injury resulting from imports.[9]

[8] Some members of the Committee replied to this that they were more concerned with protecting the interests of domestic producers who were already suffering under the Trade Agreements Program than with soothing the jitters of foreign nations.

[9] Although Secretary of Labor Durkin did not appear before the Committee, he submitted a statement in support of a simple extension of the existing Act. He stated that difficulties arising from substandard wages and working conditions overseas were receiving "the most careful handling" by the new Administration, and he offered the suggestion that competition resulting from such factors could be minimized by "promoting higher labor standards in other parts of the world."

Later in the year Secretary of Commerce Weeks argued that the United States

As already noted, national defense considerations were stressed by private spokesmen favoring the Simpson Bill and those opposing it, but no witnesses from the Defense Department appeared to give that agency's views.[1] Excerpts from a letter from the Defense Department, dated April 21, 1953, were cited during the hearings and in a House report.[2] This letter said, in part: "The national security of the United States depends not only upon the vitality of segments of our local economy such as those embraced by the petroleum, coal, zinc, and lead industries but more greatly upon the vitality of our whole national economy and the strength of the economies of friendly countries. It is for that reason that the Department of Defense strongly urges a 1-year extension of the authority of the President to enter into foreign-trade agreements uninhibited by restrictions and limitations such as those that would be imposed by [the Simpson Bill]." It should also be noted that the connection between liberal United States trade policies and a successful defense of the free world was discussed in general terms by the Administration during the hearings on the Mutual Security Program. At that time Secretary Dulles said: "if our economic policies [with respect to Western Europe] are such as, for example, simultaneously to expect a big military effort, to cut off their trade with us, to continue their imports from us, to cut off trade with the Soviet world, and get along without any economic aid . . . it is just utterly impossible to preserve anything like the unity and strength that is now represented by NATO.

could not afford to "sacrifice" the high wages and living standards of American labor. He said he was willing to see American industry face foreign competition with respect to all the "ingredients" going into a product except labor and proposed that some guide be worked out for determining tariff levels that would offset the important differences in labor costs which were not already offset by differences in labor productivity. (See *New York Times*, November 17, 1953, pp. 47 and 52.)

[1] It was brought out during the hearings that certain industries did not feel that the Tariff Commission had considered the defense aspects of their output when making decisions on applications for relief under the escape clause. The Tariff Commission itself stated that it was not uncommon for domestic interests opposing a decrease in their tariff protection, or seeking relief, to claim that their industries were important to national defense, but that the Commission had not considered that existing laws authorized it to consider national defense in arriving at a determination. (See "Trade Agreements Extension Act of 1953," *Hearings, op.cit.*, p. 1953.)

[2] *H. Rpt. No. 777, op.cit.*, p. 27.

The whole thing . . . would collapse if those things happened."[3]

During the course of the Trade Agreement hearings, the President formally recommended that a reexamination of the nation's foreign economic policy program be undertaken by a joint commission composed of members of both houses of Congress and of private citizens.[4] Some on the Committee on Ways and Means criticized the request on the grounds that it was merely a device to avoid facing issues, that numerous import-competing industries would be irreparably damaged while waiting for the Commission's report, and that the Commission would duplicate the work—and probably the conclusions—of the Bell committee. Administration witnesses denied the accusation of dilatory tactics and sought to reassure Congress that existing safeguards would be used to protect domestic industries in the meantime. As to the duplication-of-effort charge, they testified that the new group would differ from the Bell committee in that, among other things, it would include Congressmen, thus making it a more representative body and engendering more confidence in its conclusions. The witnesses also asserted that the main purpose of the new Commission would be to give the Administration a "fresh view" of the situation, but that the House Ways and Means Committee would still be the final authority on writing tariff legislation.

Opinion in the Ways and Means Committee was sharply divided, and two bills were finally reported out favorably: the first of these (H.R. 5495) was sent to the full House in early June and was a modified version of the President's request, while the second (H.R. 5496) was reported out in mid-July and was in most important respects the same as the original Simpson Bill. The first provided for a one-year extension of the Act, the establishment of a bipartisan seventeen-member joint commission on foreign economic policy (later known as the Randall Commission), a reduction from one year to nine months in the time allowed the Tariff Commission to investigate and report on an application for relief under the escape clause, and an increase in the membership of the Tariff Commission from six to seven

---

[3] "Mutual Security Act of 1953," *Hearings*, U.S. Senate, Committee on Foreign Relations, 83d Cong., 1st Sess., May 1953, pp. 86–87.

[4] For a text of the letter, see Department of State *Bulletin*, May 25, 1953, pp. 747–748.

members.[5] The Committee report contained a minority opinion by the Democratic members criticizing the provision for adding a seventh member to the Tariff Commission, asserting that this was an obvious and open attempt to "pack" the Commission with the aim of changing it from a nonpartisan fact-finding body to a vehicle for returning to the protectionist days of the Hawley-Smoot tariff. Rather than attempt to kill the bill, however, thus raising "even greater doubts among friendly foreign nations as to the future of United States trade policies," they voted for the measure "with grave misgivings," trusting that the President would use discretion in administering it.[6] Emotions ran high during the debate in the House which followed. There was little attempt at careful economic analysis in the speeches, with the issue of more protection versus freer trade revolving around the size of the Tariff Commission. An amendment to strike out that section of the bill was defeated by a vote of 152 to 115.[7] Many Republicans upheld the enlarged Tariff Commission proposal as one means of insuring more expeditious and more favorable treatment in the future than in the past for domestic producers applying for relief under the escape clause. Many Democrats strongly opposed the measure on the grounds that it would turn the Tariff Commission from a highly respected institution into a "political football," and charged that the Republican leadership of the House was opposing the program of the President and attempting to go "back to an isolationist economy."[8] Some conciliatory speeches were made on the floor by the so-called "pro-Administration Republicans" minimizing the importance of the Tariff Commission question and claiming that the essentials of the bill were the extension of the Act and the establishment of the foreign economic policy commission.[9] In the final House vote the bill was approved in unamended form by a majority of 363 to 35. It was then sent to the Senate.

[5] It was reported in the press that the President had agreed to the seven-man Tariff Commission (it being commonly assumed that the seventh member would be of protectionist leanings) as the price for an otherwise relatively unencumbered one-year extension of the Act and the establishment of his foreign economic policy commission. (See, for example, *New York Times*, June 10, 1953, p. 28.)

[6] *H. Rpt. No. 521, op.cit.,* p. 11.

[7] See *Congressional Record* (daily edition), June 15, 1953, p. 6772.

[8] *ibid.,* p. 6764.          [9] *ibid.,* p. 6735.

The Senate Finance Committee did not hold hearings but did solicit statements from interested parties.[1] Many of the private organizations and individuals who had testified previously before the House Committee submitted similar statements, and in most cases those who had opposed the original Simpson Bill also opposed the seven-man Tariff Commission, while those who had favored the Simpson Bill saw in the enlargement of the Commission a way of getting protection through less direct means. The State and Commerce departments were the only official agencies to submit their views, and both endorsed the House bill but made no mention of the increased membership of the Tariff Commission. The Senate Committee reported out the measure favorably after removing the section adding another member to the Tariff Commission and inserting in its place the proviso that (a) if one half of the Commissioners recommended the same action and on the same grounds, the President could consider this a majority decision, and (b) in the case of a tie vote in the Commission each half of which was unanimous as to action recommended and grounds therefor, the findings and recommendations of both sides would be submitted to the President for consideration, in place of the former practice of dismissing the case.[2] The Committee explained that in making these changes it had taken into consideration the fact that the to-be-established Commission on Foreign Economic Policy would study the Tariff Commission and its operations, thus giving Congress another opportunity to adopt or reject provisions concerning the Tariff Commission.

The debate in the Senate centered on the question of protecting farmers from imports. An amendment designed to speed up action under Section 22 of the Agricultural Adjustment Act, by providing for direct appeal to the Tariff Commission not only by the Secretary of Agriculture but also by other interested parties, was rejected in favor of one which gave the President authority to take immediate action to restrict agricultural imports in case of emergency, without going through the processes called for in the existing law.[3]

[1] "Trade Agreements Extension Act of 1953," *Statements on H.R. 5495*, U.S. Senate, Committee on Finance, 83d Cong., 1st Sess., June 1953.

[2] *S. Rpt. No. 472, op.cit.*, p. 8.

[3] The first amendment was designed primarily to help the wool growers and was defeated after it was pointed out that the Secretary of Agriculture had

After being passed by the Senate by a voice vote, the bill was sent to a conference committee for reconciliation of the differences between it and the House-approved version. After much discussion, the Senators finally won their point on the composition of the Tariff Commission. As finally approved in early August, Title I of the Trade Agreements Extension Act of 1953 extended the Act for one year, shortened the time allowed for Tariff Commission reports on escape-clause investigations from one year to nine months, continued the standard caveat on GATT (added in conference), and provided for emergency Presidential action under Section 22 of the Agricultural Adjustment Act. Title II followed the recommendations of the Senate Finance Committee as to action on a divided vote of the Tariff Commission. Title III authorized the establishment and spelled out the duties of the Commission on Foreign Economic Policy. The bill became law[4] almost two months after the previous Act had expired.

Most of the "safeguarding," i.e. protectionist, provisions of the original Simpson Bill—plus a new provision for putting into effect a previous Tariff Commission recommendation for relief of domestic watch producers under the escape clause—were included in a revised version of H.R. 5496 (H.R. 5894). Without further hearings, this bill was reported out favorably by the Ways and Means Committee of the House in mid-July, over the vigorous objections of the minority members, who characterized it as action to protect "specific and particular localized industries" without reference to "the implications on other interests, our national policy and our foreign policy."[5] In the House debate that followed, many of the same arguments that had been used to defend or attack the original Simpson Bill were applied to its progeny. There was much patriotic rhetoric, but the most telling argument against the bill was that it would prejudge the entire issue of United States foreign economic policy at a time when

already asked the President to have the Tariff Commission make a study of the wool situation under the terms of Section 22. (*Congressional Record* [daily edition], July 2, 1953, p. 8141.)

Senator Kefauver, in an attempt to liberalize the bill, proposed an amendment to extend the Act for three years and to eliminate certain of the restrictive features of the existing law. This was defeated.

[4] P.L. 215, 83d Cong., August 7, 1953.

[5] *H. Rpt. No. 777, op.cit.,* p. 26.

steps were being taken under another law to set up a Commission to study this problem. The bill was finally recommitted to the House Ways and Means Committee.[6]

The Randall Commission published its *Report* in January 1954, and, as noted above, the majority made a series of recommendations designed to liberalize moderately United States trade policy.[7] Although the specific recommendations showed that important concessions had been made to the more protectionist-minded members of the group, dissents were recorded to many of the individual proposals and a strongly worded *Minority Report* was issued by Congressmen Reed and Simpson.[8]

The majority *Report* called for an extension of the Trade Agreements Act "for not less than 3 years, with appropriate safeguards" and said that, on the basis of the experience gained during this period on the effects of this and other recommendations, and of the actions taken abroad, "consideration should then be given to extending the . . . Act for a longer period than 3 years, with such safeguards as experience then indicates to be necessary."[9] The Commission recommended that the peril-point and escape-clause provisions be retained in the law but that the President be "expressly . . . authorized to disregard findings under these provisions whenever he finds that the national interest of the United States requires it." The Commission recommended that the President be authorized, during the three-year period, "to reduce existing tariff rates [pursuant to multilateral negotiations] by not more than 5 percent of present rates" per year; to reduce tariffs, unilaterally or reciprocally, by not more than 50 percent of the effective rates on January 1, 1945, "on products which are not being imported or which are being imported in negligible volume"; and "to reduce to 50 percent ad valorem, or

---

[6] See *Congressional Record* (daily edition), July 28, 1953, p. 9905.

[7] See Commission on Foreign Economic Policy, *Report to the President and the Congress, op.cit.*, pp. 48-53. See also Commission on Foreign Economic Policy, *Staff Papers, op.cit.*, pp. 249-372. For a report on a conference in which a group of economists criticized the Commission's commercial-policy recommendations as being inadequate to meet the needs of the United States, see Knorr, K., and Patterson, G., *A Critique of the Randall Commission Report, op.cit.*, pp. 18-34.

[8] See Commission on Foreign Economic Policy, *Minority Report*, Wash., D.C., January 1954.

[9] Commission on Foreign Economic Policy, *Report to the President and the Congress, op.cit.*, p. 49. According to the press, the Commission had seriously considered recommending a ten-year extension of the Act.

its equivalent, any rate in excess of that ceiling," with the proviso that the above-mentioned reductions "should not be cumulative as to any commodity."[1] The Commission also recommended simplifying tariff schedules with respect to both commodity definitions and rate structures, eliminating "foreign value" as a basis for valuing imports for tariff-duty purposes, speeding up the application of antidumping duties and permitting the continuance of imports pending investigation of suspected dumping, reviewing the effectiveness of countervailing-duty provisions in the present law, continuing the unconditional most-favored-nation policy, and maintaining existing or similar sanitary and health standards for imported goods. With respect to the "Buy American" provision, the Randall Commission recommended that the President be authorized "to exempt . . . bidders from other nations that treat our bidders on an equal basis with their own nationals," and that pending such an amendment to the law procurement agencies should be directed "in the public interest to consider foreign bids which satisfy all other considerations on substantially the same price basis as domestic bids."[2]

## B. ACTION UNDER THE ESCAPE CLAUSE

The escape clause permits a party to a trade agreement to withdraw a concession which it finds has caused or threatens to cause serious injury to domestic producers as a result of increased imports. It has been included in all new trade agreements signed by the United States since 1943 and is a part of the General Agreement on Tariffs and Trade.[3] The clause is commonly re-

[1] Although the *Report* is not clear, it appears that the Commission intended these provisions to replace, and not be in addition to, the existing authority to reduce rates by not more than 50 percent of the rates in effect on January 1, 1945. For many commodities this authority was already exhausted.

[2] The President's Materials Policy Commission had criticized the "Buy American" provision in its 1952 report, and President Eisenhower had also voiced some opposition to it. But Congress took no action during 1953. For some discussion in the press about the "Buy American" Act, see *New York Times*, January 8, 1953, p. 21; April 21, 1953, p. 12; April 28, 1953, p. 28 (editorial); May 15, 1953, p. 88; May 20, 1953, p. 13; May 27, 1953, p. 22; June 16, 1953, p. 43; June 17, 1953, p. 19; June 19, 1953, p. 20 (editorial); July 28, 1953, p. 88; and January 6, 1954, p. 14; *Fortune*, July 1953, pp. 67-68 (editorial); and *The Economist*, April 25, 1953, pp. 204 and 219-220; June 20, 1953, pp. 819 and 835; and February 6, 1954, pp. 892-893.

[3] Except for direct Congressional action, the escape clause is the usual channel by which domestic producers seek relief from foreign competition. There are

garded as a manifestation of protectionism, and enlarging its scope has been a continuing aim of those favoring higher import barriers.[4] As noted above, efforts in early 1953 to obtain legislation easing the way for domestic producers to receive relief from foreign competition under the clause were unsuccessful. This was greeted with muted enthusiasm by the liberal trade elements, who asserted that the battle had been postponed, not won. Furthermore, they argued, although the existing provision had resulted in but few withdrawals or modifications of concessions, it was highly restrictive of imports in that the knowledge that concessions could be thus withdrawn served to discourage potential imports and to dampen incentives to develop export industries abroad for the American market. Moreover, the Tariff Commission is responsible for advising the President on invoking the escape clause and the appointment of two high-tariff advocates to the Commission in 1953 was interpreted by many as boding ill for more liberal import policies.[5] One of the men replaced, however, was commonly regarded as protectionist, and there was no evidence of any sharp change in Tariff Commission recommendations following the new appointments.

---

however, other measures in the hands of the Administration for giving relief; the most important of these are under Section 22 of the Agricultural Adjustment Act and are discussed in Section E of this chapter.

Section 337 of the Tariff Act of 1930 authorizes the President, on the basis of studies by the Tariff Commission, to exclude imports whose entry constitutes unfair competition. This provision has rarely been used in recent years, but in 1953 three complaints by United States producers were filed with the Commission. One concerned imports of multiple-compartment cooking pans; it was subsequently dismissed by the Commission on the ground that the facts did not warrant a formal investigation. The other two dealt, respectively, with imports of certain synthetic jewels and certain plumbing fixtures. Both of these complaints were under investigation at year's end.

Section 336 of the Tariff Act of 1930 permits the President to increase the import duties on goods not covered in trade agreements to an amount which will equal the excess of the cost of production in the United States over that in the principal supplying country. During 1953 the Tariff Commission continued to investigate the difference in production costs of certain household chinaware and kitchen utensils, but it had made no recommendations to the President by the end of the year.

[4] See *Survey—1951*, pp. 146-151, and *Survey—1952*, pp. 174-180, for brief accounts of United States escape-clause activities during those years.

[5] See *New York Times*, April 6, 1953, pp. 1 and 9, and April 7, 1953, pp. 41 and 48, and *The Economist*, August 8, 1953, p. 390. For a more moderate view of the significance of the new appointments, see Stein, H., "Next Steps in U.S. Trade Policy," *Lloyds Bank Review*, October 1953, p. 10.

During 1953 the Tariff Commission received nine new applications for relief under the escape clause[6] and had on its docket twelve applications from previous years.[7] Of these applications, the Commission dismissed two (on hard cord and twine and fluorspar) during the year, seven were still in process of investigation as the year ended, and twelve investigations had been completed.[8] In the twelve completed investigations, a majority of the Commission recommended against invoking the escape clause in the case of nine commodities, having found that imports as a result of tariff concessions were not of such amounts, either absolute or relative, as to cause or threaten to cause serious injury to domestic producers of like or directly competitive products. These cases covered household china tableware, wood screws, estrogenic substances, chalk whiting, wood-wind musical instruments, cotton-carding machinery and parts, watch bracelets and parts, rosaries, and mustard seed. The majority of the Commission did recommend that tariffs be increased on briar pipes and screen-printed silk scarves. The Commission split evenly on the application for relief for handblown glassware, and, under the terms of the 1953 Trade Agreements Act, this case was also sent to the President.[9]

The Tariff Commission's recommendation to raise the duty on imports of briar pipes had been sent to the White House on December 22, 1952, but Mr. Truman chose to leave the decision

[6] On watch movements and parts, groundfish fillets, lead and zinc, straight pins, safety pins, fluorspar, mustard seed, cloverseed, and scissors. The first two items were second applications. (See *Survey—1952*, pp. 177-178, for the statement by President Truman when rejecting the first recommendation for invoking the escape clause on watch imports.)

[7] On briar pipes, certain kinds of household china, wood screws, estrogenic substances, chalk, screen-printed silk scarves, wood-wind musical instruments, certain kinds of cord and twine, cotton-carding machinery and parts, rosaries, certain types of watch bracelets, and handblown glassware.

[8] Official accounts of escape-clause investigation recommendations are published by the Tariff Commission in a series entitled *Report to the President on Escape Clause Investigation under Section 7 of the Trade Agreements Extension Act of 1951*. For less detailed accounts, see the relevant sections of U.S. Tariff Commission, *Fifth Report on Operation of the Trade Agreements Program, July 1951–June 1952*, Wash., D.C., 1953, and U.S. Tariff Commission, *Thirty-seventh Annual Report*, Wash., D.C., 1953.

[9] In addition, the Tariff Commission, in response to a Presidential request, reviewed its earlier-accepted recommendation that the duty on dried figs be increased and recommended that the higher duty be continued for the time being. President Eisenhower approved this recommendation but asked the Commission to keep the case under review and report to him when "altered circumstances" indicated that the tariff could again be lowered.

to his successor. This case, involving a small industry, aroused great interest both at home and abroad as a possible clue to the future tariff policy of the new Administration. The prevalent view in Europe was that the future for that area's exports to America would indeed be bleak if the U.S. Government increased the existing duty (ranging upward from 75 percent, depending on the type of pipe) on imports of such a nonstrategic item. President Eisenhower, presumably aware of the implications of this case, decided to postpone his decision and asked the Tariff Commission for further facts.[1] Several months later the Tariff Commission submitted another report, repeating its recommendation that the duties be raised. Nearly three months later the President rejected this recommendation, primarily on the ground that the difficulties of the domestic industry were more the result of a decline in the popularity of pipe smoking than of increased foreign competition.[2] The President's decision was regarded as "encouraging" by foreign trading interests, but it was noted in the press that the outcome had been in doubt for almost a year and that a major complaint against United States commercial policies was their uncertainty, rather than the actual height of tariffs.[3]

The Tariff Commission recommended in April that the President withdraw all Trade Agreement concessions on screen-printed silk scarves; the effect of this would have been to double the import duty. Two months later the President stated that he "declined to accept" the Commission's recommendation at that time and asked that further study be given to the question, explaining that he was reluctant to modify concessions pending the report of the Commission on Foreign Economic Policy.[4]

The other escape-clause case presented to the President in 1953 involved handblown glassware and was of special interest because the Tariff Commission had split evenly in its recom-

---

[1] See *Foreign Commerce Weekly*, March 2, 1953, p. 28.

[2] The President tempered his disagreement with the Tariff Commission by noting that the law limits the factors the Commission can take into account in making its recommendations but that it is the President's responsibility to weigh these recommendations in the light of considerations of "public policy or national interest which lie beyond the scope of the Tariff Commission's field of inquiry. . . ." (Department of State *Bulletin*, November 30, 1953, p. 755.)

[3] *New York Times*, November 11, 1953, pp. 1 and 41.

[4] See *Foreign Commerce Weekly*, June 22, 1953, p. 32.

mendation, making this the first case to come under the provision of the 1953 Trade Agreements Act which permits the President to consider either recommendation as being that of the majority in such instances. Once again, however, after two months' study, the President declined to make a decision without further information, the effect being to retain for the time being the existing tariffs.[5]

The Randall Commission, in its early 1954 *Report*, noted that although there had been over fifty applications for relief under the escape clause, the President had invoked it with respect to only three products.[6] The Commission concluded that adequate reassurance as to the stability of the nation's trade policy would be provided by its recommendation that the escape clause and the peril points be retained[7] but that the law be amended expressly to authorize the President to "disregard findings under these provisions whenever he finds that the national interest of the United States requires it."[8]

## C. *CUSTOMS SIMPLIFICATION*

In recent years opinion has been growing in both official and private circles at home and abroad that existing United States customs regulations are unnecessarily complex, obsolete, and time-consuming, and often inequitable, in many instances constituting almost as important a deterrent to larger imports as the actual

[5] Under provisions written into the Trade Agreements Act of 1951, the President was directed to insert the escape clause in all existing trade agreements "as soon as possible." (See *Survey—1952*, pp. 179-180.) In July 1953 and again in January 1954, President Eisenhower reported to Congress that discussions with Ecuador were continuing on inserting the clause in that trade agreement but that the Administration felt it was still not "practicable," for the reasons stated in President Truman's report of July 10, 1952, to "approach" the Governments of El Salvador, Guatemala, and Honduras about including the escape clause in the trade agreements with them. (For the reports, see *H. Doc. 205*, 88d Cong., reprinted in Department of State *Bulletin*, July 20, 1953, p. 92, and *H. Doc. 296*, 88d Cong., reprinted in Department of State *Bulletin*, February 1, 1954, p. 178. Previous reports on this matter were printed as *H. Docs. 43* and *54*, 88d Cong.)

[6] Commission on Foreign Economic Policy, *Report to the President and the Congress*, op.cit., p. 51.

[7] The Tariff Commission conducted no peril-point investigation during 1953 inasmuch as the United States did not undertake any trade agreement negotiations.

[8] For a criticism of these recommendations and of the escape clause and the peril points by a group of American economists, see Knorr, K., and Patterson, G., *A Critique of the Randall Commission Report*, op.cit., pp. 19-21.

tariffs. In recognition of this, a customs simplification bill was introduced by the Administration in 1950; when that failed of Congressional approval the proposal was reintroduced in 1951, at which time it was passed by the House in amended form but died in the Senate Finance Committee. This lack of legislative approval was generally attributed more to Congressional inertia in the face of the complex technical provisions of the proposed bills and to the pressure of more urgent legislative matters than to outright opposition.[9]

One of the first recommendations to Congress by President Eisenhower when he took office was that it revise customs regulations so as "to remove procedural obstacles to profitable trade,"[1] and in May 1953 the House Ways and Means Committee held hearings on H.R. 5106, which incorporated "nearly all" of the suggestions made by the new Administration. This measure fell far short of the proposals recommended in the early 1953 Bell Report and was somewhat more diluted than the specific proposals submitted by the previous Administration in that, among other things, the controversial proposal that "American selling price" be eliminated as the valuation basis for coal tar and organic chemical products was not included. Nor did the 1953 proposal include, as had the 1951 measure, a series of provisions which were similar to the relevant articles of the General Agreement on Tariffs and Trade but which were not obviously desirable in the sense of lowering costs of customs administration without reducing protection. The general objectives of the bill were to make the administration of customs laws more economical, to simplify certain procedural requirements so as to reduce the delays and uncertainties in importing, to remove certain inequities in existing procedures, and to eliminate provisions regarded as obsolete.[2] Many of the host of specific problems dealt with in the

---

[9] See *Survey—1952*, pp. 180-181, and the references cited there for a discussion of the proposals in earlier years. See Chapter 7 of the Public Advisory Board for Mutual Security, *A Trade and Tariff Policy in the National Interest, op.cit.*, for an early 1953 analysis urging a thoroughgoing reform in United States customs procedures.

[1] President Eisenhower, State of the Union message, reprinted in Department of State *Bulletin*, February 9, 1953, p. 208.

[2] Most of the information in this section was taken from "Customs Simplification," *Hearings on H.R. 5106*, House of Rep., Committee on Ways and Means, 83d Cong., 1st Sess.; *H. Rpt. No. 760*, 83d Cong.; and *S. Rpt. No. 632*, 83d Cong.

bill were generally accepted as desirable by virtually all the witnesses. Included among these were such matters as simplification of the requirements for marks of origin, elimination of some procedures in connection with transfers of commodities between warehouses, the repeal of certain penalties for undervaluation of imports, provisions to permit correction of administrative errors *without appeal to courts, repeal of many obsolete accounting provisions,* liberalizing the free-entry provisions for travelers, widening the number of people authorized to sign ships' manifests, simplifying the procedures for verifying documents, extending the time during which samples of various goods might remain in the United States free of duty, etc. Three of the proposals, however, were controversial: changing the formula for appraising imports for purposes of assessing ad valorem duties, altering the method for converting foreign currencies into dollar equivalents, and increasing the value of duty-free entry for certain goods.

The Treasury Department, as the agency most directly concerned with customs administration, was the chief Administration spokesman for the bill. This proposal, it was argued, would be a substantial step toward improving service to the importing public at the least possible cost to the taxpayer although its passage would by no means bring a "customs millennium." Other departments of the Administration submitted written statements recommending enactment of the measure on the grounds that it would facilitate the development of mutually profitable trade and help other countries to earn their own way. It was emphasized that the existing complexities and uncertainties were particularly important as "psychological barriers" to imports.

All the private witnesses who appeared before the Committee, including those representing the American Tariff League, approved the general purposes of the bill, but specific sections of it excited extreme opposition.[3] As in the past, the proposal to substitute "export value" as a preferred basis of valuation for the

___

[3] Only a few witnesses took occasion to inform the Committee that they believed the proposal did not go far enough. The feeling of those who had earlier argued for even more changes appeared to be that the proposal under consideration was such an improvement over the existing state of affairs that its passage should not be prejudiced by adding more controversial items.

former criterion of "the foreign value or the export value, which-ever is higher," was regarded as the core of the bill.[4]

Support for this provision was based primarily on the fact that it would eliminate the necessity for detailed investigations to determine the value of imported commodities on the foreign domestic market, thus reducing the expense and delays associated with the existing system of valuation.[5] Criticism of this provision came chiefly from those who saw it as likely to reduce the amount of protection afforded the domestic producer. Their main arguments were that "foreign value" was usually higher than "export value" and thereby furnished a form of protection without which certain domestic industries could not survive; that the bill went beyond the scope of customs simplification and got into tariff legislation since ad valorem duty levels are determined by the value assigned to an article as well as by the appropriate tariff rate; and that the proposed changes, by giving customs appraisers more discretion than they had under the existing law, could, "in the hands of a free trader, who wanted to favor the importer, . . . result in great fraud."[6] Those opposing this section also questioned whether much simplification of customs administration would result inasmuch as they believed that many more investigations under the Anti–dumping Act would be requested as a result of the use of the "export-value" criterion.

The draft bill also proposed several changes in procedure for converting foreign-currency prices into their dollar equivalents for customs valuation. The Administration characterized these as merely getting rid of archaic provisions, restating the conversion rules in terms of current international financial practices,

---

[4] For brief definitions of such other criteria as "United States value," "parity value," "cost of production" (or "constructed value"), which were to be used if "export value" were not ascertainable, see *H. Rpt. No. 760, op.cit.,* pp. 13-15.

[5] In testifying before the House Appropriations Committee in connection with Treasury Department appropriations for 1954, Assistant Commissioner of Customs David B. Strubinger had said on March 25: "Delays of a year in the final determination . . . of duty . . . are frequent; delays of from 1 to 2 years are not uncommon; and longer delays do occur. These delays do not reflect any incompetence or inefficiency on the part of customs officers. . . ." (See "Treasury-Post Office Departments Appropriations for 1954," *Hearings,* House of Rep., Subcommittee of the Committee on Appropriations, 1953, p. 516.) It should be added that witnesses at the customs simplification hearings did not question the efficiency of the Bureau, given the regulations it was charged with enforcing.

[6] "Customs Simplification," *Hearings, op.cit.,* p. 72.

and simplifying the day-to-day computation of customs duties. It argued that the results of the proposed changes would be the same as under existing law. Some of these changes were unopposed, but great controversy arose over the proposal to give statutory basis to the existing practice of recognizing the fact that many countries use multiple exchange rates and of accepting the rate applied by a foreign country to a specific export as the appropriate one. Some witnesses objected to what they felt was the granting of official support to the practice of multiple exchange rates; others believed the proposed changes would give the Administration too much discretion in determining the appropriate rate if there were more than one; and others, representing firms suffering import competition, took this occasion to urge that when multiple currency practices were followed the rate used for conversion purposes should be the one which resulted in the highest dollar valuation. The currency conversion proposals were also contested on the grounds that they had been derived from the abandoned ITO Charter and from the GATT, which, it was emphasized, had never been ratified by Congress. The only other provision of the bill to receive serious criticism was that which proposed to raise the limit on the value of duty-free mail importations from $1 to $3. This was strongly opposed by spokesmen for manufacturers and retailers of inexpensive items, who expressed the fear that their businesses would be destroyed by competition from foreign mail-order houses if the proposal were made law.

Before reporting the bill out favorably, the Ways and Means Committee did alter slightly the wording of the section pertaining to valuation so as to make it clear that appraisers were granted no increase in discretionary power. The Committee also deleted the provision to increase to $3 the value of duty-free mail importations, stating that this was done in the absence of further assurances that the "undesirable results" mentioned by witnesses could, in fact, be avoided.[7]

The House debate centered on two amendments offered from the floor. One provided that the duty on reimports of certain nonprecious metal commodities which had previously been exported from the United States for further processing should be

---

[7] *H. Rpt. No. 760, op. cit.*, pp. 3-4.

based only on the additional labor and processing cost rather than the total value of the finished article. This was approved by the House. The other, introduced at the suggestion of the Treasury Department, provided that injury to American producers be a precedent condition for imposing countervailing duties. This was defeated. The bill was then passed by a voice vote and sent to the Senate Finance Committee. This Committee held no hearings, it being late in the session. It reported the bill out favorably, but only after deleting what were generally regarded as the most important sections—those which changed the criteria for valuing imports and the regulations for converting foreign currencies into dollars for valuation purposes. The Committee justified these deletions on the ground that the sections were highly controversial and indicated a need for more extended hearings than it was possible for the Senate Committee to hold at that time.

The Committee also removed the amendment introduced on the House floor relating to the duty on reimported nonprecious metal products on the grounds that the Treasury Department (which had not reported on this matter to the House Committee) had informed the Senate Finance Committee that such legislation would not simplify, and might even increase, the work load of the Bureau of Customs and that the Tariff Commission had judged the amendment to be not only confusing in language but designed essentially to provide tariff relief rather than customs simplification. The Committee further stated that its approval was in no way connected with approval or disapproval of the GATT, but a statement to that effect was not written into the measure. This diluted version was passed by the Senate on July 27 with but little debate, and in the interests of getting some kind of customs simplification law on the books, the House accepted the Senate changes on July 28. The original sponsor of the House measure immediately introduced a new bill (H.R. 6584) which contained the three deleted provisions; the Ways and Means Committee of the House reported it out favorably the next day, and on the following day the House passed the bill and sent it to the Senate, where it remained.

The President signed the Congressionally approved measure (P.L. 243, 83d Cong., August 8, 1953) and noted that the new law contained a large portion of the legislation needed to revise customs in line with his earlier recommendations. He expressed his gratification that the few Treasury proposals which had been deleted from the original bill were embodied in H.R. 6584 and said that he hoped this would receive early consideration by the Senate.[8] The new law, although much weaker than the original bill, still represented a considerable reduction in red tape and procedural requirements. On the whole it was regarded by those American and foreign businessmen, as well as foreign governments, who were urging a more liberal trade policy for the United States as a more encouraging sign of future trends than was the renewal of the Trade Agreements Act.[9] The Randall Commission supported the President's recommendation for prompt consideration of H.R. 6584 by the Senate and, in addition, suggested the Treasury Department study and report on proposals to further simplify valuation standards by using actual invoice prices, to simplify classification of articles not already enumerated in the tariff schedules, and to modify certain detailed administrative provisions of the tariff laws in the interests of efficient customs administration.[1]

## D. *EIGHTH SESSION OF THE CONTRACTING PARTIES*[2]

Since 1947, when the General Agreement on Tariffs and Trade (GATT) was concluded at Geneva, the Contracting Parties have

[8] For the text of this statement, see Department of State *Bulletin*, August 17, 1953, p. 202. For a list of interim rules applied by the Customs Bureau, see Department of Commerce, *Foreign Commerce Weekly*, August 31, 1953, p. 18.

[9] See article by M. L. Hoffman in the *New York Times*, August 5, 1953, p. 1. *The Economist* (August 8, 1953, p. 390), however, was dubious about the significance of the law, which it considered a "token rather than a real triumph for the liberal trade policies the President has supported."

[1] See Commission on Foreign Economic Policy, *Report to the President and the Congress, op.cit.*, pp. 46–47.

[2] The main sources of information for this section were the *Press Releases* issued by the European Office of the United Nations during the Eighth Session, and European Office of the United Nations, *International Trade News Bulletin*, Geneva, October 1953, pp. 406–419. Brief official accounts of the results of the session will be found in *United Nations Bulletin*, November 15, 1953, p. 467; and Department of State, *Press Release* No. 598, October 27, 1953, reprinted in Department of State *Bulletin*, November 16, 1953, pp. 677–680.

For an account of proceedings at earlier sessions, see *Survey—1952*, pp. 181–191, and references cited there. For an official account of the pre-1953 activities of the Contracting Parties, set "against a background of the main developments

held periodic "sessions" to discuss and take decisions on problems that have arisen under the operation of the Agreement. The eighth such session was held in Geneva from September 17 to October 24, 1953. The thirty-three governments comprising the governing body of the GATT all sent delegations to the session,[3] and ten non-member governments and eight intergovernmental organizations were also represented.

At the outset a United States delegate relayed to the meeting President Eisenhower's hope that all the members would remain "firmly dedicated" in their common task of raising world trade levels; reminded the group that the United States was in the midst of reassessing its own foreign economic policies; and stated that his Government believed the time had come to "reassess" the GATT. Delegates from other countries welcomed the reappraisal of United States policies being undertaken by the Commission on Foreign Economic Policy, and several asserted that fundamental changes in American policy were necessary if the rest of the world were to be able to restore equilibrium in its balances of payments. Despite the uncertainties concerning the future international economic situation, particularly as it was dependent upon United States policies, the general atmosphere in the Eighth Session was more optimistic than it had been in the 1952 meeting.

### Complaints against the United States

Criticisms of actions of the United States were again a prominent feature of the discussions, and, as in earlier years, these were primarily directed toward American policy on certain agricultural products.[4] Strong complaints had been registered at the 1951

---

in international trade," see Contracting Parties to the GATT, *International Trade, 1952,* Geneva, June 1953.

[3] Liberia withdrew from the GATT on June 18, 1953. (See Department of State *Bulletin,* June 29, 1953, p. 917.)

[4] One happy note was sounded at Geneva on this group of problems. On June 10, 1953, the United States had imposed a yearly quota of 4.5 million pounds on imports of shelled filberts under the authority of Section 22 of the Agricultural Adjustment Act. Turkey complained at once that this action nullified the benefits from concessions granted by the United States under the GATT. At the Eighth Session the abolition of the import quota as of September 30, 1953, was announced by the United States delegate. The Turkish delegate expressed his country's gratitude for this "prompt action," which, he said, indicated that the United States was fully aware of its role in securing international cooperation and was sincere in its desires to restore freer world trade. The Italian delegate

and 1952 sessions against the quantitative restrictions imposed by the United States on the importation of certain dairy products under Section 104 of the Defense Production Act. The United States delegates had acknowledged that Section 104 was in conflict with provisions of the GATT, recognized the right of others to take retaliatory action, and said the Executive Branch would continue its efforts to get Congress to repeal the offending section.[5]

Congress did allow Section 104 to expire in mid-1953, but only in return for assurances from the Administration that restrictions necessary to make the domestic price-support program effective would be imposed on imports of dairy products, fats, and oils under Section 22 of the Agricultural Adjustment Act (see Section E, below). The United States delegate reported this action to the Eighth Session of the GATT. He assured the other delegates that the United States was seeking to "correct the basic difficulties" of the domestic dairy industry but stated that the position of that industry was especially critical in 1953 as a result of an unexpected increase in domestic production. He pointed out that conflicts between agricultural and trade policies were not peculiar to the United States and were among the problems which the Contracting Parties would probably wish to consider in any future review of the GATT. He added that his Government was "very regretful" that this problem still existed but was "confident" that a satisfactory solution would yet be found.

Delegates from other nations found the new United States restrictions to be much as they had been under Section 104, and some reported that they found them even more stringent. The bitter complaints of earlier years were repeated, and the United States delegate was reminded that such restrictions made it difficult for other countries to earn dollars and so forced them to reduce their purchases of United States exports. The complaints against the United States were somewhat tempered by the knowledge that the conflicts between United States agricultural policy and trade policy were being examined by the Randall Commission.[6] The

---

associated himself with the Turkish representative's remarks. (For a summary of this discussion, see European Office of the United Nations, *Press Release GATT/156*, October 7, 1953.)

[5] See *Survey—1952*, pp. 182-188.

[6] See Commission on Foreign Economic Policy, *Report to the President and Congress*, op.cit., pp. 28-84.

mild action taken by the Contracting Parties is discussed in Section E, subsection a, below.[7]

Turkey, Greece, and Italy had in 1952 registered complaints against the increased duty on dried figs imposed by the United States under the "escape-clause" provision, and the Administration had promised to ask the Tariff Commission to review the case and to report the results of this review at the Eighth Session. At the same time, the Turkish Government had announced a decision to impose increased duties on certain United States products for the duration of the higher rate on dried figs, and discussions were initiated between the United States and Greece in regard to compensatory concessions which could be made to Greece.[8] As noted earlier, the Tariff Commission found in 1953 that the increased rate was still necessary. This was duly reported at the Eighth Session, together with Turkey's "disappointment." The Greek delegate also reported that no "satisfactory solution" had been found in their case. The Contracting Parties thereupon adopted a resolution noting that talks would be continued between the Governments of the United States, Greece, and Italy; reaffirming their conviction that the desired solution was a restoration of lower duties; and requesting the three Governments to report further action at the Ninth Session.

The United States export subsidies on raisins, in existence since 1949, had been criticized at the previous session on the ground that the United States was taking over the traditional markets of Greece and Turkey in third countries. Subsequent negotiations had resulted in a 30 percent reduction in the United States subsidy for the 1953-1954 crop period, but the Greek delegate reported at Geneva that the situation for his country had worsened because Turkey had in the meantime decided to subsidize raisin exports. The Turkish delegate explained his country's subsidy as an emergency protective measure imposed, among other reasons, because of the continuing United States subsidy. He pointed out that it was no greater than the United States subsidy. The United States delegate defended his Government's action on the

[7] For an account of the discussion and the text of the resolution adopted, see European Office of the United Nations, *Press Release GATT/135*, Geneva, October 5, 1953, and *Press Release GATT/138*, Geneva, October 18, 1953.

[8] For an account of the retaliatory measures taken by Turkey, see *New York Times*, February 22, 1953, pp. F-1 and -6.

grounds that the international dollar shortage made the "normal demand" for United States raisins ineffective and that the subsidy was not intended to increase United States production. He expressed the hope that the recent general improvement in the international balance-of-payments situation would soon eliminate the necessity for such payments.

The Italian delegate, supported by those from South Africa and the United Kingdom, complained against the United States subsidies on orange exports to European markets, charging that this policy was depriving other producers of traditional markets. In reply, the United States delegate said that the orange subsidy, like that for raisins, was designed to permit the United States to maintain its traditional markets until the return of "more normal" conditions. He pointed out that the subsidies had been reduced in recent years and that United States exports of oranges to Western Europe had not increased as much as those from Italy, Spain, or North Africa. Nonetheless, he said, the United States would be glad to consult on the issue with the Italian and South African delegations.[9]

### Complaints against Other Contracting Parties

The United States and Canada had lodged a complaint against Belgium at the Sixth Session, in 1951, charging that certain quantitative restrictions imposed on imports from the dollar area (designed to redirect some of Belgium's imports to European sources in order to reduce her European Payments Union surplus) were damaging their trade and were in violation of the GATT. Belgium gave assurances then, and again at the Seventh Session, in 1952, that these restrictions would be removed as soon as possible. At the Eighth Session, the Belgian delegate reported that in 1953 his Government had eased restrictions on imports of commodities representing approximately 70 percent of the value of total dollar imports into the Belgium-Luxembourg Customs

---

[9] Several delegates, but not those from the United States, expressed grave concern over what appeared to be an increase in the use of export subsidies. Many regarded Article XVI of the Agreement—which requests a country using an export subsidy to discuss the possibility of limiting the subsidization if its effect has been to damage seriously the interests of another contracting party— as a weak provision. The United Kingdom delegate advised the others that his Government would try to get "stronger and more precise" provisions on export subsidies incorporated in any revised version of the GATT.

Union. Both the United States and Canadian delegations welcomed this action but said they were anxious to know when further liberalization would be undertaken and asked Belgium to help exporters by publishing promptly detailed information on the administration of her import restrictions. It was agreed that additional informal consultations should be held and that the matter would be retained on the agenda for the Ninth Session.[1]

The U.S. Government noted that the French Government had included in its 1953 budget a tax of 0.4 percent ad valorem on all imports and exports of France and her territories and questioned whether this tax was consistent with France's obligations under the GATT. The French delegate told the Contracting Parties that the tax was a fiscal measure designed to provide social security for French agricultural workers and was so small as to have no significant effect on international trade. But he recognized that the tax did infringe on certain GATT provisions and stated that his Government would remove it from the next budget. This, however, was not done.

Several other complaints were heard and discussed in which the United States was not a major participant. Among the more important was the failure of Brazil to remove those features of her internal taxes which, it was admitted, discriminated against certain exports of the other contracting parties. This question had been on the agenda of the Contracting Parties for several years, and in 1953 both France and the United Kingdom "expressed great disappointment" over the "continued delay" in removing the offending provisions. The matter was put on the agenda for the Ninth Session. Much more violent criticism was directed at the failure of Belgium to remove the discrimination arising from a special 7.5 percent ad valorem tax on imports designed to countervail a system of family allowances for Belgian workers.[2] The system was first protested in 1951. Since that time the number of complainants had grown, and in 1953 the Danish delegate said that he was "beginning to doubt the sincerity" of Belgium in this matter. The Belgian representative said that his

---

[1] European Office of the United Nations, *Press Release GATT/139*, Geneva, October 14, 1953.

[2] See European Office of the United Nations, *Press Release GATT/135*, Geneva, September 28, 1953.

Government was "deeply concerned" with the problem but that it was a more complex matter than outsiders might think. At the close of the session it was announced that the Belgian Council of State was examining a draft law designed to correct the situation; the item was maintained on the agenda for the Ninth Session.[3]

### Consultations on Quantitative Restrictions

Quantitative restrictions on imports or exports are banned, in principle, by the GATT. Article XII, however, permits the use of such restrictions when found necessary to safeguard a member's external reserve position and balance of payments, and Article XIV permits the discriminatory application of such restrictions during the "postwar transition" period. Any country intensifying its restrictions—or maintaining discriminatory measures after March 1952—is required to conduct consultations annually with the other contracting parties.

Twenty-two of the thirty-three contracting parties maintained quantitative restrictions during 1953, and most of them were to some extent discriminatory. In contrast to 1952, however, when there had been a general trend toward the intensification of such restrictions, 1953 found many countries relaxing their direct controls over imports and, on balance, some decline in their discriminatory application. Little information was released as to the substance of the consultations held during the Eighth Session, but the official statements said that there was a "full and frank discussion" of the reasons for and the effects of the restrictions.[4] Apparently, as in 1952, no attempt was made to seek collective pronouncements on the justification of the policies of individual countries, but the delegates from nations whose policies were the

[3] Some complaints that had been voiced at previous sessions were settled prior to the 1953 meeting. Notable were the decision of Greece in the spring of 1953 to abolish certain "emergency" import taxes and to reduce to the GATT-bound level some import-duty "coefficients" which had been increased in 1952. The Governments of Germany and Norway reported that they had held bilateral discussions after the Seventh Session on the issue of German discrimination against Norwegian sardines and had reached an agreement.

[4] European Office of the United Nations, *Press Release GATT/146*, Geneva, October 24, 1953. See also Contracting Parties to the General Agreement on Tariffs and Trade, *Basic Instruments and Selected Documents, Second Supplement*, Geneva, January 1954, pp. 39-52.

subject of consultations promised to bring the opinions of other members to the attention of their respective governments.[5]

In these consultations the general improvement in the world's payments position was noted.[6] The United States delegate said that his Government viewed this improvement as the result of "fundamental readjustments" and as constituting "a challenge and an opportunity" for all nations to abolish their postwar discriminatory restrictions—which, he said, had distorted the pattern of United States production though they had not affected the total level of United States exports. The Canadian delegate supported the United States position, but several others pointed out that the improvement did not extend to all countries and many asserted that "special" and "temporary" factors accounted for much of the recent increase in dollar receipts by the rest of the world.[7]

### Accession of Japan

The question of Japan's engaging in multilateral tariff negotiations under the GATT with a view toward subsequent accession was discussed at the Seventh Session of the Contracting Parties in 1952. British and French delegates led the opposition to any action at that time, and the issue was referred to an intersessional committee.[8] This committee met in February 1953 and recommended that, provided certain safeguards were set up to prevent her entry from disrupting international trading patterns, Japan should become a contracting party at an early date through the normal procedure of participation in a new round of tariff negotiations. These negotiations did not take place, however, in part because the United States could not participate, and several other countries insisted that they could accept increased competition

[5] As stipulated in the GATT, these discussions were carried on in cooperation with officials from the International Monetary Fund and consideration was given to the results of similar consultations between the Fund and certain of its member nations. See Chapter IV, Section B, above.

[6] European Office of the United Nations, *Press Release GATT/134*, Geneva, October 2, 1953. See also the discussion of the International Monetary Fund in Chapter IV, Section B, above.

[7] The Randall Commission also concluded that the world's dollar problem was far from solved. See Commission on Foreign Economic Policy, *Report to the President and the Congress*, op.cit., pp. 3-5.

[8] See *Survey—1952*, pp. 188-189, and *United Nations Bulletin*, February 15, 1953, p. 134.

from Japanese exports only if the United States market were made more accessible.[9] In August 1953 Japan requested permission to accede provisionally to the GATT and to take part in GATT activities; in return, Japan said she would bind most of her tariffs and formally accept all obligations of the Agreement.[1]

The United States delegate strongly supported the Japanese application. He characterized such a provisional arrangement as "both equitable and wise" in view of Japan's position as a large trading nation, of her efforts to conform to "the spirit and objectives" of the GATT, and of her loss of the Chinese market and the ending of grant aid from the United States.[2] Several other delegates supported this position, but the United Kingdom spokesman opposed it. He warned that, rightly or wrongly, many countries still feared Japanese competition and would raise their tariff barriers against all nations if Japan became a contracting party and so were entitled to receive equal treatment with other GATT members. He argued that, given the uncertainty of United States policy and the proposed general review of the GATT, the issue should be deferred.[3] The representatives of France, Australia, and New Zealand associated themselves with the British delegate. In the end, with six abstentions,[4] the members voted to invite Japan to participate in the work of the Contracting Parties and their subsidiary bodies and a declaration was drawn up stating that, pending official accession of Japan, trade relations between signatory countries and Japan would be conducted according to GATT rules.[5] Inasmuch as the United States generalizes the

---

[9] As a condition for getting Congress to extend the Trade Agreements Act, Secretary Dulles had promised that no new tariff negotiations would be undertaken in 1953. See Section A, above.

[1] European Office of the United Nations, *Press Release GATT/129*, Geneva, September 23, 1953.

[2] Department of State *Bulletin*, October 12, 1953, pp. 495-496.

[3] European Office of the United Nations, *Press Release GATT/132*, Geneva, September 24, 1953.

[4] The United Kingdom, Australia, New Zealand, Southern Rhodesia, South Africa, and Czechoslovakia. Some observers considered it noteworthy that the Commonwealth had split on this issue. (*New York Times*, October 24, 1953, p. 8, and October 25, 1953, p. 12.)

[5] The text of the decision may be found in European Office of the United Nations, *Press Release GATT/144*, Geneva, October 23, 1953, and a synopsis of the general debate which preceded it may be found in European Office of the United Nations, *Press Release GATT/132*, Geneva, September 24, 1953.

The declaration remained open for signature through December 31, 1953, by

application of the most-favored-nation clause, this action meant no changes in her treatment of Japanese imports.

*Waiver of Obligations under Most-Favored-Nation Clause*

Article I of the General Agreement requires the contracting parties to apply unconditional most-favored-nation treatment to their tariffs; but it also permits the continuation of margins of preference existing on April 10, 1947—the most important of which are the so-called British imperial preferences. At the Eighth Session, the United Kingdom requested the other parties to approve a waiver of Article I which would permit certain goods from the Commonwealth countries to continue to enjoy duty-free entry despite any future tariff increases imposed by the United Kingdom on imports of similar goods from other countries. The British delegate insisted that the requested waiver was merely a "technical" measure designed to place the United Kingdom on an equal footing with other countries in the matter of using the tariff to protect domestic industry and agriculture. He asserted that it was not intended to divert trade from foreign to Commonwealth suppliers. Strong opposition to the request was voiced by the delegates from several European countries, who saw it not as a "technical" matter but as a question of principle and feared it was an opening wedge which might lead to a general repudiation of the rule against the establishment of new preferences.[6] The United States delegate—whose Government had frequently in the past argued for a reduction in the imperial preferences—refused to take a firm position, saying that he had sympathy with both the supporters and the critics of the British proposal.[7] The question threatened to create a serious split between the United Kingdom and the Continental countries, which in turn would have

---

which time it had been signed by twenty-one countries, including the United States and Japan.

[6] Inasmuch as Britain was committed under various agreements with the Organization for European Economic Cooperation to reduce her quantitative restrictions on imports from the European countries, some viewed this request as designed to frustrate the OEEC program by replacing quantitative restrictions with permanent tariff protection. (See *The Economist*, September 19, 1953, p. 771.) According to a *New York Times* correspondent, however, most neutral observers believed that the British were "perfectly sincere" in their statements as to the purpose of the request. (*New York Times*, September 26, 1953, p. 6.)

[7] A résumé of the general debate may be found in European Office of the United Nations, *Press Release GATT/128*, Geneva, September 28, 1953.

threatened the future of the General Agreement.[8] High-level diplomatic talks failed to resolve the issue, but a compromise was finally reached whereby the waiver was authorized, provided the resulting tariff increases did not divert a substantial amount of imports to Commonwealth suppliers and provided the waiver was applied only to such Commonwealth goods as had traditionally enjoyed duty-free entry into the United Kingdom. Procedures were also approved for consultation and arbitration in individual cases, with the GATT organization acting as the final judge on possible violations of the principle of Article I.[9] Although this was much less than the British delegate had originally asked, the United Kingdom shortly thereafter notified the Contracting Parties that it proposed to increase tariffs on about forty items under the waiver provisions.[1]

## Rebinding of Schedules

Under the existing commitments the contracting parties were to be free as of the end of 1953 to change unilaterally the tariff concessions negotiated under the General Agreement—concessions covering some 55,000 items which currently accounted for over four fifths of the world's trade. In order to avoid an "unraveling" of past accomplishments and extensive renegotiations, one of the major concerns of the Eighth Session was reaching agreement on a "tariff truce" while member governments reassessed their individual foreign-trade policies and the future role of the GATT itself. The delegates from the United States and Canada led the fight for binding the existing schedules for another eighteen months, emphasizing the importance of preventing a substantial increase

[8] For press accounts of the discussion, see *New York Times*, September 2, 1953, p. 10; September 22, 1953, p. 18; September 26, 1953, p. 6; October 23, 1953, p. 5; October 24, 1953, p. 8; and October 25, 1953, p. 12. See also *The Economist*, September 19, 1953, p. 771, and September 26, 1953, p. 878.

[9] European Office of the United Nations, *Press Release GATT/150*, Geneva, October 24, 1953.

Australia was granted a waiver of obligations under Article I with respect to imports of primary products from the Territory of Papua–New Guinea. This was justified on the grounds that the preferential treatment in the Australian market would aid the economic development of the Territory. Australia gave assurances that the waiver would not be used in such a way as to injure the competitive trade of other countries. (See European Office of the United Nations, *Press Release GATT/149*, Geneva, October 24, 1953.)

[1] *The Economist*, October 31, 1953, p. 850.

in tariffs while the United States was reexamining its international economic policies. Most of the other delegates agreed that it was desirable to have the schedules continue in force, but several gave notice that their governments might ask for a renegotiation of duties on certain items imported by themselves or their dependencies.[2] A declaration was adopted extending the life of the schedules until July 1, 1955. The declaration remained open for signature until December 31, 1953, and specified that it applied only to those contracting parties that signed it, that signatories were not bound with respect to nonsignatories, and that any negotiations between signatory and nonsignatory parties would be carried on subject to the renegotiation provisions of Article XXVIII of the General Agreement. By early 1954 all the contracting parties except Brazil, Czechoslovakia, and Peru had signed.[3]

## Review of the GATT

Perhaps the most important decision taken by the Contracting Parties at the Eighth Session was the unanimous vote that the time had come for an extensive review of the operations and the administration of the General Agreement. Virtually all the delegates agreed that while the GATT had "served international trade well," economic conditions within the participating nations and the economic relations among them had so changed since the General Agreement came into existence in 1947 that it was time to have a formal review of the institution. Opinion differed, however, as to what such a review should seek to accomplish. Some delegates, notably those from Norway, Brazil, and Indonesia, urged that the occasion be used to transform the GATT into a charter for a new international trade organization, including provisions for stabilizing prices of raw materials, maintaining full employment, promoting economic development, controlling international cartels, and so forth. There was no indication in 1953

[2] Such notice was given by the delegates from the United Kingdom, Turkey, India, Greece, New Zealand, Australia, Belgium, and the Netherlands.
[3] The general debate on the extension of the schedules is summarized in European Office of the United Nations, *Press Release GATT/127*, Geneva, September 28, 1953. Details of the declaration and the ensuing debate are contained in European Office of the United Nations, *Press Release GATT/143*, Geneva, October 28, 1953.

that the Eighty-third Congress would look more favorably on such an organization than their predecessors had when killing the Havana Charter in 1950;[4] and the United States delegate at Geneva—supported by those from Sweden, Canada, Italy, and the Netherlands—spoke in favor of more moderate objectives, urging that the review "should not be too ambitious as to the scope of activities to be covered" and should be concerned with seeing how the present provisions of the GATT could be improved.[5] The British delegate and others emphasized that there was little point in undertaking a thorough review of the GATT until the U.S. Government decided on the outlines of its future trade policy. The final decision was to convene a session of the Contracting Parties on October 14, 1954, unless the intersessional committee should recommend postponement, for the purpose of examining "to what extent it would be desirable to amend or supplement the existing provisions of the GATT, and what changes should be made in the arrangements for its administration, in order that the GATT may contribute more effectively towards the attainment of its objectives." Under the decision each of the contracting parties was asked to submit proposals and suggestions regarding this review by July 1, 1954.

The Randall Commission noted in its *Report* that the GATT had never been approved by Congress and that the questions which had been raised about the constitutionality of United States participation had created uncertainties about the future role of America in the Agreement. It specifically recommended that the organizational provisions of the GATT should be renegotiated— "with a view to confining the functions of the contracting parties to sponsoring multilateral trade negotiations, recommending broad trade policies for individual consideration by . . . the various countries, and providing a forum for consultation regarding trade disputes"—and then submitted to Congress for approval.[6] The intent of this recommendation was not clear, but some observers feared the effect might be not to strengthen and make more permanent the General Agreement and United States participa-

[4] See *Survey—1950*, pp. 172-177.

[5] For a summary of the discussion, see European Office of the United Nations, *Press Release GATT/148*, Geneva, October 19, 1953.

[6] Commission on Foreign Economic Policy, *Report to the President and the Congress, op.cit.*, p. 49.

tion in it, but rather to destroy most of the organization's effectiveness by taking away its administrative powers.[7]

## Other Major Activities

Among the many other matters discussed at the Eighth Session, the following deserve mention here. Article XX of the GATT permits the maintenance during the postwar "transitional period" of quantitative import restrictions under certain specific conditions. This permission was originally scheduled to expire on January 1, 1951, but the time limit was extended for one year at the Fifth Session and for an additional two years at the Sixth Session. With little debate, the authority was again extended, until mid-1955. The first annual report by the European Coal and Steel Community, describing those activities of the Community which were relevant to the waivers granted its members in 1952 with respect to the application of the most-favored-nation clause and the nondiscriminatory application of quantitative restrictions,[8] was discussed and received "general approval" by the Contracting Parties.[9]

Various administrative barriers to trade, including valuation methods, determination of nationality of imports, and consular formalities, continued to be studied during the Eighth Session by working parties of the Contracting Parties, assisted by representatives of the International Chamber of Commerce.[1] The Contracting Parties again extended (until December 31, 1953) the time allowed for Uruguay to study and sign the Annecy and Torquay protocols.[2] The Philippine Government announced an

[7] See Knorr, K., and Patterson, G., *A Critique of the Randall Commission Report*, op.cit., pp. 21-24.

[8] See *Survey—1952*, pp. 187-188.

[9] For details, see European Office of the United Nations, *Press Release GATT/-145*, October 28, 1953, and Department of State *Bulletin*, November 16, 1953, p. 679.

[1] A GATT convention on samples and advertising media, opened for signature on February 1, 1953, had been signed by three governments—the United States, West Germany, and Greece—by the end of the year. Twelve more signatures were needed before the convention could become operable.

For further United States action on customs simplification, see Section C, above.

[2] The Uruguayan House of Representatives met in November and approved the two protocols, and Uruguay became a contracting party in December. Brazil had signed the Torquay Agreement in February 1953 and during the year under review had agreed with the United States on a number of new tariff concessions under its terms.

indefinite postponement on any decision to accede to the GATT in view of the negotiations, then in a preliminary stage, with the United States regarding a revision in the terms of the 1946 Philippine Trade Act. The Contracting Parties, as was the practice, considered and acted upon rectifications and minor modifications of certain schedules which had been requested by various members, incorporating the approved changes in a protocol.

The Contracting Parties again discussed at some length various aspects of a French proposal calling, in general, for participants to reduce their tariffs by 30 percent in three annual stages and for the reduction of individual rates to prescribed "floors." It was agreed that the scheme required extensive study by the various governments, and the only decision taken was to submit the proposal to the member governments for "consideration and comments."[3] The United States delegate at Geneva stated that his Government would study the plan carefully and would submit it to the Randall Commission as a "possible line of approach." That Commission, however, made no reference to it in its *Report*.[4]

## E. *CONFLICTS BETWEEN TRADE AND AGRICULTURAL POLICIES*

For years the United States has pursued domestic agricultural policies that often conflicted with the nation's foreign-trade policies, such inconsistencies usually being resolved in favor of the former. The most important *immediate* source of the conflicts was the relatively rigid price supports maintained for farm products at levels frequently well above those in other markets and often resulting in the accumulation of large surpluses within the United States. Inasmuch as many of the commodities affected were ones for which the United States was either an important importer or exporter, the consequences have been that special barriers, in addition to

[3] For details of the plan, see Contracting Parties to the GATT, *A New Proposal for the Reduction of Customs Tariffs*, Geneva, January 1954. For some press discussion of the proposal, here and abroad, see *New York Times*, January 18, 1954, p. 8, and *The Economist*, January 23, 1954, p. 259.

[4] A year earlier, some observers had expressed the hope that the plan might have great appeal for the Republican Administration in Washington inasmuch as its approach differed from that of the Reciprocal Trade Agreements program —associated in the minds of most with the Democratic Party. (See, for example, *New York Times*, December 24, 1952, p. 5.)

tariffs, have been erected against imports and subsidies of one kind or another have been paid on many exports. Both practices have elicited strong complaints from foreign nations, although many of them have also followed practices with respect to the agricultural sectors of their economies which were incompatible with a system of free and nondiscriminatory trade.[5]

The year 1953 witnessed no decline in these conflicts; indeed, on balance they increased and more than the usual adjustments were made in trade policy to accommodate the nation's farm programs.

## Import Restrictions

The major authority for erecting nontariff barriers to imports of agricultural produce is Section 22 of the Agricultural Adjustment Act. This law authorizes the President, on the basis of investigations by the Tariff Commission, to apply either import quotas or import fees whenever it is found that imports are tending to render ineffective, or materially interfere with, programs being carried out by the Department of Agriculture.[6] Congress has also from time to time passed special laws designed to protect American farmers from foreign competition.

### a. FATS AND OILS—THE "CHEESE AMENDMENT"

Overriding objections by the Administration and many private importing and exporting groups, Congress in 1951 responded to pleas of dairy industry spokesmen and substantially extended the scope and intensity of existing import restrictions on various fats and oils by adding the so-called "cheese amendment" (Section 104) to the Defense Production Act. Violent objections to this law were voiced by spokesmen from many foreign countries, and the United States was found to have violated commitments it had

[5] For a survey of the conflicts between United States agricultural and trade policies in earlier years, see *Survey—1952*, pp. 192-208, and the references cited there.

See also Johnson, D. G., "Agricultural Price Policy and International Trade," *Essays in International Finance*, No. 19, International Finance Section, Princeton University, June 1954.

[6] Such import quotas may not reduce the quantity imported by more than half the quantity of imports consumed during "a representative period as determined by the President," and the import fees may not exceed 50 percent ad valorem.

assumed under the General Agreement on Tariffs and Trade. Nonetheless, in 1952, again over the opposition of the Administration, Congress modified the law only in minor respects and extended it until June 30, 1953.[7]

In 1953 the Government was accumulating huge surpluses of various milk products, including butter, under its price-support programs, and the dairy industry clamored for continued, and increased, protection from imports. The new Administration had promised to develop an "improved" agricultural program, but this had not been completed by midyear and the Executive Branch did not feel it was in a position at that time to put forward major recommendations for international policy with respect to agricultural products. It did agree that so long as farm prices were being supported at the current relatively high levels there would be a need in some instances to restrict imports.[8] Administration spokesmen urged, however, that Section 104 of the Defense Production Act be allowed to lapse and that reliance for such protection as seemed necessary be provided under Section 22 of the Agricultural Adjustment Act. They hastened to add that they were "keenly aware" of the importance of restricting the imports of dairy products and that they intended to make Section 22 more "effective" than it had been under the previous Administration.[9] The major justification offered for relying on Section 22 was that it would put the American restrictions within the framework of our international agreements, particularly the GATT, and so would

[7] For a summary of the specific provisions of the law and experience under it, see *Survey—1951*, pp. 182-186, and *Survey—1952*, pp. 192-198.

[8] Most of the information in this section was taken from the following official documents: "Standby Economic Controls," *Hearings on S. 753 and S. 1081*, U.S. Senate, Committee on Banking and Currency, 83d Cong., 1st Sess., March 2 to April 1, 1953, Parts 1, 2, and 4; "Defense Production Act Amendments of 1953," *Hearing on S. 1081*, House of Rep., Committee on Banking and Currency, 83d Cong., 1st Sess., May 21 to June 2, 1953; "Dairy Industry," *Hearings on Import Controls*, House of Rep., Special Subcommittee to Investigate the Dairy Industry in the United States of the Committee on Agriculture, 83d Cong., 1st Sess., March 17 to April 16, 1953, Part 1; "Foreign Trade in Agricultural Products," *Hearings on Agricultural Exports and Imports and Their Effect on Farm Price Programs*, U.S. Senate, Committee on Agriculture and Forestry, 83d Cong., 1st Sess., April 9 to June 15, 1953, Parts 1, 3, 4, and 5.

[9] In particular, the Secretary of Agriculture recommended that it be amended so as to permit more speedy relief by authorizing the President, in an emergency, to invoke its provisions on an interim basis pending receipt of a report by the Tariff Commission. (Such emergency authority already existed with respect to perishable agricultural commodities.)

remove some of the foreign objections to the restrictions on fats and oil. Administration spokesmen mentioned, but did not stress as their predecessors had in 1951 and 1952, that restricting agricultural imports might operate to reduce the size of the American farmer's export markets and that these import barriers conflicted with United States policies designed to liberalize world trade and to reduce the dependence of other countries on aid from the U.S. Government.[1]

Most of those associated with the dairy industry supported retention of Section 104.[2] They argued that Section 22 would not provide the amount of shelter they wished inasmuch as it applied only in the case of imports interfering with *federal* agricultural programs that were currently in operation and that the procedures for invoking Section 22 were so complex and time-consuming that it would often be ineffective. They also pointed out that in their opinion reliance on Section 22 rather than Section 104 would not quiet the complaints of foreign producers.[3]

In the midst of the Congressional discussion, President Eisenhower directed the Tariff Commission to determine if action under Section 22 would be necessary with reference to imports of dairy products, as well as of peanuts and peanut oil, flaxseed and flaxseed oil, and tung nuts and tung oil, should Section 104 be allowed to lapse. The Commission made its report in early June, and the President thereupon issued a proclamation imposing—as of July 1, if Section 104 lapsed—quotas and/or import fees on imports of these products which were approximately the same as those cur-

---

[1] These broader arguments against the "cheese amendment" were also made, with various qualifications, by several private groups, including the National Foreign Trade Council, the United States Chamber of Commerce, the National Council of American Importers, and the National Association of Manufacturers.

[2] Other organized farm groups, however, including the American Farm Bureau Federation and the National Grange, favored the repeal of Section 104 with needed protection being supplied by Section 22, "realistically administered." Their arguments paralleled those of the Administration.

[3] "Grass-roots" sentiment on the subject of direct import controls, as reported by the House of Representatives' Committee on Agriculture, which toured seven mid-Western states in the autumn, was that it was "utter folly" to develop farmer self-help until imports were effectively controlled. The farmers interviewed urged the giving of food rather than "guns, tanks, and planes" under the foreign-aid programs and did not consider this practice comparable to dumping. (See *New York Times*, October 28, 1953, p. 11.)

rently in effect under Section 104.[4] (No restrictions were imposed on imports of tung nuts or tung oil under Section.22, and token imports of butter were permitted for the first time since the war. The quota on cheddar cheese, on the other hand, was substantially reduced.)

The following day the coauthor in the House of Section 104 asked that it be stricken from the law, stating that Section 22, as interpreted by the President, "serves a satisfactory purpose until such time as we can get an amendment . . . which will permit a complete embargo on any commodity covered in Section 22."[5] Congressional support for retaining Section 104 thereupon evaporated, and it was dropped from the law extending the Defense Production Act.[6]

Two days after Section 104 lapsed, the Senate debated various proposed amendments to the Trade Agreements Act designed to strengthen curbs on imports considered harmful to American farmers. As finally approved, the Act was amended by adding under the section entitled "Emergency Action under Section 22 of the Agricultural Adjustment Act" the following new provision: "In any case where the Secretary of Agriculture determines and reports to the President with regard to any article or articles that a condition exists requiring emergency treatment, the President may take immediate action under this section without awaiting the recommendations of the Tariff Commission, such action to continue in effect pending the report and recommendations of the Tariff Commission and action thereon by the President."[7] No action was taken under this provision during 1953.

As some had anticipated, replacing one law with another failed to lessen foreign nations' criticism of United States policy. Several countries protested the various import quotas which were imposed from time to time during the year, and the Canadian Government apparently spoke for many when it stated that it wished "to make it clear that it does not regard the new restrictions as any more

[4] For the text of his statement, characterizing the new arrangements as less arbitrary and conforming "more with the . . . reciprocal trade agreements to which the United States is a party," see Department of State *Bulletin*, June 29, 1958, pp. 918-920.

[5] *Congressional Record* (daily edition), June 9, 1958, p. 6469.

[6] See *H. Rpt. No. 694*, 88d Cong., and P.L. 95, 88d Cong., June 30, 1958.

[7] Trade Agreements Extension Act of 1958, Section 104, subsection (c).

in accordance with the Trade Agreement between Canada and the United States when they are imposed under Section 22 . . . than [when they were] imposed under Section 104 . . ."[8] and that these restrictions raised "grave problems for the whole structure of international cooperation" and violated "American pledges to expand, rather than restrict, world commerce."[9]

As noted above, the U.S. Government reported to the Eighth Session of the Contracting Parties of the GATT that Section 104 had been repealed, but other members asserted that restrictions of "substantially the same severity" had been continued under Section 22. Most governments were unwilling to exercise their rights under the Agreement to retaliate against the United States, preferring to postpone any drastic new action until Washington had received and acted on the Randall Commission *Report*.[1] The Contracting Parties did officially recognize "that a number of contracting parties have indicated that they continue to suffer serious damage," and they adopted a resolution which (a) affirmed the right of the affected countries to have recourse to Article XXIII procedures so long as the restrictions remained in effect,[2] (b) authorized the Netherlands Government to continue to limit

[8] *International Trade News Bulletin*, Geneva, July 1953, pp. 287-288.

[9] *New York Times*, July 2, 1953, p. 35. Canada's concern was not limited to the curbs on dairy products. Protests were registered during the year on actual or threatened restrictions on imports from Canada of oats, groundfish fillets, rye, potatoes, beef, and wheat, as well as of zinc, lead, and petroleum. (See *New York Times*, May 7, 1953, p. 20; July 21, 1953, p. 6; August 9, 1953, pp. F-1 and -5; September 26, 1953, p. 23; November 6, 1953, p. 35; and November 17, 1953, p. 18.)

On November 12 President Eisenhower announced the establishment of a Joint Committee on Trade and Economic Affairs, composed of Cabinet Ministers of each country, to consider problems of Canadian–United States economic relations. According to the press, the first question to be considered would be the effect of the United States wheat subsidy on Canadian exports to the British market. (See *New York Times*, December 18, 1953, p. 27. For details on the formation of the Committee, see Department of State *Bulletin*, November 30, 1953, pp. 735-740.)

[1] The Randall Commission made no specific recommendations for resolving the conflicts between agricultural and trade policies, restricting itself to a statement of the problems and emphasizing the need for flexibility in agricultural policy to make it jibe with the nation's trade principles. (See Commission on Foreign Economic Policy, *Report to the President and the Congress, op.cit.*, pp. 28-84.)

[2] Under this Article, a contracting party may propose adjustments to compensate for the nullification or impairment, by acts of another contracting party, of expected benefits under existing trade agreements. If no satisfactory adjustment is reached after a reasonable time, the offending contracting party may be suspended.

during 1954 that country's imports of wheat flour from the United States, (c) recommended that the U.S. Government have regard to the harmful effect of these restrictions on international trade, and (d) requested the U.S. Government to report, before the opening of the Ninth Session in the fall of 1954, what action it had taken.[3]

## b. OTHER SECTION 22 IMPORT RESTRICTIONS

For some time United States wool producers had been complaining that their industry was declining, and, while it was recognized that competition from synthetic fibers was an important source of their difficulties, they also argued that they were suffering from import competition. In September 1952 President Truman asked the Tariff Commission to determine whether imports were threatening the price-support program, under which the Commodity Credit Corporation had accumulated a surplus of nearly 100 million pounds of wool. President Eisenhower ordered this particular investigation dropped in June 1953, the specific price-support program for wool in effect when the investigation was ordered having ended, but directed the Commission to undertake another investigation for the 1953 wool-marketing season.[4] During the subsequent Tariff Commission hearings, Department of Agriculture spokesmen recommended a 7 cents per pound increase in the duty on imports of raw wool. Representatives of the domestic wool growers argued for an increase of between 12 and 15 cents a pound, plus a quota. Wool manufacturers opposed any increase in import barriers, declaring that it would not only add burdens to the domestic consumers but would increase the advantage already held by producers of synthetic fibers, and recommended instead direct subsidies to the wool growers.

In the meantime the Secretary of the Treasury, under Section 303 of the Tariff Act of 1930, had imposed a countervailing duty of 18 percent—in addition to the existing tariff—on wool tops from Uruguay. This action was taken on the ground that through

[3] European Office of the United Nations, *Press Release GATT/133*, Geneva, October 18, 1953.

[4] At the same time he asked the Secretary of Agriculture to make a broad and thorough study of the factors responsible for the declining sheep population in the United States. (See *Foreign Commerce Weekly*, July 20, 1953, p. 28.)

the operation of its multiple exchange rate system Uruguay was subsidizing the export of wool tops to the United States. Domestic wool growers found little relief in this measure, inasmuch as Uruguay had accounted in recent years for only about 4 percent of American imports. On March 8, 1954, the Treasury reduced the countervailing duty to 6 percent, following a revision of the Uruguayan exchange rate practices.[5]

In early March 1954 the Tariff Commission completed the study requested in June and recommended that, under the authority of Section 22, the President impose on top of the existing duty an import fee of 10 cents a pound on wool and 11¼ cents a pound on carbonized wool and wool tops. The President, however, refused to implement this recommendation, pending Congressional action on his own recommendations, made in January 1954, that the price for domestic wool be set in the open market and that direct payments be made to domestic producers in amounts necessary to raise the total payments received by the grower to the current parity price.[6]

In mid-1953 the President requested the Tariff Commission to carry out a Section 22 investigation on oats. Six months later the Commission recommended the imposition of severe quotas. Before the President had formally acted on the recommendation, however, Canada "voluntarily" agreed to limit its exports of oats to the United States during the crop year ending in October 1954 to 23 million bushels—about one third of the exports during the preceding year—on the understanding that should large quantities be imported into the United States from other sources the situation would be "reviewed" by the Canadian and U.S. governments. Later in the month the President ordered a quota of 2.5 million bushels imposed on imports from non-Canadian sources during the current crop year.[7] About the same time the President also asked the Tariff Commission to investigate the effects of rye imports (coming largely from Canada) and to make recommendations as to whether Section 22 should be invoked for this commodity. In March 1954 the Tariff Commission recommended the

[5] *Foreign Commerce Weekly*, May 18, 1953, p. 28, and March 15, 1954, p. 10.
[6] *Foreign Commerce Weekly*, March 15, 1954, p. 9. For the text of the President's proposals, see *New York Times*, January 12, 1954, p. 8.
[7] *Foreign Commerce Weekly*, June 22, 1953, p. 82, and Department of State *Bulletin*, January 4, 1954, pp. 21-22, and January 11, 1954, pp. 56-57.

imposition of import quotas, and the President thereupon applied the suggested quotas for the period ending in mid-1955.

Severe quota restrictions, amounting to virtual embargoes, had been in effect since 1939 on most types of cotton and since 1941 on wheat, wheat flour, and other wheat products. These were maintained unchanged during 1953.

President Truman had refused in late 1952 to put into effect a Tariff Commission recommendation that imports of shelled filbert nuts be limited to 4.5 million pounds during the current crop year. President Eisenhower, however, reversed this decision and imposed the quota, stating that production and inventories had reached a new high and that imports were interfering with the Department of Agriculture's program.[8] Turkey filed a complaint that this action nullified concessions the United States had granted under the GATT; and on September 29 the President announced that he was not acting on a Tariff Commission recommendation to continue these import restrictions for the 1953-1954 crop. Earlier the President had proclaimed that the existing fees on imports of almonds, which had been put in effect in 1952, would be continued for the year beginning October 1, 1953, but he did not accept the Tariff Commission's recommendation that the fees be imposed for subsequent years.[9]

C. RESTRICTIONS ON MEAT AND LIVESTOCK IMPORTS

The United States sometimes restricts imports of certain agricultural products for the avowed purposes of enforcing domestic sanitary and health requirements and preventing the spread of animal and plant diseases.[1] The most important of these restrictions have been the embargoes applied on meat and livestock imports from countries whose herds were suffering from foot and mouth disease. On March 1, 1953, the United States removed the embargo which had been placed on Canadian beef during the previous year,[2] but at the same time it reestablished certain tariff quotas on meat imports.[3] The ban on imports of meat and live-

[8] Department of State *Bulletin*, June 29, 1953, pp. 917-918.
[9] Department of State *Bulletin*, November 2, 1953, pp. 602-603.
[1] It has been charged that these restrictions are sometimes imposed for protectionist purposes only.
[2] See *Survey—1952*, pp. 198-199.
[3] See *American Import and Export Bulletin*, April 1953, pp. 277-278, for details.

stock from Norway, in effect since 1951, was lifted in October when the Department of Agriculture declared that country free of foot and mouth disease. This action was expected to have little effect on trade between the two countries inasmuch as Norway, a net meat-importing country, has historically sold only small amounts to the United States. A new outbreak of the disease in Mexico in May brought about the reimposition of the embargo—raised only the previous September after a six-year duration—on imports of meat and livestock from that country.[4]

d. SUGAR QUOTAS

Although United States growers provide only about a quarter of the sugar consumed in this country, imports of sugar are subject to a rigorous quota system designed to guarantee a "fair and equitable" market for domestic producers and to maintain "not excessive" prices to consumers.[5]

Under the terms of the Sugar Act of 1948, as amended, the Secretary of Agriculture late each autumn estimates the total domestic "requirements" for the following year and then announces quotas for both domestic and various foreign suppliers. The usual practice in recent years has been to allot about 28 percent of the total requirements to domestic producers, although they often do not fill it. In December 1953 the Secretary of Agriculture announced a total quota of 8 million short tons for 1954, assigning nearly 29 percent of this to the American growers. The

---

Canada lifted her direct controls on meat and livestock imports in early 1953, and for the first time in six years relatively large amounts of cattle were exported by the United States to take advantage of the higher Canadian prices.

[4] See *Foreign Commerce Weekly*, June 1, 1953, p. 24, and *New York Times*, May 24, 1953, p. 89. See also *Congressional Record* (daily edition), June 1, 1953, p. A3288, for a charge that the embargo was imposed for other than quarantine purposes.

Imports of canned meat in hermetically sealed containers, as well as of cured meat from federally inspected plants in Mexico, were permitted to enter the United States. All fresh, chilled, or frozen meat imports were prohibited.

Three American experts on the disease were sent to Mexico by the Department of Agriculture to assist in dealing with the outbreak, and the U.S. Government contributed $2.8 million during the year to a cooperative effort with the Government of Mexico for controlling and eradicating the disease. Since the end of World War II, the U.S. Government has contributed over $90 million to this program.

[5] The U.S. Government also participates in the work of the International Sugar Council, as discussed in the following chapter.

total quota was initially set at some 400,000 tons below the estimated requirements, a practice followed in the past and primarily designed, apparently, to provide a price stimulant to domestic production.[6] In March 1954, again in keeping with past practices, the total quota was increased, by 200,000 tons, following an increase in domestic prices.[7]

### e. TARIFF QUOTAS AND MISCELLANEOUS RESTRICTIONS

The Tariff Act of 1930 provides that tariff quotas may be imposed by the United States, and provisions for such quotas, usually on agricultural products, have been included in several of the trade agreements negotiated by the United States under the GATT. But few changes were made during 1953 in the existing quotas. Those on fresh and sour whole milk and cream were unchanged during the year, while that on butter was made ineffective by the measures described above. In keeping with the GATT provision that 15 percent of the average domestic consumption of groundfish (cod, haddock, hake, pollock, cusk, and rosefish) over the previous three years should be permitted entry at the lower trade-agreement rate, the tariff quota on this item was increased by nearly 8 percent in 1953. The tariff quota on seed potatoes was unchanged, but the amount of other white potatoes permitted to enter at the reduced trade-agreement rate during the year ending in mid-September 1954 was reduced from the 13.3 million bushels permitted in the previous crop year to 1 million bushels as a consequence of an increase in domestic production.[8]

The Philippine Trade Act of 1946 provides for specific import quotas on rice, cigars, scrap and filler tobacco, coconut oil, pearl or shell buttons, hard-fiber cordage, and sugar. These were not altered during the year, and no action was taken under provisions of the Act which authorize the establishment of quotas on other

---

[6] The large commercial users of sugar objected to this "negative allowance" formula. (See *New York Times*, June 19, 1953, p. 34, and November 17, 1953, pp. 47 and 49.)

[7] See *New York Times*, March 17, 1954, p. 43.

[8] *Foreign Commerce Weekly*, October 5, 1953, p. 25. The *Survey—1952*, p. 201, was in error in reporting the tariff quota for that crop year. The statement should have been that the quota was raised in 1952 from approximately 4.0 million bushels to nearly 13.4 million bushels.

Philippine articles which cause or threaten substantial competition with like articles produced in the United States.[9]

## Export Subsidies

It has long been the practice of the United States to subsidize the export of many agricultural products. The authority for much of this subsidization is granted by Section 32 of the 1935 Agricultural Adjustment Act, which also set aside 30 percent of the receipts from all import duties for the encouragement of exports of farm goods. Additional funds have been made available, and Congress has also provided, from time to time, additional authority for subsidizing such exports. As the surpluses of many agricultural products continued to mount during 1953, pressure in Congress for special measures to dispose of them increased.

Export subsidy payments under Section 32 totalled nearly $14 million in 1953, as compared with $16 million during the previous year. (Not included are the $106 million in subsidies required to fulfill the nation's obligations under the International Wheat Agreement, discussed in the following chapter.) These Section 32 payments were made on exports of fresh and processed oranges and grapefruit, honey, fresh pears, raisins, and a small amount of wheat and wheat flour outside the wheat exported under the International Wheat Agreement. The amount of subsidy on honey was reduced twice during the year and was terminated in October, but that on wheat was increased slightly early in the year and was expanded still further in December.[1] The subsidies on certain types of raisins were removed early in the year but were renewed in September. The subsidy program on

[9] In 1953 the Philippine Government formally requested the U.S. Government to review and to make certain changes in various provisions of the Philippine Trade Act of 1946. Under the provisions of this Act, the free-trade status accorded most commerce between the two countries is scheduled to be replaced by gradually increasing mutual import duties, beginning in mid-1954. By 1974 all customs preferences are to be removed. Details of the Philippine requests were not made public, but—so far as trade policy was concerned—it appeared from the press that they contained proposals that free-trade treatment be extended for some commodities after mid-1954 so as to permit certain major Philippine export industries to continue their favored position in the American market. The United States established a special committee to study this problem during the year, but any changes in the Act will require Congressional approval. (See Department of State *Bulletin,* September 7, 1953, pp. 316-318, and October 19, 1953, pp. 523-525.)

[1] See *Foreign Commerce Weekly,* December 14, 1953, p. 20.

fresh pears, omitted in 1952, was reinstated on September 25, 1953.

Although it has been the usual practice to make Section 32 payments only on shipments to traditional export markets and not to countries which commercially produce the goods or which border on the United States, Greece, Turkey, Italy, South Africa, and the United Kingdom (on behalf of its dependent territories) again complained, at the Eighth Session of the GATT in October, that the United States subsidy programs on raisins and oranges were depriving them of traditional markets in third countries.

As noted in Chapter I, the President was directed in a 1953 amendment to the Mutual Security Act to use a portion of the funds provided under that Act for the purchase of surplus agricultural commodities to be sold to friendly foreign countries for local currencies. The press reported that most countries were reluctant to receive their Mutual Security aid in this particular form, but some $60 million had been allocated for this purpose by the end of the year, although only $8 million—of tobacco to Britain—had actually been shipped.[2] Congress also passed a law in June authorizing the gift of up to 1 million tons of Government-held wheat to Pakistan; three fifths of this amount had been shipped by year's end.[3] In August Congress passed another law, authorizing the President to use up to $100 million of Government-held surplus agricultural products to aid foreign countries in time of famine or emergency. A few million dollars of such gifts, in the form of wheat, were made during the year to Bolivia, Jordan, and Libya.[4]

In his farm message to Congress in early 1954, President Eisenhower recommended that the existing large surpluses of farm commodities be "insulated" from the commercial markets and asked for authority to "set aside" $2.5 billion worth of these products currently held by the Commodity Credit Corporation for use

[2] For reports on views abroad on this policy, see *The Economist*, December 5, 1953, p. 774, and *New York Times*, July 7, 1953, p. 15; November 18, 1953, p. 8; November 21, 1953, p. 8; November 22, 1953, p. 6; December 11, 1953, p. 57; and December 30, 1953, p. 26.

[3] P.L. 77, 88d Cong., June 25, 1953.

[4] P.L. 216, 88d Cong., August 7, 1953. See also Foreign Operations Administration, *Report to Congress on the Mutual Security Program*, Wash., D.C., December 31, 1953, pp. 8, 20-21, and 30-31.

in school lunch programs and disaster relief, as stand-by reserves for use in national emergencies, and for aid to other countries. He stated that one of the largest potential outlets for the existing surpluses was in friendly foreign nations and asked for authority to continue "substituting to the maximum extent food and fiber surpluses in foreign economic assistance and disaster relief."[5] Many in Congress were on record as favoring such substitutions, but foreign nations had, to say the least, made clear their preference for aid in a less restricted form.

[5] *New York Times,* January 12, 1954, p. 8.

# VI · STRATEGIC ASPECTS OF COMMERCIAL POLICY

ALTHOUGH the international economic policies of the United States since 1934 have centered around the Reciprocal Trade Agreements Program, certain important policies and activities, such as those concerned with international commodity agreements, have always been more or less outside this program. Moreover, in time of war, or when the threat of war has been great, the long-term objectives of the Trade Agreements Program have been overshadowed by policies designed directly and immediately to strengthen the ability of the United States and her allies to resist aggression. In the years following 1948, and especially after the outbreak of the war in Korea, great emphasis was placed in the United States on restricting the exports from all free nations of goods which might strengthen the capacity of the Soviet bloc to wage war and on stockpiling strategic materials so as to reduce the nation's wartime dependence upon foreign sources of supply. The goals of these programs were frequently short-run, and they often conflicted at points with the repeatedly reaffirmed long-term goals of freer and nondiscriminatory international trade. Where these conflicts occurred, the various strategic programs usually ruled.

## A. *EXPORT CONTROLS*

For several years the U.S. Government has required a license for the export of various commodities. The purposes and extent of these controls have varied, but the major objectives in the post-World War II years were (a) to prevent an undue drain of scarce commodities from the domestic economy and (b) to protect and strengthen the national security by preventing exports of strategically important goods to potential enemies and by directing such exports to friendly foreign nations.[1] The law authorizing

---

[1] See *Survey—1952*, pp. 204-206, and the references cited there for a brief discussion of American export control policies in 1952 and earlier years.

most of these controls—the Export Control Act of 1949—was due to expire on June 30, 1953, and in April the Administration asked Congress to extend the authority for five more years.[2]

There was general agreement inside the Government, and no recorded opposition to it by the public, that the policy of restricting certain exports was an integral part of the defense preparations of the nation.[3] Some in Congress, however, argued that export controls were unwise as a "general policy" and favored extending the authority for only one year. Others maintained that a longer period was desirable in order to enable exporters more easily to make their plans.[4] The law, as finally approved after little debate, extended the 1949 Act for another three years.[5]

The continued disappearance of materials shortages in the United States during 1953 permitted the relaxation and removal of the controls which had been applied to many commodities in the preceding years for the purposes of preventing "excessive" drains and reducing the inflationary impact of foreign demand. By the end of 1953 less than 160 of the 1624 individual commodities listed on the Department of Commerce Positive List of Controlled Commodities were controlled exclusively for short-supply reasons.[6] In addition, the quantitative export quotas on many of the remaining items were enlarged or removed during the year.

[2] The Department of Commerce is primarily responsible for administering the Export Control Act, but other agencies are also charged, under other laws, with controlling certain United States exports. Important here are the Treasury Department (narcotics and gold), the Atomic Energy Commission (fissionable materials), and the State Department (arms, ammunition, implements of war, and helium). All of these agencies cooperate and coordinate their activities with those of the Foreign Operations Administration, which administers the Mutual Defense Assistance Control Act, described in Section B, below.

[3] The more important official documents used in preparing this section were "Extension of Export Control Act of 1949," *Hearing on H.R. 4882*, House of Rep., Committee on Banking and Currency, 83d Cong., 1st Sess., April 29, 1953; *S. Rpt. No. 207*, 83d Cong.; *H. Rpt. No. 335*, 83d Cong.; and the quarterly reports of the Secretary of Commerce entitled *Export Control*, Wash., D.C. The *Foreign Commerce Weekly*, published by the Department of Commerce, also reports many details of the program.

[4] See *Congressional Record* (daily edition), May 6, 1953, p. 4747, and May 7, 1953, p. 4865.

[5] P.L. 62, 83d Cong., June 16, 1953.

[6] As of January 1, 1954, the Positive List contained 1624 separate commodities, as compared with 1723 a year earlier. Virtually all of the net reduction was due to decontrolling commodities no longer in short supply. (These figures on number of commodities under control are not comparable with those given in earlier volumes of this *Survey* due to changes in classification practices.)

The improved supply situation in the United States and abroad, together with a lifting of domestic distribution controls, reduced to minor importance the Government's task of allocating the scarce goods to friendly countries where their use would contribute most to the security of the United States. The major continuing problem in this sphere was the procurement and allocation of electronic equipment needed by friendly foreign air forces.

Attention of the export control authorities during the year under review was focussed predominantly on preventing shipments to potential enemies which might increase their military capacity. The number of items subject to these security controls decreased slightly during the year, but efforts were made to control more effectively the nearly 1500 such items remaining on the Positive List.[7] The embargo which had been placed on *all* shipments to China and North Korea in 1950 was not lifted at the time of the armistice in Korea and was still in effect at year's end. Indeed, during the year the United States issued regulations prohibiting foreign-flag ships and planes calling at Far Eastern Communist ports from receiving fuel in the United States during the next 120 days except under individual export licenses. American oil companies east of Suez had been required for some time previously to file similar applications with the U.S. Government before bunkering such carriers.

For several years the United States had required that a license be issued for *all* goods exported directly to the Soviet bloc in Europe and had maintained an embargo on shipments of what the Administration regarded as "strategic" goods. This policy was continued throughout 1953. These security export controls were "selective" as well as "flexible"—that is, they were imposed on commodities which the United States officials concluded had strategic value to the Soviet Union and the Eastern European satellites at a particular time; if world conditions and the relative strategic importance of the goods altered, the restrictions on ex-

---

[7] Certain restrictions on trading with Czechoslovakia were lifted by the United States when William Oatis was released from prison. These particular restrictions had originally been imposed to exert pressure for Mr. Oatis's release, however, so that the net effect of relaxing them, according to a State Department spokesman, was to restore Czechoslovakia to "equal footing" with the rest of the Soviet bloc. (*New York Times*, June 6, 1953, p. 4.)

ports could be changed accordingly. In practice, the controls since 1950 had been so administered as to constitute a near-embargo, the Soviet Union and its satellites having displayed little interest in obtaining clearly nonstrategic goods. The total value of United States exports, including reexports, to the European Soviet bloc during 1953 was estimated at about $1.8 million, well above the $1.1 million in 1952 but only a portion of 1 percent of the $340 million shipped in 1947, including relief as well as commercial shipments. East Germany received over half the total and Poland most of the rest. The bulk of the shipments were of tobacco, second-hand clothing, and inedible tallow.[8] United States imports from this area totalled about $36 million in 1953, largely Polish and Danzig hams and Russian furs, as compared with $40 million in 1952 and $108 million in 1947. In addition, United States imports from the Soviet bloc in Asia totalled $9.3 million in 1953 as compared with $27.7 million in 1952 and $120.3 million in 1948. A large part of the 1952 and 1953 imports were strategic goods specifically licensed for import.

In an attempt to prevent United States exports from reaching the Soviet bloc indirectly, export licenses were also required for the export of many strategic goods to all destinations—except Canada, with which close and constant coordination of policies on these matters was maintained. The general policy was to refuse to license exports to a country if that country was not adequately controlling similar exports to the Soviet bloc. In this connection, increasing reliance was placed during 1953 on the Import Certificate–Delivery Verification scheme. Under this system, export licenses were granted only upon certification by a

[8] Considerable publicity was given in the press early in 1954 to a request by a private American exporter for a license to ship to Russia relatively large quantities of butter—to be purchased from the U.S. Government-held stocks under its price-support program. (See *New York Times*, January 13, 1954, pp. 1 and 6; January 14, 1954, p. 28 [editorial]; January 16, 1954, p. 3; January 20, 1954, pp. 1 and 5; January 21, 1954, p. 4; January 26, 1954, p. 34; and February 11, 1954, pp. 1 and 5.) The Secretary of Commerce later announced that the Department had decided "as a matter of policy" to deny licenses for the export of Government-owned surplus agricultural and vegetable fiber products to the Communist bloc for cash. He pointed out, however, that this did not eliminate the possibility of granting export licenses for such crops if they were obtained in the open market. (Department of State *Bulletin*, March 1, 1954, p. 321.) It is to be noted that the Secretary's statement did not preclude bartering of Government-held agricultural surpluses for imports from Russia, and it was unofficially reported that such trade was being considered.

foreign importer to his government assuring that the item in question would actually be imported within the customs territory of that country. In some cases the United States exporter was also required to secure a statement (that is, a Delivery Verification) issued by the foreign government certifying that the goods had, in fact, entered that country.

There was little criticism—or discussion—of these export control activities either in the press or in Congress during 1953. It was generally recognized, however, that the success of the program depended in large part on similar action being taken by other countries of the free world. The officials administering United States export controls therefore worked closely with those charged with administering the Battle Act, discussed in the following section.

## B. RESTRICTIONS ON NON UNITED STATES EAST-WEST TRADE

Beginning in 1948, when the view became widely held in Washington that the Soviet bloc was bent on aggression, the U.S. Government urged its allies to restrict their exports of strategic items to Russia and its satellites in a manner similar to that being used in the case of exports from the United States. The Administration unsuccessfully opposed the technique favored by Congress for obtaining the "cooperation" of other friendly countries: denying United States aid to any nation which shipped certain goods to the Soviet bloc. Following, and replacing, certain other laws based on the same general principle, the Mutual Defense Assistance Control Act (the Battle Act) was approved in October 1951; among other things, this Act provided that no economic, financial, or military aid from the U.S. Government should go to any nation which knowingly permitted the export of goods characterized in the Act as of "primary strategic importance" to potential aggressors.[9] The President was authorized, however, to

[9] For details on this law and an account of developments in East-West trade policies after its passage, see *Survey—1952*, pp. 206-214, and the references cited there. Most of the information in this section on developments during 1953 was taken from Foreign Operations Administration, "World-wide Enforcement of Strategic Trade Controls," *Mutual Defense Assistance Control Act, Third Report to Congress*, Wash., D.C., September 1953, and Foreign Operations Administration, "East-West Trade Trends," *Mutual Defense Assistance Control Act of*

waive the termination-of-aid provision in the case of certain—but not all—of these items if he found that discontinuance of the aid "would clearly be detrimental" to United States security. The Act also directed the Administration to negotiate with recipients of United States aid for the purpose of restricting exports of certain other goods which, while not under an actual embargo, were regarded as having "secondary strategic importance." The Administration was also authorized to invite nations not receiving assistance from the United States to cooperate in the control of shipments of goods of primary and secondary strategic importance to the Communist countries. Through 1952 no aid had been terminated under this law, and the Administration reported that it had, by and large, received commendable cooperation from other countries and concluded that the export controls exercised by the non-Communist nations had decreased the rate of Soviet military build-up. Nonetheless, it insisted that the export control systems were not perfect and that even if they were they could only slow down—not prevent—Russian progress in building up a tremendous war potential.

In January 1953 the sponsor of the Battle Act published a report of his observations on the effectiveness of the law and its administration.[1] In general, he concluded that the Act had been well administered, that foreign governments had cooperated reasonably well, and that the Act had operated to delay or prevent "millions of dollars" of shipments of strategic goods to the Soviet bloc. Nonetheless, he asserted, certain defects existed, including legal loopholes in the law itself as well as some administrative shortcomings. He also cited the unfavorable and, in his view, largely unfair publicity at home and abroad on the policy. To help remedy the shortcomings, the report recommended, among other things, that some items be classified into a higher strategic category and that more stringent controls be applied to prevent transshipments.

---

*1951, Fourth Report to Congress,* Wash., D.C., May 1954. A description of East-West trade controls and their implications is also contained in Commission on Foreign Economic Policy, *Staff Papers,* Wash., D.C., February 1954, pp. 440-452.

[1] "Progress in the Control of Strategic Exports to the Soviet Bloc," *Committee Print,* 83d Cong., 1st Sess., January 29, 1953.

Congressman Battle also recommended that responsibility for administering the Act be more centralized than in the past.[2]

No Congressional hearings were held on the Battle Act per se in 1953 and the law was not amended, but the East-West trade issue was discussed in certain other hearings during the year. A few members of Congress believed that the United States should do everything in its power to prevent all exports from the West to the Communist countries. Officials from the State Department and the Mutual Security Agency, however, explained, as had their predecessors in the previous Administration, that United States policy was and should be designed to stop the flow of *strategic* materials to the Soviet bloc, to make sure that existing *nonstrategic* East-West trade resulted in a net security advantage for the West, and to maintain close and friendly relations with other free nations.[3] These officials also asserted that in urging the diminution of trade between the free world and the Soviet bloc consideration must be given to whether the United States had a responsibility to help the Western nations find alternative markets and sources of supply, and, if so, whether Government funds should be spent for such purposes. The Secretary of State declared that the Administration should not press at that time for curtailed East-West trade in Europe because such trade, properly

[2] While not disputing the benefits of concentrated administrative responsibility, the new Mutual Security Director pointed out that the problems of East-West trade were so far-reaching that effectiveness in administration called for coordination among many government agencies with different Departments assuming primary responsibilities in connection with different phases of the work. (See "Mutual Security Act Extension," *Hearings on H.R. 5710*, House of Rep., Committee on Foreign Affairs, 88d Cong., 1st Sess., March 11 to June 6, 1953, pp. 187-188. For the views of Mr. Stassen's predecessor, see the letter from the Director for Mutual Security appended to the report cited in the preceding footnote.)

Administrative responsibility was vested in both the Secretary of State and the Director of the Foreign Operations Administration on a "coordinated" basis. For a description of the various committees and working groups, in the United States and abroad, which were concerned with the administration and daily operation of the strategic export control program, see "East-West Trade," *Hearing*, House of Rep., Subcommittee on Foreign Economic Policy of the Committee on Foreign Affairs, 88d Cong., 2d Sess., February 16, 1954, pp. 4-8.

[3] See, for example, *Hearings on H.R. 5710, op.cit.*, p. 121. See also "Control of Trade with the Soviet Bloc," *Hearings Pursuant to S. Res. 40*, U.S. Senate, Permanent Subcommittee on Investigations of the Committee on Government Operations, 83d Cong., 1st Sess., March 30 to May 20, 1953, Parts 1 and 2, and *S. Rpt. No. 606*, 88d Cong.

handled, could "show to the captive world the far greater advantages of our free society in terms of better economic well-being."[4]

In keeping with the new Administration's general practice of reassessing every major foreign policy, the National Security Council undertook a review of all aspects of United States economic defense activities. The Council's report, completed in July, reaffirmed the views put forward by the State Department and the Mutual Security Agency.[5] It emphasized the importance of maintaining political unity within the free world, declared that the opinions of other sovereign nations on these questions must be considered, and advocated that East-West trade be disrupted only where a clear security advantage for the free world would result from such interference. The report also upheld the opinion that restrictions on exports of strategic materials could not seriously impair the Soviet bloc's economy in the long run; at most they could only retard the growth of the Soviet war potential.[6] While supporting the basic policy and objectives of recent United States policy on East-West trade, the report advocated a change of emphasis in the direction of simplifying the lists of controlled items and concentrating on controlling more effectively those commodities and services deemed to be making a "significant contribution" to Soviet military potential.[7] This policy was supported by

[4] *Hearings on H.R. 5710, op.cit.*, p. 181.

[5] See "East-West Trade," *Hearing, op.cit.* The report itself was not made public, but witnesses made frequent references to it throughout the above-cited hearing.

[6] In discussing the effects of strategic controls on East-West trade, the Randall Commission research staff wrote that the injurious impact of these controls on both Eastern and Western Europe should not be exaggerated. Given the possibility that Eastern Europe might not have been willing to export very much "even under the most favorable circumstances," and the fact that Western Europe (as long as its production facilities were operating at full capacity) would have had to pay for its imports with machinery and industrial materials which now save or earn dollars by remaining in Western Europe, "the net dollar cost to Western Europe of East-West trade controls . . . must be calculated modestly, probably . . . on the order of one hundred or two hundred millions a year." It was also pointed out that an "unavoidable adverse byproduct" of these export controls was that they helped the Soviet authorities to detect and repair "vulnerable points" in their economy. On balance, however, the Commission's staff felt that the Soviet bloc was "probably hurt more than the free world" by the restrictions. (Commission on Foreign Economic Policy, *Staff Papers, op.cit.*, pp. 447-450.)

[7] According to the press, in early 1954 the Administration was engaged in an extensive "pruning" of the secret list of strategic materials currently denied

the majority of the Randall Commission, who recommended that "so far as it can be done without jeopardizing military security, and subject to the embargo on Communist China and North Korea, the United States [should] acquiesce in more trade in peaceful goods between Western Europe and the Soviet bloc."[8]

The question of trade between Western Europe and Communist China and North Korea was the subject of much publicity during the year.[9] It was generally acknowledged that Western European trade with Communist China was at a relatively high level and that in some cases this trade had increased during 1952 and 1953. Most Administration spokesmen, however, asserted that such trade was almost wholly in nonstrategic goods and emphasized that many of the nation's allies were heavily dependent on the revenues and commodities obtained from such traffic.[1] Spokesmen for the Defense Department, on the other hand, characterized such trade as "indefensible" and stated that it had made the Korean war more difficult and more costly for the United Nations.[2] Officials of the State Department and the Mutual Security Agency did not deny that this trade did have some adverse effects on the Korean war effort, but they maintained that the United States must of necessity contend with international political reality and that these allies had not been able, for reasons they held to be valid, to accept the position of the United States as it applied to *nonstrategic* items. Administration spokesmen opposed the suggestion that the United States "blacklist" any shipping concerns engaged in the China trade. In 1951 and 1952 ·the Administration had nego-

---

to the Soviet bloc by the free world, in preparation for discussions with the Western European nations. (*New York Times*, March 14, 1954, pp. 1 and 23.)

[8] Commission on Foreign Economic Policy, *Report to the President and the Congress*, Wash., D.C., January 1954, p. 66.

[9] Early in the year the Director for Mutual Security announced a seven-point program to tighten up East-West trade controls as a result of Communist participation in Korea. The main lines of this program concerned the prosecution of persons conducting illegal trade, "peaceable but effective measures" to prevent transshipments, cooperation with appropriate Congressional committees for purposes of investigation and writing legislation, and coordination among the Executive departments concerned. (See Department of State *Bulletin*, March 23, 1953, pp. 485-486.)

[1] *S. Rpt. No. 606, op.cit.*, p. 7.

[2] In its interim report, the Senate Subcommittee supported this view and criticized what it described as the lack of determined official action to dissuade our allies from engaging in this trade. (See *ibid.*, p. 19.)

tiated agreements with Panama, Costa Rica, Honduras, and Liberia whereby those governments agreed to follow the United States practice of prohibiting its flag ships from carrying strategic items to Soviet bloc ports and, in particular, from calling at ports in Communist China and North Korea. The Greek Government made a similar commitment during 1953, as the result of discussions with the U.S. Administration.[3] In March 1953 the British and French governments announced the adoption of "voyage controls" whereby British and French ships would not be allowed to carry to Communist China goods embargoed under the United Nations resolution of May 18, 1951.[4] The British Government also tightened its controls over bunkering of vessels proceeding to Communist China so as to prevent bunkering of ships of any flag that were carrying embargoed items. Similar controls were subsequently adopted by the Netherlands, Norway, and Denmark.

As in the preceding year, no cases were reported during 1953 of an aid recipient's knowingly permitting the shipment of those items whose passage, under the Battle Act, made the termination of aid mandatory. Six countries—Denmark, France, West Ger-

[3] The Director for Mutual Security therefore labeled as unnecessary, and challenged the wisdom of, Senator McCarthy's widely publicized action in obtaining a "voluntary agreement" from certain Greek shipowners in New York to stop transporting goods to Communist China. Regardless of the good intentions involved, said Mr. Stassen, this action confused the issue as to official responsibility for administering trade controls, increased the difficulties of the Executive Branch's efforts to obtain agreements from other governments, made it harder to obtain necessary information for investigation and appropriate legal action against these owners and their ships, and strengthened the arguments of certain elements abroad who opposed effective control laws on the ground that they were unnecessary. ("Control of Trade with the Soviet Bloc," *Hearings, op.cit.*, p. 39. For details of the "informal agreement," see *New York Times*, March 29, 1953, p. 34.)

Further discussion on this matter took place between Senator McCarthy and the Secretary of State. In a subsequent statement the Secretary gave but little public support to Mr. Stassen's stand and expressed his appreciation of the cooperation received from Congress on these matters. He noted, however, that administration of the Battle Act was the Mutual Security Director's responsibility and "pointed out the dangers" of having Congressional committees enter the realm of foreign relations, which should be under the "exclusive jurisdiction" of the President. (Department of State *Bulletin*, April 13, 1953, p. 532.) Public disagreement between Senator McCarthy and the Executive departments on this question continued throughout the year, receiving sporadic publicity in the press. The Senator repeatedly accused the Department of State of sending "perfumed notes" to allies when, he declared, it should have taken a "strong" stand against this "blood traffic."

[4] For details of this resolution and developments thereunder in previous years, see *Survey—1952*, pp. 213-214, and the references cited there.

many, Italy, Norway, and the United Kingdom—however, shipped so-called "Category B" items to the Soviet bloc during 1953. Most, but not all, of these were in fulfillment of contracts entered into before the Battle Act embargo became effective. In each of these cases, President Eisenhower notified Congress, as had his predecessor in similar circumstances, that "cessation of aid would clearly be detrimental to the security of the United States."[5] President Eisenhower did not publicly spell out his reasons for this conclusion, as President Truman had,[6] and said only that termination of aid would adversely affect the strength of the Western alliance.

Throughout the year, representatives of the Soviet Union made overtures to the Western European nations urging an increase in East-West trade and asserted repeatedly that the problems of the so-called underdeveloped areas would be greatly lessened if trade with the Soviet bloc were encouraged. Such proposals had been made before, but some observers thought that they could detect in 1953 evidence of genuine attempts to attract imports of consumer goods and basic commodities needed for industrialization. (In the past these proposals were generally regarded as propaganda moves in the Soviet "peace offensive.") The official reaction of the U.S. Government was one of great skepticism, but the Russian suggestions capitalized on the shift in Western Europe from a producers' to a buyers' market, on the growing concern felt by many in Western Europe over future United States trade policy, and on Western European fears of an American depression.[7] Many reports appeared in the press concerning trade pacts between the free world and the Communist bloc for the exchange of nonstrategic goods, and widespread publicity was given to visits by unofficial Western European business missions to Moscow and Peiping. At the end of the year, however, it was found that the value of Western trade with the Communist bloc, including China, had declined in 1953. Western exports to the entire Soviet bloc (unadjusted for price changes) were estimated to have totalled the equivalent of some $1.3 billion in 1953, com-

[5] *Mutual Defense Assistance Control Act of 1951, Third Report to Congress, op.cit.,* pp. 78-77, and *New York Times,* March 6, 1954, pp. 1 and 5.
[6] See *Survey—1952,* pp. 208-209.
[7] See *New York Times,* April 26, 1953, pp. 1, 28, and 25, and April 28, 1953, p. 9.

pared with $1.4 billion in 1952 and $2.0 billion in 1948. Western imports from the bloc were similarly estimated at $1.6 billion in 1953, $1.6 billion in 1952, and $2.0 billion in 1948. Furthermore, although free-world trade with Communist China did show a substantial rise during early 1953, this trend was halted in the second half of the year, and the resulting increase in such trade for the year as a whole was considerably below the original estimates. Western exports to Communist China were estimated at $280 million in 1953 (compared with an early estimate of $375 million for the year) and $268 million in 1952, while Western imports from the area were estimated at $425 million in 1953 and $366 million in 1952.

The staff of the Randall Commission reported that a decline in postwar East-West trade up to and through 1953 "might have been expected," even in the absence of Western strategic controls, because of Soviet efforts to reorient satellite economies toward Russia in order to make the bloc more self-sufficient, because state-controlled Communist prices for exports have normally been higher than free-world prices, and because Communist suppliers have often failed to fulfill delivery schedules. It was added, however, that even if existing Western export controls were not relaxed, the 1953 Soviet drive for imports of consumer goods (shipment of which is restricted least, if at all, by the West), if genuine, would probably lead to an increase in East-West trade in 1954.[8] There were some indications in late 1953 and early 1954 that, barring new evidence of aggressive designs by Russia, the controls on exports of marginally strategic goods might be relaxed in many of the Western European nations.

## C. STOCKPILING[9]

Experiences during World War II convinced the U.S. Government of the necessity of having a readily accessible supply of strategic and critical raw materials, sufficient to fill the gap between estimated minimum needs (both military and civilian) and probable supplies, should another large war occur.[1] The emphasis

[8] Commission on Foreign Economic Policy, *Staff Papers*, *op.cit.*, p. 446.
[9] Fissionable materials are stockpiled by the Atomic Energy Commission. Data on these operations and policies are secret and are not included in this discussion.
[1] For a summary of developments relating to stockpiling policy and activity in earlier years, see *Survey—1952*, pp. 214-221, and references cited there. Most

in the program, reformed in 1946, has been on reducing the *wartime* dependence on foreign sources, and, to this end, about three fourths of the stockpile additions have been imports. The program has several aspects and is carried out under several laws, chief among which are the Strategic and Critical Materials Stockpiling Act of 1946 and the Defense Production Act of 1950. It has involved both the procurement of strategic and critical goods and the development of sources of supply—domestic and foreign.

## Program

Anticipated civilian and military requirements for raw materials are constantly changing as new weapons and materials are developed, as strategic assumptions are altered, and as the nation's industrial capacity changes. The stockpile objectives are therefore subject to continuous review. As of the end of 1952 seventy-four commodities were on the stockpile list, and during 1953 the objectives for twenty-one of them were reviewed. One new item—selenium—was added to the list, and lower goals were set for eight of the twenty-one items as a result of increased possibilities for using substitute materials and because it was concluded that

---

of the material in the present section is taken from U.S. Department of Defense, *Stockpile Report to the Congress,* Wash., D.C., August 15, 1953, covering stockpiling activities from January through June 1953, and U.S. Office of Defense Mobilization, *Stockpile Report to the Congress,* Wash., D.C. [May 1954], covering stockpiling activities from July through December 1953. Other major sources used were "Independent Offices Appropriations for 1954," *Hearings,* House of Rep., Subcommittee of the Committee on Appropriations, 83d Cong., 1st Sess., Part 3, pp. 819ff.; "First Independent Offices Appropriations, 1954," *Hearings on H.R. 4663,* U.S. Senate, Subcommittee of the Committee on Appropriations, 83d Cong., 1st Sess., April 21 to 25, 1953, pp. 136ff.; "Third Annual Report of the Activities of the Joint Committee on Defense Production," *H. Rpt. No. 1097,* 83d Cong., pp. 62-67; U.S. Office of Defense Mobilization, *Defense Mobilization Report to the President,* Wash., D.C., October 1953, pp. 12-14; "Stockpiling—Palm Oil," *Hearing Pursuant to S. Res. 40,* U.S. Senate, Permanent Subcommittee on Investigations of the Committee on Government Operations, 83d Cong., 1st Sess., February 25, 1953; *S. Rpt. No. 689,* 83d Cong.; and "Stockpile and Accessibility of Strategic and Critical Materials to the United States in Time of War," *Hearings Pursuant to S. Res. 143,* Parts 1 and 2, U.S. Senate, Special Subcommittee on Minerals, Materials and Fuels Economics of the Committee on Interior and Insular Affairs, 83d Cong., 1st and 2d Sess., October 20 to 24, 1953, and September 28, 1953 to February 2, 1954.

For a background study of United States minerals policy in relation to defense, see Commission on Foreign Economic Policy, *Staff Papers, op.cit.,* pp. 219-248.

previous estimates of availabilities in wartime were, in the light of changed assumptions, unduly pessimistic. In addition, the specifications for three items were revised. As a result of these fresh appraisals, together with some price changes, the value of the total stockpile goal was again reduced. It had been $9.3 billion at the end of 1951 and $7.5 billion at the end of 1952; it was set at $6.8 billion as of December 31, 1953.

In the budget presented by the outgoing Truman Administration for fiscal year 1954, Congress was asked to appropriate $225 million for stockpile purposes.[2] The new Administration, however, reported that as a result of "the diversion to industry of materials contracted for from stockpile funds, price decreases, short deliveries, and changes in . . . purchase programs and objectives," there would be some $400 million of previously appropriated and unencumbered funds available at the end of June 1953, and it therefore did not request any new appropriations.[3]

## Procurement and Supply Development

During 1953 the new Administration reshuffled once again the administrative structure responsible for formulating and carrying out the national stockpiling policy and placed the major burden of responsibility for the program in the new Office of Defense Mobilization. The review of stockpiling policy which had been started in 1952 was completed in mid-1953 and reached the conclusion that, in general, existing policies should be continued.[4]

**a. PROCUREMENT**

Deliveries to the stockpile during 1953 were valued at some $733 million (at December 31 prices), as compared with $918 million during 1952 (at then current prices). Thus, at the end

---

[2] Of this, $37 million was to be used to liquidate previous contract authorizations. Congress had been asked to appropriate $225 million for fiscal year 1953 but had actually provided $204 million.

[3] "First Independent Offices Appropriations, 1954," *Hearings, op.cit.,* p. 150. For a foreign view on stockpiling policy under the new Administration, see *The Statist,* September 12, 1953, pp. 838-839.

[4] Several relatively minor recommendations were made, including, among others, the suggestion that many of the operating rules be formalized and several of the criteria for selecting materials for stockpiling be clarified. For more of the details, see U.S. Department of Defense, *Stockpile Report to the Congress, August 15, 1953, op.cit.,* pp. 13-14. The text of the report resulting from the review was not made public.

of 1953, such materials on hand were valued at $4226 million (current prices) or about 62 percent of the total program. An additional $879 million of materials were under contract for future delivery, bringing the value of the total stockpile, including goods in inventory and under contract, to approximately 75 percent of the over-all objective. Of the seventy-five materials being actively stockpiled at that date, quotas for thirty-nine were reported as being completely filled, taking into account both inventories and items under contract, while the goals for thirteen other materials were at least 80 percent completed, leading to the conclusion that it was possible to shift from a policy of "massive expansion or accumulation" to one of "flexible and selective management" of the stockpile.[5] The Office of Defense Mobilization late in the year issued a general policy directive stating that the stockpile objectives should be achieved in the shortest possible time but that this should be done without interfering with the rearmament program and without creating "undue hardship" within the civilian economy.

Apparently it was not found necessary during the year under review to withdraw any materials from the stockpile for current use, as had happened in 1952, although in some instances materials originally intended for the stockpile continued to be directed into current industrial consumption.[6]

Foreign nations again in 1953 urged the United States to increase its stockpile purchases as a means of stabilizing prices and of helping them to increase their dollar earnings. Mr. Milton Eisenhower, in his report to the President on United States–Latin American relations, recommended that serious consideration be given to building larger stockpiles of storable commodities during periods when world prices for such commodities were falling. Such a policy, said the report, would help achieve the dual purpose of "protecting the long-term economic future of the United States" and providing "some degree of stability in world

[5] See *H. Rpt. No. 1097*, *op.cit.*, pp. 62–67.

[6] Beginning in the summer of 1951, all domestically produced aluminum had been diverted to private industry, but stockpiling of such supplies was resumed during the second quarter of 1953. The supply situation continued tight, and the Government announced in late 1953 that it was waiving the provisions of the "Buy American" Act with respect to imports of aluminum in any form. (*New York Times*, October 22, 1953, p. 45.)

market prices of raw materials."[7] However, strategic considerations continued to dominate stockpiling activities, and there was but little public evidence during 1953 that policies were being greatly influenced by considerations of the welfare or convenience of the foreign suppliers.[8]

As in past years, the Emergency Procurement Service of the General Services Administration was the official purchasing agent for stockpiling under the program and the bulk of the funds used were direct appropriations by Congress for this purpose. Relatively small amounts continued to be supplied by other methods and sources. The Commodity Credit Corporation, authorized to barter certain surplus agricultural products in exchange for foreign-produced materials for subsequent sale to the General Services Administration for the national stockpile, acquired or put on order about $24 million of such materials during 1953, bringing the total value of such transactions to $74 million. The Foreign Operations Administration, as the Economic Cooperation Administration and the Mutual Security Agency had done previously, made available to the General Services Administration some of the counterpart funds reserved for United States use for the direct purchase of strategic and critical materials. The equivalent of some $17 million were so spent during the first nine months of 1953, raising the total from 1948 to the equivalent of nearly $92 million. In addition, the U.S. Government received strategic materials valued at nearly $18 million in repayment of interest and principal on various dollar and local-currency counterpart fund loans which the Foreign Operations Administration and its predecessors had made to foreign producers for the purpose of increasing their production of critical materials.[9]

[7] Department of State *Bulletin*, November 28, 1953, p. 716. Other measures designed to stabilize international raw material prices are discussed in Section D, below.

[8] In early 1954 the U.S. Government completed formal negotiations with the Chilean Government for the purchase of about 100,000 tons of "surplus" Chilean copper with the aim, in part, of relieving a financial crisis in that country.

[9] P.L. 152, 81st Cong., provides that Government agencies may accept strategic materials instead of cash in payment of rents, principal, or interest on the sale or lease of Government surplus property. Apparently 1953 saw no new items added to the 86,450 tons of pig aluminum previously acquired for the stockpile in this way. Similarly, commodities seized by the Customs Bureau which are

b. SUPPLY DEVELOPMENT

A general policy was established in 1950 that whenever it was judged that there would not be enough of any of the listed strategic and critical materials to meet the current requirements—or those it was anticipated would arise during a period of full mobilization—for at least (a) military and atomic energy production in the United States and in allied countries, (b) defense-supporting and "essential" civilian production, and (c) the stockpiling program, the Government should prepare and carry out programs for expanding the production of such items. Most of these programs were under the authority of the Defense Production Act of 1950 and applied to increasing domestic capacity; they are therefore outside the scope of this document. It may be noted, however, that during 1953 the new Administration carried out a review of this materials-expansion program and considered that it would be possible to reduce by large amounts the investments planned, some concern being felt lest the output from the already expanded facilities produce "serious adverse market effects."[1]

Several methods have been used to expand the production abroad of strategic and critical materials. One of the more important has been the placement of long-term purchase contracts. The Export-Import Bank has helped, authorizing in 1952 some $115 million in loans out of its own funds for expanding the production of strategic materials abroad. But, as discussed in Chapter III above, during 1953 new authorizations fell off sharply, totalling only about $32.3 million. Of this total, $30 million were to several South African gold-mining companies to facilitate the construction of plants and related facilities for the production of uranium for sale to the Atomic Energy Commission. In addition, during 1953 the Export-Import Bank authorized $28.4 million of new loans for especially risky raw materials ventures abroad out of

useful for stockpiling may be transferred to the stockpile free of charge. No such transfers were reported during 1953.

Surplus Government-owned materials valued at $5 million were transferred to the stockpile during 1953. These materials included magnesium, nickel, opium, platinum and other platinum-group metals, tantalum, and vanadium.

[1] H. Rpt. No. 1097, op.cit., pp. 65-66, and U.S. Office of Defense Mobilization, *Defense Mobilization Order—V-3*, Wash., D.C., March 18, 1954 (mimeographed).

funds made available under the Defense Production Act of 1950, as amended in 1951. All of these latter loans were authorized in the first half of the year. However, during the year earlier authorizations of $28.5 million were cancelled. Thus, the net amount authorized since the beginning of the program remained at just under $44 million. The 1953 authorizations were for the production of cobalt, copper, molybdenum, and bismuth. (Actual disbursements under these loans for the Office of Defense Mobilization totalled $7.7 million in 1953, as compared with $0.2 million in 1952.) Most, if not all, of these loans carried with them an option by the U.S. Government to purchase some of the output.[2]

The Foreign Operations Administration, in cooperation with the General Services Administration and continuing the practice of earlier years, provided some dollars and counterpart funds to expand the output of strategic materials abroad, largely in the dependent overseas territories of the European countries. During the year the equivalent of nearly $25 million—mostly in counterpart funds—was disbursed for such purposes, raising the total since the beginning of the program in 1948 to the equivalent of nearly $107 million; however, virtually no new *commitments* were entered into during the year. In addition, the Foreign Operations Administration disbursed $3.7 million under the "basic-materials development" program approved by Congress in 1953 and the General Services Administration, under a program initiated in 1952 and financed from funds provided under the Defense Production Act, disbursed $2.8 million to expand the production of deficiency materials abroad, raising the total to $6.9 million.

## D. INTERNATIONAL COMMODITY ARRANGEMENTS

The U.S. Government has had a long history of opposition to intergovernmental commodity agreements on the ground that they tend in practice to result in higher prices, restrictions on output, and misallocation of resources. This opposition has been somewhat tempered during recent years, and the U.S. Govern-

---

[2] The International Bank, as noted in Chapter IV, continued to make some loans for expanding the production abroad of strategic and critical materials, and, as discussed in Chapter II, some help was given foreign countries in their production of these goods under the technical assistance program.

ment has not only participated in various international study and advisory groups but, faced with a large Government-held surplus of wheat, has been an active participant in the International Wheat Agreement.[3]

Spokesmen for many foreign nations, especially those whose economies are heavily dependent upon the export of a few raw materials, often have argued for such agreements, stating that in practice normal market forces are not capable of preventing burdensome surpluses, low prices, and unemployment, followed by extreme shortages and skyrocketing prices. The results, they assert, are not only periodic internal economic crises for the producers, but also serious international economic maladjustments.[4]

This issue has been discussed frequently, especially in the United Nations, in connection with the problem of the economic development of the so-called underdeveloped areas. Spokesmen for the United States have in these discussions accepted the argument that more stable prices *and* output for raw materials could increase the ability of poor countries to finance economic development but have emphasized the great difficulties in practice of enforcing commitments and of reaching agreement on safeguards to protect consumers and on appropriate prices. While not openly hostile to intergovernmental agreements in these discussions, American officials usually have found the specific proposals offered unacceptable.[5]

The Paley Commission in mid-1952 stated its conviction that the solution of the problem of instability in the raw materials market must be sought through international agreements in which the United States would have to play a major role. A year later the Douglas report, though less outspoken in its support of such agreements, advised President Eisenhower that measures must

[3] In the ill-fated Havana Charter, the United States accepted "in principle" that such agreements might be desirable in peacetime under certain safeguards.

[4] It has also frequently been alleged that the terms of trade have worsened in recent years for the raw-material-producing countries; this allegation has been questioned and denied by United States officials, who have also asserted that the U.S. Government would not commit itself to supporting proposals to apply international controls over the prices of most of the important goods moving in international trade.

[5] See, for example, *United Nations Bulletin*, January 1, 1953, pp. 3ff. and 88-89.

For a study of many of the issues involved in international commodity agreements, see United Nations, *Commodity Trade and Economic Development*, UN Publication Sales No.: 1954.II.B.1.

be developed "to abate the violent fluctuations in the prices and the volume of the major raw materials that enter into international trade." "Without recommending intergovernmental commodity agreements," it added, "the history shows that this is a problem that deserves more study."[6] On the other hand, the early 1954 *Report* of the Randall Commission, although there were some dissents, took what most regarded as a hostile attitude toward such agreements. The Commission asserted that it did not believe that "extensive resort" to "intergovernmental commodity agreements, involving export quotas, import quotas, price limits, reserve stocks, price stabilization purchases and sales (buffer stocks), production controls, or some combination of such devices" would solve the problem of price instability for raw materials; on the contrary, the Commission felt that such agreements would only serve to "introduce rigidities and restraints that impair the elasticity of economic adjustment and the freedom of individual initiative, which are fundamental to economic progress."[7]

Although there was little change in stated policy by either Congress or the Administration on the issue during 1953, there were some indications that in practice more support than in the past was being given to specific proposals for intergovernmental commodity agreements of one kind or another.

### International Materials Conference[8]

Following the outbreak of the war in Korea in mid-1950 and the resulting scramble for many raw materials, the United States, the United Kingdom, and France—in response to concern expressed by many countries—took the initiative in creating the International Materials Conference, whose functions were those of recommending to governments measures for distributing scarce commodities equitably, conserving supplies, and increasing production. The organization, composed of a Central Group and a

---

[6] Department of State *Bulletin*, August 31, 1953, p. 278.

[7] Commission on Foreign Economic Policy, *Report to the President and the Congress*, op.cit., p. 35. For background data, see Commission on Foreign Economic Policy, *Staff Papers*, op.cit., pp. 188–212.

[8] It should be noted that although this organization also dealt with the distribution of raw materials, its purpose was quite different from that of the "peacetime" international commodity arrangements, described elsewhere in this section.

series of commodity committees, had no authority to apply sanctions, and the member and cooperating nations, which accounted for over 90 percent of the free world's production and consumption of the affected materials, were free to accept or reject the Conference recommendations. In the event, the Conference limited its activities primarily to recommending allocations of scarce materials, and its recommendations were generally implemented by the members.[9]

The Conference received much praise from the Administration and from many unofficial observers, who found that it had made major contributions to the reduction of hoarding and panic buying of scarce materials and had been remarkably successful in encouraging the distribution of relatively scarce materials in a manner calculated to provide the maximum defense for the free world while maintaining a spirit of cooperation and good will among the participating governments. Some members of the U.S. Congress, on the other hand, strongly criticized the institution in 1952 on the grounds that it was causing unemployment in some industries by making insufficient allocations of certain materials (notably copper) to the United States, that it was an international cartel, and that it was a "backdoor attempt" by the Administration to bring into being the International Trade Organization. All these charges were denied by the Administration.[1] Partly as a result of this Congressional opposition, but more importantly because of the increase in production and, in some cases, of declining demand for many of the commodities, the Conference, which from the start had been viewed by its members as a temporary organization, had begun in late 1952 to dissolve itself.[2]

[9] For a summary account of the Conference, its problems, and its accomplishments through 1952, see *Survey—1952*, pp. 222-226, and the references cited there. For an official account of developments from March 1952 through February 1953, see International Materials Conference, *Report on Operations, 1952-1953*, Wash., D.C., 1953. A similar account, for March 1953 through September 1953, when the last commodity committee was terminated, may be found in International Materials Conference, *Report on Operations, Final Report*, Wash., D.C. [1954]. Other official sources which were used in the preparation of this section were the press releases and information bulletins issued during 1953 by the Conference.

[1] See *Survey—1952*, pp. 224-225.

[2] The Defense Production Act Amendments of 1953 (P.L. 95, 83d Cong., June 30, 1953), removed certain restrictions which Congress had previously placed on

During the first quarter of 1953, copper supplies were judged adequate, and the Copper-Zinc-Lead Committee was terminated in March; the Sulphur Committee was similarly dissolved in April. A substantial increase in the supply of molybdenum during the second quarter of 1953 made it possible for the Tungsten-Molybdenum Committee to end its activities in July. Nickel was kept under allocation through the second and third quarters of 1953, but the Manganese-Nickel-Cobalt Committee, the last one operating, was disbanded as of the end of September. The Central Group continued in existence on a stand-by basis, but in December, following a review of the raw materials situation, it was decided that the International Materials Conference had accomplished its purpose and should be formally terminated as of December 31, 1953. At this meeting, the members agreed that the Conference had developed methods which might provide useful guides in coping with future problems and agreed to hold consultations, at the initiative of any member, should the threat of shortages arise at some future date.[3]

### Commodity Study Groups and Agreements[4]

#### a. INTERNATIONAL COTTON ADVISORY COMMITTEE

At the second session of the twelfth plenary meeting of the International Cotton Advisory Committee, convened in Washington in November 1953, consideration was given to various schemes for an intergovernmental agreement on cotton which had been prepared following a first session in May.[5] Four different plans were considered: a multilateral contract similar to the International Wheat Agreement, a buffer-stock program, a combination of the two, and a quota-type pact similar to the Sugar Agreement. No accord was reached, and the views of the United States delega-

---

United States participation (see *Survey—1952*, pp. 224-225), on the basis of Administration statements that these provisions were unnecessary "since the administration was relaxing controls and had no intention of using the powers which these sections forbade or restricted" (*S. Rpt. No. 138*, 83d Cong., p. 16).

[3] See Department of State *Bulletin*, January 11, 1954, p. 60.

[4] See *Survey—1952*, pp. 227-232, for a summary of developments during that year. For an official report of the work of these groups, including some on which the United States was not represented, see United Nations Interim Co-ordinating Committee for International Commodity Arrangements, *Review of International Commodity Problems 1953*, U.N. Publication Sales No.: 1954.II.D.8.

[5] *New York Times*, May 18, 1953, p. 48.

tion were not published, but it may perhaps be presumed that the United States representatives wished to postpone taking a position pending the report of the Randall Commission. Resolutions were passed, however, directing the organization's standing committee to continue its examination of the proposals by hiring one or more technicians to prepare an objective report on the problem and to study methods of increasing world consumption, including aid to nations requiring additional cotton but unable to pay for it, in order to overcome the existing 10 percent production surplus. The standing committee was also asked to watch the effects of internal actions by both member and nonmember nations with a view toward coordinating such actions through intergovernmental cooperation. The group was asked to report its findings at the next session, scheduled to take place in Brazil in June 1954.[6]

## b. WOOL STUDY GROUP

The Wool Study Group did not meet during 1953. In January the International Wool Secretariat announced that prospects for the wool trade in 1953 were promising and noted that wool consumption was rising. At year's end it was reported that 1953 had been a year of "marked stability" for the commodity. However, as noted in the previous chapter, United States wool growers insisted theirs was a declining industry, and late in the year President Eisenhower recommended a major change in American policy with respect to locally produced wool.

## c. RUBBER STUDY GROUP

The working party set up in 1952 to consider the practicability and necessity of taking international measures "to prevent burdensome surpluses or serious shortages of rubber" recommended in 1953 a buffer-stock type of agreement. The Rubber Study Group met in Copenhagen in May to consider this proposal, but there was so much opposition to the plan on the part of the United States and certain other consumer nations that further discussion was postponed until a later meeting.[7] Meanwhile great concern

[6] *New York Times*, November 13, 1953, pp. 35 and 37.
[7] For some criticisms by American businessmen, who characterized the scheme as a cartel, see *New York Times*, May 11, 1953, pp. 35 and 38. See also *Foreign Commerce Weekly*, July 13, 1953, p. 6.

was being voiced by producer nations over the fall in the price of natural rubber, a development which they attributed in large measure to what they charged were the below-cost sales of synthetic rubber by the United States and which they feared would be further aggravated by the passage of legislation providing for the sale of Government-owned synthetic rubber plants to private concerns.[8] The price of natural rubber continued to fall as the year progressed, and an increasing number of reports appeared in the press of proposed negotiations for the sale of rubber by certain Southeast Asian countries to Communist China. Nonetheless, when the Group met again in the fall, it proved impossible to effect a compromise between the views of the producer and consumer nations, and the buffer-stock scheme was abandoned, at least for the time being.[9]

### d. TIN STUDY GROUP

The International Tin Study Group held its seventh meeting in London in late March and appointed a working party to consider reopening negotiations for an international tin agreement, the last negotiations, in 1950, having come to nought in the face of United States objections to one set of proposals and the unwillingness of the producer nations to accept United States counterproposals.[1] It was reported that during the 1953 negotiations the United States representatives were "noticeably sympathetic" toward the idea of an agreement, although warning that the U.S. Government could not commit itself prior to the report then in prospect from the Commission on Foreign Economic Policy.[2]

[8] P.L. 205, 83d Cong., August 7, 1953.

[9] Some members of the Group suggested that the United States raise the price of synthetic rubber, reexamine its methods of rotating its strategic stock, and revoke a 1952 directive setting the conditions under which mandatory consumption of synthetic rubber could be reimposed.

[1] Department of State *Bulletin*, May 18, 1953, pp. 724-725. For a summary of the 1950 discussion, see *Survey—1950*, pp. 225-227.

[2] World tin production had exceeded current consumption each year since 1948, and some anticipated that United States stockpile purchases, which had hitherto been very helpful in absorbing the surplus, would probably cease in 1954. Certain sectors of the press, however, concluded that the changed United States attitude, if indeed there were a change, toward an international agreement resulted "more from recognition of the political dangers of low tin prices in South East Asia and elsewhere than from any sudden tenderness for producers as such." (*The Economist*, July 4, 1953, p. 58.)

A five-year International Tin Agreement was duly drafted at Brussels and submitted to the November-December meeting of the International Tin Conference. The stated major objectives of the Agreement were: the prevention or alleviation of unemployment in the tin-producing industry, the achievement of "a reasonable degree" of price stability, the insurance of "adequate supplies at reasonable prices," and the promotion of economic development in producing countries and the conservation of tin resources. The proposal called for an international council on which both producing and consuming nations would be represented, with important decisions requiring a majority vote by both groups;[3] a 25,000-ton (or equivalent) buffer stock, administered in such a way as to keep price fluctuations within the limits of $.80 and $1.10 per pound; export quotas for each producer country; and commitments by consumer countries not to dump governmental stockpiles on the market without adequate notice and consultation. After some minor changes, the Conference adopted the Agreement and it was opened for signature until June 30, 1954. The United States did not take a position on the Agreement at the Conference but agreed to study it.[4]

Although the Agreement could enter into effect without United States ratification, many believed that an unfriendly attitude on the part of the United States would probably deter other consumer nations from joining. Following the Randall Commission's critical appraisal of international commodity agreements in general, the State Department announced in March 1954 that the U.S. Government would not sign the Agreement. It added, however, that this Government "was aware of the importance attached to the agreement by other governments" and "would not object if other governments decided that this [agreement] was in their interest."[5] Assurances were also given that the United States would not dump its excess tin stocks on the market, but would hold them "in insulation," subject to withdrawal at the direction of the President. Details as to the actions of other governments in

[3] This was the main difference between the 1953 tin pact and pre-World War II tin control systems, the latter being exclusively producers' arrangements.
[4] For a more detailed description of the Agreement, see Department of State *Bulletin*, February 15, 1954, pp. 239-247.
[5] Department of State *Bulletin*, March 15, 1954, p. 398.

the face of the United States position were not available as this document went to press.

### e. INTERNATIONAL SUGAR AGREEMENT

In late 1952 the International Sugar Council requested the Secretary-General of the United Nations to call a conference in 1953 for the purpose of negotiating an international sugar agreement to replace the long-since-inoperative 1937 Agreement. The new agreement was to be designed to cover international trade in the so-called "free market"—that is, foreign trade in sugar not covered by existing special trading arrangements— which, in effect, excluded virtually all sugar imports by the United States, the British Commonwealth, and the Soviet Union. Not quite half of the sugar moving in international trade is currently traded in the "free market."

The conference convened in London during July and August. After a series of difficult and "stormy" negotiations and compromises,[6] accord was finally reached on a five-year Agreement, scheduled to take effect on January 1, 1954. Its main objectives were "to assure supplies of sugar to importing countries and markets for sugar to exporting countries at equitable and stable prices; to increase the consumption of sugar throughout the world; and to maintain the purchasing power in world markets of countries or areas whose economies are largely dependent upon the production or export of sugar by providing adequate returns to producers. . . ."[7] To accomplish this, the Agreement established price limits (3.25 to 4.35 cents per pound) and set annual quotas

---

[6] The total yearly export quota was finally set at 5,390,000 metric tons, instead of some 7,000,000 tons as originally requested by the exporting nations. The Peruvian delegate walked out of the conference (though he continued to keep in touch with negotiations) in protest against the quota assigned his country, and the Indonesian delegation threatened to take similar action.

[7] See United Nations, *United Nations Sugar Conference, 1953: Summary of Proceedings,* UN Sales No.: 1953.II.D.3, p. 25. For a review of the general arguments for and techniques of international commodity regulation, with particular emphasis on the special problems of sugar, and the International Sugar Agreement, see United Nations Food and Agriculture Organization, *Observations on the Proposed International Sugar Agreement* (Commodity Policy Studies, No. 4), Rome, June 1953. Further information on the Agreement and its background appear in Department of State *Bulletin,* October 26, 1953, pp. 542-546.

For a criticism charging, among other things, that the Agreement did not come to grips with the basic problems of the world sugar market, see Commission on Foreign Economic Policy, *Staff Papers, op.cit.,* pp. 207-211.

for each exporting country. Producer nations were obligated to restrict production to the amount necessary to satisfy local consumption, fill their export quotas, and maintain the stocks allowed under the Agreement. Importing countries were obligated to buy a given proportion of their sugar needs from participating exporting countries and to restrict purchases from nonparticipating exporting nations to the quantities bought from these suppliers during a given base period.[8]

The Administration appeared before the Senate Foreign Relations Committee in March 1954 in support of ratification of the Agreement, characterizing it as a "constructive step" in the solution of the world's sugar problems and a measure "dictated by both domestic- and foreign-policy considerations."[9] It must be remembered, however, that virtually all United States imports are excluded from the regulations under the Agreement inasmuch as they take place within special arrangements.

f. INTERNATIONAL WHEAT AGREEMENT

The 1952 negotiations on extending the International Wheat Agreement beyond its expiration date of August 1, 1953, reached an impasse, principally because the importing countries refused to accept the higher prices urged by the United States and the other exporting nations.[1] The talks were resumed in early 1953, and after prolonged discussions a three-year draft Agreement was prepared.[2] The new Agreement followed the same general lines as the earlier one, the most important change being that the minimum world market price at which the importing countries agreed to buy specified amounts was raised from $1.20 (in the last

[8] The new Agreement was more flexible than its prewar predecessors in that the International Sugar Council was authorized under certain conditions and within limits to modify the price range and to adjust quotas.

[9] "International Sugar Agreement," *Hearing on Exec. B*, U.S. Senate, Committee on Foreign Relations, 83d Cong., 2d Sess., March 18, 1954, p. 48.

[1] See *Survey—1952*, pp. 281-282, and the references cited there for the techniques of the scheme and the issues that had arisen under it.

[2] For details of the Agreement, see *Congressional Record* (daily edition), July 18, 1953, pp. 8890ff. Other official documents used in the preparation of this section include "International Wheat Agreement," *Hearing on Exec. H*, U.S. Senate, Committee on Foreign Relations, 83d Cong., 1st Sess., June 26, 1953; *S. Exec. Rpt. No. 4*, 83d Cong.; "International Wheat Agreement Amendment," *Miscellaneous Hearings . . . on S.J. Res. 97 . . .* (vol. 1, pp. 47-72), House of Rep., Committee on Banking and Currency, 83d Cong., 1st Sess., July 20, 1953; and *H. Rpt. No. 893*, 83d Cong.

year of the old Agreement) to $1.55 per bushel in each year of the new Agreement and the uniform maximum market price at which the exporting countries agreed to sell specified amounts was raised from $1.80 to $2.05 per bushel.[3]

The United States and other exporting countries thus won their major objective. But this victory was at the great cost of having the United Kingdom withdraw because she was unwilling to accept a maximum price higher than $2 per bushel.[4] The refusal of Britain to accede was of primary importance inasmuch as her quota as an importer was equal to nearly 30 percent of the total.

President Eisenhower in early June asked the Senate to ratify the Agreement, and the Administration was supported in its request by spokesmen for the major farm organizations. The chief arguments offered for ratification were that the pact, while not a cure-all for the world's wheat problems, had demonstrated its practicality as an instrument to bring some stability into international wheat trade without injecting too great a degree of official interference with normal private trading activity; that it had helped to strengthen free world cooperation;[5] and that it had made possible the "legitimate" disposal on the world market of United States wheat, export of which was largely dependent on subsidies to make it internationally competitive so long as the current price-support policies were in effect.[6]

The National Foreign Trade Council was the only group to oppose the new Agreement at the hearing, asserting that it allowed governments to adopt practices which United States laws denied to private enterprise, such as output restriction, market allocation, and price regulation; that it prejudged the outcome of the Ran-

[3] See the sources quoted in the previous footnote for details on the many other, relatively minor changes in the Agreement.

[4] All of the other forty-five countries that had participated in the 1949 Agreemen signed the new pact.

[5] However, the staff of the Randall Commission reported: "If anything, the agreement has tended to strengthen individual nations in going their own several ways in wheat policies, rather than to bring their policies into economic harmony." (Commission on Foreign Economic Policy, *Staff Papers, op.cit.,* p. 206.)

[6] Administration witnesses emphasized that the subsidy under the Agreement, which had averaged about 62 cents per bushel under the 1949 pact, would be only about 40 cents per bushel under the new pact, for the first year at least. It was subsequently reported that the actual subsidy payments under the Agreement for calendar year 1953 amounted to $106 million, as compared with just over $150 million in 1952 and $199 million in 1951.

dall Commission's study of the problem; that the Agreement would be unworkable without the accession of the major importing nation, the United Kingdom; that the pact imposed a heavy burden on American taxpayers who had to pay the subsidy involved; and that it was unfair to single out wheat for special aid.

There was, however, virtually no important opposition in Congress to the Agreement, though several members regretted the unwillingness of Britain to join and some suggested that Mutual Security aid to that nation be terminated if she continued to refuse to cooperate in the wheat scheme. Administration spokesmen successfully countered this suggestion by arguing that stopping aid to the United Kingdom would be a blow to United States security and that it was hoped that the British Government would reconsider its decision and sign the pact. (This did not take place during the period under review.) Following a brief debate, the Senate approved the pact, and the President signed the implementing legislation on August 1.

In its January 1954 *Report*, the Randall Commission concluded that the Wheat Agreement had contributed little to the solution of the wheat problems of either the United States or the world and that its chief significance for the United States had been to accord "official sanction" by other nations to American export subsidization. The majority of the Commission therefore recommended that the Agreement "be kept under critical review . . . and that its termination in 1956 be given consideration."[7]

## E. *TEMPORARY SUSPENSION OF IMPORT DUTIES AND TAXES*

President Eisenhower's Administration during 1953 followed the same general policies as its predecessor in encouraging and approving Congressional efforts to reduce or remove import duties and taxes on several metals considered vital to the rearmament program and for which the United States was heavily dependent on foreign sources.[8] The United States had been increasingly

[7] Commission on Foreign Economic Policy, *Report to the President and the Congress, op.cit.*, pp. 29, 30, and 32. For background, see Commission on Foreign Economic Policy, *Staff Papers, op.cit.*, pp. 201-207.

[8] For a discussion of the issues and the Legislative and Executive actions on this policy in 1952 and earlier years, see *Survey—1952*, pp. 282-284, and the references cited there.

dependent on foreign sources of copper for several years, and the 2-cent-per-pound import tax had been suspended, despite some opposition from domestic producers, from 1947 to mid-1950 and, again, from April 1951 to February 1953. The Eighty-third Congress, at the request of industry, considered renewing this suspension for another year. The Administration supported the request for continued suspension, pointing out that current domestic supplies of copper were able to fill only two thirds of the estimated requirements for military and civilian production and asserting that a reimposition of the tax would increase consumer prices on many items. Opposition to the measure was moderate and was registered by spokesmen for some of the domestic producers and some members of Congress, who declared that because of lower costs abroad, nontaxed imports had a "repressive" effect on internal production in an industry vital to national defense. Evidence that existing domestic producers could produce profitably at 24.5 cents per pound led to the provision that the import tax would automatically be reimposed if prices fell below 24 cents. With the addition of this provision, there was virtual unanimity in Congress and industry that the tax be suspended until June 30, 1954.[9]

Virtually all kinds of metal scrap have been scarce in the United States for many years, and the duties and import taxes on them have been suspended most of the time since 1942. In 1952 Congress approved an extension of the suspensions, excluding lead scrap, until mid-1953. The Executive Branch supported a simple one-year extension of the 1952 law, stating that the commodities, except lead and zinc, continued to be in short supply and were selling at high prices. Congress approved a renewal of the legislation to mid-1954, after excluding zinc scrap from its provisions.[1] A special bill suspending the duty on zinc scrap through June 1954 was introduced in the House but was not reported out of the Ways and Means Committee.

[9] P.L. 4, 83d Cong., February 14, 1953. For further details, see "Copper Import Tax Suspension," *Hearings on H.R. 568*, U.S. Senate, Committee on Finance, 83d Cong., 1st Sess., February 3 and 4, 1953; *H. Rpt. No. 4*, 83d Cong.; *S. Rpt. No. 35*, 83d Cong.; and *S. Rpt. No. 35*, Part 2 (Minority Report), 83d Cong.

[1] P.L. 221, 83d Cong., August 7, 1953. The law continued the suspension of import duties on zinc scrap purchased under written contracts entered into prior to July 1, 1953. (See *H. Rpt. No. 879*, 83d Cong., and *S. Rpt. No. 636*, 83d Cong.)

A bill was also introduced into Congress calling for a two-year suspension of the duty on crude bauxite. It was passed unanimously by the House, but the Senate took no action on it.[2] Another bill, suspending for one year the duties on aluminum and aluminum alloys, was reported out favorably by the House Ways and Means Committee but was later recommitted.[3] No attempt was made during 1953 to extend the 1950 laws suspending the duties on imports of unmanufactured lead and zinc—the tariff on these having been reimposed by President Truman after domestic prices fell below the minimum stipulated in the law—nor did the new Administration renew its predecessor's request for the suspension of import duties on tungsten.

The majority *Report* of the Randall Commission noted the increasing dependence of the United States on many raw materials imported from foreign sources and recommended that "our tariff policy toward the needed materials should be such as to offer them reasonably easy access to the United States market" and that if it were found "necessary" solely on military grounds to expand domestic production, this should be accomplished not by tariffs on imports but "by other means, the cost of which should be borne in the Defense budget."[4]

[2] For details, see *H. Rpt. No. 876*, 83d Cong.
[3] See *H. Rpt. No. 878*, 83d Cong.
[4] Commission on Foreign Economic Policy, *Report to the President and the Congress*, op.cit., pp. 39-41.

# VII · UNITED STATES BALANCE OF INTERNATIONAL PAYMENTS, 1953

THE trend toward a greater degree of balance in the rest of the world's financial relations with the United States which became noticeable during the latter part of 1952 continued throughout 1953. The improved situation reflected the increased demand in this country for the goods and services of other nations and the increased ability of foreign producers to meet demand in their own countries and abroad.[1]

Perhaps the most outstanding feature of the year under review was the ability of foreign nations to accumulate some $2.3 billion of long- and short-term assets through their transactions with this country. This was nearly double the amount accumulated during the previous year and, for the entire postwar period, was exceeded only by the $3.6 billion recorded in 1950—a year of exceedingly high prices for many of the raw materials imported by the United States and a year in which economic, as distinct from military, aid of one kind or another provided by the U.S. Government was nearly $2 billion greater than in 1953. On the other hand, "extraordinary" expenditures abroad by the U.S. Government in 1953 (in the form of disbursements by military and civilian establishments, including offshore procurement and stockpiling activities) were well above those in any year since 1949, totalling some $4.6 billion. These expenditures, of course, were usually quite different from aid in that they represented

[1] Official publications of the U.S. Government provide accessible and excellent accounts of the balance of payments of the United States, and only a brief summary of the major developments is given here. More detailed information may be found in the following documents, the source of most of the material in this chapter: Department of Commerce, *Survey of Current Business*, Wash., D.C., June 1953, pp. 4-8; September 1953, pp. 11-12; October 1953, pp. 8-10; December 1953, pp. 5-7; February 1954, pp. 23-24; and March 1954, pp. 20-24. See also Department of Commerce, *Foreign Commerce Weekly*, March 22, 1954, pp. 16ff.; March 29, 1954, pp. 25ff.; and April 12, 1954, pp. 15ff.; and Board of Governors of the Federal Reserve System, *Federal Reserve Bulletin*, October 1953, pp. 1039-1047, and March 1954, pp. 237-245.

purchases by the United States of goods and services abroad and required the use of foreign productive resources which, in part, might otherwise have been used to expand "commercial" exports and to reduce imports.

The value and volume of United States imports and exports of goods and services reached postwar highs in 1953. The current-account export surplus, at $4.7 billion, was the lowest of any postwar year and exceeded by less than $0.5 billion the value of military supplies and services provided on a grant basis.

The effects of the mild recession in the United States during the last few months of the year were apparently largely offsetting. The decline in imports during a period when there is normally a slight seasonal increase was roughly matched by a change from a net inflow to a net outflow of private portfolio capital as the abandonment during the last quarter of the Administration's previous tight credit policy favored the flotation of new issues in the American market by Canada and the International Bank. These capital movements, however, were more or less special in nature, and many feared that a continuation of the decline in United States business activity might soon lead to a reversal in the approach toward world economic balance.

Statistical details on movements in the major items of the United States balance of payments are given in Table 15, below.

## A. *CURRENT ACCOUNT*
### *Merchandise Trade*

**a. EXPORTS**

The merchandise exports of the United States during 1953 totalled over $16.4 billion. This was the highest dollar value on record and was some $0.6 billion more than in 1952. Excluding shipments of grant-aid military equipment and supplies, however, American exports *declined* by approximately $1 billion from 1952 to 1953, continuing a trend which began in the last half of 1952. Furthermore, this fall took place during a period when there was some relaxation in import restrictions by several foreign countries. Inasmuch as prices were, on the average, approximately the same in both years, the decline was all in the volume of exports.

Nearly two thirds of the fall in nonmilitary exports was accounted for by the shrinking demand abroad for American agricultural products as output in other countries increased and as prices abroad, in many instances, continued to run below the support prices in the United States. The 40 percent decline in the value of raw cotton exports and the 37 percent decline in wheat exports were only partially offset by the increase in tobacco sales abroad as Britain relaxed the stringent import limitations applied in 1952.

Although there were many exceptions for specific commodities, the 1953 commercial exports of nonfarm products as a group were some 3½ percent below the level of the previous year. The major declines during 1953 were in nonmilitary exports of coal, steel, and petroleum products. These reflected the closer balance achieved in Europe between demand and domestic output of the first two commodities and, in the case of oil, new production from the expanded refinery capacity in Europe, together with the continuing tendency of other countries to buy oil from nondollar sources, wherever possible.

Taking both the commercial and military-aid shipments, but excluding reexports and exports which were not shipped from United States customs areas, nearly 70 percent of the value of United States exports in 1953 was finished manufactures, the balance being almost evenly divided between the other three major classes of goods: crude materials, foodstuffs, and semimanufactures. In the years just preceding World War II only about half the value of American exports was accounted for by finished manufactures, nearly one quarter by crude materials, one sixth by semimanufactures, and only about 10 percent by foodstuffs.

The decline in United States commercial exports extended to every area of the world except Canada, which received no aid and increased its imports from the United States by nearly $200 million (7 percent) over 1952 as Canadian investment, production, and income continued their rapid rise. Europe recorded the largest decline in purchases from the United States—nearly $500 million—reflecting the continued rise in production there. Latin America also reduced its purchases by nearly $500 million, but the major reasons for the smaller market for United States exports in the nations to the south were inventory adjustments in several countries and the curtailment of imports by Brazil as she paid off

## TABLE 15

### International Transactions of the United States, 1951-1953
#### (millions of dollars)

| Type of Transaction | 1951 | 1952r | 1953p and by Quarters | | | | |
| --- | --- | --- | --- | --- | --- | --- | --- |
| | | | Total | I | II | III | IV |
| **Exports of Goods and Services** | | | | | | | |
| Merchandise, adjusted[a] | 15485 | 15806 | 16437 | 4256 | 4508 | 3717 | 3956 |
| Income on investments | 1992 | 1886 | 1899 | 440 | 450 | 439 | 570 |
| Transportation | 1487 | 1348 | 1287 | 317 | 333 | 328 | 309 |
| Travel | 420 | 524 | 545 | 112 | 149 | 172 | 112 |
| Miscellaneous services | 834 | 1085 | 1168 | 300 | 310 | 273 | 285 |
| Total Exports | 20218 | 20649 | 21337 | 5425 | 5750 | 4929 | 5233 |
| **Imports of Goods and Services** | | | | | | | |
| Merchandise, adjusted[a] | 11668 | 11503 | 11904 | 2984 | 3125 | 2916 | 2879 |
| Income on investments | 398 | 432 | 448 | 111 | 112 | 101 | 124 |
| Transportation | 933 | 1075 | 1117 | 264 | 302 | 297 | 254 |
| Travel | 722 | 822 | 908 | 143 | 236 | 373 | 156 |
| Miscellaneous services[b] | 1333 | 1962 | 2251 | 535 | 538 | 599 | 579 |
| Total Imports | 15054 | 15794 | 16628 | 4037 | 4313 | 4286 | 3992 |
| **Surplus of Exports of Goods and Services** | | | | | | | |
| Merchandise, adjusted[a] | 3817 | 4303 | 4533 | 1272 | 1383 | 801 | 1077 |
| Income on investments | 1594 | 1454 | 1451 | 329 | 338 | 338 | 446 |
| Transportation | 554 | 273 | 170 | 53 | 31 | 31 | 55 |
| Travel | —302 | —298 | —363 | —31 | —87 | —201 | —44 |
| Miscellaneous services | —499 | —877 | —1083 | —235 | —228 | —326 | —294 |
| Total Export Surplus | 5164 | 4855 | 4709 | 1388 | 1437 | 643 | 1241 |

| Type of Transaction | 1951 | 1952r | Total | I | II | III | IV |
| --- | --- | --- | --- | --- | --- | --- | --- |
| | | | | | 1953p and by Quarters | | |
| *Net Means of Financing Surplus* | | | | | | | |
| Foreign liquidation of gold and dollar assets^c | —442 | —1188 | —2296 | —758 | —898 | —747 | —398 |
| U.S. Government sources: | | | | | | | |
| Grants and unilateral transfers^b | 4501 | 4657 | 6198 | 1788 | 1943 | 1226 | 1241 |
| Long- and short-term loans | 168 | 477 | 221 | —10 | 84 | 178 | 19 |
| U.S. private sources: | | | | | | | |
| Remittances^c | 412 | 433 | 487 | 120 | 122 | 128 | 117 |
| Long- and short-term capital^d | 1066 | 1067 | 869 | 219 | —100 | 23 | 227 |
| Total Net Financing | 5700 | 6451 | 4979 | 1859 | 1601 | 808 | 1211 |
| *Errors and Omissions* | —536 | —596 | —269 | 29 | —162 | —165 | 31 |

Details may not add to totals because of rounding.

p) Preliminary.

r) Revised.

a) Includes goods sold to or bought from other countries that have not been shipped from or into the United States customs area (e.g., with respect to imports, purchases abroad by U.S. Government agencies for transfer to third countries under various foreign-aid programs and purchases abroad for the use of American military establishments overseas; with respect to exports, commodities furnished by the U.S. Government from overseas stocks—such as surplus property—and goods sold from overseas purchases, particularly under the various foreign-aid programs). The United States customs area includes the continental United States, Alaska, Hawaii, Puerto Rico, the Virgin Islands, the Panama Canal Zone, American Samoa, and certain minor American islands in the Pacific.

b) Infrastructure expenditures under the military assistance program are included in this balance-of-payments statement as miscellaneous services. In the tables in Chapters I and II of this document these expenditures were classified as grants.

c) Includes net dollar disbursements by the International Monetary Fund and the *difference* between the dollar disbursements by the International Bank and the net purchases in the United States of debentures sold or guaranteed by the International Bank.

d) Includes net purchases of debentures sold or guaranteed by the International Bank.

Sources: Department of Commerce, *Balance of Payments of the United States, 1949-1951*, Wash., D.C., 1952, p. 118, and Department of Commerce, *Survey of Current Business*, Wash., D.C., June 1953, p. 4, and March 1954, p. 22.

accumulated commercial debts to United States suppliers. Again excluding military aid, Canada, Western Europe, and Latin America each took about one quarter of the value of United States exports, compared with 15 percent, 42 percent, and 17 percent, respectively, in 1936-1938.

b. IMPORTS

Both the value and volume of total United States merchandise imports, including goods purchased abroad by U.S. Government agencies for transfer to third countries, were at an all-time high in 1953. The volume increased by some 6 percent over 1952 and the value by about 4 percent. However, as with exports, the growth of imports for the year as a whole lagged behind the expansion in the value of the nation's total output, imports for consumption being equivalent to only 3 percent of gross national product.[2] Most of the increase over 1952 in United States payments for imports went to Western Europe—especially Western Germany, the United Kingdom, and the Benelux countries—with the result that the area as a whole had regained nearly the same share of total United States merchandise imports as it had before the war, that is, 23 to 24 percent. Canada also increased its sales to the United States, but the Latin American countries recorded virtually the same amounts and the Far Eastern countries—especially Malaya, India, and Indonesia—earned fewer dollars in direct trade with the United States than they had in 1952, due to the fact that the prices of some of their major exports fell. The downward trend of United States business activity in the latter half of the year, accompanied by some liquidation of inventories, resulted in relatively sharp declines in the value of imports. During the last quarter of 1953 the value of imports was approximately 6 percent less than during the same quarter of the previous year. Moreover, it was anticipated that the prices per unit paid for several important metal imports would decline once the deliveries under existing long-term contracts were filled.

[2] For a discussion of "The United States Demand for Imports," see *American Economic Review, Papers and Proceedings*, May 1953, pp. 134-166. A. C. Harberger here argues that the commonly used techniques have in the past grossly underestimated the United States price elasticity of demand for imports. H. P. Neisser, on the other hand, finds that the techniques used in the past provide, by and large, acceptable explanations and reasonably accurate forecasts.

Although the total was higher, the value of several major imports declined during 1953. Most notable was crude rubber, the import payments for which were some 45 percent below those of the previous year as the result of a one-third decline in price accompanied by a curtailment in Government stockpiling purchases. Imports of sisal, henequen, and burlap also dropped sharply, mainly because of lower prices, and wool imports declined moderately. These decreases were more than offset, however, by the continuing rise in value of imports of several crude metals and petroleum, demand for which was closely linked to rearmament. An increase in total volume and price of coffee imports accounted for much of the increase in the value of total food imports, but more sugar, whiskey, meat products, and fruit and vegetables were also purchased abroad as incomes in the United States continued to grow. Foreign producers of many other commodities—including newsprint, watches, fertilizers, cotton and wool manufactures, and electrical apparatus—were also able to increase their sales to the United States during the year.

As compared with prewar, changes in the composition of imports varied much less than changes in the composition of exports. In both periods foodstuffs accounted for approximately 30 percent and finished manufactures for about 20 percent of the total value of American imports. Semimanufactures, however, rose from about 20 percent of the total before the war to nearly 25 percent in 1953, while the proportion represented by crude materials fell from approximately 31 percent in the 1936-1938 period to 24 percent in 1953. Geographically, and excluding purchases for offshore use, Latin America supplied 32 percent of United States merchandise imports in 1953, Canada nearly 23 percent, and Western Europe 21 percent; these figures may be compared with 22 percent, 14 percent, and 28 percent, respectively, in 1936-1938. Asia and Oceania supplied 32 percent in the prewar period but only 17 percent in 1953. Other areas of the world supplied only small amounts to the American market.

*Invisibles*

a. INCOME ON INVESTMENTS[3]

At $1900 million, United States income on foreign investments during 1953 was $80 million more than that estimated for the previous year.[4] Approximately half the increase represented interest on Government loans, and the other half, income from manufacturing investments abroad. The latter was partially offset by the decline in income associated with the lower prices received for many of the minerals (other than petroleum) and agricultural commodities produced abroad by American-controlled foreign enterprises. Payments to foreigners on their investments in the United States totalled $448 million, which also was slightly more than in 1952.

Details on investment income during 1953 are not yet available, but revised estimates for 1952 show that during that year the United States received $1419 million from private direct foreign investments and $196 million from private portfolio investments, while the U.S. Government received $204 million from its various foreign loans and credits. Approximately two thirds of the portfolio income during 1952 was received from Canada, with Western Europe and Latin America accounting for most of the rest. Just over 80 percent of the interest on Government loans was paid by the Western European countries. As Table 16 shows, the income from private direct investments was, as it had been for several years, concentrated in the petroleum industry and in Latin America, Canada, and the Middle East.

In *addition* to the income on foreign investments shown in the balance-of-payments statistics, foreign-incorporated subsidiaries

[3] "Income" is defined in the official statistics as the sum of interest and dividends from portfolio investments and dividends, interest, and branch profits from direct investments. Income from direct-investment companies excludes undistributed profits of subsidiaries, which are, however, included in "earnings." All income as officially reported for balance-of-payments purposes is calculated after the payment of any foreign taxes thereon.

For much detailed information on United States income from foreign investments in recent years, see Pizer, S., and Cutler, F., "Income on United States Foreign Investments," *Survey of Current Business*, December 1953, pp. 8-14. This is the source of much of the summary data given here.

[4] The revised figure given in Table 15 was subsequently revised downward again, but inasmuch as the other items have not yet been publicly revised, income from investments was not changed in that table.

## TABLE 16

*United States Equity in Direct Investment Earnings and Income Receipts,*
*by Area and Industry, 1952*[a]

(millions of dollars)

| Industry | Latin America | Canada | Western Europe | Western European Dependencies | Other | Total |
|---|---|---|---|---|---|---|
| Petroleum | | | | | | |
| Earnings | 438 | 12 | 79 | 112 | 371 | 1018 |
| Income receipts | 303 | —20[b] | 33 | 93 | 268 | 677 |
| Manufacturing | | | | | | |
| Earnings | 156 | 257 | 169 | 2 | 59 | 648 |
| Income receipts | 64 | 139 | 56 | 1 | 26 | 286 |
| Mining and Smelting | | | | | | |
| Earnings | 96 | 54 | 5 | 31 | 23 | 209 |
| Income receipts | 81 | 36 | 1 | 27 | 14 | 159 |
| Distribution | | | | | | |
| Earnings | 55 | 34 | 33 | 4 | 21 | 146 |
| Income receipts | 25 | 14 | 24 | 3 | 14 | 79 |
| Agriculture | | | | | | |
| Earnings | 84 | 1 | * | 8 | 24 | 118 |
| Income receipts | 73 | * | * | 1 | 11 | 86 |
| Public Utilities | | | | | | |
| Earnings | 32 | 9 | * | * | 7 | 48 |
| Income receipts | 35 | 11 | * | * | 8 | 49 |
| Miscellaneous | | | | | | |
| Earnings | 26 | 53 | 20 | 2 | 8 | 109 |
| Income receipts | 18 | 41 | 14 | 2 | 7 | 82 |
| | | | | | | |
| Total | | | | | | |
| Earnings | 888 | 419 | 305 | 154 | 513 | 2280 |
| Income receipts | 599 | 222 | 129 | 127 | 343 | 1419 |

Details may not add to totals because of rounding.
Less than one-half million dollars.
[ ] For definitions of "earnings" and "income receipts," see p. 280, n. 8.
[ ] Exploratory expenses charged against branch profits.
Source: Pizer, S., and Cutler, F., "Income on United States Foreign Investments," *Survey of Current Business*, Wash., D.C., December 1953, p. 11. The above data should not be compared with those given for 1951 on page 278 of the *Survey—1952* inasmuch as the latter figures were preliminary and have since been revised. The revision may be found in the source cited for this table.

of United States companies had other "earnings" that were retained abroad. The United States equity in such undistributed subsidiary profits during 1952 was about $860 million—some 20 percent more than in 1951—and preliminary data indicate that a similar amount was retained in 1953, despite the general trend toward higher income tax rates in many of the foreign countries. Thus total earnings from United States direct investments during 1952, after payment of foreign taxes, were nearly $2.3 billion on a total investment of about $15 billion—an average rate of return of approximately 15 percent. For the postwar period as a whole, the amount of earnings which foreign-incorporated subsidiaries retained abroad equalled approximately half of total earnings. Moreover, this proportion increased each year after the end of the war and in 1952 it rose to 62 percent. Information on the reasons for such retention and the uses to which the funds were put is incomplete, but the Department of Commerce has concluded that the greater part of such earnings were voluntarily left abroad and used to expand existing investments; the balance were more or less idle while awaiting permission from local authorities for remittance to the United States and/or were used for intercompany loans and advances to parent companies.

During 1952 about 25 percent, by value, of total United States commodity imports came from United States-controlled productive facilities abroad; the proportion was about 30 percent for all imports from Canada and Latin America. The proportion varies greatly from commodity to commodity, and over three quarters of American imports of crude oil, copper, paper-base stocks, bananas, nickel, aluminum, and bauxite were from United States direct investments abroad.

b. TRANSPORTATION[5]

Balance-of-payments *receipts* on transportation account continued the decline registered in the previous year while *payments* on this account continued their steady postwar increase, with the result that the export surplus on this item totalled only $170 million in 1953 as compared with over $1 billion in 1947. The United States ran a deficit on transportation transactions with Western Europe, had a modest surplus with Canada, and had

[5] For a detailed statement of postwar changes in this account, see Smith, J. E., "Transportation in the Balance of Payments," *Survey of Current Business*, September 1953, pp. 20-24. This article is the source of most of the information given here.

Earnings by American carriers in foreign trade are greater than the balance-of-payments statistics show inasmuch as carriage payments on United States imports transported in American bottoms are not counted as international transactions. The transportation account in the balance of payments is dominated by ocean transportation, but it also includes air and rail activities as well as traffic with Canada on the Great Lakes.

somewhat larger surpluses with Latin America and the other major areas of the world.

The fall in transportation earnings in 1953, as in 1952, was attributable to several factors, the most important being the decline in United States exports of coal and grain, together with intense competition for bulk cargo from foreign tramp steamers. The latter charged rates so low as to leave American flag vessels little of such bulk-shipment business other than that assured by the provision in the Mutual Security legislation that at least 50 percent of aid-financed cargoes be shipped in American bottoms. Although rates on other dry cargoes were maintained at their 1951 high level by carrier conferences, the United States' share of this trade and of the tanker traffic also declined as foreign fleets grew in size and speed and as many countries continued to give preference to foreign ships in their efforts to reduce dollar expenditures.

The larger payments to foreign vessels for transportation services were in part offset by larger port expenditures by such vessels in the United States. In 1951 and 1952 (data for 1953 are not available) foreign port expenditures in the United States equalled some 80 percent of the foreign dollar earnings from carrying freight to the United States and from passenger fares provided by United States tourists. Foreign port expenditures have in recent years been running over twice the amount of United States port expenditures abroad, due in large part to the practice of many ships of all nations' bunkering at American ports and frequently purchasing equipment here. The relatively high cost of stevedoring in American ports also has been a contributing factor.

Although American tourists in 1952 spent nearly six times as much for fares on foreign vessels as American liners received from foreign travelers, United States airlines received nearly twice as much from foreign travelers as American residents paid to foreign airlines. Nevertheless, payments received from foreigners by American airlines were almost balanced by the carriers' foreign expenses.

C. TRAVEL[6]

United States residents spent an estimated $908 million while traveling abroad during 1953—about 10 percent more than in the previous year—continuing a postwar trend. Foreign travelers in the United States spent an estimated $545 million—about 4 percent more than in 1952 but below their expenditures in the years 1948-1950.

The greatest increase in American tourist outlays in 1952 and 1953 was in Western Europe, including the Mediterranean area, the coronation in the United Kingdom contributing to the rise. Canada also increased its dollar earnings from this source, but Western Europe, with its improved travel and hotel accommodations and more ample food supplies, was challenging Canada as the favorite tourist area for Americans; in 1953 the American expenditures in the two areas were almost identical, together accounting for two thirds of the total.

Canada continued to be by far the most important source of tourist income for the United States, accounting for nearly 60 percent of total travel receipts in 1953, and was the only major area with which the United States had an export surplus on this account. Residents of Latin America contributed just over one quarter of the total tourist outlays in the United States, while Western Europeans accounted for less than 8 percent of the total.[7]

d. MISCELLANEOUS SERVICES

Expenditures abroad by the United States for "miscellaneous services" continued the spectacular increase noted in the previous year and totalled an estimated $2251 million in 1953, making a major contribution to the improved dollar position of the rest of the world. Nearly $2 billion of these, including all of the nearly $300 million increase over 1952, were expenditures by the U.S.

[6] See Sasscer, F. P., "One Billion Travel Dollars Go Abroad," *Survey of Current Business*, June 1953, pp. 9-11, for much detailed information on the travel account during 1952 and earlier years.

[7] The long-term downward trend in the number of foreign-born United States residents traveling to Europe continued, but in 1952 (data for 1953 are not yet available) they still accounted for nearly half of the total. In that year the foreign-born residents stayed in Europe 71 days on the average, compared with an average of 49 days for native-born residents. However, the average expenditures, excluding fares, by the foreign-born were less than $8 per day, as compared with $19 per day by the native-born.

Government.[8] Included were some payments by civilian branches of the Government, but the bulk of these expenditures represented that portion of their pay which American troops spent abroad, purchases of various services by the United States military groups, and payments to foreign residents by the United States for services required in connection with the building and operation of various airfields, bases, depots, and so forth.[9] Nearly half of the Government payments were made in Africa, Asia, and the Far East, and a little less than 40 percent were made in Europe.

Private payments on this account totalled an estimated $266 million, the same as in 1952; four fifths of these in recent years have been in Europe and have been mostly for reinsurance and for communications services.

*Receipts* by the United States on the miscellaneous services account also increased during 1953 and totalled $1168 million, $83 million more than in the previous year. Just over 40 percent of this total was on Government account and was apparently composed mostly of services provided foreigners under the various military assistance and technical assistance programs. As in earlier years, receipts on private account were accounted for largely by film rentals, management fees and royalties, reinsurance services, and private foreign representation expenses in the United States.

### Export Surplus

The net result of the above international transactions by the United States was a current-account export surplus in 1953 of some $4700 million, less than $150 million below that of the previous year and only about $450 million less than in 1951. However, if the value of military supplies and services provided other governments by the U.S. Government is excluded from the calculations, then for the first time in many years the current accounts of the United States were nearly in balance, the export surplus being

[8] The Department of Commerce estimates that total United States expenditures abroad for both goods and services amounted to about $4.6 billion in 1953, more than in any other year since 1949. (*Survey of Current Business*, Wash., D.C., March 1954, p. 24.)

[9] Included are the payments by the United States for its share of the infrastructure program in Europe, discussed in Chapter I. The payments made under the offshore procurement program are excluded, being covered in commodity imports.

TABLE 17

*United States Current Account Export Surplus, by Area, 1951-1953*

(millions of dollars)

| | 1951 | 1952r | Total | 1953p First Quarter | Second Quarter | Third Quarter | Fourth Quarter |
|---|---|---|---|---|---|---|---|
| Canada | 698 | 821 | 895 | 271 | 349 | 109 | 167 |
| Excluding military aid[a] | (698) | (821) | (897) | (271) | (349) | (110) | (168) |
| Latin America | 1033 | 618 | 193 | —107 | 17 | 31 | 253 |
| Excluding military aid[a] | (970) | (559) | (157) | (—113) | (9) | (16) | (246) |
| Western Europe | 3168 | 2804 | 2857 | 972 | 907 | 373 | 606 |
| Excluding military aid[a] | (2057) | (661) | (—607) | (—34) | (—220) | (—296) | (—56) |
| Western European Dependencies | —475 | —472 | —465 | —131 | —121 | —100 | —114 |
| Excluding military aid[a] | (—475) | (—472) | (—465) | (—131) | (—121) | (—100) | (—114) |
| Eastern Europe | —64 | —25 | —14 | —8 | —9 | 2 | 1 |
| Excluding military aid[a] | (—51) | (—25) | (—14) | (—8) | (—9) | (—2) | (—1) |
| All Other Countries | 798 | 1093 | 1220 | 379 | 284 | 239 | 318 |
| Excluding military aid[a] | (497) | (697r) | (435) | (109) | (35) | (107) | (184) |
| International Institutions | 6 | 21 | 20 | 12 | 10 | —11 | 9 |
| Excluding military aid[a] | (6) | (21) | (20) | (12) | (10) | (—11) | (9) |
| Total | 5164 | 4855 | 4709 | 1388 | 1487 | 648 | 1241 |
| Excluding military aid[a] | (3702) | (2262) | (425) | (106) | (52) | (—172) | (439) |

Details may not add to totals because of rounding.

p) Preliminary.

r) Revised.

a) The data on military aid here were taken from different sources than those used in Chapter I and differ by small amounts from the data on "military end-items" as given in Chapter I. Most of the differences are accounted for by the fact that the contributions to the infrastructure program in Europe are excluded from the data in this table and included in the other tables. It has not been possible to reconcile the other differences, but they probably arise because of varying treatment given administrative expenses under the military-aid programs and perhaps some differences in the date of recording actual expenditures.

Sources: Department of Commerce, *Survey of Current Business*, Wash., D.C., June 1958, pp. 4-5, and March 1954, pp. 22-23, and Department of Commerce, *Balance of Payments of the United States, 1949-1961*, Wash., D.C., 1962, pp. 118-119.

only $425 million compared with nearly $2300 million in 1952 and $3700 million in 1951. This decline was attributable in part to the huge "extraordinary" expenditures of the U.S. Military Establishment abroad, already noted, but it was also a reflection of the decline of about $1 billion in commercial exports and the increase of some $400 million in imports. A part of the increase in imports, however, represented the rise in offshore procurement of military supplies under the aid program. It must also be noted that the export surplus, excluding military aid, during the last quarter of the year not only was higher than during any other quarter since the spring of 1952, but exceeded that for the year as a whole, a substantial import surplus having been recorded during the summer of 1953. Available data do not permit confident conclusions as to the significance of these last-quarter developments, but the business recession in the United States was a contributing factor.

Geographically, as Table 17 shows, the most striking change during the year was the emergence of a Western European export surplus—excluding grant-aid military supplies—with the United States during every quarter. For the year as a whole, the import surplus of the United States with Western Europe, excluding transfers of military supplies, exceeded $600 million, compared with export surpluses of $661 million in 1952 and over $2 billion in 1951. Latin America cut her current-account deficit with the United States to almost a quarter of that for the previous year, but Canada's deficit increased slightly.

## B. *CAPITAL ACCOUNT*

### *Foreign Gold and Dollar Assets*[1]

The greater balance in the current-account position of the United States, noted above, combined with a continued net outflow of both official and private loans and grants, permitted the rest of the world to increase its known gold and dollar assets (both long- and short-term) in its transactions with the United States

---

[1] Most of the information in this section was taken from "International Gold and Dollar Movements" in Board of Governors of the Federal Reserve System, *Federal Reserve Bulletin*, Wash., D.C., March 1954, pp. 237-245, and from Department of Commerce, *Survey of Current Business*, Wash., D.C., March 1954, pp. 20-24.

by approximately $2300 million during 1953. This was nearly twice the increase recorded in 1952 but was well under the $3600 million rise which took place in 1950. Of the 1953 accretions, only about $100 million took the form of long-term assets, $2200 million constituting additions to the *liquid* international reserves of the rest of the world.[2]

The lion's share—over 90 percent—of these liquid reserves were accumulated by continental Western Europe and the sterling area. The Latin American countries added approximately $270 million to their holdings in their transactions with the United States, but Canada, which repurchased sizable amounts of its outstanding long-term securities in the United States when bond prices here fell, lost approximately $125 million in liquid reserves to the United States. The Asian and African countries not included in the sterling area were able to accumulate only small amounts of gold and dollars by trading with the United States. The international institutions, especially the International Bank, added an estimated $76 million to their reserves, largely from sales of securities in the United States market.

Of the $2200 million of liquid assets accumulated by foreign countries in their trade with the United States, some $1200 million took the form of gold purchases, nearly $550 million were in the form of short-term U.S. Government securities, and about $150 million were bankers' acceptances and similar assets. Foreign deposits in United States commercial banks rose by over $425 million, but deposits at the Federal Reserve banks declined by approximately $125 million.

The rest of the non-Soviet world also added an estimated $400 million to its official gold reserves through new production and from gold sales by Russia. Thus the liquid gold and dollar holdings of the free world outside the United States increased by some $2600 million during 1953. Taking into account the new gold production, plus transactions among foreign nations as well as between foreign countries and the United States, the continental Western European countries and the sterling area together accounted for over $2400 million of the increase, as Table 18 shows. Every

[2] Here, as in the official statistics, liquid holdings are defined to include gold, bank balances, and securities having a maturity of twenty months or less at the time of purchase.

TABLE 18

*Estimated Foreign Gold Reserves and Dollar Holdings, 1938-1953*a
(millions of dollars)

|  | 1938 | 1945 | 1952 | 1953p |
|---|---|---|---|---|
| Sterling Area | 3900 | 4086 | 3283 | 4046 |
| Continental Western Europeb | 7300 | 8131 | 8868 | 10060 |
| Eastern Europec | 425 | 515 | 307 | 306 |
| Canada | 395 | 1726 | 2492 | 2416 |
| Latin America | 950 | 3778 | 3369 | 3625 |
| Asia | 760 | 2417 | 2367 | 2309 |
| Other | 95 | 111 | 283 | 282 |
|  |  |  |  |  |
| Total, Foreign Countries | 13825 | 20764 | 20469 | 23044 |
| International Institutionsd | — | — | 3287 | 3342 |
|  |  |  |  |  |
| Grand Total | 13825 | 20764 | 23756 | 26386 |

p) Preliminary.
a) Dollar holdings represent both official and private holdings as reported by United States banks and include deposits, short-term U.S. Government securities (those maturing in twenty months or less after date of purchase), and certain other short-term liabilities. Gold reserves are the estimated holdings of central banks, governments, and international institutions. These data do not include long-term dollar assets, gold in private hoards, or private holdings of United States currency, as distinguished from deposits.
b) The Continental OEEC countries, Finland, Spain, Yugoslavia, the Bank for International Settlements, the European Payments Union, and the Tripartite Commission for Restitution of Monetary Gold.
c) Excludes gold reserves, but includes dollar balances, held by Russia.
d) Primarily the International Monetary Fund, International Bank, and United Nations. The Bank for International Settlements and the European Payments Union are included in "Continental Western Europe."
Sources: Board of Governors of the Federal Reserve System, *Federal Reserve Bulletin*, Wash., D.C., March 1954, p. 245.

continental European country shared in the rise, but Germany was the biggest gainer, adding some $534 million to her reserves. Most of the 23 percent increase in reserves recorded by the sterling area arose out of its transactions with the United States, but gold production in South Africa also contributed and $115 million were received from the EPU.

As a group, the Latin American countries increased their reserves by just over $250 million, this being slightly more than their accumulations from transactions with the United States. Most of these countries shared in the gain, but Argentina and Venezuela accounted for about 60 percent of the total. Canada suffered a small drain on her liquid reserves, primarily as a result of the large repurchase of Canadian securities in the United States market, mentioned above. Although Japan continued to benefit from large dollar expenditures by United States military forces, her imports rose substantially and she was able to register a rise of only $22 million in her gold and dollar reserves. Indonesia, on the other hand, used up some $112 million of her hard-currency reserves during the year, and the Philippines also recorded a small decline in dollar holdings. A few of the other Asian countries recorded modest increases, but the area as a whole—excluding sterling area members—reported a slight decrease.

At the end of 1953 the known gold and dollar reserves held by other nations were at an all-time high—over two-thirds greater than in 1938 and three times as large as in 1928. Including the gold and dollar holdings of the International Monetary Fund and Bank, the known reserves of the rest of the world were over 90 percent greater than they were just prior to World War II. Prices and the volume of world trade had, of course, also increased substantially during the interval, and most observers agreed that it could not be concluded that the reserves were adequate to meet the requirements for a general and rapid dismantling of import and exchange restrictions throughout the world. Nonetheless, there was broad agreement that this increase in international liquidity was a prerequisite for freer trade and payments policies.

### Other Items

The various means by which the United States financed its export surplus and a large part of the increase in the reserves of the rest of the world—official grants and loans, private loans and remittances, and dollar disbursements by international institutions—were discussed in some detail in Chapters I through IV and need not be summarized here.

### C. ERRORS AND OMISSIONS

Known dollar payments by the United States exceeded known dollar receipts during 1953 by an estimated $269 million. Taking into account the many estimates that are necessarily involved in compiling the United States balance of payments, this was a relatively small item for errors and omissions. As usual, it probably represented in large measure unrecorded capital movements into the United States, but a part may have resulted from an undervaluation of exports in official statistics and an overvaluation of imports.[3]

[3] A Department of Commerce study completed in 1953 showed that for the month of April 1950, at least, most of the errors in calculating the value of imports were offsetting. (See *Foreign Commerce Weekly*, August 24, 1953, p. 20.)

# SUMMARY

In 1953, for the first time in twenty years, governmental responsibility for the formulation and execution of the nation's international economic and financial policies was in the hands of a Republican Administration and a Republican-dominated Congress. A basic theme of the Republicans during the 1952 election campaign, and one with much popular appeal, had been that it was "time for a change," not only in personnel but also in policies. Much time and effort were given during 1953 to reassessing past policies, but there was little public evidence that there had been, by the end of the year at least, many major changes, although some differences in emphasis were apparent. Perhaps this was to be expected during the first year—even assuming the policies of the past were indeed seriously wanting in important respects—for there was little alteration in the broad nature and dimensions of most of the problems facing the country, previous policies and programs had an immense momentum of their own, and many of the new senior officials were for the first time wrestling with problems of the sort which confront a nation playing a leading role in the free world's economic affairs. Nonetheless, the current policies had been the subject of growing dissatisfaction both at home and abroad in 1952, and some of those who, with no partisan political motives, had characterized the last year of the Truman Administration as one of a "paralysis" in policy determination were no more charitable in characterizing the first year of the Eisenhower Administration as one of a "vacuum" in policy formulation.

There was virtually no serious questioning in 1953 by the new Administration and Congress (or by most of the vocal public) of the major premise of their predecessors, that the threat of aggression by the Soviet bloc was the overriding foreign-policy issue facing the nation and that national security considerations therefore must rule in determining the nation's foreign economic policies. As before, the major economic weapon used by the United

States to strengthen the defenses of the free world was the granting to friendly countries of huge amounts of military assistance. Similarly, this help continued to take the form not only of military end-items but also of civilian-type goods, the latter being designed to permit the recipient to devote his own resources to rearmament in some multiple of the American aid. Both the Executive and the Legislative branches of the Government were determined, however, that the amount of such military assistance should fall from its current level, and the new appropriations for these purposes were some 30 percent less for the fiscal year beginning in mid-1953 than they had been for the previous twelve months. This decline in appropriations resulted in part from the efforts to more nearly balance the federal budget while reducing United States taxes—a much-stressed "promise" by the Republicans in the 1952 election campaign. Its feasibility was enhanced by the existence of large amounts of unspent funds carried over from previous years and the increased ability of the Western European nations, in part due to previous American aid, to meet their rearmament needs from their own resources. Moreover, this reflected what the new Administration regarded as one of its major policy decisions of the year: inasmuch as the time of maximum Soviet threat could not be determined, rearmament of the West should not be directed toward reaching a predetermined year of maximum strength but must be on a scale which could be maintained for an indefinite period; this, in turn, meant that the previously established objectives for the NATO forces for 1953 should be reduced. Administration spokesmen frequently chose to describe this as a change in emphasis from quantity to quality.

From the beginning of the free-world-wide military assistance program in 1949, Europe, including Greece and Turkey, had received the lion's share of the military aid; but following the outbreak of war in Korea, increasing emphasis had been placed on helping various Asian nations—especially Nationalist China and Indochina—to strengthen their defenses. This trend was accelerated in 1953 with the share of new military assistance appropriations scheduled for Europe falling, as compared with the previous fiscal year, from some seven eighths to less than two thirds of the total, while that destined for Asia and the Pacific increased from about one eighth to over one third. Because of the lag between appropriations and the actual provision of goods and services, however, these policy decisions to decrease the total amount of military assistance and to increase the share destined for the Asian nations were not fully reflected in the grants actually utilized. In fact, the amounts of this type of assistance provided rose from $4.4 billion in calendar 1952 to $5.8 billion in 1953, as diversions to Korea ended and as the pipeline began to spout goods ordered in earlier years. The share of the Far Eastern nations in the total rose from less than one eighth in 1952 to nearly one sixth in 1953. Total net transfers to foreign countries during 1953 under *all* grant *and* loan programs amounted to $6.4 billion. This was one-fourth more than during the previous year and higher than in any earlier postwar year; by the last quarter of the year, however, the outflow had fallen to an annual rate of just over $5 billion.

Details on rearmament in the aided countries and on American contributions thereto were not available to the public, but such information as was released indicated that the Administration was pursuing policies very similar to those of its predecessor on such important matters as the types of goods and services being furnished, the conditions on which they were provided, offshore procurement, and the infrastructure program. Both Congress and the Administration did stress a bit more than in earlier years the importance attached by the United States to an early ratification of the European Defense Community Treaty.

The European countries continued to strengthen their defense capabilities as the actual flow of military aid deepened and their own production increased, but it was officially stated at year's end that the NATO forces were still unable to withstand a full-scale assault by the Soviet bloc. Although Germany, Belgium, Luxembourg, and the Netherlands took some of the necessary steps to ratify the European Defense Community Treaty, little if any progress was made in overcoming the reluctance of the French and Italian parliaments to approve it, and German forces had therefore still not been incorporated into the mutual defense effort by the end of 1953. With the deterioration in the position of the French and Vietnamese forces in Indochina, the U.S. Administration announced plans to increase greatly the already enlarged program of military aid to that area, but as the year ended the Communist forces there appeared to be in a stronger position than at any time in the seven years of war. The strengthening of the Nationalist Chinese forces on Formosa continued throughout the year, and, for the first time, the shipment of military supplies to Japan was authorized under the Mutual Security Program. Except for Greece and Turkey, little military aid was given to the Near Eastern countries, and the 1951 plans for the creation of a Middle East Defense Command appeared to have been abandoned, for the time being at least, in the face of the continuing Arab-Israeli hostilities and the Anglo-Egyptian dispute. The new Administration continued to hope, however, that some form of regional defense organization might be created in that area and saw new prospects for this in the early 1954 mutual defense agreement between Pakistan and Turkey, following the signing of which the U.S. Government announced plans to send, for the first time, military aid to the former, despite strong protests from India.

While being careful to leave the door open for the judicious extension of economic aid, the new Administration asserted even more strongly than its predecessor that Government aid designed directly to improve economic well-being was no longer justified for the Western European nations, and only small amounts of such assistance were provided in 1953. The Eisenhower Administration accepted the previously established position that it was in the economic, political, and security interests of the United States for this Government to help reduce poverty and misery in the poorer areas of the free world, provided this did not become a "big-money" program. Although stressing their opposition, in principle, to giving large amounts of commodities, as distinct from "pure" technical assistance, to the poorer areas of the world, both the Executive and Legislative branches agreed in 1953 that, as in the past, substantial amounts of "emergency" economic aid were justified for several nations of the Near East and Asia— notably Israel, the Arab States, Iran, India, Pakistan, and Korea.

Somewhat more attention than in the recent past was given to the Near East, especially the Arab States, and early in the year the new Administration announced its plans to approach the economic problems there on an "area-wide," rather than a country-by-country, basis. In the event, the attempts to encourage economic-development projects which involved the cooperation of both Israel and at least one of the Arab States were largely frustrated, and the aid was used for much the same purposes as in the recent past. The amount provided Israel, however, was only about one-half the previous year's figure. While United States aid going directly to the Arab States increased somewhat, American contributions to the United Nations agency charged with helping to meet the relief needs and encouraging the resettlement of the Palestine refugees amounted to less than half those of the previous year as the agency found virtually no prospect of permanently resettling many of these refugees so long as the political difficulties between Israel and the Arab States remained unresolved. Economic aid to Iran was much larger than in the previous year, with most of the increase taking place after the overthrow of the Mossadegh Government and upon the request for emergency assistance from the new Premier. Economic aid to India and Pakistan, the maintenance of whose newly formed democratic governments continued to be regarded as of major importance by the U.S. Government, also increased during the year. Relief and rehabilitation aid to Korea was expanded, but the new Administration apparently planned to provide a sizable part of the post-hostilities help directly to Korea, rather than through the United Nations Korean Reconstruction Agency as had been planned previously. Senior Administration officials frequently spoke of doing more than in the past to help the Latin American countries, but both new appropriations and net grants to that area declined in 1953 as compared with 1952.

Somewhat larger amounts than in the previous year were spent on the technical assistance aspects of the bilateral program for helping the so-called underdeveloped countries, as many of the individual projects passed from the planning to the execution stage. On the other hand, contributions to the United Nations technical assistance program were slightly below those of the previous year, and spokesmen for many of the poorer countries expressed great disappointment at the failure of this program to reach the previously scheduled scale of operations.

There was some criticism in the press that the new Administration was in the process of "smothering" its bilateral technical assistance activities under the military-aid program and of diverting their purpose from one of helping others help themselves to create decent conditions of life in which they could find social and political security and stability to one of directly strengthening the military potential of the United States and the aided countries. These allegations were denied by the Administration, and there was little public evidence to indicate that there had been any major shift in the immediate goals, primarily improving health and expanding food production. The accomplishments of the program were still being reported mainly in terms of individual instances of success in reducing the incidence of certain diseases or increasing the production of specific commodities. It was still too early to determine whether the broader objectives of decreasing the number of people living in misery, reducing the appeals of Communism, and strengthening the political ties of the aided countries with the United States were being met.

Although relatively large quantities of "emergency" economic aid continued to be supplied to some of the countries receiving technical assistance, the new Administration was more insistent than its predecessor had been that most of the foreign capital—as distinct from technical services—wanted and needed by the underdeveloped countries must come from sources other than the U.S. Government. In the latter years of the Truman Administration the Export-Import Bank had made many so-called long-term development loans to foreign governments, sometimes in direct support of Point Four activities. In 1953 the Bank virtually withdrew from this field and largely restricted its new commitments to medium- and short-term loans to help finance specific United States exports. This policy, however, apparently had not yet become firmly established, and there were some indications in early 1954 that the Bank might reenter the field of long-term development loans.

The U.S. Government continued to express general satisfaction with the scale of operations of the International Bank and its policy of concentrating on long-term development loans to poorer countries. Spokesmen for many of the underdeveloped nations continued to insist that the World Bank was unable or unwilling to meet their capital requirements and urged the United Nations to create a Special United Nations Fund for Economic Development and an International Finance Corporation. The strong opposition of the U.S. Government to the immediate creation of either institution rested on essentially the same considerations put forward in 1951 and 1952, and again it was successful in having both proposals remanded for further study. Nevertheless, United States spokesmen continued to emphasize their Government's sympathy with the economic-development aspirations of the poorer countries and their desire for more help from abroad and, amid much publicity, proposed that all the member governments of the United Nations agree to ask their peoples to devote a portion of the savings which would result from an "internationally-supervised, world-wide disarmament" to an international fund for economic development. A resolution embodying this proposal was approved by the United Nations General Assembly after many delegates insisted it must not be interpreted, as some feared, as implying that economic development and rearmament were alternatives. Many clearly regarded the United States proposal as a delaying tactic which offered no help in the foreseeable future. United States officials did not pretend to be optimistic as to the time when such rearmament savings would be available and stressed, even more than had their predecessors, that private capital exports must be the main channel through which the foreign needs for American investment would be satisfied. To this end, previous efforts were intensified during 1953 to encourage such investments by the negotiation of investment treaties and tax conventions, by the broadening of the areas and circumstances for which government guaranties would be issued against various nonbusiness risks in foreign investment, and by exhortation. Consideration was also being given to asking Congress to approve a series of tax concessions on income from foreign investments. No one expected these devices to have an immediate effect, and many observers expressed skepticism as to the ability of such techniques to overcome many of the known barriers to larger private long-term investments. During the year such new capital outflows totalled only $517 million, which was well below the 1952 level.

For several years the United States had been more or less marking time in its foreign-trade policy. But a convergence of forces, much discussed in 1952, continued during 1953 to push many trade problems to the surface and to add to the numbers of those who believed the need for a reformulation of the nation's international commercial policies was clear and urgent. Included among these forces were the already-noted policy of reducing and quickly terminating most official grants and loans for other than strictly military purposes and the failure of private capital outflows to grow. Although rarely discussed in official statements, many observers believed that the growth throughout the world of managed economies had invalidated some of the crucial assumptions underlying the Trade Agreements Act—the core of American commercial policy. The policy of urging friendly foreign countries drastically to reduce their exports to the Soviet bloc, which was continued with but few changes by the new Administration, also brought to the fore the question of trade policy, for easing access to its internal markets was considered to be one way in which the United States could lighten the burden on its friends of keeping East-West trade at low levels. Purchases abroad for the official stockpile declined in value during 1953, and, barring some new and major international crisis, the prospects were for a continued tapering off of such imports in the future. At the same time, the growing awareness of the increasing dependence of the United States on foreign sources for many metals and minerals to meet current demands led to more insistent questioning of the wisdom of some of the existing import barriers. Furthermore, American trade and tariff policy engendered growing concern among foreign nations during 1953 as they increased their ability to produce goods for export, and spokesmen for many foreign countries repeatedly asserted that action by them on many important economic policies awaited firm indications from Washington as to how the United States planned to conduct its foreign-trade affairs.

Although few disputed that the nation had only the remnants of a foreign-trade policy, there were great differences of opinion within the United States, and within the Republican Party, as to the proper aims of commercial policy and the means of obtaining them. And the new Administration was unprepared in its first year to put forward new proposals. It was successful in its efforts to defeat a strong movement in Congress to amend the Trade Agreements Act so as greatly to increase the barriers to imports. The Act was extended, with only minor amendments, for one more year on the understanding that there would be no important tariff and trade negotiations during the interval and after it had been agreed to create a special Commission to examine, and to make recommendations to the President and Congress on, the entire field of foreign economic policy. The Administration thereupon adopted a general policy of deferring or postponing action on any problem being studied by the Commission.

Early in the year Congress did approve a customs simplification bill, repeatedly requested by the previous Administration, but only after the most controversial item—replacing "foreign value" with "export value" as the favored method of valuing imports for purposes of assessing ad valorem duties—was deleted. The highly controversial 1950 amendment to the Defense Production Act authorizing stringent import quotas on many fats and oils—the "cheese amendment"—was allowed to expire, but this was virtually without significance inasmuch as restrictions with practically the same effects were immediately imposed under other legislation. Moreover, several new barriers were erected against agricultural imports and Congress was more energetic than usual in attempting to dispose of surplus agricultural products abroad under various aid programs, making even more intense the long-existent conflicts between the nation's agricultural and foreign-trade policies. The Contracting Parties to the General Agreement on Tariffs and Trade again found the United States in violation of some of its international commitments, but most foreign governments reluctantly agreed to postpone retaliatory action in the hope that Washington would soon formulate new trade and tariff policies along more liberal lines.

The trend noted during 1952 for the rest of the world to achieve a greater balance in its financial relations with the United States continued throughout 1953, and other nations accumulated some $2.3 billion of gold and dollar assets in their transactions with this country. Although many "extraordinary" and nonrecurring factors helped to account for this improvement, it did reflect to an important extent the substantial economic progress made by foreign countries (due in part to past aid from the U.S. Government) and the increased ability of foreign suppliers to compete with United States producers, especially in third markets. As the so-called dollar problem for most foreign countries became less acute, increasing attention was given throughout the world, and especially in Western Europe, to the possibility of taking important new steps toward dismantling many of the restrictions on international trade and payments. This had long been an avowed goal of American policy, and many discussions were held between American and foreign officials on the contributions the United States could make to helping other nations give their people greater freedom of choice as to where they buy and sell goods and services. United States officials gave assurances that they would welcome any such moves and declared that their Government recognized the important bearing American policies had on the problems and welfare of other countries; but they also stated that they were not yet ready to put forward proposals for changes in American policies.

# INDEX

GPSR Authorized Representative: Easy Access System Europe - Mustamäe tee
50, 10621 Tallinn, Estonia, gpsr.requests@easproject.com